TESTIMONY

Edited by

DAVID ROSENBERG

T I M E S **T** B O O K S

R A N D O M   H O U S E

TESTIMONY

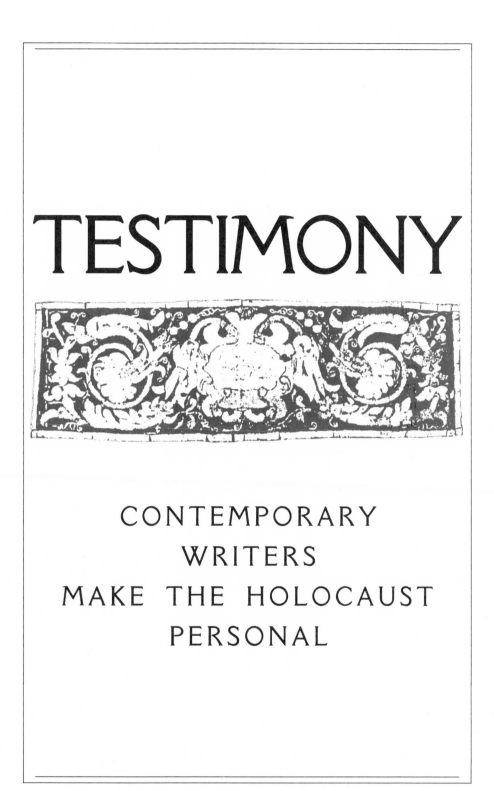

CONTEMPORARY
WRITERS
MAKE THE HOLOCAUST
PERSONAL

Acknowledgments for previously published material appear on pages vii-ix.

Library of Congress Cataloging-in-Publication Data

Testimony: contemporary writers make the Holocaust personal/edited by David Rosenberg.
    p. cm.
   ISBN 0-8129-1817-7
   1. Holocaust, Jewish (1939–1945)—Influence. 2. Jewish authors—United States—Biography. 3. Jews—United States—Intellectual life. I. Rosenberg, David, 1943– .
D804.3.T47 1989
940.53'18—dc20   89-40185

Text design by Levavi & Levavi, Inc.
Manufactured in the United States of America

9 8 7 6 5 4 3 2

First Edition

Permissions
Acknowledgments

Grateful acknowledgment is made to the following for permission to reprint previously published material:

The Ecco Press and Penguin Books Ltd: "Song on Porcelain" by Czeslaw Milosz from *The Collected Poems, 1931–1987,* first published by The Ecco Press in 1988. Copyright © 1988 by Czeslaw Milosz Royalties, Inc. World rights excluding the United States, the Philippine Republic, and Canada administered by Penguin Books, Ltd. Reprinted by permission.

Doubleday, a division of Bantam, Doubleday, Dell Publishing Group, Inc.: "The Song of Songs" from *Chosen Days* by David Rosenberg. Copyright © 1980 by David Rosenberg. Reprinted by permission of Doubleday, a division of Bantam Doubleday Dell Publishing Group, Inc. British Commonwealth rights administered by Sanford J. Greenburger Associates.

Editions Gallimard: Excerpt from "Le Dernier Poeme" by Robert Desnos from *Collected Poems.* The excerpt is translated into English by David Shapiro. Reprinted by permission of Editions Gallimard.

Faber and Faber, Ltd.: Excerpts from "Buna" and "For Adolf Eichmann" from *Collected Poems* by Primo Levi, translated by Ruth Feldman and Brian Swann, published by Faber and Faber, Ltd. Reprinted by permission.

Harper and Row: Excerpt from the retranslation of Psalm 137 from *Blues of the Sky* by David Rosenberg. Copyright © 1976 by David Rosenberg. Reprinted by permission of Harper and Row, Publishers, Inc.

Contents

CONTENTS

III.

Introduction:
In a Forgotten Mirror

There are many surprising approaches to personal history in *Testimony*: it's as if we've begun to learn from the survivors, still among us, how crucial it is to pass on whatever one has seen. At first few survivors talked in public about their experiences; our strength to listen had to grow as well. But can that allow us to forget the ways in which we ourselves, at a distance, experienced the most painful subject of our times? The immediacy of testimony can be kept alive—especially when we look through our own eyes at the Holocaust's aftermath.

To make personal is a form of testimony, and I began to envision this book listening to complaints that the Holocaust is overdramatized yet underremembered, its major scholarship unread. Academic symposia may furnish large amounts of words but for limited audiences. I shared the sense that a different approach was needed. And what can be done by imaginative writers exclusively is to reexamine our American lives in the Holocaust's wake, its unending trail of absence. To be avoided are the dangers of remoteness, of sentiment that entrenches cliché, of talking too much without making the connections to personal experience.

Still, if you brought together a group of our bravest writers, unafraid to look critically at personal history, how would you ask them to look again? Once, I thought writers would resist making themselves vulnerable to the Holocaust. However strong the documents of witnesses and survivors, the incongruity between their lives and ours remains. We may all be hypothetical survivors, but for us, for whom Western history still comes through the Enlightenment, the catastrophe proves too complex —yet too naked also, too bedrock a despair for conventional literature. To represent the interplay of history, memory, and myth against a cardboard background—too much to ask for. And that's how I first thought society must appear in the ashen Holocaust spotlight: fragile as cardboard.

However lightly, the Holocaust has touched all Americans, at the least in a richly Jewish anxiety Elie Wiesel has mirrored: "With the invention of nuclear weapons the world has become Jewish." *Testimony* takes a step forward by including a majority of writers born during and after the war, who describe—in many cases for the first time—the shadow of the Holocaust on their own lives. Confronting this history, they challenge the youngest generation of emerging writers, whose brush with the consequences of the Holocaust is still embryonic, as yet unexamined.

For a writer from a Jewish family, the connection to literal events is like a faded photo, and the contributors to *Testimony* examine their lives for what is missing: relatives, friends, but also culture, history. And more than that: childhoods silently touched. Symbolically as well as literally, the dead could not be buried, but *Testimony* suggests how each of us, however young, can look back on our lives and still trace the loss. Can it be enough to hand children the books I myself once read? Or must the facts of life be told personally, no matter how poorly known, and even though the times seem to change. Even to say we are still living in the generation of witnesses is important, and further: We've become transmitters, whatever we say.

"When did you first learn of the Holocaust?—and at what stages in your life did the education proceed? How has it shaped

—or been absent from—your career as an American writer? Has it been abused or forgotten in ways that affected you?" These were among the questions I put to writers whose courage to face the subject led me to choose them for this book. They are questions that most Americans can ask of themselves about an event that has shaken our perception of humanity, yet for Jews they hit closer to home. "For those of us not contemporary with the event, it could only 'dawn' upon us—but even if you were influenced by the aftershock of the event itself, I would want to know what mute life was then set speaking (or what sensitivity silenced), what dread was reawakened, what strength or necessity found."

When *Testimony* was conceived I built on the previous collection I edited, *Congregation*. In both, the most challenging task for a writer, the most engaging for a reader, is the contrast between childhood and adult knowledge. In *Congregation*, it is knowledge of the Bible; in *Testimony*, it is of the Holocaust. In either case the subject was encountered by us—even in youth, even as it happened—as mythic in proportion to the everyday. To expand our sense of personal history, we need the talent of accomplished poets and novelists. The candor of a creative memoir, as it fights for maturity, can reflect a reader's own unfolding sense of the past.

Since the center of Jewish culture shifted after World War Two, from Europe to Israel, it has been easier for Americans to presume the culture was dying, or so it seemed in the United States after the deaths of major Yiddish poets and writers. Among the contributors to *Testimony,* not many know even a handful of Israeli writers—or any other non-American Jewish writers—of their own generation. Forgotten in America is the taproot to an extraordinary Jewish genre of lament, as if blacks were to forget the blues.

Yet this book sets off in a new direction. Some of the writers find themselves retracing the Jewish culture missed in childhood. They modify the notion that the Holocaust is the sole catalyst for reviving Judaism in secular America. Philip Roth wrote recently, "The willful amnesia that I generally came up against whenever I tried as a child to establish the details of our pre-

American existence was not unique to our family." Still, the postwar amnesia that troubled the best American Jewish writers is breaking up. Many contributors to *Testimony* no longer feel estranged from the words of the Ba'al Shem Tov, a Hasidic authority whom their grandparents may have respected: "Forgetting lengthens the period of exile. In remembrance lies the secret of deliverance." Some contributors found these words engraved on visits to Israel—carved above the entrance to the memorial hall at Yad Vashem, Israel's multilayered complex of Holocaust archives, educational resources, and memorials.

There were other writers I contacted—most of the celebrities who spring to mind—and many expressed interest in contributing to *Testimony,* only later to deny, like Roth, an ability to link up with the European history of parents and ancestors. Contrast Isaac Bashevis Singer, still the master of American Jewish writers—writing in the 1950s in *The Family Moskat,* and in later works—for whom the Holocaust is always ahead of us, the dark center of an impending war, casting its shadow backward and forward. Yet in most American war novels until very recently, the Holocaust is a peripheral event; even German history is more engaging than Jewish history.

A writer's ear can evoke a contemporary context for feelings as extreme as dread or paralysis—feelings repressed in childhood. There is nothing human in the Holocaust—only the inhuman, the doing of evil—that is foreign to us. Yet the unconscious trouble of childhood is easily denied, as easily as it is lampooned by those denying their own self-betrayals. It is easy to defend oneself from a Holocaust that is buried in the past.

Yet not so easy in this book. The testimony of these writers swerves away from the common route of denying connection. Connecting, they may reopen routes to Freud but also an ancient prayer book, the Jewish Machzor. Leading up to Yom Kippur, the prayers indict the self, judge it for the repressed wishes of the heart; avoidance especially, hiding, denial. Though none wraps itself in piety, many of these essays approach the best in Jewish writing by mirroring origins, recalling an obsession with truth. When you turn to the imaginative writing of these authors, you again meet an obsession with unmasking denial. The masks that fall may be small but nevertheless grandiose, made to distort memory.

This book includes a converted Jew who looks back to an unusual past in rural Georgia and one who recalls Judenrein towns in West Germany—yet they seem no more exotic than those Jewish writers in New York and Los Angeles whose parents tasted every life-style. Their children grew up with all sorts of dreams; some embraced Israel, some Hollywood, some an inner escape. All kinds of Jews were destroyed in the Holocaust; by reflecting that diversity our past can retain some immediacy. There are writers in this book who escaped Europe, losing immediate family and mother tongues in the Holocaust—while others, exposed only to English, hardly knew they were Jewish.

Does anyone go up to the attic anymore, to look through the old family albums? The pain has sunk in, rests buried in an old cemetery in an old neighborhood. In the early postwar years, it was riveting to point out snapshots taken in Europe, to hear, "This one and this one died soon after. This sweet-faced one was twelve. She wore a leg brace from polio. When they took her away from her mother, Aunt Yanka told us she screamed, 'I can work, I can work!' "

Now when we refer to the Holocaust, it's a more complex event—earlier ages seem more innocent. Sodom and Gomorrah may have lost power—except in poetry, where progress is illusory. But *Testimony* does rescue from attics the bond to a deeper past. The purpose is not nostalgic; rather, a context for a voice in Claude Lanzmann's *Shoah*: "Suddenly you're not what minutes before you were—part of a family, father, son, husband, brother, cousin, uncle, nephew. All gone. There was nothing, they were dead, the ones who came to weddings, to funerals."

In fashionable styles of thinking, things may be different. The ability to forget a painful past—or to erect facades that re-create pre-Holocaust days—predominates. "Postmodern," most accurate in its irony that we are less than modern, barely registers the black hole of the Holocaust as significant gravity in Western culture. And probably it is in America that the greatest distance from the Holocaust has been achieved. In Europe there's an audience educated in the war, but in America Primo Levi was shocked to find that the sold-out audiences on his American lecture tours were entirely Jewish, as if the Holocaust were a subject Jews kept to themselves.

Rediscovering the Holocaust in college in the sixties, where Raul Hilberg's groundbreaking *Destruction of the European Jews* was all but unknown, I was unprepared for the jolt. The major American authors were still alive and even writing—Eliot, Auden, Williams, Bishop, Hemingway, Faulkner, Frost, Pound—yet you could read them along with those in their prime and never come across the Holocaust. There was little in our education to point out how sheltered their lives had been. I do remember a course in anthropology, and trying hard to imagine the headhunter tribes, the few who were cannibals, as if they were alien. But even they—who read no Heidegger, listened to no Wagner—were conscious of the awesome role played by those whom they cooked.

Then I found instead, as if underground, a Jewish literature in which the vanquished were remembered with tenderness, the victors hardly at all. Greek and Roman massacres of Jews—cultures I had routinely studied—were recorded in grim detail in the Talmud, as if by Holocaust survivors. Other books in the post-biblical Jewish library mirrored Western history with a counterculture for which no literary equivalent exists: instead of the politics of Crusades, I found trembling accounts of catastrophe. It is a form of witness, a lament which the civilizations I knew best—knowing dominance, imperialism—could not articulate. Through it, along with the negative inversions of inner life—anxieties of the Kabbalah—and then Medieval and Modern Hebrew literature, I found windows, strange to American culture, onto Islam as well as Christianity, Russian power as well as Arabic—from a context of vulnerability, a culture apart.

In the same way, the synagogue's "Service of the Heart" remains an underlying spirituality in all Jewish denominations. Steadily refined since pre-Christian times, it is also Judaism's least understood aspect in a historically Christian society. Even when our greatest cantors sing, they are as if engulfed by sobs.

Why does it scare me when the Holocaust is explained away as genocide? Some authors in this book are not frightened by it —am I overdramatizing? It's my own ignorance that frightens me: What I've understood is missing in American culture makes me fear how much more is lost in the extermination of European Jewry. Precious lives were obliterated in other genocides, yet a Christian or a humanist or even a Muslim has lost through the Final Solution his own links to Jewish origins. The Jewish culture in their midst is gone. I don't want to beg for curriculums, though I support struggles to grasp in imagination what otherwise cannot be saved. Perhaps the leading Holocaust thinker today, Saul Friedlander in Israel, is chilling when he contrasts the impact of World War One on the intellectual life of the West, with the Holocaust: "None of the major cultural currents which have developed in the West since the war have been directly influenced by it."

Perhaps I fear a damaged sensibility lies behind the journalese that can equate—not warily compare—atrocities. Isn't it a shortcut to repression? Forget for a moment the sum of atrocities in the Holocaust, or in any other genocide—I want to see the Holocaust, instead, as an historical process. I want the lives and history behind it, not to crave so much selfish distance that I can't see past the burning fires, the smoke. I would also welcome with deep affection the Cambodian historians—those who would enrich me with the culture lost, alongside the dread tales of survivors we can't stop listening to, a dialogue of past and present.

I would embrace Soviet or Polish poets who may yet negate the amnesia that denies a specifically Jewish loss. Behind a gauze of half-truths that covers the Soviet sphere of influence, a soccer team from Lodz, Poland—a city built and peopled with a larger proportion of Jews than New York, comes to play internationally, and even the players and their spokesman have no idea why the Jews alone did not come back after the war. Oh, the Jews? They were killed by the Germans, along with the Poles. But there are Poles on this Polish team—where are the Jews? Where is the Jewish graveyard?

What am I asking for—an interruption of soccer? No, I want

the poets to come and be interviewed first, the poets, scholars, and historians. In the United States recently, the Russian poet Yevgeny Yevtushenko was raising money for "Memorial," a group building a monument to Stalin's victims. I was reminded of the Israeli poet Abba Kovner's fund-raising many years ago in America for the Scroll of Fire, to little interest. I was suspicious myself of working with institutions that think they know what they want from poets. Still, this is no longer a generation that is shocked by the dark age we've lived in, to which the atrocities return us. *Testimony* is not about establishing the soul-chilling facts—though that is still a crucial work—and not about anyone else's atrocities, though that must also stiffen one's attention. The Holocaust, as it burns in Western memory, gives off a sadness carried within now. We may only be taking first steps in the heart's ascent from it.

Entering the sixties, the focus remained on the perpetrators, not the victims: Eichmann as a Nazi bureaucrat was a demonic type for all bureaucrats. Testimony meant standing up to the bureaucracies, from the House Un-American Activities Committee to Watergate. Now we can acknowledge that testimony goes deeper, to the pain of not having known the victims as individuals within their culture, once our culture. Their absence outlines the fragility of civilization. Recognizing naive visions of the future—superficial political dreams, technological daydreams, religious fantasies—it's easier today to identify the wish for quick, even brutal, fixes.

This book's different testimony represents a generation linking up with its childhood by describing what could not then be expressed. In that respect, we led sheltered lives (that, in fact, was the working title of this book).

Yet the predilection of others to look away, to resist the probing of original myths, is still with us. In postwar Europe, those who view themselves as having been seduced by evil can still observe a taboo of silence, passing the abuse on to their children. Or, instead of sharing the burden of complicity, the parents wish the damage away in a faulty admission: they were victims, but as if the crime were the robbery of a cash register that blind work will restore.

A brief eruption of recognition, as in the speaker of the West German parliament's speech marking Kristallnacht's fiftieth anniversary, was lost under questions of appropriateness. Some of his words read: "Who could doubt that in 1938 a majority of the Germans stood behind Hitler? Many allowed themselves to be blinded and seduced by National Socialism. Many made the crimes possible through their indifference. That is why the call to 'finally put an end' to our past is senseless. Our past will not be quiet, it will not go away." If one's parents were mentally raped by Hitler, one's youth today would still deserve a therapy, a chance to acknowledge damaged origins. This is not a charge of collective guilt at all; it's a wish for therapy, to counter what the philosopher Theodor Adorno once discerned in Germany: "The hatred for Freudian theory is directly of a piece with anti-Semitism, not just because Freud was a Jew but because psychoanalysis consists precisely of a critical self-reflection that puts anti-Semites into a seething rage."

Earlier last year, West Germany's president had mentioned, "Auschwitz remains unique. It was perpetrated by Germans in the name of Germany." So now what? One can only live with it in unease, and expressions beyond these noble words are few. Unused to such self-consciousness, most face the catastrophe by distancing it, reducing it to a familiar crime in history. It's hard to blame anyone for seeking comfort in distance, in declaring himself absent from the scene, unborn even, yet the inner wound festers when crimes are left repressed. About the actual victims, "Jews are only accepted when dead"—so the media recently quoted a well-meaning teacher in Germany. What the teacher must have meant is that there is still little education in Germany of why Jews are more than victims, why Jewish culture has continued to grow throughout history, surviving Christian and even Communist myths.

And then there is the German chancellor, who declared that "this crime of genocide is without parallel in its cold-blooded, inhuman planning and its deadly efficiency," and "we Germans have to live with the terrible fact." Yet how? The survivors have shown us that asking the question is more than a lifetime's work. Merely accepting a presence of bureaucratic evil, as some may have done in the sixties—imagining it everywhere around us—

goes only so far. In a front-page review of a controversial book, the *New York Times* reviewer quotes the author, historian Arno Mayer, and adds for the rest of us: " 'The Judeocide remains as incomprehensible to me today as five years ago, when I set out to study and rethink it.' Who does not share this feeling and the sense of despair it engenders?" Yet what is five years?

In *Testimony,* the anger is sometimes addressed openly. Toughened by the sixties, many authors share the strength of the Holocaust's major historian, Raul Hilberg, who declared on Bill Moyers' television special, *Facing Evil,* "I have not despaired, always remembering the words of Sigmund Freud in 1915: 'Do not despair over what you see now, a First'—only in those days they didn't say First—'a World War, for mankind has not risen very highly, and therefore it has not fallen so much.' And so I say to myself, 'Oh my, how many years are still left me to continue this research? Forty years is not a long time.' "

If art emerges from the breakup of old faiths, it also gains energy from the desire to remember them. That desire is sensed budding in this book, in the shelter of memory. Within it, Jewish history can't begin or end with the Holocaust; instead, it returns even through Thorstein Veblen's old description of the cosmopolitan Jew of the mind, through Freud, and to the meetings between secular and religious modes, to Americans and Israelis redrafting Jewish culture, a Harold Bloom or a Moshe Idel.

Proceeding in their own ways, the authors of *Testimony* redefine the myths of their private lives, to find the Holocaust woven among them. Sometimes it's hard to forgo a swipe at one's vexations, from the latest in television styles to Israeli hippies. Yet these writers have avoided using the Holocaust as a cheap parallel to yesterday's headlines. At the same time, these pieces were not written to be etched in stone, and I discouraged any potential contributor who felt compelled to strike a pose of censorious reverence. I wanted to avoid at all costs the false notes of the academic, and perhaps I went too far; for instance, of the hundreds of immensely important books and films recording the Holocaust, few are mentioned. But I encouraged contributors to improvise, to take tentative steps of personal engagement. Even as the library of serious studies expands, built on heart-stopping accounts by the original witnesses, *Testimony* follows, by suggesting we can look more closely at our own lives—not just the lives of others—to see where the shadow continues to fall.

A Note

Authors may have their own preferred terms for the Final Solution, or the war against the Jews. I accept the term "Holocaust" as the common one in English and the earliest—especially for the painful irony of its many origins. (In the collected edition of Freud he edited, A. A. Brill noted in 1938: "As these pages are going to the printer we have just been startled by the terrible news that the Nazi holocaust has suddenly encircled Vienna and that Professor Freud and his family are virtual prisoners.")

Acknowledgments

This project has many friends, and I am especially indebted to those whose support only grew stronger: Grace Schulman, Barbara Rogan, Jody Leopold, Gail Labovitz, Walter Brown, Harold Bloom for his probity, and two who always took this book personally, Lew Grimes of Janklow & Nesbit Associates, and Sandee Brawarsky of Times Books. My mother, Shifra Asarch, mothered this book even by telephone. I also wish to thank Cynthia Ozick, who introduced me to the young German-born writer Susanne Schlötelburg.

—*David Rosenberg*

I

To Feel These Things

LEONARD MICHAELS

1

My mother was seventeen when she married
and said good-bye to her parents in Brest Litovsk. She then
sailed the Atlantic to New York and settled in an apartment in
Coney Island. Soon afterward, the year Hitler came to power, I
was born. Roosevelt had been elected president a bit earlier.
These two names, intoned throughout my childhood, belonged
to mythical deities. One was evil. The other was the other.

My mother's family expected to follow her to America, but
the day her father went to get their emigration papers he was
attacked in the street by a vicious mob. They left him for dead.
He didn't recover quickly and then it was too late to get out of
Poland. In photos he is pale and thin. The skin pulls tight across
sharp facial bones. He looks ill-nourished but sits posing in the
old style, as if a photo is serious business. My mother says they
threw his unconscious body into a cellar. I heard the story
around the time children hear fairy tales, as if it too were make-
believe. Once upon a time my grandfather . . .

The beating occurred during a pogrom, before the official
beginning of the Holocaust, when it was still possible to know

---
3

what was happening in Poland. I heard about pogroms from my mother, who had been a witness. Years later I would hear that organized terrorism had been reported for centuries in Europe, Russia, and the Middle East, and that rabbinical commentaries engaged questions as to whether the community should surrender a few to save the rest, die with the few, or resist. Rabbis consulted the commentaries while the S.S. prepared gas chambers and worked out train schedules. When the Nazis seized Brest Litovsk, my grandfather, his wife, and his youngest daughter were buried in a pit with others.

My mother thought she had lost her whole family in Poland. I was all she had left of close blood. As she sat in the living room waiting for my father to come home from work, she sometimes cried. This was my personal experience of the Holocaust, though only the effects of it thousands of miles away, in a small apartment, amid claw-footed furniture covered by plastic to protect the fabric. I saw her crying, but mainly I imagined things. To understand, I was obliged to imagine, to dream up the world from little clues, the story about my grandfather, my mother crying.

I came to understand that it was always bad for the Jews, the way "it" is said to be raining. I didn't know what it was, but I was sure it was more than a man called Hitler. He was the leader of the Nazis, the latest manifestation, but it was far greater than he, infinitely more pervasive, and much older. It was cruel, unreasonable, strong, able to fix the plumbing and paint the walls. It didn't speak Yiddish. It was like animals and trees more than a person, though it appeared in persons, anywhere, anytime. It lived for pleasure and murder, especially the murder of Jews because they were everything it wasn't. No other reason.

I came to understand all this because my mother, an adolescent without her own parents, siblings, or friends, was very intimidated by her surroundings in America, even fearful of going out alone in the streets. She had long black hair and gray-blue eyes. Strange men wanted to approach and talk to her. She kept me close. We were constantly together, I was constantly sick with respiratory diseases and ear infections; many colds, bronchitis, pleurisy, and pneumonia twice. She sat at my bedside saying *"Meir fa deir,"* again and again, which meant "Let me die rather than you." I never thought I was going to die, only that I'd be weak and feverish forever, unable to compete in playground games with other boys, always skinny, timid, badly coordinated, burdened by sweaters and scarves and winter coats buttoned to the neck. If I loosened my scarf or undid a coat button, my mother would fly into a state of panic as though millions of germs were shooting through the gap I'd made in my clothing. My mother was beautiful and hysterical. She told me about pogroms.

After we moved from Coney Island to the Lower East Side of Manhattan, my mother and I were separated for the first time. I began going to school. There I was quickly singled out as an exceptional child and subjected to intelligence tests. They were to determine whether I was a moron. I, too, was intimidated by everything. During the war I began to change.

I put a large map of Europe on my bedroom wall. When I read about Allied bombing raids in Germany, Poland, Italy, or elsewhere, I would find the city and stick a red pin into it. I imagined myself as a pilot or a bombardier in a B-17. When I saw, in the movies, the doors of the bomb bay swing open and the long bombs with tails and the sticklike incendiaries fall away toward factories and railroad tracks, or whole cities, I felt satisfaction and enormous relief. The great work was being done. Ordinary Americans, plain folks, regular guys from Brooklyn and Kansas, were winning the war. I saw it in the movies.

My mother took me to the movies on Friday afternoons when school let out. I waited all day through math, history, reading, drawing, and assembly with bombers and fighter planes raging in my head toward Germany, and the minutes passed slowly, so slowly they didn't seem to pass at all, but then, suddenly, school ended and I was free to run home. Before we left for the movies, I had to drink a glass of milk. I hated its whiteness, the whiteness of its taste, and the idea of it as good for me. "Finish the whole glass. It's good for you." She watched until the whole glass, like a column of liquefied teeth, went down into me. To the last nauseating drop. But then came the B-17, a big dark bird stuck with machine guns in its ribs, nose, belly, and tail. It was a primordial winged reptile dragging long flaps and lugubrious claws for landing gear, lumbering up into the gray dawn among its thousand sisters, each of them bearing a great load of bombs. It was my image of the good, love's fierce answer to evil. The B-17 was the best thing I had with which to hit back hard. An image. Almost an action; almost my action. I carried it about for years in my head and heart, the feeling of that clumsy mass of aluminum sculpture called "flying fortress." It was how I revenged my mother's grief, how I did something to ease my sense of responsibility, my need to act, be effective.

After the war, her brothers' names appeared in the Yiddish newspaper, *The Forward,* which was published a few blocks from where we lived, in a tall white building opposite the Seward Park Library. It seemed miraculous that my uncles' names had come from Europe to the *Forward* building, which I'd passed many times going to the library or to my father's barbershop around the corner on Henry Street. But the distant, the exotic, the un-imaginable was in these streets, even in the Garden cafeteria near the foot of the *Forward* building, where I sometimes sat with my father and ate whitefish on black bread with onion, and stared at the dark Jewish faces of taxi drivers, pickle salesmen, dry goods merchants, journalists, and other urban beings who sipped coffee or borscht, and smoked cigarettes and argued, joked, or com-plained in Yiddish or in such English as had been mutilated into the nuances of sense and feeling required by Yiddish, grammati-cal niceties flung aside so that meaning could walk on the earth.

The names of my uncles, Yussel and Srulke Czeskies, had appeared among the names of survivors who had been gathered in camps for displaced persons, in Italy and elsewhere, and who now sought relatives in America. One uncle had been in the Russian army, the other in the Polish army.

I was happy. I was also worried. My mother would bring them to America, but would she be held guilty for what they had endured? She hadn't been with them. She hadn't been able to save the family. But they hadn't seen how she cried, and they couldn't know what it was like to live amid American greatness and be unable to do anything for them, or even to know what had happened to them. When they came to America, says my mother, my character changed. I became a "cold boy."

There is injustice, more imagined than real, against which

nothing can be said. We'd done nothing bad, and yet I felt a weight of blame and had an early notion of guilt as fundamental to life. It was wonderful to see her brothers in our apartment, and I felt very happy, but I retreated to corners, looking cold and sullen, as if absorbed in private shadowy thought, like a neighborhood cat. A strange mechanism of feelings drew me away from simple happiness into inward complications, like one who is depressed by holidays.

My parents didn't disclaim our religion, and nothing strange or skeptical entered their orthodoxy, but the father of a friend of mine, as a result of the Holocaust, began to detest all organized religious expression. He developed his own interpretations and religious practices, as if he were the only Jew who really understood what was on God's mind. His life was reduced to secret study and his tuxedo-renting business. To his mind, the Jews had been punished for some grotesque mistake. He sacrificed himself to putting things right and spent no time with his children or, if he had any, friends. Nothing but God and the wretched distraction of business.

Maybe he wasn't exceptional. Even as a child, I thought we were obsessed with meaning. We didn't just eat, sleep, work, study, play, but wanted the meaning of these things and everything. Meaning as such, as if it had inherent practical value, like wood or gold. We sought it with brain fingers, loved how it felt in the elaborations of talk. At the heart of talk and all meaning was the religion, the law, forever established, yet open to analysis and explanation. My parents sent me to Hebrew school and I was bar mitzvahed, and I made a speech, though I had nothing to say. A rabbi wrote it for me. I only demonstrated that I could talk, make the sound of meaning.

I went to Hebrew school in the late afternoon every weekday, every weather. It was in a low-ceilinged room of dull yellowish light, reflected off thickly varnished wood desks and paneled walls. The room was in the bottom of a tenement on East Broadway. To sing in public, in the synagogue, was a frightening prospect, since I couldn't carry a tune, but I entered a delirium of Hebrew prayer, as if I'd acquired an ear and become a believer. The idea of sacrifice works for Christians; the

Holocaust worked for me. I believed if you flip a coin and it comes down heads, Hitler murders Jews. If it comes down tails, nobody cares.

I could tell one Jew from another according to whether they believed as I did. They were lucky or frivolous if they didn't; or, in their indifference to plain truth, they were self-annihilating. Believe it, I thought. Your life is at stake. If it isn't true about the endless murdering, who knows? So believe it anyway. Feel Jewish. Improve your chances against being murdered. Thus, I advanced to a higher level of thought.

Seeing my mother alone and helpless in her grief, I'd also felt alone, strangely invisible. It was as if we'd been abandoned, like her family and the others, to the nature of things, wherein there is a general complicity with murder. It was in the concrete sidewalks, the grass, the weather, and the human heart, not to mention all the fish in the sea, a need to murder, a need for the pleasure in it. I remember pictures of President Roosevelt, his long handsome face, with its insouciant smile, his cigarette holder aloft in a white aristocratic hand, perhaps in the manner of S.S. officers outside the windows of the gas chambers, chatting and smoking as we died in agony visible to them. Of course I wasn't there. I had nothing to fear. I had only a sense of ubiquitous savagery, the inchoate nightmarish apprehensions of a child, much like insanity or the numinousness of a religious vision where ideas have the force of presence, overriding logic. I heard Yiddish-speaking relatives discuss the president's tepid reaction to Kristallnacht and his decision to turn away a ship of Jewish refugees from American shores. From those who could make a difference, I figured, came indifference. Knowing nothing about immigration laws or the isolationist politics of America, I understood only an aesthetics of power, the weird mixture of comfort and sadism in the president's smile. In the very capacity to do something, lived the frisson of doing nothing, of not caring. I could not have articulated this understanding any more than I could have said how I tie my shoelaces.

"Take care," writes Primo Levi, "not to suffer in your own homes what is inflicted on us here." He means don't let his experience of Auschwitz become yours. Don't let it happen again. He is very clear, but I had to read the sentence repeatedly before I understood that is all he means, and that he doesn't mean: NOT TO FEEL THESE THINGS IN THE DAILINESS OF YOUR LIFE OR IT WILL POISON EVERYTHING ELSE.

Thus, misreading a few words, I discover primitive egocentric apprehensions in myself long after the Holocaust. Levi isn't talking about feelings. He doesn't mean what I thought. Still, not to have felt these things in my own home wasn't and isn't easy. A governor of feelings would have had to be screwed into my head. But I confess to misgivings. I must literally remind myself that nothing happened to me. I wasn't with my grandparents and other relatives in Poland, or with the children in the trains to the death camps. Local citizens didn't hear my screams. My childhood was touched by the horror, nothing more. I cannot claim too little.

2

In the early sixties I lived on 104th Street, near Riverside Drive, a short walk to Columbia University, where, one afternoon, Hannah Arendt was to make a personal appearance and talk about her book on Eichmann, which had caused dismay and outrage in Jewish literary circles. I couldn't imagine what an impersonal appearance might be, but this one would certainly be personal. Arendt would surrender authorial invisibility and come forward, testify. With her physical presence she would take responsibility for her book, as if to say, "Here I am. I really mean what I wrote. Jews conspired in their own destruction, etc." In this New York setting, to say it was more courageous than to write it, since the audience was likely to be hostile. She'd already been abused in print. Some said her book was ill-informed; others said worse. Maybe she would offer a few more words about what she called "the banality of evil," but I was less interested in her ideas than in the drama of the occasion, and I wondered if she would find a way, within the scope of her dignity, to apologize for the book. To me, it issued from a kind of snobbery, suggested by her use of the word "banality." For the sake of an off-rhyme jingle, she'd written "banality of evil" instead of a less surprising, but adequate, less clever, less self-regarding qualifier.

Snobbery, if that's what it was, seemed an odd response to

Holocaust matters, like a refusal to feel common things or to identify with the grief and rage of survivors. I supposed every Jew felt grief. It seemed inevitable, but I was eventually to learn there are more ways not to feel things, common and otherwise, than to feel even what seemed inevitable. To me, that is. To me, whatever it's worth, being told that Eichmann was a dull, ordinary fellow was like being told Nazi murderers took pleasure in Mozart. In the light of their crimes, neither dullness nor refined taste seemed a fascinating perplexity. I'd heard people say that the Nazis had undermined Western civilization, had brought meaning itself into question. If so, I hadn't noticed. Too big; an idea like the sky; too vague. Western civilization was a course in universities, a hypothetical construction invented by professors. Grief and rage were real; beyond question. Then came the Eichmann book, its ironical tone, the word "banality." Nazis were merely contemptible. The snobbish air certainly wasn't unique to Arendt, but part of a familiar tone, something like a protective coloration that is often discovered in the prose of intellectuals, and it is typically associated with irony.

Along with other colors of rhetoric, irony derives from the camouflage techniques of animals. To hide or kill, they become indistinguishable from their environment. A twig is a snake. A light-streaked bush is a tiger. A rock is a lizard. An innocuous comment is a deadly cut. Irony feeds on doubleness, separating you from your subject, your outside from your inside. It can be hilarious or chilling. It shades easily into snobbery. Even Socrates, original master of irony, if he applied his manner to the Holocaust, would seem insufferable, especially if he carried on about allegiance to the state, the necessity of obeying orders.

Arendt described the effects of terror as unimaginably awesome in her previous book. In this book about Eichmann, the agent of terror, it was an ordinary, shabby, boring business. Perhaps in the talk she would insist on distinctions. What she seemed to say as opposed to what she said in fact. All this gave interest to seeing and hearing her. I had another interest, too, that was entirely emotional. It had to do with my marriage to Sylvia Bloch, a brilliant German Jew whom I considered crazy. She had refused to go with me to the talk, but then she couldn't read more than a few pages of Arendt without having a fit and railing at me for bringing the book into the apartment, for calling it to her attention, for thinking about huge evils when we had so much else to think about of far greater immediate importance, like our relationship, the source of daily trouble, violence, and gloom. In a way, then, against Sylvia, I went to the talk.

It was a beautiful sunny day, like an open mind, and I looked forward to enjoying the drama of Arendt's appearance, even to being edified, though my life was a mess and I was confused and unhappy about everything. Recently, in a doctor's waiting room, I'd read a magazine article about Patagonia and I'd begun to dream of going there, living in a bleak lovely place that was incessantly cleansed by fierce winds and the corrosive air of the tumultuous Pacific. Then I remembered that Nazis fled to Argentina after the war, establishing pockets of poison in even the remotest areas.

The auditorium was nearly full when I arrived, and soon it became overcrowded with people sitting on the floor and window ledges, mostly students, young, nicely dressed, respectful of the occasion, long trained to listen to authorities, or whoever happened to be standing in the front of the room. A few years later, during the war in Vietnam, this would change.

Arendt paced the stage and, with her arms crossed on her chest, she stopped to face her questioners. Her posture was defiant and defensive at once. It became apparent that she was a strong proud woman who intended nothing like an apology, and that the event would be only serious and too polite. Academic. It could have been conducted by telephone. I began to lose interest and to drift away on my interior cloud of anxieties. There was no drama to hold me, no agon. Then, toward the end, in response to some question, I think she said, "We must wait for the poets." I sat right up, tried to focus, to re-create the context, but hands were already in the air with new questions, new remarks.

It was a long time ago. I didn't take notes. If indeed she said, "We must wait for the poets," perhaps she meant they would teach us how to speak about the Holocaust without exploiting the subject, without assimilating it to advertisements of our sensibility, without bad rhetoric, without risk of any other obscenity. The poets would transform what isn't even anybody's subject

—except for victims and scholars—into a language free of all narcissism. They will speak with correct impersonality, which is by no means unfeeling, of the hideous abomination. In this future speaking, we will rediscover our humanity. If indeed she said, "We must wait for the poets," it might count as an apology, a good thing to say. Whatever she said, I carried that phrase back down Riverside Drive and into the small hell of my three-room apartment on 104th Street, and I've thought about it many times over the years while waiting for the poets.

Dreaming of Hitler:
A Memoir of Self-Hatred

DAPHNE MERKIN

1

For a number of years during my late adolescence and early teens I dreamed about Hitler. These dreams
occurred irregularly, but they always took place in a verdant
setting—the same green glen to which I summoned other male
figures, Bob Dylan and Franz Kafka, whom I longed to meet.
(Why the mind of an inveterate city girl like myself should have
found it easier to spin fantasies in a rural setting is a curiosity to
me still: Do country dwellers place their dreams in bustling metropolitan areas?) In these dreams I stood at the end of a long
vertical of grass and from the other end a man walked toward
me. The man was dressed in a khaki uniform and tall, glossy
black boots; his eyes were a piercing light blue with tiny pupils,
and he sported a perky, abridged mustache. The man coming
toward me could have been anyone, a father or a boyfriend, but
he was recognizably none other than Adolf Hitler. Adolf Hitler
was smiling at me!

What took place in these dreams amounted to a miracle, a
miracle performed not by God's hands, as I had been taught, but
by my very own: I convinced Hitler that he didn't really hate the

Jews. I did this by talking to him softly, against a sun set low in the sky. Our conversation seemed to take up in the middle, as though we had been interrupted only recently. It involved a lot of gentle argument, of the sort two lovers might engage in. At one point during our conversation Hitler even stroked my hair —the hair of a Jewess, I remember thinking deep within the dream, the wrong color hair, not an Aryan blond. The thrust of my argument with Hitler was very personal, almost embarrassingly intimate. It had little to do with what I considered to be the pompous male line of thinking about the world, with theories of a humiliated post–World War One Germany or of an entrenched national anti-Semitism.

I believed entirely in private wounds. After all, I had enough rage in me to decimate whole races, and I was only a girl. Having been fascinated by Hitler for years, I had read enough about his background to know that the real object of his fury was his father, Alois, who had beaten him with Teutonic conviction.

"Don't you see," I said, "it's not us you can't stand, not me. It's your anger at your childhood that makes you want to kill all the Jews."

Oh, the serene imperialism of dreams, where Adolf Hitler nodded his head, comprehendingly, and 6 million lives were about to be spared! How much we can undo in dreams. I would wake up with a secretive glow, a sense of mastery that I never experienced in my everyday life.

I first learned about the Holocaust at an age when I had difficulty assimilating it as other than a natural extension of the hostility I felt directed at me by my own parents, siblings, and schoolmates. The effect of that hostility—or at least as it was perceived by me—had landed me in a hospital for extended psychiatric observation at the age of eight. The given reason for my two-week stay was that I suffered from anemia, but my siblings—my brothers, especially—were not fooled by the medical cover my mother put on my emotional distress. They looked at me strangely when I returned home and started referring to a "brain operation." Nothing much changed after this—nothing that would have alleviated the family situation—except that I started seeing a psychiatrist. The second psychiatrist I went to believed in "play therapy," and I remember my frenzied beating up of dolls in her office.

Although I don't connect the growing despair of my childhood with anything so remote from it as Hitler's destruction of the Jews, I think an awareness of that massive, external effort contributed to my innate feeling of houndedness. For children, the world begins at home, and in my home there was a lot of terror. My parents were both German Jews, of authoritarian inclinations. I was one of six tightly spaced children who pretty much toed the line, except that in my case a sense of internal protest expressed itself in incessant tears, and I was sent off for repairs. It seems to me now that the fact of the Holocaust did not come to me as a revelation so much as a confirmation of something I already fatally knew: the world was full of pain, might made for right, and everywhere lurked insinuating ironies. *Arbeit Macht Frei*—Work Will Set You Free—was the inscription mockingly emblazoned on the entrance gate to Auschwitz; if there was no actual gate to our apartment, there might as well have been, for we were an unusually isolated family enclave, barricaded by money and religion.

Even before I learned about the specific brand and virulence of Hitler's hatred, I was aware of a certain fragility about the whole enterprise of being Jewish. The Upper East Side of Manhattan, which is where I grew up, was—and still is—a bastion of genteel money. The Jews who live there are a fairly assimilated bunch, given to stringing Christmas lights along with their Christian neighbors. My family, on the other hand, was strictly Orthodox, given to lighting Hanukkah candles and to the observance of deeply separatist rituals such as those of kashrut and Shabbat. Although there is much about the nature of Orthodox Jewish life that is self-ghettoizing, this tendency is less obvious —certainly less noticeable—in neighborhoods where like-minded Jews live together. But in the fifties and sixties, the years in which I reached adolescence, there were few like-minded Jews in the neighborhood who shared my family's ways. To walk along Park Avenue on Yom Kippur in dressy clothes and the requisite sneakers (this was well before the Age of Reeboks) induced in me a state of morbid self-consciousness: *everyone* who passed on the street could tell I was Jewish, as clearly as if I were wearing a yellow star.

But nothing was clear about the subculture of being Jewish in the larger culture of America, anyway. There was no direct route to unambivalent ethnic pride because there was something I imbibed very early on about the possibility—even in my highly identified family—of seeming *too* Jewish. My father wore his yarmulke at home but not outside or at business. My brothers wore theirs at home and in the Jewish day school they attended, but on the street they sported baseball caps, the better to mingle with the populace. If being Jewish was all right, why wasn't it *completely* all right? Why, for instance, did I detect an admiration in my mother for an aesthetic that was quintessentially "WASP," a love of understatement and a disdain for flash? My brothers wore Eton suits—gray or navy wool shorts and jackets—in the traditions of the sons of the British upper classes, and my sisters and I were outfitted in the guileless, unfrilly clothes favored by patrician mothers everywhere. Floating always among us was an awareness of the importance of avoiding, if one could help it, too "Jewish" an appearance, the dreaded stigma of too "Jewish" a voice. My sisters, accordingly, emerged with carefully modulated accents that sounded vaguely foreign, a mix of German and British. I, by some cruel twist of fate, developed in my high school years an accent that sounded unmistakably, harshly "New Yawk." My mother and sisters wanted to know why I talked like I came from Brooklyn, but somewhere in me I must have wanted to shed all vestiges of the dominant culture and get back to the lusty Jewish core. Most resoundingly of all, everyone I knew admired the sort of looks—in both men and women—that are thought of as quintessentially non-Jewish: the Irish handsomeness of a John Kennedy, the sweet-featuredness of a Donna Reed. My sisters and I venerated the blond and blue-eyed child actress Hayley Mills. Who among these icons displayed the prominent nose, darker coloring, or intensity of gaze I associated with being Jewish?

Can racial self-hatred be passed along, like a bad gene?

16

In a theater in the Upper West Side, somewhere in the middle of *Hotel Terminus,* Max Ophuls's movie about Klaus Barbie —the infamous "Butcher of Lyons," a rabid Nazi but also the father of a pretty blond daughter who speaks lovingly of him— the following statement is made: "Only Jews and old Nazis are interested in Jews and old Nazis."

It is an observation that stays with me after the film is over, another of those insinuating ironies, chilling the night air. The person I saw the movie with was struck by different aspects of it than I was. A friend of long standing, she says she had not noticed the pervasive, cool anti-Semitism expressed by many of the Americans and Europeans interviewed in the film. I accuse her, as we wait for the light to change along Broadway, of insufficient Jewish self-awareness, a cultivated disinterest inherited from *her* parents. It occurs to me even as I point this out, that ethnic consciousness of a high order—who is less or more Jewish —is a relative luxury. In Lyons, in the early forties, we would both have been equally vulnerable, equally prey to Klaus Barbie's arbitrary acts of brutality. But is such a realization conducive to a sense of solidarity or of isolation? To be pressed into a group identity by animus alone, by the sheer weight of ostracism, is probably sustaining cause for de-identification. The old Groucho Marx line about not wanting to belong to any club that would have him as a member could only have been said by a Jew. In a way, it is a dead man's joke, the sort of hopeless truth that could make one scale barbed wire.

Perhaps to be Jewish is to be trapped always with *other* Jews, even with those other Jews one doesn't like. There is a stifling quality to enforced tribalism, a negative air space, like being in a gas chamber. It is difficult, for instance, to conceive of having the luxury of disliking the person standing next to you in a gas chamber. Still, must one embrace one's fellow victims? The Resistance fighters in Ophuls's movie, the heroic men and women, Jews and non-Jews, seem to harbor deep suspicions, one toward the other. Resisting a greater, evil force does not seem to have brought these people closer together, but rather to have drawn them further into themselves. I am reminded of the way I felt after watching *Let My People Go,* one of the early documentaries about the Holocaust, which was shown to my high school once a year, on the day officially consecrated to remembrance. The film was in sober, archival black and white, narrated by a basso profundo male voice, a voice like Gregory Peck's or Orson Welles's. As I recall, it was full of stark imagery:

Overweight Jewish women standing before open pits, covering their pubes with their hands in a last gesture of dignity before they will be struck down by bullets; scrawny hirsute Jewish men wearing the hideous striped pajamas of the concentration camps; families amassed for transport at railway stations, mothers holding on to the hands of children dressed in their best coats, beneath the eyes of the S.S. men with their ominous leashed dogs. The grimmest shot comes near the end, with a dump truck unloading emaciated, genderless corpses from a liberated camp, the unrecognizable dead.

Sitting in the auditorium among my classmates, I found myself wondering which of my friends would grab a crust of bread out of my hand, which of the boys and girls who didn't like me would cunningly survive, which of the ones I didn't like would become *kapos*. It is a heavy burden, this being hated for being Jewish, and there is no assurance that it will produce in someone as conflicted as myself any overriding sense of community, of oneness.

Under circumstances of extreme duress, do untrusting souls become more trusting? Or is the larger Jewish family like the smaller, nuclear family in which I have been raised—a worthy but untenable concept?

I have dreams of making Hitler pay attention to me, but in waking life my father is permanently out of reach, a figure who mostly frightens me, a German Jew whom I eye with distrust, who is given to ear-splitting displays of temper. Sometimes I think inside every German Jew—like the proverbial thin man trying to get out of every fat man—is a German trying to get out: a Nazi manqué. Around my father I feel the helplessness of appeal; the attack dogs of his derisive impatience are barking inside me, straining at the leash, ready to jump if I make the wrong move.

Only Jews and old Nazis are interested in Jews and old Nazis: a relentless, claustrophobic-inducing thought, like being stuck in a bad childhood even after one has chronologically grown out of it. Certainly, many of the Jews I know are ceaselessly interested in reading about the Nazi period, myself included. Goebbels and Göring, Himmler and Hess, Mengele, the names mean something, one can put them together with faces and idiosyncrasies, wives and children. Julius Streicher and his inflammatory cartoons. Eichmann and his clerk-like personality.

Questions that occur to me over the years about the Nazis range from the most trivial to the most basic:

- Did all of the Nazis have a fondness for music, dogs, and chocolate?
- Can one generalize that no Jewish mother will henceforth name her son *Adolf*?
- Can there ever be another Adolf without that telltale twitch of a mustache?
- Did any of the Nazis have sleepless nights?
- Was a messy Nazi viewed jokingly as a kind of Jew?
- Did Nazis work an eight-hour day in the death camps?
- What did a Nazi think about when he stood naked in the shower?
- What did the Nazis eat for breakfast?

I have read somewhere that one of the children who survived Josef Mengele, the Auschwitz doctor who harbored an obsession with twins, upon whom Mengele performed fastidious experiments, wishes nothing more in adulthood than to be able to be with Mengele, to set him straight. The ravaged self looks for sustenance from those who have ravaged it. Even within death camps there are havens, or the insinuating irony of a haven: Mengele's "hospital," wherein resided a form of malign beneficence.

More questions occur to me over the years about the Holocaust, questions addressed from a different angle, as though another twist of the evil kaleidoscope might bring a better picture or truer colors:

- Would I have survived?
- Would I have *wanted* to survive?

- What did you have to do inside your own head in order to survive?
- What did you do with the wish to die?
- Would anyone I know in the present have tried to hide me then?
- If it were to happen again, now, would any of the non-Jews I know be willing to risk their own lives in an attempt to save mine?
- Would I have been willing to risk my life to save another?
- What was it like to wake up in the morning in a concentration camp?
- What did you do with your memories?
- What did you do with your hopes?
- Did you, sooner or later, stop dreaming?
- If you did dream, did you dream of the concentration camp, or was it doubly shocking to wake up and find yourself there?
- How bad was the smell?
- If you couldn't adapt, did that mean you were weak?
- If you adapted, did that mean you were bad?
- Why did the act of survival seem to confer an honorary status?

The basic question, of course, is this: Do the good survive? (Primo Levi survived to write about his experience in an everyday voice with a searing directness, only to commit suicide.) If we accept that it is in the nature of evil to be banal, we must also accept that it is in the nature of goodness to be eternally precarious. As Claude Lanzmann's mercilessly lengthy film, *Shoah,* demonstrated over and over again, the Holocaust was nothing if not a precise equation, a particular set of circumstances, a certain brand of lethal gas, a certain number of people per train, the perfection of logistics: Against such calibration, what hope has goodness?

From *King of the Jews,* a 1979 novel by Leslie Epstein about the Judenrat (the Jewish council responsible to the Germans) within the Polish ghettoes: *"I am a dog, a dog,* Leibel Shifter had said. But everyone knew he had been mad. No, no cure for Judaism. It was a sentence for life."

What becomes difficult to separate out is the process whereby the Nazis become internalized as part of the apparatus of self-loathing. Although I don't think I ever mitigated the factualness of the Holocaust, at some moment in time the historical reality becomes overwhelming evidence, a shadow identity tagging along, obscuring the light. At various points I wonder, disloyally, what it would be like to grow up without an awareness of "the Jewish problem," what it would be like not to have to take in an event so vast and so pernicious it remains obdurately uninstructive.

There is no experience that is untouched by reference to it—this black clot of history—and even the literature I come to embrace in college as an alternate way of seeing, the civilized cadences of the modern British tradition, seems tainted by traces of the full-fledged virus of anti-Semitism. What am I doing studying the elegant malaise of T. S. Eliot's poetry, identifying wildly with his tenuous Prufrock, when Eliot's was an art that blossomed in, as the critic Robert Alter has called it, an "imagination of exclusion"? And those capacious clauses of Henry James's novels in which I hoped to park myself—the endless permutations of sensibility in which I would enfold and assuage the grief and disappointment of my existence—there, too, lay a closed path. For I knew in my heart that I was not Jamesian, not the slightest bit. Henry James would find my native experience rude and insufficiently transmuted. I spoke Hebrew, for God's sake, and not as an academic exercise but as a living language to be spoken on the dusty streets of Jerusalem! What Henry James would find me, I feared, was what Hitler declared the Jew to be, in a word of his own devious coinage: *Artfremdt*. Inalienably alien.

Can there be "a Jewish problem" without the hostile prompting of circumstance? Is it possible to feel inordinately persecuted without the Nazis? By the age of ten, even earlier, self-loathing comes off my skin like a stench. (I think of the skin of concentration camp inmates, the fat content reduced into soap, a neutral sudsing bar purified of Jewish essence, capable of cleansing all unwanted smells.) Perhaps self-hatred is no more than a genetic mutation, DNA coding gone wrong, passed on from one generation to the next—Alois Hitler to Adolf, my parents to me—until the only way out is to dump the whole burden onto the shoulders of the next available victim. That process we define as *identification with the aggressor* is easier to classify than to track, much less understand, but what it seems to provide is an escape hatch from an intractable emotional agenda of humiliation and rage; it is a way of warding off the guard dogs that bark within the brutalized mind. For the act of displacing the Bad in oneself—involving both disassociation (from one's feelings of negative self-worth) and projection (of those feelings onto some other person or group)—someone's got to pay: If one can't kick one's father to death, six million Jews will do. My dreams of stopping Hitler from his dire deeds were also dreams of reparation, of saving my abject self. Spare me, spare my race, spare me from me. Who knows at what point within the developing personality the furies within become the furies without: *Juden Raus! (Jews out!)*

2

I cannot remember with any exactness how I first became aware of the Holocaust. Did it, for instance, impinge slowly or did it come as a flood, drowning out all prior views of the world? It seems to me that my earliest inkling was connected with a cousin who used to visit my family while still a bachelor, one of two unmarried male relatives who used to spend weekends with us. Although this cousin was the less playful of the two, and therefore of less immediate interest to me, he came crowned with a halo: He had been in one of the "camps" as a young boy, together with his mother, brother, and sister. Now he sat in our living room, and I occasionally sat on his lap and grilled him along with my siblings on the details. We asked him about his experience in the valley of death as though we were questioning him about a thrilling adventure, a lark, but that is the even-handed curiosity children have. We asked to see the number burned into the soft underside of his arm again and again, as though we were looking at a marvel, something of value to be ceaselessly admired. I knew that cattle were branded for purposes of identification but I had never seen a person so branded. There must have been something titillating, even pornographic, about those blue digits tattooed on white flesh—a violent confusion of the usual, rigidly maintained categories of childhood. We had learned that there was the human and that there was the animal; they were separate kingdoms, although once in a while the human and the animal banded together for safety, as in Noah's ark. But this numbered human arm was a glimpse of something different and wholly adult: behavior that partook of the bestial.

Although I always expected this cousin to show great emotion when recounting what he had been through, he seemed singularly muted, as though his responses had been overworked a long time ago. And did he really tell us anything about the daily life of a ten-year-old in the abattoir? When I think back I can remember nothing except that vast knowledge we had about him—a halo of darkness above a pale, wry presence.

. . .

However many inklings I had (and there were other cousins, other stories of harrowing escapes over barbed wire), they didn't add up to an indelible impression—not, that is, until my mother showed me a pair of books she kept on a shelf in my father's study. She had purchased the books in Germany when she stopped there for a day or two in the early fifties on some European trip with my father. As my mother explained it, these books were in effect photo albums of the war assembled for the benefit of Nazi documentation, as testament to the successful process of racial genocide. It seems to me now that these books were like no others I would ever see, not precursors of other images but final gravures, admitting of no worse horrors. The photos were in black and white—shot without sentiment or judgment. What they presented was dramatic evidence of the camera's neutrality but also—and this latter possibility suggested something too frightening to be fully grasped—of the neutrality of the recorded event itself.

An old, frock-coated Jew whose beard was being clipped with a large pair of scissors stood with passive pleading as a group of cackling S.S. officers watched; another old Jew, shorn of all dignity, danced a jig in the middle of the street to some invisible Nazi's command. I looked at these pictures and felt the doctrinaire humiliation, the programmed dehumanization behind them. But what did the people for whom the photographs were meant feel about these images? Nothing, it suddenly became clear to me, was absolutely terrible; everything was absolutely subjective, including the perception of evil. It was entirely possible that the upstanding Germans, proud believers in the Aryan ideology, who observed these small tortures—preludes to what larger tortures—felt a kind of satisfaction, a grim contentment at the settling of ancient scores. Anti-Semitism used as a tool to redress the tyrant-parent within, the politicized healing of private wounds; it made a horrible, rabid sense to me. Germans, as I knew well from my own upbringing, are keen disciplinarians, intent on instilling in their offspring a fear of their own childish willfulness and an awesome reverence for adult authority. What greater pleasure—what more ecstatic sense of reparation—than to see that parental model of authority that the Nazis represented play childishly—*disobediently*—with the natural order of things, vandalize and subvert the peace, bully people who were smaller than they?

Sitting on the sofa next to my mother, my mother who spoke German to my father, who spoke often and nostalgically of her native Frankfurt, my mother whom I would one day write a novel about and compare—in an effort to understand her cool disregard and arbitrary cruelties—to Ilse Koch, the lantern-jawed Nazi who oversaw the women's barracks at Auschwitz, everything appeared to me to be too large and too confusing. How German, I wondered uneasily, was a German Jew? (All the German Jews I knew, unlike Jews of Polish or Hungarian descent, seemed to feel a connection with the dominant mother culture that tried to erase them from the earth.) Did my mother secretly endorse the anti-me, the ridiculed Jew? How else to explain her morbid fascination with Nazi culture, her occasional singing of the Nazi anthem (the melodious Horst Wessel song), her determination for her American, post-Holocaust children to be familiar with the desolate details of the Final Solution, crushing though the information might be to a young and vulnerable mind. There, in my father's study filled with *s'forim,* his books of Jewish learning, the realization dawned on me: The only road to safety was to identify with the aggressor. Spare your hide and join forces with the enemy, even if the enemy happens to reside inside of you. *What an ugly race Jews are,* I thought, looking at the photographs, turning resolutely away from empathy and self-acceptance toward the open arms of mockery and self-abnegation.

And so I was well on my way to embracing *Artfremdt.* Hitler would have been proud of me, an Orthodox Jewish girl ready to sign up with the storm troopers, with the brown-shirted S.A. (led by promiscuous Ernst Roehm) that preceded the S.S. The irony of the situation, if I had been able to see it, was an insinuating one, like the Jewish orchestras that played cheerful Strauss waltzes for their fellow prisoners in Theresienstadt—the sort of macabre sentiment only a Nazi would relish.

The trouble with imbibing the black draught of the Holocaust so early was that it unfairly upped the ante: *How unbearable could anything be if it wasn't being in concentration camp?* As if it weren't enough that I reasoned this way myself and thus was given to slighting my own adolescent misery, my mother used it is a constant refrain. "Just imagine you're in concentration camp," she would blithely suggest to me about any situation I found unbearable. There were, admittedly, many: Whenever I went away from home for more than a night or two at a time, I experienced the acute separation anxiety with which children who have never experienced enough acceptance at home tend to respond to new situations. I would find myself calling from sleep-away camp or my first trip on my own to Europe in a state of dazed panic, pleading to come home, only to be told that these discernibly enjoyable experiences that I was failing to enjoy were best viewed as a foretaste of unknown horrors to come, pallid tests of my endurance, of my will to survive. *Just imagine you're in concentration camp*: It was my mother's unique form of tongue-in-cheek consolation, but against such consolation, what hope had my flimsy, self-indulgent despair? Even I could see, without my mother's dramatizing the point, that my angst, purely psychological in origin, was a luxury when set against the life-or-deathness of concentration camp. But the comparison seemed unfair in its extremeness, a means of inducing shame rather than of inspiring fortitude—or, God knows, cheer. In a rather strange twist of events, a historical occurrence that appeared to me to represent everything *un*instructive, to symbolize a nadir of human behavior, was used for my mother's bewildering pedagogical purposes.

If, in the course of my childhood, the Holocaust began to take on the quality of a fatal object lesson, it also threw up one or two less horrific scenarios, intriguing possibilities for my further investigation. Chief among these was the example of Anne Frank, the soulful-looking Dutch girl who hid with her own and another family for several years during the war in an Amsterdam attic until the Gestapo, tipped off to their presence, tracked the group down and deported them. Her adolescent diary was found by a gentile neighbor after the war and given to her father, Otto, the only surviving member of the family; it was published in 1947 and became an acclaimed masterpiece. I read Anne Frank's diary when I was about ten or eleven, only a little younger than she was when she wrote it. I loved the way she addressed her diary by a name, "Kitty," as though it were a real person, a living and breathing companion. I started to keep a succession of abortive diaries myself; I gave them all names, in admiring emulation and in the hope that this gesture would keep me going, but every name sounded hollow next to the sacral "Kitty" and I could never convince myself after the first couple of entries that my diary was worth keeping.

There was another aspect of Anne Frank's diary that pleased me, an aspect that suggested my mother's lessons in the self-diminishing value of the Holocaust weren't necessarily the right ones to draw: The fact was that Anne Frank didn't in the least appear to think that the Holocaust—although it howled like the hungriest of wolves right at her doorstep—devoured the intensity and dignity of all other, private experience. In the almost daily communications with her dear "Kitty," Anne's brooding, introspective nature was given free and writerly play. Her dissatisfactions with her mother; arguments with her older sister,

Margot; sharp-tongued observations about the other family in hiding: These carefully delineated problems were important to her (and, by implication, became important to her readers), as important in their way as the claustrophobic and fearful conditions the family was living under. The reality of her own mind was as valid as the life-threatening reality external to her mind. *How unbearable could anything be if it wasn't being in concentration camp?* I had before me now in Anne Frank's diary the glimmer of a different answer: You could be living right in the eye of the Nazi storm and still take your own little angst seriously. Better yet, you could emerge from the Holocaust a literary heroine! The thought was exhilarating.

The other scenario the image of the Holocaust set before me only evolved as I grew older; it wasn't nearly as reparative a possibility as becoming a famous writer, but it suggested a different direction in which to look for the resolution of what seemed to me to be a historically vexed sense of identity. In my teens, as the dance of the sexes began its first, fumbling two-step all around me, I pondered the aesthetics of Jewishness. I had always been fleetingly aware that the elusive ideal of beauty as perceived by me and my familiars—the Hayley Mills ideal of my childhood—had little to do with the facial physiognomy I thought of as classically Jewish. As I grew older this perception only deepened: I'd yet to meet a Jewish girl or woman of my acquaintance who didn't take it as the highest accolade to hear it observed that she didn't look Jewish. This wasn't to say that there wasn't, in due fairness, an admission of a genus of Jewish prettiness (usually having to do with shiny dark hair and lustrous eyes) but not to look Jewish, to look *un*-Jewish—that, it seemed, was to be golden, to be truly desirable.

There was something even more interesting—more disturbing, if you will—that I noticed as I entered my early twenties. This was a phenomenon I will call "shiksa hunger": the longing for the non-Jewish, the crystallinely Christian, woman on the part of Jewish men. And what Jewish men they were! All the best, most creative ones—Woody Allen in his movies, Philip Roth in his novels—steered clear of the besmirched, mother-polluted Jewesses in their midst and cast yearning eyes upon the blond, Aryan fantasy. In a toss-up between having Anne Frank or Eva Braun (Hitler's mistress) as a date, it was clear to me whom these men would choose.

Then, too, I began to notice, as I became intrigued by the workings of power, that the more successful a Jewish man was, the more likely he was to marry a woman who wasn't Jewish. The first marriage, maybe; but the triumphant second marriage —the one in which the money or fame finally poured in—was generally to a woman outside of the faith. It made a tragic kind of sense, actually: If biology was destiny—and the Nazis staked their entire empire of destruction on the most exacting, fractionally accounted definition of this claim (one-quarter and one-half Jews being as good as "whole" ones)—then what simpler way to escape your destiny than by denying it at its source. Judaism, in its more traditional Orthodox and Conservative factions, traces religious ancestry only through the mother. If your father is Jewish and your mother isn't, you, ergo, aren't; similarly, if your mother is Jewish and your father isn't, you, ergo, are. For a male to marry a non-Jewish female is to ensure, the zealotry of the Nazis notwithstanding, his children's futurity as non-Jews. If to be Jewish is to be trapped always with other Jews, then to marry a woman who isn't Jewish is to locate the beginnings of an exit, a route into the heartland where the Holocaust is just another black mark in the pernicious history of mankind rather than the seminal, never-to-be-forgotten event of Jewish times.

3

Finally, last fall, I got to Germany. In my midthirties, a writer and book editor, I attended the Frankfurt Book Fair for the first time. I was put up at the Frankfurter Hof, an elegant and icily run hotel considered to be one of the city's best. From the moment I arrived I felt on the alert—as though, more than forty years after the Holocaust, I might pass a half-open door along the hotel's wide and richly carpeted hallway and spot a decadent cocktail party of S.S. officers, their telltale swastika patches winking out at me amid the tinkle of glasses.

The New York publishing world, which attends this international gathering en masse, is largely composed of Jews; many of these Jews have been coming to the Frankfurt Fair for years, seemingly without self-consciousness, with nary a wrinkle in their smoothly arranged professional identities. But then again, most of the Jews I have encountered since I began both writing and working in publishing are what I consider to be "closet" Jews—Jews with little or no background in Judaism and with a bemused, fiercely secularist attitude toward the many rituals that are the foundation of their religion. The extent of these Jews' evident disinterest in their own heritage puzzled me initially, just because they seemed so tolerant—so curious—about everything else, from Buddhism to deconstructionism. Only the arcana of Jewish life struck them as humdrum. (Although this attitude began to change some years ago, when Judaism—especially in its more esoteric, intellectual form—took on a newly fashionable aura: Literary critics who had formerly confined themselves to the great lights of the Western tradition, to Blake and Milton and Wordsworth, suddenly found themselves intrigued by biblical authorship and the secret codes of the Kabbalah.) To be an even modestly "literary" Jew, to be a magazine or book editor, seemed to go hand in hand with an arrogant ignorance of Jewishness. And the genuine Jewish "literati," the name-brand critics and writers I met in passing—their disregard for an almost-six-thousand-year-old tradition was nothing short of dazzling.

I can't really claim, then, to have been surprised by the ease with which the Jews of publishing moved around a city that had once burned books written by Jews. (I knew there had been an organized protest within the past several years of a fair that had been held on Yom Kippur: This quite estimable gesture seemed to have cleared the decks for some time to come.) What I was surprised by, rather, was how vigilant—on behalf of Jewishness, not only my own but the generic article—I felt. Everywhere I noted the brusque efficiency of a people who believed in imposing an iron-clad sense of order—on their children, on their hotel guests, on their public transportation. The bellmen at the Frankfurter Hof could not be engaged in anything other than the most succinct dialogue about directions and restaurant reservations; they did not bend their ear to any attempt at friendly banter, nor did they crack an extra smile. I wondered, uneasily, whether they knew I was Jewish, that old stench coming off me.

At dinner one night with an executive from another New York publishing house, a Jew brought up in the Midwest who told me he had joined a synagogue and had recently been bar mitzvahed as part of a belated discovery of his roots, I referred in passing to my qualms. After dinner we walked back to the Frankfurter Hof, where he too was staying, and found ourselves on a small back street. The street was empty, spotless, and suddenly it seemed full of menace. I made a nervous comment about there seeming to be no homeless in Frankfurt, or at least not anywhere I had been. "The homeless have been exterminated," my companion joked. And then he pointed at the small apartment building opposite to us and asked me if I had noticed a woman standing by a window. "She looks," he said, "like a Nazi," only his tone wasn't jocular this time. I peered upward and after several seconds I made out the figure of an elderly woman, holding a curtain back with her hand, staring down at us. Something about her face, about the hardness of her gaze, seemed unutterably hostile. "Maybe she's Ilse Koch," I said.

On a cold and gray Saturday afternoon of my last night in Frankfurt I set off with a colleague for the Israelitscher Friedhof at the far end of the city. I had with me a small index card on which my mother had written the address of the Jewish cemetery and drawn the tri-arched headstone that marked my great-grandfather's grave. The cemetery, my mother had warned, was hard to find, and so were the individual graves; she had said to make sure and summon the old Jew who maintained the graves by ringing at the tiny gate to the right of the main entrance. The cemetery was kept locked and this beadle (I kept thinking of the shammes in my parents' synagogue) was not only in possession of the key but would also be able to guide me to the spot where my great-grandfather was buried.

The sky seemed to darken even as we took the long taxi ride through neighborhoods that grew increasingly less affluent the farther we got from the Frankfurter Hof. There was a starkly concrete, postmodernist quality to the area the taxi finally stopped in—few visual adornments and a pervading atmosphere of urban gloom, like George Orwell's vision of the future. We alighted across the street from the cemetery and walked to the all but invisible gate. We rang and rang for the cemetery-keeper but he did not come: It was Saturday, after all, Shabbat, and I had known in the back of my mind that there was a good possibility he wouldn't be there. But it was the only opportunity in a frenetic week of appointments that I had, and I had somehow reasoned to myself that a Jewish cemetery in Frankfurt in the year 1988 wouldn't be closed in recognition of ancient laws.

I felt profoundly disappointed: I had imagined engaging in a long, gossipy dialogue with this keeper of old graves. My mother's family had been one of the most influential within the petit-bourgeois Orthodox community that flourished in Frankfurt until the early thirties, and I had pictured myself discovering all sorts of details about a bygone life that I had heard much about. I was disappointed, but I wasn't ready to give up. I suggested that we go into the small florist's across the street and see if there was any way we could obtain entry without the caretaker. Inside the flower shop I used my best garbled German to explain the nature of our expedition to the young man who was wrapping flowers for a customer. Much to my surprise, he seemed to understand me and handed over a large key. In gratitude we bought several bunches of flowers—"to place on the graves," as my colleague explained to me, although I in turn pointed out to him that this was a Christian rather than a Jewish custom.

At last we found ourselves inside the cemetery proper. The wind had come up and the vista before us looked desolate. There were many more graves than I had envisioned—what looked to be acres of graves, erect and broken headstones stretching in every direction as far as the eye could see. I had expected a more modest and containable expanse: If the Nazis had been too busy destroying living Jews to destroy the burial place of dead ones, I still hadn't expected to find such a multitude of resting souls. I studied my mother's primitive illustration to see if it would help me, but the type of headstone she had drawn—like three, rather than two, Mosaic tablets—seemed to have its duplicate in every other row. The two of us started off for a section of the graveyard all the same; I had the name and the dates, and I was certain we'd stumble across it.

As the minutes passed and the wind moaned in the bare and wintry branches, my helpful companion and I became absorbed in the graves, pausing to study dates and to decipher inscriptions. After a while we agreed to separate for efficiency's sake and I soon found myself wandering around, lost in contemplation of the lives—many tragically brief—that the inscriptions attested to. I wondered what the furniture had looked like in the houses these men and women had lived in; what clothes they wore; how they felt about being Jewish. More than half of the epitaphs were in German rather than Hebrew, which suggested that many of the dead had been fairly assimilated. There were headstones that marked empty plots, with epigraphs that spoke of dearly loved kin who were deported as late as 1944: These, I gathered, had been erected in memoriam after the war. (The cemetery is still in use.) I became conscious of my very contemporary clothing, my jeans and sneakers and black leather jacket, so different from the wardrobe these proper-sounding German women would have been used to.

Somewhere within the stillness of the graveyard lay the bones of my ancestor, a devout late-eighteenth-century Jew; I thought if I could find him I would perhaps find a missing piece of myself, a way of casting off the shadow identity of Jewishness for something more sustaining, something that would let in the light. When I came to the northernmost corner of the cemetery I suddenly realized I had no idea where my partner in sleuthing was. I called out to him, but he didn't answer. I called out again, more loudly, and there was only the echo of my own voice in return. All around me was silence, and the impassive dignity of death. I looked around me—by now evening had set in—and felt a chill, a rustle of fear. What if my colleague weren't able to find me or I him? What if I were left here, locked in at evening's end with the Jewish corpses of Frankfurt?

I gazed out into the haunted night and thought I saw someone moving toward me, a ghostly figure. "Control your imagination, girl," I told myself firmly. And then, to distract myself from my growing panic, I decided to make *use* of my always vivid imagination. Imagine, I instructed myself, that you are directing a movie, a gritty Fassbinder-like movie about corruption and guilt, set in the Jewish cemetery. I quickly wrote a script in my head, some vague story line involving an alienated American Jewish photographer who stumbles into this graveyard she hadn't known of. I turned, readily imagining myself in the role, to the young man coming toward me. He was of medium height, with piercing blue eyes and a dark thatch of hair. He walked toward me, this angry young painter and reader of Marx, in improbably tall and glossy black boots. He took me in his arms and—in the magical way of cinema, where past and present can be artfully cross-framed and all of life can be viewed as a flashback—I found myself in the embrace of the young Adolf Hitler. He played with my hair, the hair of a Jewess, the wrong color hair, not an Aryan blonde. I was about to convince him out of something enormous and evil when I heard someone shout out my name.

The welcome figure of my colleague, in his navy-blue slicker, came toward me. There was a light rain coming down. I reluctantly agreed that it was getting too dark to look anymore, although it seemed to me that my great-grandfather was expecting me. We placed the bunches of flowers on several graves, anonymous but somehow familiar, and then we left the cemetery.

These days I find myself dreaming less of Hitler. The grandiose fantasy of redeeming the man in the mustache and boots —and, in the process, myself—seems to have lessened its hold on my unconscious life. Part of me misses these dreams, and the wondrous sense of accomplishment they brought: there I was, the same girl who feared her own father, reversing the tide of history, demonstrating powers of understanding and persuasion that were unguessed at in my observable existence.

Perhaps the passing of these dreams suggests no more than that I have grown older and more resigned, that I have made some realistic accommodation with the forces that rage within and without. Just as there is no sign that the world has grown more fond of the Jews, so there is no sign I will ever be free of a certain fascination with the darker impulses at work in myself and others. Still, I sense of late a slight shifting of the focus, a lifting of the onus of hostility. There is some kind of relief in being able to recognize the aggressor, even identify with him for a while, and then walk on. Like tipping one's hat at one's enemy, it may not be a grandstanding gesture, but it's definitely a civilized one.

In the Holocaust Gallery

DAVID LEHMAN

My mother did everything she could to save her parents. In Vienna just after the Anschluss, you could still escape, though Buchenwald and Dachau had already opened their gates; you could escape if you had luck on your side and could raise enough money to bribe minor officials, secure exit visas, buy a berth on a boat crossing disputed waters. But the price of a bribe like the cost of an ocean passage kept going up and my mother arrived penniless in England and penniless again in New York. "I could have saved them but before I got the money it was always too late." She was still trying long after her parents were deported from Vienna in 1941. They were killed in Riga on March 12, 1942. Karl Lusthaus was sixty-five; Dora (Berger) Lusthaus, the daughter of a Torah scribe, was fifty-three. They were driven in a truck to an open field, where they dug their own graves and were shot.

During Yizkor, *only the mourners remained inside the dark synagogue. The children standing talking in front of the building still had both parents living. Standing among them in the bright morning sunlight, I thought about the difference between us out here and the*

others inside; they were literally, we figuratively, in the dark. I also
remember wondering about the act of imagination necessary to con-
template your own father's death. I still cannot do it, and my father
has been dead these many years.

I asked my mother how she found out that her parents had
been killed in Riga. "Many years later, from a woman I knew in
Vienna, I met her in Fort Tryon Park, I was married and already
had Joan and you, and she told me she was with my parents in
Riga, that she had kept the records there. You know the Germans, how exact they are. That's how we know the date. They
had to write down all the names and everything that happened."
The coexistence of such a passion for precision with such grotesque hysteria is one of the evilly fascinating contradictions of
the German mind under National Socialism. "They took children and threw them in the fire. How could a normal person do
that?"

On the blackboard in the Yeshiva,
Blood, frogs, lice, wild animals, pestilence, boils, hail,
Locusts, darkness, and the slaying of the first born.

One of the boys, the sandy-haired Captain Snowball, quoted
Dostoyevski: If God is dead, everything is permitted
On the blackboard in the Yeshiva.

The boys in Professor Kafka's class had to argue the proposition.
"Isn't it the other way around," said Ezra.
"Because everything is permitted, God is dead."

The boys in the back row of Professor Kafka's class
Traded condoms and cigarettes and baseball cards. Joshua said:
"It is Nietzsche's fault." Not that God was dead but

Nietzsche identified morality with Jews,
The Jew as ugly Socrates, the weakling with the fine mind
Who stood in the way of tragic strength, heroic will-to-power.

"Socrates killed tragedy, and the Jew with his morality
And his Ten Commandments duped all of Europe
To adopt an ascetic ideal." The Nazis went where Nietzsche

Directed: a land beyond good and evil, during the twilight
Of the idols. "For what else is Fascism but the glories
Of the all-conquering will, the rapist's conquest of the anus?"

Samuel said: "They burned the books. Action was language
Minus meaning, which is why Hitler believed it best
Never to write a thing down if he could say it."

Daniel agreed that the philosophical core of Fascism
Is nihilism. "Then you're at sea and at the mercy
Of any lifeboat that comes along." "It's Heidegger's fault,"

Aaron said and would have said more if not for
The sudden laughter from the back row of Professor Kafka's class.
One boy stood up. "It's Professor Kafka's fault," he said.

Then he walked to the blackboard and erased it.
General chaos. Soon all the pupils were shouting, giving
Kafka his chance to slip away. Let the starving artist

Make a virtue of his need: Let him fast. That is his art.
And thus Kafka's Hunger Artist was born.
Crowds at his cage in the carnival

Admired him. "But you shouldn't admire me,"
He said, dying. "And why shouldn't we?"
"Because I could never find the food that I liked!

If I had, I'd have stuffed my face like everyone else."
Famous last words. The attendant tossed a steak
To the panther in the next cage, whose jaws contained freedom.

In the dust of his dormitory windowsill
At Columbia University, the bearded Jewish bard wrote:
"Fuck the Jews!" And was expelled.

And when the geniuses were fasting for peace
On the steps of Low Library, Holocaust
Sounded like Holy Ghost, *if you said it fast enough.*

One year I was teaching at Swell College, one of the few remaining all-girls' colleges. I asked my freshman students to write a paper on an abstraction "such as honor or justice." Laura, a very pretty and very pale Irish girl, wrote an earnest paper on laughter, which she criticized on the grounds that a good deal of humor occurs at the expense of another person or group. For example, the other day she had heard this joke. What's the difference between a pizza and a Jew? And the answer is: the pizza doesn't scream when you put it in the oven. I read the paper; I corrected the grammar; I gave it a grade. A few days later, Laura came to my office and said, "I'm sorry. I didn't know that you're Jewish." "No apologies are necessary," I replied. "You weren't telling the joke, you were condemning it." But she blushed. And looked at me funny for the rest of the semester.

The teenage girl was asked if she knew what the Holocaust was. Yes, she said. Isn't that the Jewish holiday they had last week?

That was the year I conceived of the Holocaust Gallery. The Holocaust Gallery is where I put the pictures and quotations and ideas I collect on the subject of the Nazis and the Jews. In the Holocaust Gallery these images and words are allowed to collide. The technique of dislocation and disjunction is primary. The result may be art or it may be the cut I got on my face while shaving this morning; it doesn't matter in the end. Everything has its place here, everything is testimony, from overheard phrases to whole essays, riddles, and nightmares. That is the way of memory, and our one imperative in the Holocaust Gallery is *never forget*. Stray facts, key names: the Night of the Long Knives, Kristallnacht, the Anschluss, Lebensraum, Zyklon B, Operation Sea Lion, Wolf's Lair, the Final Solution. Incongruity: Hitler was a vegetarian, didn't smoke, didn't drink. Yes, said D. (who wore a pink triangle), Hitler was a "tee-totalitarian." Philosophical dead ends: the ontological status of poetry after Auschwitz. Intractable dilemmas: the case of the thinker on the mountaintop who remained a member of the Nazi party right to the end of the war (card number 312589, Gau Baden) and how does that knowledge modify our understanding of Heidegger's work, for there must be some vital connection between the life and the work, for if there weren't, of what interest to us could his philosophy be? Notable attempts to write about the catastrophe: Isaac Rosenfeld's "Terror Beyond Evil" and "The Meaning of Terror" in *An Age of Enormity*; Charles Reznikoff's *Holocaust*, poems based on testimony from the Nuremberg trials; Arnost Lustig's short story "The Girl with the Scar"; Art Spiegelman's comic book *Maus*. Memoirs: Primo Levi's. Speculations: why the Nazis chose the swastika as a symbol, and what was its relation to the cross—diabolism? Sign of the Anti-Christ? The swastika's relation to the red star of Russian Communism, the yellow star of Judaism. Also, the element of primitivism in Nazi ideology: a woman giving birth is equal in greatness to a soldier killing his enemy. Allegories: The history of Nazi Europe from 1933 to 1945 considered as the plot of a pornography movie with uniformed officers and venereal whores. The Madame pretends to be a dog, gets whipped and likes it.

Several years later we got a postcard from Germany saying, "Death is a postcard from Germany." They offered to send us his ashes in a box if we paid the shipping and a nominal handling charge. I remember reading somewhere that the Nazis always billed their victims' relatives for the cost of detention and trial. The executioner's fee came out to a flat 120 marks.

I heard it: a baby cried and then
A man with a voice like my own
Answered the phone with a demonic laugh.

I heard the sound of canned laughter.
The immediate family gathered round.
Twenty-two minutes of news

And eight minutes of commercials
For headache remedies, neuritis and neuralgia,
Had put them in the right mood, neurosis and nostalgia.

I heard the victim cry: "Answer me!"
The death threat that came in that morning's mail
Was in his own illegible handwriting.

One place to find truth is in the recurrent nightmare of a seven-year-old boy in 1955.

One day when I was too sick to go to the Yeshiva, I turned on the television and there it was, in black and white, *The Holocaust*, not the multi-part soap opera with the pro-PLO actress playing the bald soprano, that came many years later, but something altogether different and really quite revolutionary: a mixed-media extravaganza featuring scratchy newsreel footage of Hitler and cronies, official Nazi propaganda films, fragments of portentous BBC dramas (young Albert Speer in his three-piece suit and impeccable Oxbridge accent decides to cast his lot with the führer), recordings from Berlin's *Judenrein* Philharmonic (Herbert von Karajan conducting Brahms's First), an academic panel discussion on collaborationism in Belgium and France, Nuremberg trial transcripts read in a monotone, interviews with death camp survivors, the Kol Nidre service. In sum, the most advanced collage devices, violent montages, and shock effects went into *The Holocaust*. An undercurrent of hysteria ran through it all, galvanizing the viewer while keeping him continually off-balance.

I never found out who was responsible for *The Holocaust*. Whoever it was had a capacity for paranoia that astounded me and a tolerance for pain that scared me. The work was clearly the product of an imagination that characteristically defended itself with irony. But the irony, and this is what I liked most about it, was corrosive; it was radical; it doubled as a way of going beyond defensiveness, beyond the pathos of "survivor's guilt" and the other clichés with which we deaden language so that it ceases to explain us or even to chronicle our day-by-day activities and thoughts. The irony hurt.

For example, a close-up of a gas chamber dissolved into a fake Ivory Soap commercial featuring healthy bodies and lots of suds. The juxtaposition though glib was oddly disturbing, as if the idea were simply to deliver a shock, and sustain it—*The Holocaust* as a musical comedy!—it being hard enough to shock a modern audience. Other sequences were designed to dramatize one dialectic or another. A split panel showed the 1936 Olympic Games on the left and an ordinary day in Buchenwald on the right while on the soundtrack you heard the choristers burst into the fourth movement of Beethoven's Ninth Symphony. *What was the relation between these striking images and events? If we knew the answer to that, maybe we'd have a better sense of art's proper relation to history.*

Suddenly I pulled back from the picture on the screen and thought about the screen itself. And suddenly I understood what Walter Benjamin meant when he wrote, in the conclusion of "The Work of Art in the Age of Mechanical Reproduction," that "the logical result of Fascism is the introduction of aesthetics into political life." Mass-production robs art of its "aura" (Benjamin's term) in the sense, perhaps, that photography robs the subject of his soul—a common fear among so-called primitive tribes. In the absence of this "aura," this soul-like stuff, there is little to prevent art from becoming a branch of technology. The state has gone beyond good and evil; the Fascist state, "with its *Führer* cult," proffers a mythology of power in which strength-versus-decadence substitutes for good-versus-evil. Rhetoric stripped of all moral ambition becomes propaganda in the service of a counterfeit reality, a script designed to mesmerize the masses with man-made myths of supermen, a master race, a new Siegfried and a new Brunhilde in the dawn of a new age. All this I now understood.

In that visionary moment, I was luckily able to imagine a more benign future for television. I even had a glimpse of our present age of hysteria, where the soap operas have laugh tracks and you can't tell the past from the present, the shows from the commercials, one cliché from another tautology:

> In the men's room of the Kafkaesque museum, a woman of Junoesque proportions is waiting for the hero. She will conduct him to his Orwellian fate: Room 101. You'll never guess what happens to him there. *Fade* to woman in dentist chair, reproving her dentist for his bad breath, in a commercial for a certain mouthwash, I forget which one, whose subliminal message is that the patient can turn the tables on the guy in the face mask with the drill in his hand, the woman can get the better of the man, the servant can beat the master, *this is America, where soda jerks get to be president!*

A comparative analysis demonstrates, in other words, that the so-called aestheticization of politics needn't be fatal. There's a considerable difference between advertising in a democratic society and propaganda in a totalitarian state.

Yet a more profound lesson couldn't be evaded, or could be evaded only so long as one remained a child. It was clear, or should have been, from the day we clicked on our sets and watched Lee Harvey Oswald get shot to death in 1963: *nothing is real except what's on television, yet television makes everything unreal*. The more enterprising and dogmatic of our colleagues spent years proving that the problem wasn't limited to television but was indeed a structural trait of language in general. They concluded by asserting a doctrine of despair that made themselves feel strangely giddy and left no one, friend or foe, unmoved. The implications were devastating. Not only was it impossible to speak the truth, it was impossible to postulate a truth, it was impossible to know anything with certitude. *The traveler between two cities can never reach his destination. As for the artist, there can be no unmediated vision.*

All the professors agree. The words we use mean less and less; the more we use them, the less they mean. Take *holocaust*. To have made a cliché out of the century's greatest nightmare is, it may be argued, language at work. If so, surely the individual artist's job is to rebel against this linguistic fact, to use language against itself (though *language against itself* has itself become a dreadful cliché), to interrupt this program to bring you a special message (don't believe the hype). Wherever reality is mass-produced for mass consumption and life is lived between quote marks, then (said Ben Zoma) "the artist's first obligation is to his own existence, his own imagination, for the force that would abolish it is strong. Therefore he yokes images together with the violence necessary to create irreducible enigmas on paper. Meaning resides there, in that margin of resistance to the material world. There we live our individual lives, unsponsored and free."

On the one hand, the new knowledge was indispensable, since it made us realize what we were in for in talking about the Holocaust. On the other hand, it was dangerous knowledge—you knew it could be used by fanatics to deny the whole thing, history in general, the death camps in particular.

I turned on the television and saw oaths and bloodshed as before, with more barbed wire than ever, violins and nervous breakdowns: phantasmagoria as never before shown to the masses, drug-induced nightmares of ultimate nihilistic fantasies, death's-head dictators, black masses, unrepressed negative id, the triumph of the will, as television discovers the monster of the past and tries to re-create it in the lab. *Be prepared, ladies and gentlemen, to oscillate between states of perplexity and of sadness so intense it threatens always to turn obsessive and mad. Understand that the ironies are history's, not the author's; that one place to find truth is in the recurrent nightmare of a seven-year-old boy in 1955. And now, without further delay: the Holocaust, day one.*

On the third day of the Holocaust,
They cut off her hair & sent it back to Germany.
They took out her teeth & sent them back to Germany.
She said one word: Revenge!

Before they hanged her
And made the other women watch.
Angel of delirium and death!
Nobody heard the scream.

The shades in the window are about to attack,
The shades are heavier than sails under water,
And we've been commanded to lift them up
Though that means going without air underwater:

What else can you expect from God
Who ordered Abraham to slay his son?
I am seven years old, feverish in bed,
And hear the chanting of the mob outside.

Are they praying are they wailing psalms and lamentations
Or are they cheering the invaders in their uniforms?
Angel of Mercy, show no mercy!
Angel of Death, pass over my house!

By a coincidence that was not uncommon in those days, my future parents arrived in New York City within a few weeks of one another at the end of 1939. They met for the first time a year later, at a social evening held at a "Friendship Club" for refugees, where my father gallantly gave my mother his seat. They danced; they took long walks; and one spring afternoon my father bought my mother an ice cream soda and had to go without lunch for a week. Joseph Lehman and Anne Lusthaus were in the rabbi's office in Washington Heights, arranging the details of their wedding, on the Sunday morning when Japan bombed Pearl Harbor.

March 1942. There was an announcement, my mother explained. "Everyone over sixty-five had to go to another camp, where the work was lighter, so my father had to go and my mother volunteered to go with him. She didn't have to go. She was only fifty-three. She didn't know they were going to be shot."

"Today's subject is The Problem of Evil, part three.
Parts one and two, for those of you who were absent,
Consisted of the Book of Job. Part three

Begins with a restatement of Job's predicament, stressing
That Job, the 'perfect' man, was chosen to suffer
Not by chance but precisely because he didn't deserve to suffer.

In a word: if you believe in God, a God
Presumably benevolent and omnipotent (for if
He's neither of those things, what kind of god would he be?)

How do you account for the existence of evil
In the world? Notice, moreover, how frivolous is this God
Of yours, the God of Job, who takes away all the man has

In the spirit of play, a wager with the devil, a whim.
You say we must revise our notions of God?
Yes, that's very likely. In practice, however, this means that

Nobody believes in God anymore. Let's say you were one
Of the survivors of Treblinka. Look at it from
The prisoners' point of view: starving, beaten, lined up to die.

Now let's say Roosevelt had authorized bombing strikes
On the camps and the railway lines leading there. Do you see
What I'm getting at? What do those prisoners make

Of the planes flying overhead, dropping their bombs
Like a prophecy fulfilled?" I see the beauty of the question
But it's hard to concentrate. I am thinking of the man

Who tried to throw a piece of bread over the barbed-wire fence
To his brother; the bread didn't clear the fence,
And the brother was electrocuted trying to get it,

And the first man survived with blue numbers on his arm
And came to America and raised a family in Pennsylvania
And now his daughter plays the guitar and has red hair

And is the nurse who slaps an i.d. bracelet on my wrist
When I arrive. I'll have to stay here for a year. At least
There are plenty of books on the wall, brandy enough for two.

Vienna, 1938. The fear, said my mother, stays with you all your life. Your friends would say to you: it's not you it's the others. Yes you're Jewish but you're different. It's the others we hate. Please forgive me I can't help it, said our landlady, crying, when she put the swastika in the window. And everywhere you went there were signs, faces with long noses and grasping hands. Buy German not Jewish! German not Jewish! It's the Jews' fault that we're so poor! They killed Christ and they want to kill your children!

This is the bread of affliction . . .

In *The Thanatos Syndrome*, a novel by Walker Percy, there is a crazy character, a priest who speaks with the clarity of a madman, who says there is only one word in the American language that hasn't lost its power and you can tell it hasn't lost its power because that word still means something it means more than the sum of its associations it is irreducible and now the priest is haranguing the hero and do you know what that word is? That word is Jew, Jew is the only word that hasn't lost its power.

. . . that our forefathers ate in Egypt.

Jews unlike cats have three lives, says a character in "Rosa," a story by Cynthia Ozick. She's right: for the survivors, there's "the life before, the life during, and the life after." The life after is right now. The life during was the Third Reich. And the life before was life when it was real, in places that no longer exist, in a language no longer spoken, before they came to America, land of amnesia.

Let all who are hungry join our feast!

It is possible that we live in the shadow of a building looming high over the street—and that only the shadow exists, not the building. Under a lamppost the two American writers are rapping, arguing, competing for who can write the best essay on the Holocaust. One of them says: Do you know what they did at Buchenwald? They had a cage with an eagle and a bear inside. Every day they threw a Jew into the cage. The bear would tear him apart and the eagle would pick at his bones. "That's amazing," says the other writer, appreciatively. "Think of the symbolism."

This year we remain slaves.

The debate has gone on for many years. Should the United States and Britain have bombed the camps and the railway lines conveying the Jews to their destruction? I keep visualizing the

Jews in line, in rags, their heads like grotesque skulls with missing teeth, their bodies emaciated, lined up for the gas chambers, when suddenly, out of the blue, come the Allied bombers! At first it seems like pure hallucination: are the planes simply clouds worked upon by a feverish imagination? Then you hear them and you know. They're real, all right. And here come the bombs. *We* know what is happening, we who watch the newsreel of our parents' lives and then discuss the issues in philosophy class. But to the men and women still standing in line, waiting for the wait to end, do these planes and their bombs represent salvation or simply a swifter form of annihilation?

Next year we shall be free.

It was, thanks to the truth serum, July 1934.
Everyone knew the phone would ring, and it did,
As did the doorbell simultaneously. "Hi, Kid."
It was Uncle Joe. "Does the immortal soul exist?"
He wanted to know. So I answered the door
And there he stood, shivering like a skeleton,
Having kissed the age on its feverish forehead.

He was the condemned poet, and I was his advocate,
And Uncle Joe was Uncle Joe, wanting to know
What I thought he should do, and why.
Stalin was enraged by Pasternak's equivocal reply.
"Had Mandelstam been my friend, I'd have had more
To say for him," said Uncle Joe. Then he hung up
And had Mandelstam sent to Siberia to die.

Back to the phone. It was my sister Joan,
Another trick question up her sleeve. "If a plane crashed
On the border between Canada and the United States,
On which side would they bury the survivors?"
It was, thanks to the truth serum, July 1958.
I was ten years old. I said I didn't know.
I wanted to kiss the age on its feverish forehead.

If you asked me to choose the paradigmatic nineteenth-century sentence, I would single out—for its poetry, its exactness, and the centrality of its insight—the sentence in *Madame Bovary* in which Rodolphe, with his vast amorous experience, ponders the relation of love to language. He knows that the exaggerations of poetry can go together with tepid emotions—but he knows, too, that the full heart may nevertheless overflow in the emptiest metaphors, "since no one can ever give an exact measure of his needs or his thoughts or his sorrows, and human speech is like a cracked kettle on which we tap out tunes for bears to dance to while we long to make a music that will melt the stars."

Ask me to choose among twentieth-century sentences, and I may well opt for one that has neither beauty nor truth but with an epigrammatic precision describes a collective delusion. Consider the three-word sign hanging over the entrance to Auschwitz: *Arbeit Macht Frei*—Work shall set you free! Consider these words, this concept, in relation to the machinery of death going on inside the camp, the bodies sticking to each other in the gas chambers. The relation of sign to circumstance, of words to desolate place, is as terrifying as the dry bones of Ezekiel. It is a graver and eerier monument to human vanity than the ruined sculpture of a tyrant—"Look on my works, ye Mighty, and despair!"—surrounded by desert vastness in Shelley's "Ozymandias."

The man dragging his dead father on the ground stops for a minute, exhausted, and the dead man sits up and says: "Why didn't they kill me, too?"

Suddenly it was as though observation were action,
The one form of action that fatalism allowed
Since it left one's innocence intact or
Cloaked it in skepticism: and we who had always meant
To believe in the will stood helplessly by
Like relatives of the deceased, listening to lawyers deny
Our right to contest the old man's testament.

So it was decided: history had already happened,
And all we could do was watch a batch of old film clips
Chronicling the catastrophe: armistice signings
In railway cars, barbed wire borders,
The stunned faces of the American soldiers
And the grinning skeletons that greeted them where
They had dug their own graves: and here

Was one who had escaped in the night
And crawled and then walked and then ran in the night
Until he reached a nearby farm and knocked on the door
And stood there, wondering whether he'd be saved,
When a shrill voice from behind the shut door
Uttered its unequivocal reply: Jew, go back to your grave.
It was, thanks to the truth serum, July 1944.

In *The Holocaust in History* by Michael R. Marrus, I read that the chief of the Jewish section of the German Foreign Office was a man by the name of Martin Luther, "an archcareerist with a talent for organization, but no pressing anti-Jewish vocation." Nazi bureaucrats like Luther were motivated, I gather, by the careerist's desire to anticipate the wishes of his superiors. When such a man ordered Jews killed by the truckloads, he felt he was following orders even when in fact he was initiating them. The historian's point in talking about such cases is the very pressing possibility that so heinous a crime could be laid at the door of something other than fanatical devotion to a leader or his creed, something like opportunism: that is, the most prosaic form of human ambition.

I, of course, felt free to imagine *the other* Martin Luther as a Nazi bureaucrat, and once I did so, it followed inevitably that I would try to figure out the destiny the Nazis might have arranged for the namesakes of other German historical figures. Hölderlin was easy; he would die a suicide on the run—on, say, the border between France and Spain, which he wouldn't be able to cross because of a technical error, a missing affidavit, something like that. The syphilitic Nietzsche would die during the Night of the Long Knives, June 30, 1934. Heine would not survive Buchenwald. Then I decided to contemplate certain great German writers, thinkers, and composers wearing Nazi uniforms, brown shirts or black shirts with little Nazi eagles on them.

I remember walking with my father in Fort Tryon Park and asking him questions. What is a Jew? And why must I wear a hat? And how did you get those scars on your hands? You've told me about Milan and Paris but never about Cuba. Tell me about the year you lived in Cuba. Why did you choose America, not England? Tell me what you think. If the Jews have been living in exile since the Bible, does the Diaspora need to be experienced anew, by later generations as by earlier ones, so that the scattering of our people happens again and again and again? Is that why attempts to massacre the Jews take place periodically? If Hitler wasn't the first, wouldn't it be foolish to imagine that he'll be the last? My father didn't want to talk about it, any of it. My father refused to speak German at home, except for curse words, bathroom expressions, and when my mother spoke to him in rapid Viennese and he had no choice. My father wanted to consign Germany and the German language and his own childhood in Bavaria to oblivion.

"Havana, October 24, 1939. My Dear Parents! I hope you are all quite well and can tell you the same of me. I beg you to send in future English post cards with English form [?] and not with German one. Last week I received a letter from N— and her husband [illegible] that they can be there without any trouble. About me I can tell you only the old things. I was today at the American consulate for seeing that my papers will be sufficient. The consul believes that all will be in order. I hope too and especially that my turn to enter the States will be in two months. But who knows the future? Today is as hot as Europe in August. All good things and my heartiest wishes, Joseph."

In the school playground they were marching
Chanting marching around in circles bearing pickets
Saying "No poems after Auschwitz! No poems

About Auschwitz!" while in the back row
The poet sat dreamily and stared out the window.
A woman I met at a writers' conference

Told me she was working on The Holocaust and Memory
At Yale. The question she had was this:
Are American Jews making a fetish out of the Holocaust?

Has the Holocaust become the whole of Jewish experience?
"You go to shul on Yom Kippur or Passover
And everything is the Holocaust." I shut my eyes and hear

The old prayers made new: "Shame is real," said Ida Noise.
Hear, O Israel. The Lord is One. *I prefer a temple*
Carved out of water and stone: the rage of a waterfall,

The melody of a brook. But back-to-nature as a strategy
   failed
When the phones started ringing in the forest,
And only a child would think of collecting dead leaves

And trying to paste them back on the trees. So I returned
To the city, married, settled down, had a child of my own,
Pretended that I was just like anybody else.

Yet I feel as if my real life is somewhere else, I left it
Back in 1939, it happened already and yet it's still going on,
Only it's going on without me, I'm merely an observer

In a trenchcoat, and if there were some way I could enter
The newsreel of rain that is Europe, some way I could return
To the year where I left my life behind,

It would be dear enough to me, danger and all. To him,
An emissary of a foreign war, London was unreal. He
   wondered
Which of his fellow passengers would make the attempt.

He knew now that they would try to kill him,
Tomorrow if not today. How could he have been such a fool?
Herr Endlich said: "We have our ways of making a man talk."

In the last forty-eight hours he had learned two things:
That you couldn't escape the danger, it was all around you,
And that the person who betrays you is the one you trusted
   most.

The clocks in de Chirico's railway station proclaim
That everything since then is a mere diversion, a mirage,
An entertainment: slightly unreal, often quite trivial.

That is its blessing, you say. Maybe. But the boy
In the back row of Professor Kafka's class doesn't believe it
For a moment. He knows the truth. He is a maker of paradoxes.

I spent a summer at Camp Concentration, a Catskills theme resort devoted to simulating episodes from the Holocaust. I was known as the Camp Philosopher. That's because I read books and was known to be keeping a journal. People liked talking to me, and I liked interviewing them for the camp newspaper, which everyone read on the long bus ride home.

I asked everyone I knew: How could it happen? *It happened because they hate us.* All right, then: why do they hate us? Why do they want to kill us all? I wrote down everything I was told, by Jew and gentile alike, even the stuff that was meant as gallows humor or was indisputably paranoid.

The St. Sebastian point of view: "When I see our people vote for an enemy, because they like the candidate's program and can overlook a little thing like anti-Semitism, I know why they hate us. It's because we're better than they are! We're too good for this world! Everyone else votes their self-interest. But we, we insist there are things more important than our self-interest. And that's why they hate us. People will always throw stones at martyrs. And so we collaborate in our own destruction."

Because of money. Because of who they are. Because of what they say. Because they resent us. Because the Jew will always jew you. Because the Jew capitalist is in league with the Jew Communist to turn the world into NATO versus the Soviet Union. Because of money. Because we don't have enough. Because we have too much. Because, said Hitler, *he* believes in nationalism and militarism, one nation, one people, one leader, and the Jew stands for the opposite. Internationalism means Communism and is a Jew; pacifism means woman and is a Jew; democracy means decadence and is a Jew. When you look at my enemies, you smell Jew.

Because of the thirst for blood, for human sacrifice. The Holocaust proves that Germany—"a highly civilized invader," as one Belgian journalist put it—remains an essentially barbarous people, a pagan people. This argument is frequently made in order to refute optimistic assumptions about progress, modernity, and the perfectibility of humankind. The Holocaust is cited as the culmination of something, not as an aberration. It is an expression—albeit a perverted one—of civilization considered as a triumph of technique: not an advance on barbarism but a technical refinement of the most ancient tribal impulses. Proponents of this view sometimes widen the focus of their argument until it includes all of Europe, not on the grounds that the Germans are representative but because they are not held to be uniquely monstrous. A massacre of Jews in the beautiful medieval castle city of Blois is entered into evidence, as are accounts of various pogroms in Eastern Europe and expulsions from Spain.

Because machines are in control of our lives and we who made the system are its victims. Because of technology. Because we live in the penal colony Kafka described. Because, said Heidegger in 1949, the mass manufacture of canned goods was analogous to the manufacture of corpses in the gas chambers of the death camps.

Because the Germans are fundamentally insane. The Holocaust is cited as an historical aberration. Death is a postcard from Germany. Said a student of medieval German literature: In retrospect, one can see that the fulfillment of Germany's primal myth would have to take the form of total destruction—of one's enemies together with oneself—in flames, preferably.

Because *we* represent the Higher Morality. We say we are

better than the animals, and the others hate us for it—it is so much easier, and in the short run so much more gratifying, to wallow in the mud like animals, to eat with our hands and drink without restraint and sleep like animals after fucking each other up the ass. It is so much more tempting to retreat to the caves where erotic shadows dance for our pleasure than to enter the synagogue of the ear of corn.

Because *they* are many and *we* are few. Therefore they lust for us, for sexual relations with us. Therefore they want to kill us. Therefore *Jew* is the only word in the language that hasn't lost its power. Say it to the next person you meet and you'll see.

Because of Marx Freud Einstein and most of all because of Jesus, who was a Jew.

Because (said Ezra Pound) of Franklin Rosenfeld and Weinstein Kirschberg (alias Winston Churchill). And you know what else Pound said? He said, "All the jew part of the Bible is black evil."

Because who stole the atom bomb and gave it to the Russkies? The Jews, that's who!

Because by God Hitler was a Jew! Only a Jew could have thought it up! Only a Jew would have had the brains! The Holocaust was a hoax! A Zionist plot! What's more, only a Jew would have exposed the hoax, only a Jew could have been such a fucking genius!

Because we call ourselves the Chosen People. And so we are: chosen for destruction. The destiny of Israel is the destiny of Joseph, who was sold into slavery by his brothers, because they envied him his father's favor. Now where's your God, O, Israel, in your time of need?

Because the psychology of anti-Semitism requires a victim that a faceless mob can hate. In *Anti-Semite and Jew,* Jean-Paul Sartre describes the anti-Semite as a triumphantly mediocre man: "This man fears every kind of solitariness, that of the genius as much as that of the murderer; he is the man of the crowd. However small his stature, he takes every precaution to make it smaller, lest he stand out from the herd and find himself face to face with himself. He has made himself an anti-Semite because that is something one cannot be alone. The phrase, 'I hate the Jews,' is one that is uttered in chorus; in pronouncing it, one attaches himself to a tradition and to a community—the tradition and community of the mediocre."

Because it was the will of God. You will ask: What kind of God would permit such a thing to happen? I will answer: What kind of God commands the father to murder his son? You remind me that the God of the Torah promises us, His chosen people, that we will be the beneficiaries of His favor in this world, not the next; that the God of Abraham saved Isaac and the God of Job gave the man back all that was taken away; for Jews, therefore, there can be no defense of martyrdom because there can be no appeal to an afterlife as the, so to speak, enforcer of morality. I confess I do not know how to reply.

Because "Holocaust" derives from *Holokaustos,* from the Greek translation of the Torah, third century B.C. It means: "the burnt sacrifice dedicated to God and to God alone."

The maker of paradoxes, asked to expose
His worst fears and ours, omits the roses
And stars and Spanish wars and guitars

On Venetian balconies. Instead of an epiphany,
He offers the heightened state of perplexity
That many an artist has wished on us in pity,

And we love him for it, before dying
In his arms, like a chastened Cordelia, crying—
But with her virginity intact. Asked to expose

The secret agenda of our nightmares, the boy
In the back row says everything's up for grabs,
Negotiable, "on the table," but first we must decide

The shape of the table, and time is running out.
He has a sense of humor, and a headache.
He never got over the problem of evil, the problem of

The philosopher's brown shirt, and the irrational
Nostalgia a man of forty feels for his childhood,
Which was full of torment at the time.

To those who phone him, asking for an explanation,
The maker of paradoxes is unfailing polite.
He knows there is nothing else he can do.

"When I was born, the third child to my parents, they were not overjoyed, since they already had a daughter and a son. But my mother told me I was so pretty that they didn't mind too much.

"We lived in Vienna in the sixteenth district. It was not a very Jewish district. Jews lived mostly in the second and twentieth districts. And in my class in school were only three Jewish girls out of thirty students. Of course from an early time we were made to feel different. Yet I had many gentile girlfriends and I remember one of them I was pretty close to. Her parents had a little garden with a hut in the outskirts of Vienna and she invited me to sleep over. Yet when Hitler came to power and I met her on the street, she acted funny and held her hand over her bosom until I found out she was wearing a swastika! This was years before Hitler overran Austria—she must have been an underground member in order to have the swastika. This gave me a real shock.

"The police came one day and asked for Adolf. They had orders to take him to the police station. Why, we asked. We need him as a witness, they said. He was present at an accident, they said. We told them: As soon as he comes home we shall send him to the police station. But of course when Adolf came home he told us there had been no accident. He was on a list. The Nazis wanted to send him to a camp. You see, Adolf was the president of some idealistic university organization, a good socialist. And from that day on, he went underground until he got a visa to go to America.

"It was a nightmare to live in Vienna at that time. Every time the doorbell rang, we were afraid—*they're coming for us!*

"A friend of mine got me a permit to go to England as a mother's helper. This way I got out of Nazi Germany. These people, Wright was their name, lived in Southsea. He was a shipbuilder and she was a dentist. They treated me very well, and he gave me English lessons every day. But I was lonely there, so after a few months I went to London, where I had some friends from Vienna. My friend Trude and I found work in the home of an English theater producer by the name of French. Trude was supposed to be the cook and I was the parlormaid. Once Rex Harrison came to dinner. He was very friendly, a real gentleman.

"I was in England when the war started and we all received the gas masks and instructions for the air raid shelters. The American consulate closed and we had to move to a refugee home. When I saw how bad the situation was and my parents were still in Vienna, I tried to get them out to England. For America they had to wait too long, their quota was very small, since my parents were born in Poland. And we did not know when Hitler came how important it was to be registered in the American consulate. In March 1938 Adolf went to register himself and in April Bert went. I only went in June to register, but at least while I was there I also got the papers to register my parents. Later I found out that each month meant one more year to wait for the visa. But it took even longer if you were born in Poland. So I asked the French people and they filled out a lot of papers which would have enabled my parents to come to England. Everything took so long, when I finally got everything together England was at war and my parents couldn't come. I had no way of getting in touch with them.

"But the American consulate finally opened its door again and I received my visa to go to America. How happy I was. Naturally I was worried to travel on an English ship, so my cousin from America sent me additional money and I changed my ticket to an American ship, the *President Harding*. I think it was the last Atlantic crossing it ever made. It took us ten days of the most terrible shaking. Everyone on board was sick and wanted to die. We were so sick that we weren't even afraid of hidden mines, and as in a dream we did all the safe drillings, etc. The last day was Thanksgiving. We had, and for me it was the first time, a delicious Thanksgiving dinner with turkey and all the trimmings, they played, 'Oh, say, can you see,' and when I finally saw the Statue of Liberty, I was really grateful to God, that he let me live and see America."

Hitler's World

JANE DELYNN

It was not until I was twenty, walking through Riverside Park on the Upper West Side of New York City with a date on a warm May afternoon, the park full of Barnard and Columbia students like ourselves, that I experienced myself as a Jew. It was the spring of 1967, the year before the campus rebellion, when Vietnam was the big story and everyone I knew considered himself part of the New Left. My date, in fact, was an English radical, quite anti-American in his ideas if not his life-style, so it was not surprising that we stopped by a group of people who were listening to a young black man in a paramilitary uniform and black beret discuss—rather orate—certain tenets of Black Power ideology. Several other young men were with him, handing out leaflets and perhaps buttons; I don't remember if any of them were white. My mind wandered, as it tends to do during most sorts of speech-making, but subliminally I must have been listening, for I suddenly became aware that the subject the young man was talking about was the destruction of Israel. He was in favor of it.

According to my ideas about myself at that time, this should not have bothered me. I knew I was a "Jew"—in the sense that my parents were Jews and I had put in my obligatory time at (Reform) Sunday school before being confirmed, but this meant nothing. In fact, it meant less than nothing, for I had long since ceased to believe in God (and was enraged by those who did with an intensity I can now only attribute to envy), and the hypocrisy with which I felt my parents and other members of the temple attended their services two days a year (the women seemingly more concerned with their hats and dresses than the prayer book; the men roaming around talking to each other in the aisles and in the lobby) made me feel that the whole thing was a conscious sham. I was studying philosophy, and my interest was in things permanent and universal, rather than contingent and accidental—as I classed the religion and nationality one was born into, physical appearance and other personal attributes, the particularity of one set of parents over another, etc. It seemed absurd to me to inherit a particular set of allegiances or affections merely because you came out of one body rather than another (though it did not seem to me absurd to prefer one person over another for just these reasons); I considered myself, in short, a citizen of the world.

In addition, I was truly passionate about the Vietnam War and gave at least lip service to other ideas of the New Left, though some deeper part of my being knew that my sense of marginality and alienation was not to be alleviated by anything so simple as these groups of self-righteous, manipulative, boring, rather unattractive young men. *Self-righteous*: because to disagree with them meant you were "bourgeois" and otherwise backward in your thinking; *manipulative*: the proposed building of a gym on a strip of rocky "community" land in Morningside Park which no one cared about before or since the mere pretext for the Columbia sit-ins (characteristically, what I objected to was not the strategy but the dishonesty); *boring*: the strategic and intellectual convolutions of an SDS meeting's being virtually inaccessible to the uninitiated; *unattractive*: my double marginality (as Jew and closet gay) had me yearn for the kind of prototypically handsome male WASP who would protect me from these unpleasant, contingent sides of myself. I distrusted the New Left, yes—but back then I distrusted myself in all things, and usually acted according to the opposite of my preferences. So the fact that my then still-unconscious feminist and homosexual instincts were disturbed by the (also unconscious to me) heterosexist and oppressive aspects of the New Left was cause for me to reject not the New Left, but my instincts. In fact, I have never before or since felt such totalitarian urgings to conform as in that presumably liberating "counterculture," which was in fact the "culture"—the meaning of the terms becoming reversed according to which community you considered yourself part of.

But back to the sunny afternoon, the young black man speaking in favor of the destruction of Israel, student faces expressing agreement in a kind of lackadaisical, spacey fashion. (Surely at least some were high on marijuana.) Only one face was energized —mine. Only one voice was angry—mine.

I can't remember my exact words (I was reminded of the incident only a few years ago, when I saw that former English radical for the first time in maybe fifteen years), but I do remember that I began shouting. In fact, I totally lost my temper— something I do fairly often now, and did almost daily during my extended adolescence, but rarely during that time of near total personal repression, when my main efforts were directed toward being invisible so that women would not look at me and induce me to perform some unspeakable, irresistible act: say, pouncing on them in the midst of Contemporary European Lit. (My notions of lesbian behavior were derived from male-oriented texts in which men lurked in bathrooms and dark doorways; this was beyond the pale for me, and I did not expect to sleep with a woman for the rest of my life.) So it was rather out of the ordinary, for me at that time, to begin shouting. I don't remember my precise words, but they were on the order of something like: Six million Jews got murdered while the world did nothing, no "legitimate" country would take them in, where the fuck were they supposed to go? Again, I don't know if it's memory or imagination that tells me the black man at whom I was shouting asked me if I was Jewish—and that when I admitted I was, a smirk appeared on his face, as if to say "Oh, well, so *that* explains it!" I was a partisan, and therefore my opinion could be dismissed. (Why being black did not de-legitimize the opinions of blacks concerning their oppression was an inconsistency I did not then begin to question.)

It was the first time I used that argument concerning the existence of Israel, though I have used (hopefully more sophisticated) variants of it many times since. I did not stop shouting until my embarrassed boyfriend dragged me away. Kindly he did not attack me in front of the others, but when we were alone, and I demanded his support, I saw I did not have it: he was British and an extreme leftist—two categories (despite the Balfour Declaration) particularly inimical to Zionism. Our memories of what followed differ significantly: he says I began shouting at him too, whereas I remember apologizing for the vehemence (perhaps even the content) of my expression. In any case, we were both shocked: he by what he considered the reactionary nature of my position; me by a totally unsuspected and unwelcome realization of my intense identification with a group of people and a religion that I had thought meant nothing to me. For better or worse, it seemed, I was a Jew.

It was ironically appropriate, I suppose, that a contingent historical event (or perhaps not—who knows what twists of irony lie in that word "chosen"?) brought me to such an unexpected place. Up until that moment I had thought much less about the Holocaust than about other, more recent contingencies of history such as the Vietnam War—and certainly far more of my time was spent thinking about the French *nouveau roman* and my own nascent prose (not to mention my sex life) than anything that was happening in the so-called real world. Yet I suspected, in the anger and distress that persisted long after my date dropped me off at my apartment (this was clearly the wrong time to make love), that something important had occurred, that my reaction was not just the result of temporary ill-temper or "being on the rag" (to which my "official" boyfriend in Ohio elegantly attributed all instances of ill-temper), but was the sign of something long repressed and profoundly important that had forced its way to the surface.

I did not like this realization. It was not my conception of myself—in all my universal splendor—to be a Jew, a member of a group of people with kinky black hair, dark skin, big noses, funny accents, and intonations. Despite the obligatory temple-going and Passover dinner (which we raced through at record speed), it did not seem to be my parents' conception of themselves either. My mother was proud that her Austrian-born parents spoke German rather than Yiddish and *kvelled* embarrassingly over Abba Eban's impeccable British accent. My father's parents, in the euphoria of having made some money in the twenties—not unlike much of the rest of America—had dropped the "ski" from "DeLynnski"—and virtually their religion as well. It had been made clear to me that if one had to be Jewish it was better to be a light-skinned Ashkenazi than a dark-skinned Sephardi. In general I disliked ethnicity: in Italians, in Irish, in blacks. I hated folk dances, native arts and crafts, idiosyncratic customs, folklore. More than anything, I yearned to assimilate. Did I not attend classes on Jewish holidays to prove that such "ethnic contingencies" meant nothing to me? Had I not posed myself in my high school graduation picture so that the pendant around my neck might be interpreted as a cross? Had I not seriously thought, during my freshman year of college, of converting to Catholicism (although this was mostly for the alleviation of guilt that would follow the confession of my homosexual impulses)? Did I not know in my heart of hearts that what I wanted most in the world was to *have* (since I could not *be*) a blond shiksa?

Add to this the weight of my liberal, "humanist" education. Had not my literary studies taught me to consider myself part of a community of erudite and cosmopolitan writers? In the Barnard of those days, this meant Modernist English and French plus a sprinkling of avant-garde Americans—none of them had ever, to my knowledge, used such a word as shiksa or goy. (When I read *Portnoy's Complaint,* it did not fit into my narrow definition of "literature.") Were not the anti-Semitic Pound and Eliot and Céline among the foremost of Modernist gods? How could I object to them, when the New Criticism taught us to speak only of the formal qualities of the text? Where in any of my history texts had I read that the Vatican had collaborated with Hitler, or that the Red Cross had had no major problems with Theresienstadt (nor found it necessary to visit any of the other camps), or that from Pearl Harbor until the end of the war (i.e., the years of the Final Solution) the Roosevelt administration allowed into the United States no more than 21,000 refugees from Axis-controlled countries—only 10 percent of the already low quota?[1]

I was reminded of my uncle Ben, constantly talking about the goyim (*good* goyim—his business partner; *bad* goyim—the rest of the Jew-hating world). I had always thought his notions narrow-minded, exaggerated, even paranoid—contingent in the worst sense. But what if, after all, he was right? What if the world didn't give a shit about Jews or our suffering (and could you separate these)? Certainly my outburst had not brought the slightest sense of approbation from anyone in the park—not the young black men in their paramilitary uniforms, not my date, not the Barnard and Columbia students listening silently in the sun. I felt, instead, like a "typical" pushy, whining, arrogant, self-pitying Jew. Of course, it was the Vietnam War and American oppression of the blacks that was on everybody's mind. But if you were a Universalist, the fact that Vietnam and black oppression were *currently* happening in America (a country in which we happened by historical accident to be living) was *just* as contingent as the fact that the Holocaust had happened some twenty-odd years previously, in Europe. Why should all one's empathy be reserved for the Palestinians or the Vietnamese—with nothing left over for Israel or the Jews?

I had no answer for these questions. In typically Jewish dialectical fashion, I argued against what I felt I believed or thought. Perhaps I was secretly a racist—more despicable even than my openly prejudiced father. Was there a side of me in favor of the war—the side that as a young girl had loved *The West Point Story,* or who wished I had the guts to talk to the (presumably lower-class, dyke-y) WACS sitting alone at their recruitment table at Barnard? If only I were the kind of person who could chuck it all and join the WACS so I could finally have someone to have sex with. (I remember envying two Sarah Lawrence students who were arrested during a demonstration and were "internally searched"—that is, finger-fucked—by a female guard at the old Women's House of Detention; the papers made a scandal of it but at the time I thought it might be the only way

---

[1] This figure is from David S. Wyman, *The Abandonment of the Jews: America and the Holocaust 1941–1945* (Pantheon Books, 1984).

I could ever get myself "legitimately" touched by a woman.) Perhaps my sense of alienation from the New Left came, not from "valid" intellectual reasons, but because I was lazy and hated marches, or because I was bourgeois and didn't have the guts to renounce my parents and possessions, or because I fastidiously resented the coercion to open my legs to all males (and specifically black males—as a kind of reparation for white and, especially, *Jewish* oppression) holding "politically correct" opinions.

I argued this, but I didn't believe it. In fact, I resented the articulation of my incipient distrust of the New Left; was there no organization to which I could comfortably belong? I had always been appalled and horrified and fascinated (in the rather sick way one is by horror) by the Holocaust. But not until that moment had I seen how it affected *my* life, as a historical event different from other—*all* other—historical events. At the time it had nothing to do with religion, though it has, over the years, brought me back to what I suppose I must call religion. (I belong to a synagogue that I attend several days a year; I pray—a few Jewish prayers mixed in with my own—in the morning.) But the instrument of my return is not religion, but the Holocaust. It is where my identity as a Jew lies—my chosen identification with an event in history that I have declared to be of significance as no other. (*Chosen,* because there are Jews who do not share this feeling; for example, extreme leftists such as Noam Chomsky.)

Indeed, I will go so far as to declare, no other event could ever be of equal significance. If the realized eschatology of Christianity can declare that the eternal exists in the here-and-now, then I declare that Armageddon has already occurred. (The Christian historian Franklin Littell believes that the true crucifixion was the Holocaust.[2] For who, after this, could truly be surprised to see nuclear missiles and bombs unleashed? We have already had our "type"—and that type is the Holocaust. To me, the Holocaust is not a symbol—even the biggest symbol—for oppression—but Oppression itself: the yardstick by which all

---

[2] Franklin H. Littell, *The Crucifixion of the Jews* (Macon, Ga.: Mercer University Press, 1986).

other "instances" and "examples" (Cambodia, for instance) must be defined.

I will go further. I do not believe that the Holocaust is in any way "vindicated" by the existence of Israel, but I believe, in a retrospective (perhaps even biblical) sense, that the existence of Israel is the reaffirmation of Jews as the chosen people—as well as the most concrete example of the world's "reparation." (What would it be like *not* to be chosen? Could we stand this?) Thus, the existence of Israel is for me suffused with a moral meaning absent from the existence of any other nation in the world. If there were a war between the United States and Israel, I would choose Israel. Sometimes I think I am secretly glad for its occasional brutality so that the world will know there is a monster out there—a monster who will never forget. Although in general I believe in nuclear disarmament, I am *glad* Israel has the atomic bomb, and the continued existence of Israel is the *only* cause for which I consider it justifiable to use nuclear weapons. Let me put this in its starkest and ugliest light: I am not sure, but I believe, that if the choice were between the survival of Israel and that of the remaining 4 or 6 billion peoples of the world, I would choose the 4 million. Fool me once, shame on me; fool me twice, shame on you.

How I got to this place is a mystery. I am not the child of survivors. Only very distant members of my family—sisters of my grandfather—were gassed and burned. In my childhood I never spoke with a Holocaust survivor. When I saw a tattooed number under the arm of a woman on a beach in Miami in 1968, I had to ask what this meant. My parents, though not unintelligent, were wholly unintellectual. Only rarely were topics discussed, and then in the most predictable and superficial manner. I never heard my parents utter an original thought about any political, social, or cultural issue. My mother has "heart"—what one might call the standard liberal sympathies of a typical Jewish woman: tragedies of all sorts upset her, she had affection for the black and Spanish children she encountered as a substitute teacher; my father, pessimistic and less conventional, was a rather reactionary, strongly anti-Communist Republican—in the fifties and sixties not a common position for a Jew of no more than average income. Intellectually I approved of my mother's views, but temperamentally I had an unpleasant suspicion I was closer to my father. I shared his cynicism and his logic—if not the right-wing conclusions to which these at that time led him. We fought about politics for years and years, until Nixon's resignation and the "loss" of Vietnam somewhat took the wind out of his sails.

But what my parents were most interested in were not intellectual issues or the external world, but their personal life: family, friends, their home, their leisure. Their faith (and the faith of their friends) in what I can only call the American Dream (they never referred to it as such) seemed unbounded. Weekends during my childhood they would drive to Scarsdale or New Rochelle to look at houses—not because they could afford to buy one, but merely, I suppose, to partake, however vicariously, of the upwardly mobile aspirations they knew as good Americans they were supposed to have. In the same vein, they tried to get me into private school, but I never was offered a large enough scholarship. Year after year I was sent to summer camp with Jewish girls from South Orange or Brookline or the Five Towns of Long Island (wealthier girls interested in clothing and makeup, for whom I had a mixture of envy and contempt)—this at a time when my mother (then in her upper forties) still had not gotten to Europe. At a young age I had my own television and a bigger allowance than most of my friends. In short, my parents "spoiled" me—as much as their limited income would allow. But as they never even hinted at financial problems, I naturally assumed I had more money than my friends, which created in me an often inappropriate sense of noblesse oblige that persists to this day—regardless of the actual financial circumstances I happen to be in. Only years later did I realize it was all part of the facade of well-being with which they felt forced to clothe their existence. The truth was far different; I know now that at one time my father was so broke he told my mother he thought they should move in with her parents in their house in New Rochelle. She refused.

Naturally, in the narcissism of adolescence I could appreciate none of this. After my Hunter High School–instilled intellectual snobbery had taught me to sneer at rather than envy the bourgeois values of my summer camp friends, I merely switched my anger at my parents for not being wealthy enough to not being intelligent enough. Why couldn't they read *The New York Times* instead of *The New York Post* (then a liberal "Jewish" newspaper —which I now, alas! still have a sickening fondness for), or drag themselves to the opera instead of *Fiddler on the Roof*, or read *War and Peace* instead of *Exodus?* They did not so much defend themselves as confess that, though I perhaps had better taste than them, this was still their taste. I considered (and called) their normative desires bourgeois and conformist—even as I counterphobically ran through boyfriend after boyfriend in an attempt to prove to my friends and myself that I was as heterosexual and "normal" as any of them. But more than anything, I hated their blandness, the predictability and banality of all they thought and said. They weren't crass and vulgar like the girlfriend's family in *Goodbye Columbus*; they weren't Yiddish-speaking Lower East Side Jews with embarrassing long curls and wigs; they weren't former Commies making amends. Their sins were hopelessly venial; they weren't a worthy enough opponent for the magnificent rebellion I yearned to stage. God knows what I would have done had not the Vietnam War come along to provide a structure for my anger (as well as provide perhaps the sole discussable topic of my college years; the rest of my life— drugs, sex—being of course verboten).

And yet from a very early age (certainly in elementary school, and perhaps before) I felt that behind their seemingly unquestioning faith in all things "American," behind their intense desire to be as mainstream as possible in every way (which unfortunately included their even more intense desire for *me* to be as mainstream and "normal" as possible) lay something else— something dark, and unarticulated, and embarrassing. At the time I called it the "void"—and attributed it to my parents' lack of love for, or at least boredom with, each other; since then I've decided it was fear. Fear that ostensibly concerned itself with money and moving "up" in the world, but fear, I now think, that was fueled by the Unthinkable, which became the Unspeakable, which included nearly everything of interest (because what was interesting was dangerous), such as sex (oral, anal, premarital, homosexual); religion (my parents refused to admit they didn't believe in God); money ("none of my business" what they made); morality (doing as everybody else did); truth (which lay in the middle rather than the extremes); intelligence ("if you're so smart, why can't you be nice?"). With all these subjects circumscribed, it is easy to see why our dinner conversations were so tedious: my father's recitations of his day at business, my mother's gossip about their friends or, when she was teaching, repetitious anecdotes and complaints about the kids and teachers at school. I had early learned how dangerous was the expression of my true (invariably subversive) feelings; being a wretched liar, and disgusted (unduly, as my parents told me) by hypocrisy, I soon learned to say nothing. The house was silent too, except for phone calls and my compulsive listening to pop radio; none of us was a television addict, and my parents rarely listened to music. I prayed for these silent meals to be over, but unfortunately I was a slow eater, and so the silence luxuriated. (I begged but was not allowed to bring books to the table.) The memory of these meals haunts me still, in that I am rarely able to be alone in my apartment (any apartment), in the evening, in the dark, without music or television on in the background. I am as scared of the silence as my parents were of speaking.

But just because something is not articulated does not mean it is not there. And what I think was there, the source of all that repression and fear, the intensity of their normative desires for which I expressed such contempt, and of which I now realize (first by my childhood silence, then by my adolescent and young adult attempts to disguise my sexual predilections) I was a total co-conspirator—was the Holocaust. The boredom of our conversation was a kind of trade-off for safety, so that the terrible truth that hovered over us and that we did everything to deny might never come to consciousness: the recent attempt of part of the world to wipe us off the face of the earth, and the indifference of nearly all the rest of the world (even our beloved America!) to such an attempt.

All this, you must realize, is my story—an interpretation I've invented to explain (but perhaps serves only to romanticize) the otherwise hopelessly dull texture of my childhood. My parents deny this utterly. They insist there is no subtext, that the Holocaust had little impact on their lives except to make them more aware of being Jewish. The minor anti-Semitisms of my youth —the "Jewish" quota at the Ivy League colleges (particularly for public school Jews), my mother's calm acceptance of my first-grade teacher telling her I couldn't be in the Brownies because the "quota" had already been filled—are never discussed.

You probably are not aware of this, but my father was the most important soldier in the entire U.S. Army. This is true not just contingently but *logically*—as he has proven to me on more than one occasion by an incontrovertible process of deduction. First of all, he was in the spearhead of the Allied forces—the Third Army—landing at Omaha beach about a month after D day. He was in what was probably the most important branch of that army—the artillery. Infantrymen shot Germans, true enough, but it was the big guns that were effective against tanks, factories, as well as—of course—people. Of all the artillery weapons, the 105 howitzer was the most important—being both light enough to be highly maneuverable and yet powerful enough to be effective against tanks (surely neither of us has to remind you of the importance of the panzer divisions). Needless to say, my father was in a 105 howitzer battalion—and not just any old howitzer battalion attached to any old regiment, but a howitzer battalion attached to the Third Army itself. The battalion went anywhere the action was, and was in the front lines longer than any other before being relieved. Of the five batteries in the battalion—three firing batteries, one Headquarters, and Service, my father was in Service. The firing batteries were important, naturally, and so was Headquarters, but nothing was more important than Service—which delivered food, ammunition, clothing, gasoline, and mail to the rest of the unit. What would the army be without K rations? In this most important of batteries my father had the most important job—communications. Nor was he content to just set up the radio—he organized and wrote the battalion shows, managed the baseball team, and (according to him) ran the battery in the captain's absence (did this unit have no lieutenant?). He received five battle stars: Ardennes, Central Europe, Northern France, Normandy, the Rhineland. He is the unsung hero of the war.

My father likes to look on the bright side of things. Most of the time, to hear him talk, you would think the war contained the best years of his life: French farmers gave him champagne; he hid under a bridge as Germans marched overhead; on a furlough to Nice he stayed in a hotel that was the former German HQ. Only a few weeks ago did I learn, in response to a direct question, that during the war he had passed by a camp. This was Dachau—strictly speaking, a concentration rather than an extermination camp. Although he did not go inside, he could tell what had gone on in there. All the soldiers could tell what had gone on in there. "How?" I asked him. "You could tell," was all he could bring himself to answer. It was I who was forced to utter the words: "By the smell."

Like me, my father tends to vengeance. Not for us is turning the other cheek. Whereas my mother wishes the A-bomb had never been used, my father and I regret the European war didn't go on a little longer—so maybe we could have tested the A-bomb on Germany rather than Japan. (I'm leaving aside the question of whether the United States would have in fact used such a weapon on a European country.) In the light of such feelings, I asked my father if he had ever felt like killing a specific German—for instance, one who was attempting to surrender. He told me this was a decision you didn't make ahead of time, but on the spur of the moment—according to circumstances and one's mood. Apparently the circumstances were not right, for I gather he would have been in the mood.

I was not born until after the war. I very much doubt I will ever go to Germany or Poland. If I do, I would expect—and hope—to have a thoroughly unpleasant, infuriating time.

Unless prodded, my parents do not speak of the Holocaust. Recently publicized revelations concerning the U.S. failure to ease immigration requirements before the war or bomb the rail lines to Auschwitz have resulted in converting their former admiration of Roosevelt to hatred, but they hold no particular grudge against America for failing to do more to help the Jews: other countries were just as bad—or worse. Whereas I, born in

1946, become each year a little more *consciously* obsessed with the Holocaust, my parents say they dwell less and less on what happened "such a long time ago"—except when current events call it to mind.

I do not understand my parents, but then, I never have—and not only in this area. My choice is to take them at their word —and consider them unimaginative and unfeeling—or to view their statements in the light of a repressed anxiety and fear so deep it still cannot rise to the surface. Surely it is not surprising that I have chosen the latter explanation—if only from an understandable desire to have my parents be "deeper" than they appear, or perhaps merely because my preference is for the complex rather than the simple. Certainly it is odd that an event that took place so "long ago" for those who lived through it grows more vivid to me every day, that their anger recedes as mine grows. Or perhaps it is merely that they are old, and this is the process by which memories are passed from one generation to the next.

When I was very young my mother's parents bought a large brick house in a suburb of New York called New Rochelle. At the house itself I alternated between reading (once I was old enough to do so), playing outside, or sitting around the breakfast room table listening to my (mostly) female relatives talk. Surely other topics must have been discussed, but Death is the one I remember. My grandfather was seventy-two years—three generations—older than me, and most of my great-aunts and -uncles were nearly as old. Due to the great number of these relatives (not to mention their spouses and in-laws and friends and the spouses of their friends and in-laws, etc.) and the great age gap between them and me, it is scarcely surprising that funerals, heart attacks, and operations for the "disease that had no name" (I don't mean homosexuality, but cancer) should have been almost constantly on someone's tongue. These discussions petrified me, but something else must have been operating also, for I did not always escape them as quickly as I could have—even once I had learned to read. I had little to contribute, but in an odd sort of way it was pleasant to sit there, half invisible, with nothing to do but listen to this litany of disasters.

Whether due to these influences, or merely neurotic ones of my own, I developed an early and persistent fear of death that first manifested itself at the age of seven, when my parents went on a vacation to Atlantic City. My grandmother was staying with me; I told her I couldn't breathe. Rather, I was breathing, but I wasn't getting any air. Unable to calm me, she enlisted first the next-door neighbors to reassure me, then the doctor (you could still get house calls in those days), who told me it was "nothing —just an anxiety attack." True words, no doubt, but scarcely efficacious for an adult (Valiums are quicker), let alone a child. The symptoms recurred with ferocious regularity in high school and college, and have persisted—in varying degrees of intensity —to this day.

Let me make my meaning clear. I was gulping air, but I felt I was not getting enough to keep me alive. Or if I was breathing, it was not oxygen I was inhaling, but something else. Carbon monoxide, perhaps (in honor of Chelmno, Belzec, Majdanek, Treblinka, Sobibor), or prussic acid (Auschwitz)?

This may sound unduly metaphorical, but I do not believe I am being farfetched in my assertion that my breathing spells and the constant discussions of death were my family's unconscious way of dealing with the Undiscussable. My family, for all its articulated optimism, is in the process of exterminating itself. My mother's parents had three daughters. Each of these daughters (my mother and two aunts) had one child. Only one of those children—my cousin John—ever managed to get himself married. He has two daughters, one of whom is married with two children of her own. Two parents—three children—two grandchildren—two great-grandchildren: what is usually a pyramid has become a straight line. My father's side is even worse. His parents had two children, only one of whom (my father) married. He had one child—me. I am not married, and although I'd like a child, I'm probably too old to have any. Two parents, two children, one grandchild, no great-grandchildren.

Is this coincidence, or an unconscious reworking, in an insignificant, personal way, of a trauma our family pretends so hard to deny?

Sometimes in life certain events, once seemingly definitive, cease to exert their hold over us. Not because the event has changed, but because we have changed. Suddenly—for the decision is sudden, even if various awarenesses on the way to it are not—we decide something is no longer important; we can let go. Such epiphanies, such changes, can occur in areas we consider the deepest of our lives; it is what happens, for instance, when the grand reconciliation between parent and child occurs.

The Holocaust is not in this sense epiphanic for me. I can envision a psychological state where such an epiphanic letting go would be useful—but not only do I do nothing to achieve that state, I do not even *desire* to achieve this state. Perhaps in some sense I consider it morally irresponsible *to be able to achieve* this state. It is a wound I want constantly to fester.

For if it does not fester, then it means I forget. Who am I, who am alive and living a relatively comfortable and pleasant life, to forget? Peace is not mine to make. Whose it is to make (if anybody's), I feel incompetent to say: perhaps survivors of the camps, perhaps children and relatives of the dead. Perhaps no one's. Perhaps God's.

Numbers are a large part of this. (Large, but not definitive: it is irrelevant to me whether Stalin's victims surpass the number of Jews killed by Hitler.) The number—6 million—numbs me. All comparisons (again except perhaps for Stalin) are found wanting: 6 million is 5 million more than 1 million Cambodians; 5¾ million more than ¼ million starved Bangladeshis; 5,975,000 more than 25,000 Armenians killed in the recent earthquake; 5,999,668 more than 332 Palestinians and Jews killed in the *intifada*; 5,999,999 more than 1 American murdered on the *Achille Lauro*.

It is morally debasing to think like this. But I find it impossible not to. We like to pretend that every life is important, and there are just enough special instances of individual lives being important (workers spending days to pull a little girl out of a well; a poor child from an Eastern bloc country flown in for a transplant) to maintain the pretense that individual lives matter. But I resent this sentimentalism; extraordinary efforts to save individual lives seem almost obscene in the light of total indifference toward the deaths of millions of Jews—or the millions of other children whom we are content to let starve or otherwise die or become handicapped from preventable or curable diseases simply because they haven't managed to become the celebrity victim of the week. We sit glued to our televisions, enthralled as a battered woman describes how her common-law lover beat their "adopted" child, and watch indifferently as Pol Pot returns to Cambodia. Sometimes I even resent sympathy and reparations offered those whose sufferings have been less than the Jews', such as blacks or Indians or Vietnamese or Salvadorans—particularly when members of those groups did nothing to help the Jews during the Holocaust.

There is another way to think of it, I know: that it is the consciousness of the Holocaust that has made possible the existence of such things as the Sanctuary movement. But I do not believe it. Even after the war and knowledge of the camps (and despite the Balfour Declaration) the British refused to let into Palestine ships filled with *refugee Jews from the camps*! At least until a few years ago, over *half* the resolutions in the UN General Assembly concerned Israel. Let me put it this way: I am not interested in justice for anyone, unless there is justice—*first*—for the Jews.

Poland has yet to enact a memorial to its 3 million murdered Jews. I was glad when Solidarity was crushed, and Poland was placed in a state of martial law.

It is commonly said that World War One destroyed the civilized world. But the deaths during that war (excluding those who died of starvation in Russia) fell almost exclusively among soldiers. It is the events of World War Two—the bombings of civilians, reprisals against innocent citizens, the dropping of the atomic bomb, but especially the Holocaust—that mark the true end of our civilization. Or perhaps one might say that whereas World War One destroyed the civilized world, World War Two destroyed Mind itself. Atrocities no longer seriously possess the power to shock or surprise, and if on occasion we imagine they do—if we find ourselves being titillated by the latest serial or mass murderer or individual killer of particular repugnance—it is not because their acts are unimaginable but precisely because they remind us of who we are, what we tolerate, and what we are willing to forget.

To paraphrase a Yom Kippur prayer, if it was the Holocaust that inscribed the world in the Book of Death, it was the world's response to the Holocaust—or, rather, the world's lack of serious moral response to the Holocaust, both during and after the war—that closed the gates on the world. Evil will always exist; it is not evil itself that destroys society, but society's tolerance of it. In America, this moral degradation is evidenced in the failure of our judicial system, our appalling amount of crime (the murder rate in New York City—let alone Washington, D.C., or Detroit—is higher than that of the Palestinians killed by their own people and by Israeli soldiers during the *intifada*), a bureaucracy so complex—with areas of responsibility so overlapped and cloudy—that it is impossible to place accountability for any action on anyone. Where does Oliver North's defense come from, with its excuse of following orders and the transference of responsibility onto those who are dead. Who inspired our presidents (with their tape systems and millions of classified documents) never to commit their most serious and incriminating orders to paper? Where did the kind of terrorism that is now standard operating procedure for both right and left in much of the world acquire its "legitimacy"? Hitler may be dead, but the world he created lives on.

I speak of the world's lack of serious moral response to the Holocaust as being what doomed us. What, practically speaking, can one do with a nation in which virtually everyone over the age of ten, twelve, fifteen—it is impossible to assess the precise age at which knowledge becomes culpability—was either a participant in or accessory to murder?

One imaginative moral response would have been to run the concentration camps—with Germans as victims—for a short while. That is, ordinary German citizens—men, women, and children arbitrarily "chosen"—would have been dragged out of their houses in the middle of the night without warning and sent —in filthy and crowded railroad cars—"to work at labor service in an unknown destination in the East." They would have been forced to sign over their possessions to the government and to pay for their passage themselves. No official notice would ever have been given of their deaths; their mass graves would lie unmarked, their ashes conscribed to no urn. Some would be machine-gunned to death after digging their own graves; others would be "spared" for the "humane death" by carbon monoxide or prussic acid; still others—the most fit—would fuel the ovens and search for gold fillings in the mouths of the dead.

This sounds barbaric, but the truth is, traditional legal concepts of responsibility, intentionality—even sanity (as Hannah Arendt demonstrates in *Eichmann in Jerusalem*)—are meaningless when it comes to dealing with the most serious of twentieth-century crimes: state-committed terror. (The greater the magnitude and the larger the number of victims, the more likely the crime is to be ignored.) In turn, the rest of the world, by its forced and conscious witnessing of this second extermination (which, despite the far fewer number of people involved, no doubt would have raised a larger outcry than the first), would have had its complicitous silence toward the Holocaust revealed in a manner admitting of no rationalization or excuse. You could call it a particularly grisly form of political theater.

That particular moral response did not, of course, come to pass. The nations of the world prefer their barbarism to be disguised by other names: "war," "ignorance," "expediency," "anticommunism" (or "anti-capitalism"). I myself believe in a literal interpretation of biblical forms of retribution—"life for life, eye for eye, tooth for tooth, hand for hand, foot for foot, burn for burn, wound for wound, bruise for bruise" (Exodus 21:23). (I take this to justify the torture of those who torture.) I make no pretense that such retribution is for the purpose of deterrence (or, in lesser crimes, rehabilitation). The function of such retribution is to serve not the guilty but the innocent: to demonstrate to the members of a society that the taking of their life is considered such a serious matter that it can only be atoned for by the taking of another life.

This approach is hardly universally shared, and there are certainly theoretical and practical objections to such a plan. You might even say that the suggestion is not entirely serious. But a serious and nonpunitive moral response to the Holocaust *was* possible: a response that would have been "redemptive"—insofar as something such as the Holocaust is open to the possibility of "redemption." And that would have been for Germany, Austria, Poland—the countries most responsible for the Holocaust—to have become moral exemplars for the world. That is, the nations as a whole and each individual within could have become living examples of repentance and good works. For example, the adult citizens of these countries could have been forced to serve a number of years in a kind of international Works Progress Administration, building roads, dams, hospitals, irrigation projects and factories in underprivileged countries around the world (including Palestine or Israel) or serving as health workers or teachers. Out of extraordinary evil could have come extraordinary good.

That this did not happen, that it was not even suggested that this happen, that the United States spent billions of dollars to rebuild Germany, that Germany was not even permanently disarmed (as was Japan), that Nazis were eagerly incorporated into the espionage and scientific establishments of both East and West, that former high-ranking Nazis could live openly not just in South America but in Germany itself, that Kurt Waldheim could have been Secretary-General of the United Nations and is now president of Austria, that Israel opened relations with Germany while former Nazis were serving in the Adenauer government, shows how far the world will go to keep up with the pretense of "business as usual." (Ironically, if any country is called upon to be a moral exemplar, it is Israel, in its relations with the Palestinians; when it does not behave as the world thinks it should, it is immediately attacked for hypocrisy—on the grounds that Jews supposedly have a "higher" morality. Whether the world really believes this or not is of course open to question.)

While writing this essay, I have come to realize that all my life I have had a chip on my shoulder—call it a log, if you will—and it is Auschwitz. Sometimes—I don't know how to say this—I'm almost *glad* of instances of anti-Semitism: because it "proves" we're right, that the world really *does* hate us, that the Holocaust was not so much an anomaly as an extreme expression of the world's feelings toward us Jews. Anti-Semitism excuses my self-righteousness, relieves me of the hideous need to forgive, and enforces my innate feeling that the world "owes me something." I welcome the continuing gnawing at the wound, as if only by so doing will I get it through my skull that life really *is* unfair—that the fairy godmother will not come through at the last moment to make it all better, that I will never hear the world whisper in my ear those (somehow) soothing words: "Yes, it was terrible, the worst thing ever, and it *will never happen again!*"

Since the world won't provide us with our reassuring bedtime story, we incant it to ourselves over and over—*"Never again, never again"*—as if repetition will ensure it must be true.

How does a Jew continue to exist in a world in which the Holocaust has occurred? To my mind, there is only one possible genuine response: rage. But continuous rage is not productive, and so the mind alternates between it and a "German-style" forgetting, which enables us to talk and behave in a "rational" (i.e., "irrational") manner; most of the time we function both in our actions and in our feelings as if the Unspeakable did not occur. That is, for Jews to exist in the world requires the very Nazi inversion of normal patterns of thought that made psychologically possible the enactment of the Holocaust itself.[3] In this way, also, the world Hitler created lives on.

When I was a child and was taught in Sunday school not just religion but the history of the Jewish people, I didn't understand why a special connection was being made between me and a group of people that I was only contingently related to, and to whom (if, for instance, I converted to another religion) I might someday have no relation. I looked at Judaism as a religion, as I might have looked at Catholicism or Protestantism or Hinduism. But the Holocaust has convinced me that "being Jewish" means more than just being a practitioner of a certain religion; it means being part of a community, perhaps even a nationality.

---

[3] "And just as the law in civilized countries assumes that the voice of conscience tells everybody 'Thou shalt not kill,' even though man's natural desires and inclinations may at times be murderous, so the law of Hitler's land demanded that the voice of conscience tell everybody: 'Thou shalt kill,' although the organizers of the massacres knew full well that murder is against the normal desires and inclinations of most people. Evil in the Third Reich had lost the quality by which most people recognize it—the quality of temptation." Hannah Arendt, *Eichmann in Jerusalem: A Report on the Banality of Evil* (Viking Press, 1963).

(What other religion has a homeland to which its adherents can automatically become citizens?) Jews tend to be rather proud of the conversions of such celebrities as Elizabeth Taylor, Sammy Davis, Jr., and Rod Carew—and yet I wonder, if one cannot choose *not* to be a Jew, can one really choose to be a Jew? Are these people "Jews" in the same sense I am? To discuss the above in these terms, of course, means to speak about Judaism and Jewishness in terms set out not by the "enlightened" Jews of Germany—but by Hitler.

There is yet another sense in which the ideas of Hitler have triumphed. It is 1989, and Europe is pretty much Judenrein.

Selfish Like Me

HERBERT GOLD

While I was thinking about writing this chronicle, it happened that I spent a weekend at a quiet retreat in northern California. At the outdoor swimming pool, which is fed by hot springs and situated with stringent beauty atop a cliff overlooking the Pacific Ocean, the custom is nudity. It's almost a rule. Nudity keeps the microbes down—no fermenting man-made materials in the pool. It also serves well for overall sunning.

As I stripped off my clothes, I noticed a pensive woman looking out over the sea. She was very attractive, she had no book by her side, she was just concentrating on her thoughts. I swam, and then I found myself—perhaps it was no accident— sitting on my towel near her. The nudity of strangers provokes unspoken rules of discretion and sobriety. Privacy is respected. Nevertheless, we began to talk.

She was a German psychoanalyst, visiting California to at-tend a conference. When we introduced ourselves by name, she remembered the German translation of my book *Fathers*. She began to speak of her own father, whom she lacked, whom she never knew. He committed suicide a few months before she was born. It happened during the last days of the war, he was a general, and she still didn't know why he killed himself. "Perhaps it was because he saw Auschwitz," she said. I said nothing. "Perhaps he had been given orders to fight on and he knew it was useless, just to do more killing." I said nothing. "Perhaps he was afraid of the Russians."

I nodded. That could have been the case.

She burst out: "Maybe he was only sad that we lost the war!"

We sat in silence for a while. I found her attractive and the situation was peculiar. I didn't try to console her for this event, raw for her still, which occurred more than forty years ago. I didn't ask if he was a Wehrmacht general or in some other service, such as the S.S. I moved my towel to cover my circumcised penis, and then thought, What a foolish expression of embarrassment. Her nudity was without other gesture or meaning—it was just what it was. And then I decided: But it would also be embarrassing and obvious to remove the towel now that I'd covered myself.

Then I thought about what it must be like for a child to come into the world with no father, no brother or sister; to learn she is the last of a line; to know she lost her father in this way— he chose to abandon her. He may have loved her or, lost in his own chaos, he may have given her no thought at all. And of course, this confusion explained why she went into the cure-of-souls business. As most doctors do, she sought to cure herself. What can have been the life of such a person—intelligent, pretty, fatherless, first in the defeated and bereft Germany of her childhood and then in the triumphant one of its present prosperity? I was thinking about the miracle of metabolism that doesn't mark such a person with smudges and scars, but allowed her to be long, lanky, athletic, healthy-looking, with fine eyes. Well, perhaps the mark of grief was that pensiveness, and in this case the loss had only made her more attractive. I was still thinking about my stupid towel. And I wondered what my book about the history of an American Jew meant to her, but of course I wouldn't ask for anything more than the shy acknowledgment she had already given me.

"Do you know any Jews in Germany?" I asked.

I managed to let the towel fall away.

"There aren't any! They're gone! We killed them all!"

Suddenly, at this point in our conversation, after the calm recitation with which she began, her words seemed to come out of her mouth as a cry.

"But there still are some in Germany," I said.

"I met a Jew who lives two hundred kilometers away! I never see him! We lost all our Jews!"

There was a time of silence. We listened to the Pacific Ocean rolling up against the cliff, listened to the children playing in the pool as they called out to each other, splashing and laughing. We paid attention to the lovely bee-humming summer afternoon. "You're a scholar," I said. "It should be easy to find some of your father's fellow officers—there must be some of them still alive—and ask what could have been on his mind."

We had found an odd rhythm. Someone spoke, there were silences between our sentences, and then a reply finally emerged. But this time the question was different. She didn't answer. I went on:

"You could ask his fellow officers, couldn't you?"

She waited and waited. We sat in a version of the yoga position, cross-legged and naked facing each other, and then she said, "I don't want to know. That's the whole trouble. I still don't want to know."

My sitting there naked with the German general's beautiful daughter is an exaggeration of the condition of American Jews —and of its extreme manifestation in an American Jewish writer's precarious comfort amid the astonishing natural bounty of northern California. How can a person come all this way and so quickly from an egg-dealer grandfather in Kamenetz-Podolsk to a hatcher of stories in San Francisco? Rhetorical questions are for editorials. I prefer to recount: I'm here and it's amazing.

Surely some young men have larger feelings than I had. I was a soldier during the war, 1943–1946, and glamorized to myself by weapons, military intelligence training, risk. I heard of horrors; perhaps I even believed in them. What I really believed in was my own needs. At eighteen when I entered, I was thrilled by the luck of finding a good war, benefiting from pure hatreds; history did me this favor. I was looking for girls, comrades, fun.

I imagined heroism for myself; I sought hazard as a means to waking up. *Please* make me a fighter pilot like my college friend Marty Rosenberg (shot down, killed on the ground because he was a Jew); please make me a paratrooper—I've got good ankles, like to jump—which they promised to do, once I learned Russian. I could jump with our gallant Soviet allies.

Since I was immortal, I feared nothing but boredom or deprivation. Danger, even discomfort was a kick to the metabolism. The suffering of others left me somewhat astonished.

Other young men are different, maybe more generous. This is how I was. Later, I've admitted to my children that at first I felt no joy about the idea of becoming a father; it seemed to be a distant and irrelevant form of immortality; I let it happen because somebody nearby seemed to want it. Who said I needed this help toward living forever? I could manage by myself.

My daughters taught me to love my daughters. My sons taught me to love my sons. The love of children is a common human experience, but this one had to learn it from his kids. It seemed that I had to experience events before I could value them.

If no one in my family had happened to survive in Europe, I might not have missed that family. But two did, one of them a French doctor, Alain Waynberger, gone to Paris as a boy from Eastern Europe when most of the relatives chose America. He liked the idea of dozens of varieties of cheese, he said; also French painting, French girls, the nervous language. He became a French doctor, served in the French army. When France collapsed, he was one of the few who found his way across the Swiss border, paying for the chocolate he was offered by official Swiss police hospitality. "Paid enough for *many* cups of chocolate—for chocolate, a watch, and a cuckoo clock." He was able to bring his wife and their child.

When the war was over, he found no surviving relatives in Europe. His wife had no surviving relatives. They had their son. And so when the GI Bill, Fulbright scholar-cousin appeared from Ohio, during those days of rationing, no heat, black market, I became instant family, to be fed, entertained, and fathered by a man who had lost almost everyone. The trials of *les collabos* filled the newspapers. *What did he do?* was what you asked about any new acquaintance.

My cousin still loved French wine and cheese. When I refused cognac at dinner, he looked shocked. "*Zut*, if you don't want to drink it, I must give it to you by injection."

He made me laugh and he also told what he knew about how our relatives died. Because I loved him and he was living, these absences had meaning. They were real because I found a survivor. I discovered grief for the imagined deaths.

I met other survivors, the people who sold fruit in the market on the corner, with their tattoos on their wrists. Because I saw the tattoos, it was real. Despite my swagger of a young man who had merely found a pretty girl, in due course I was being instructed by an infant in the unsimple and unpredictable turmoils and stillnesses of love. I was beginning to see what lay around me. I felt the need of replenishment; I felt the replenishment my first daughter gave me. Smelling clean and laughing after her bath, she made the news of the world more than an entertainment, a movie—we were in it now together.

A stubbed toe—or a caressed arm—can easily obscure the rest of history. Through the fog of youth, when a person feels his own hungers most clearly, I began to notice that something unusual had happened.

My few lonely cousins, surviving and remembering, taught me what to treasure and what was lost.

My life as a Jew has been eccentric and not abnormal for the times. I grew up in a non-Jewish town, a western suburb of Cleveland where there were no Jews. The combination of the long streetcar ride into Cleveland and a rabbi who stood with his belly too close and hectored a boy who asked questions made me defiant. Probably my questions were foolish and inciting. But I sincerely wanted to know why the devil I was there. I preferred to play baseball on Sunday mornings. It was said that the only separation between the Euclid Avenue Temple and the Euclid Avenue Unitarian Church across the street was Euclid Avenue.

When bar mitzvah time came, I wasn't. I said no. Preoccupied with becoming Americans in a difficult isolation, with making a living in a depression, my parents didn't need more fights with a willful son. I'm still astonished that I won (lost) this small family war.

Nevertheless, I was made to know I really was Jewish. An open herring can, with a note attached to it, broke through the window when I lay in bed with chicken pox. The herring smell reflected a touch of neighborly imagination. The woman next door forbade her son to play with me. Later he brought my brother and me upstairs, his mother not yet home, and wanted to "wrestle" with us. He was bigger, he was a couple years older, he knew things we didn't know yet. When a sudden smell of punk occurred, a bitterness in the air, like fireworks, or like sour herring, I realized that something strange was happening, grabbed my younger brother, and escaped. My brother and I never told anyone about this incident. We sensed confusion in the matter for both Jack and Jack's mother. We learned about sex later—what little we learned.

The police came regularly to our house to say there was a report of loud talking. "Who, officer?" my father asked.

"Maybe it wasn't talking, maybe it's running the lawn mower on Sunday."

"This is Friday," my father said.

The cop looked around, grinning; shrugged; went away. We could see Jack's mother stationed behind her curtains.

As I reached adolescence, I was no longer invited to birthday parties. The same girls offered interesting and secret invitations. I was kissed and pressed against the walls of homes I could not enter. In due course we studied these matters together without any discussion—Donna and Pattie and Maggie, a trembling wild creature whom I wanted to take to a dance but couldn't. Her parents wouldn't permit it. But silently and greedily we could share, after school, our books spilling from our arms, the smell of dead leaves and punk rising about us in the midwestern autumn.

The equation in those days was: Sex is the devil's work; the Jew is the devil; therefore, if you want sex, you have to go to the devil. At Lakewood High School, curious anatomists wondered if I had a hidden tail. Maggie asked me to carry her books home again, then asked to see my foot. Did I have five toes or only two?

I made friends among the other loners and oddballs. There were the early drinkers, the ones who wrote poetry, despised their parents, had secrets—those in the fighting crisis of adolescence. There weren't so many of them in those times. My parents and name had handed me a ticket of admission. I decided it wasn't really a disadvantage to be a Jew. I still didn't know what it *was,* however.

My father, who owned a food market, carried a ball-peen hammer in his back pocket. I loved to see the silvery forked glint sticking out of his pants. It was for opening fruit crates and hitting enemies.

The Black Legion, out of Jackson, Michigan, and William Dudley Pelley's Silver Shirts, out of Lake Paranoia, America, and the German-American Bund were popular allegiances. Bundles of their newspapers were thrown against front doors of Emerson Junior and Lakewood High School. In the samples left in my locker, in case I had missed them, I found cartoons of hook-nosed exploiters. I learned that President Rosenfeld was a member of the Tribe, along with a diverse crew that included Jack Benny, Judas, and a strange creature called Lilith, who stole the strength of men's loins while they slept. Of these, the only one I knew personally was Lilith.

An exchange program between German and American schools returned a classmate who spoke to an assembly about his year in Heidelberg: "I didn't see any Jew persecution. But I didn't have to see any Jews, either."

There was laughter and people turned around to look at me.

The principal of the school, when he finished, thanked the boy for reporting so well on a broadening experience that contributed to bringing about better understanding of a nation which was often unjustly attacked in the controlled American press.

I suppose I had two choices in dealing with all this. One was the reaction I met later: the Jews who crossed Euclid Avenue to become Unitarian, changed their names, hid from the storm. The other was defiance. I wanted to discover the meaning of this secret power that I was credited with and blamed for. I realized it was more than the bellying rabbi had explained, more than the fights about "Christ-killer," the herring can through the window, the sweating boy next door, the girls greedy in the afternoon after school, the mysteries of being different in a different way from my friends among the other oddballs of Lakewood High School.

It was a rickety matter to decide it merely wasn't a disadvantage to be a Jew. That wasn't enough. I found something as unreal and fantastic as a traveling carnival in the fights with boys I didn't even know, the kisses from girls who wouldn't let me come to their parties. Too many negative enticements around here. Yet I liked my friends. I liked the kisses, too. Perhaps the name "Gold," my father and mother speaking with their accents —nobody else in Lakewood seemed to have an accent—came together to make a disadvantage that I liked.

There was a third option that I wasn't yet ready to discover. It was in the air I breathed, the life I lived at those ages, in that time and place. It would have been to make a life as a Jew on grounds more solid than exotic defiance.

I found a book to love even more than I adored the books of Thomas Wolfe ("Oh lost and by the wind-grieved ghost, return"—lovable stuff for a seventeen-year-old) and James Branch Cabell (elegant fencing among undefined yearnings in cloud-cuckoo land, or maybe Virginia). The book was a collaborative series of novels by Paul Eldredge, a professor of French at New York University, and George Sylvester Viereck, a German propagandist through several wars, who claimed to be the illegitimate son of the kaiser and was imprisoned for Nazi activities during World War Two. These were an eccentric choice for a seventeen-year-old's favorite literature. George Sylvester Viereck's masterwork, *My First Two Thousand Years,* was the story of the wandering Jew, romantic, awed, hyper-heated, crediting me with miracles. I took it personally. As a midwestern adolescent, I liked the idea of that special Jewish talent, "the secret of infinite pleasure indefinitely prolonged."

The sequels didn't live up to the first book; sequels seldom do. Later, after the war, after his release from prison, I lived on the same slum block of Manhattan with Mr. Viereck and used to see the senile old man stumbling past my ground-floor apartment. And then, at the age of forty, after a second marriage and new children, I wrote a book, a memoir and essay about how I grew into being both a Jew and a writer, and called it *My Last Two Thousand Years*. The old Nazi was one of the featured players in my story. I was still inventing myself as a Jew out of unpromising materials. Every writer needs to be the hero of his own myth, no matter how unheroic the raw material. ("I'm writing an autobiography," the writer says, and his friend answers: "I hope you find a subject worthy of it.")

The war was over and I was demobilized after three years in the army. I was twenty-one, but in the ways that matter for peacetime, the clock had stopped and I was still eighteen. I was ready to start education again, start courting and flirting again, start a realer life than stripping and firing weapons, jumping from parachute towers, interpreting for Russian prisoners who had chosen to fight on the German side. The army had trained me as a Russian expert, and along with these skills came the notion of our-gallant-Soviet-allies as one long, smiling block of word (siege of Leningrad, haunting flights of geese, meadowlands). The lost souls of General Vlasov's volunteers puzzled me.

I was a bookish child, bookishly puzzled, and ready to catch up with the serious business I had missed. My first summer out of the army was devoted to loafing, tennis, chasing girls, and reading Proust; an uncle bought me six ties to welcome me home. Meanwhile, my parents heard from a distant Polish cousin who had managed to survive. They filled out forms, wrote affidavits, sent money. He arrived in Shaker Heights.

He had been an eye surgeon on the staff of hospitals in Warsaw, Berlin, and Paris. Alone of our family in Poland, he came through the events because he was assimilated to Polish life, blue-eyed, without close family attachments to hinder him, and he passed through the German occupation as a Polish bricklayer. When he was finally sent to a camp, he was sent as a Pole, not a Jew. He was called Henry. He was only betrayed near the end. He lived.

When he arrived in America, he wanted to be a doctor again. He studied, took exams, and failed the English part of it. Okay, he studied some more. In late middle age he was going to learn enough English to be a doctor in America. He thought he would be an eye surgeon again.

In the mysterious isolation in which a world like the suburbs of Cleveland envelops itself, a scheme developed among several families. A neighbor also had a relative, a survivor, a woman who had suffered, lost her loved ones, and lived. What a sweet idea to put these two together, make a match! Okay, they weren't young, but it's never too late.

Better not let them in on the plan. They were both shy; who knew how nervous some people get? Absolutely better not to warn them. This was grown-up business. After all they had gone through, they were like children, timid kids. They were dependents now—we had to consider this.

"You will come to tea with some friends," my mother told Henry.

Obediently, like a good child, he assented.

We arrived at the house of the neighbor. In his courtly way, Henry bowed and touched the hand of our hostess. And then she introduced Henry's fellow survivor. He stared, and then he spat on her.

I didn't ask for the details and he never offered them. It was enough that he had known her in the camp. I had read about what it meant to be a *kapo,* and in the widening horrified pale blue eyes of my cousin, I caught a glimpse—not enough—of what it was to be a victim. I couldn't see the expression in the woman's face because I was ashamed to look.

There was consternation in the little group of neighbors and friends. They thought the war had ended with minor changes, mostly conciliatory—now Russian Jews were admitted to the country club that previously was limited to German Jews. I'm not sure what they learned from their consternation except maybe not to set out match-making as if the rest of the world were Shaker Heights, Ohio.

For the few months more that I knew Henry he seemed silent and withdrawn, oddly smooth-faced with the weight he had gained suddenly. He passed the state medical language exams and was licensed to practice medicine, went to work in a hospital, and almost immediately suffered a stroke and died. He is remembered now more for that act of spitting on a fellow Jew than for anything else. Those who might have remembered him in Poland, of course, were gone before we met him.

In 1949, when I arrived as a student in Paris, everything was magic, and the magic was all mixed up: the ancient rusted bicycle I bought with the shrewd idea that it needed no lock because no one would bother to steal it; my wife hiding under an umbrella in a corner of our room because I was trying to give myself a shower by splashing water from the sink; the thrills of rationing and the black market, where we could trade our American clothes for the luxuries of theater tickets; my French tutor, who first called me *"mon vieux"* and caused a blush of pride, a heat I can still feel in memory; reading Sartre's essay on how to treat the German occupant in various hypothetical situations (give him a light for his cigarette if he asks, because he's a human being and it would be degrading not to; lie to him when he asks a direction, because he's the enemy and he is performing as the occupant); the birds twittering in the courtyard of the little Hotel de l'Univers on the rue Notre-Dame-de-Lorette and the smell of the breath of the hotel manager, which I thought was tooth rot but finally learned was only garlic, a substance I had not grown up with in Ohio.

And my fellow students who invited me to dinner at their apartment and then pulled out their yellow stars.

And the woman who sold us cheese at the corner shop with the numbers tattooed on her wrist.

And then the jovial French tutor, who fondly said *"mon vieux,"* told me he had been a member of the Pétainist Blue Shirt youth brigade. He invited me to hear a recording, in secret, up a stairway of the rue Mouffetard, along with his fellow veterans, with candles burning in front of each of us, of a screeching speech by the revered marshal.

The events of the war were still the day's news and the day's life. They were not yet history, and perhaps, if one attends closely to the world, they are not merely history now, either.

In my twenties, I was still immortal as far as I was concerned. Any other solution besides eternal life didn't fit into my plans. Death was a rumor that didn't apply. Yet it gradually came to dawn on me that the same wasn't the case for others.

In Paris in 1949, I met a man with an odd disease. He looked like one of those freak wrestlers, Man Mountain Moise, with a granite jaw, protruding nose, stone ears; all the cartilage was growing and solidifying. He had no hair, eyebrows, or lashes. His tongue was enormous. It impaired his speech and, I was told, he would die choked by his own organs.

With thick sounds he tried to tell me about his life in French, in Yiddish, which was a bewilderment to me, in English. He had been a prisoner. There had been experiments, meshugas, making meshuga experiments with knives, no anesthetics, and he was one who lived. God alone could understand. Even God couldn't understand.

He wanted it to be known. He thought it could be written down.

I listened, but mostly I watched, astonished by the physical process of his trying to get words past his tongue. It was a stumbling, breathless procedure. His head looked as if it were carved out of a block of encrusted bone.

The condition is called acromegaly. Couldn't something be done for him? No, they said not. Perhaps his story could be told; perhaps someone could be found to tell it. But nothing could be done for his body. He was the result of a doctor's sport and imagination and there were no doctors to undo these games.

There is a story about Clare Boothe Luce complaining that she was bored with hearing about the Holocaust. A Jewish friend of hers said he perfectly understood her sensitivity in the matter; in fact, he had the same sense of repetitiveness and fatigue, hearing so often about the Crucifixion.

A few years ago I was put on the mailing list of a Holocaust revisionist mystic in Los Angeles. In a long Xeroxed letter ("copies to Opinion Leaders") he described driving up one of the barren mountains looking out over the sprawling city, studying the lights below, realizing that many of those lights represented Jewish houses and businesses, and suddenly being struck by an insight that he found overwhelming. He was out of a job, and there were so many Jews out there, living, working, breeding! If there really had been a Holocaust, why were they there?

He knew, he explained in a series of bulletins, that this revelation would make difficulties in his life, especially since now he was called by duty to devote all his energies to the cause of the truth he had discovered one sleepless night on a mountaintop overlooking a city crammed with Jews. But the Truth demanded to be told. Tom Paine and Benjamin Franklin would understand. And he had found a little contemporary circle of colleagues, others who in different fashions had come to knowledge. They would carry the battle to the enemy and the misled sheep of America.

Okay, he's crazy, he's paranoid, absurd. But he also has comrades in his struggle. He has fellow logicians. If Hitler with all his discipline was such a big deal, why do the Jews still take our jobs, our women, make our movies, decide what we'll see on the tube—tell us what to think? If the Jews were destroyed, why are they still so much with us? It makes their power even more oppressive. It means even extermination can't help. Like the devil, the Jew survives his death.

In this madness there is a certain truth. Judaism revived, Israel happened, a world and a history were lost but something both new and old came into the hollow place.

As the years go by, the story disseminates into myth and politics. The nation of Israel disturbs the world's comfort. These years, some feel like Clare Boothe Luce, weary of the matter; some come to a more efficient form of denial. I learned from a personal acquaintance about the power of that peculiar form of philosophy, Holocaust Revisionism, and its appeal to the sophisticated and well-meaning. At a dinner party in San Francisco, a lady turned to the Jew at her right with a question that troubled her. "Herb, have you heard? It seems the so-called Holy Coast of the Jews during World War Two, you remember, is just a propaganda. I was talking to a professor from L.A. the other day, he's a real expert and he made a study, he told me a lot of books prove . . ."

My fork, lifting asparagus, paused as she chattered on.

"The Zionists made it all up, you see, to get people upset and then they could do what they wanted."

This woman is university-educated, energetic, devoted to the arts. She was the wife of a colleague. During our twenty-five years of sociability, I've seen her give energy and money to a succession of causes: young playwrights, blacks, the environment, health foods. There was no ill-will or spite in her announcement between the soup and the fish that the murder of the six million did not take place. There was curiosity. There was the never-ceasing need for dinnertime conversation. There was a pleasure in discovery and the sincere wish that I might share her joy.

"Now I understand something, Herb. I wondered why so many of my friends are Jews, I mean if they were supposed to all be killed by the Nazis. I didn't stop to realize, Herb . . ."

Normally I am impatient, impolite, and abrupt. In this case, perhaps because of the occasion and because I have known the lady so long, I merely mumbled that I preferred to discuss the subject when we could speak privately.

Charlotte is a perfectly decent woman in the mode that keeps the average prosperous American world in order. She pays some attention to her children; she enjoys serving soup and salad to her friends; she grieves when she quarrels with her husband. If you prick her, she bleeds; she asks you politely not to do that again. She doesn't need to be deeply emotional or profoundly intelligent for these events to occur. She is a person who seeks style and comfort. For Charlotte, it's more comfortable not to be troubled and to accept the drift of sentiment away from the once-delicious images of Paul Newman in *Exodus*. The Charlottes go along on whatever trip happens to be offered by fashion. There were now new scenarios.

I didn't mind playing tennis with the wife of a friend, no matter that her spirit was not saintly. Mine isn't, either.

How Charlotte puzzles me is that her decently callous, ordinarily selfish life is what we can expect of human beings everywhere. She was ready to find something appealing in the madness of denial because it supported her average prosperous expectations in life. The Jews have brought around enough trouble already—no offense meant, of course.

In spite of my request, she sailed on with bright good humor: "I realize this isn't the greatest dinner conversation for you, being a loyal Jewish person and all, Herb, but when you consider what a raw deal the Arabs are getting as a result of faked photographs and exaggerations and blackmail, Herb . . ."

It happened that I had heard of a showing of the French film *Night and Fog,* a documentary of the concentration camps. We don't need to rehearse this story now: the living skeletons staring at the camera or stacked like cordwood, the dying, the trembling heaped bodies; the shovels and tractors pushing flesh into manageable heaps; the captured German footage and still photographs. I telephoned my friend Charlotte, and said, "We have a date."

"That's terrific," she said. "Just because I'm a married woman is no reason I can't have a night out with an old friend."

We did it very formally, with no discussion of the movie beforehand. A little supper, no wine, a cappuccino; I wanted to keep her alert. During the film she was silent. When it was over, tears were running down her cheeks. She hunched her shoulders, pulling her coat around her face as we hurried to my automobile. I took her home directly. She was still crying.

A few months later, at a dinner sponsored by the English-Speaking Union, I happened to sit near Charlotte. The drift of social life had arranged things so that I had seen little of her. She looked at me and a light of greeting came into her face. "You're just back from Israel, Herb! Tell me, what's the real situation from the inside? I hear—well, I guess they're trying to brainwash us. . . . Say, have you heard about how all that propaganda about the murdering of Jews during the war is just that—Zionist propaganda? Now I don't blame individual loyal Jewish persons like yourself, but . . ."

This time I was less cautious, no asparagus on my fork. "Charlotte! Don't you remember that film we saw together?"

She looked at me with friendly, interested, concerned, blinking confusion. "What film, Herb?"

"*Nuit et Bruillard.* We saw it together."

"That means *Evening Mist* in French, doesn't it? I don't remember that film. Who directed it, who was the *metteur en scène?*"

"You don't remember, Charlotte?"

She was puzzled. She leaned toward me with her intense pale blue eyes. She looked into my eyes with absolute honesty. "I go to a lot of screenings, Herb, but I try to keep my mind clear and only remember the good ones. I saw a darling Swiss-French film, *Claire's Knee* or something, is that the one? I mean, whatever's right, but if I went to a movie with you, Herb, surely I would remember, wouldn't I?"

Charlotte doesn't have to be like the man who wrote that he had driven to a height overlooking the grand city of Los Angeles and sat there all night with his revelation: Los Angeles is full of Jews; the Holocaust couldn't have happened. Charlotte needs no revelation. She prefers adjustment. There is too much to deal with and we have to make our comfort as we can. In the economy that makes her moral metabolism go, all she requires is the cutoff, the amnesia of convenience, working for her as efficiently as the tools of her beauty and her money.

In Russian, there is a verb that means to-perform-the-act-of-falling-silent. The verb is active—a positive withdrawal. It's the last phrase in Pushkin's play *Boris Godunov,* a stage direction as the crowd shrinks from its awful feeling. The choice is forced, but it suits the crowd's needs. Charlotte, not pressed in the same way, nevertheless has learned the human talent of performing the act of convenient forgetfulness. Those of us who have children have seen that this is a natural human talent. On the subject of the Jews, there is plenty of incentive to practice the skill of making things run right along.

Even Jews have difficulty imagining their history and matching their lives to it. A few years ago a homosexual friend, an activist in gay causes, normally sensible enough, sought free space at a Jewish community center for a gay support group. For whatever reasons—perhaps, for all I know, homophobic ones—the request was denied. The activist wanted to put an advertisement of protest in a local Jewish newspaper and the paper rejected his ad. He fell into a state of violent despair. He had found an issue. He wanted me to join his protest, perhaps to picket the newspaper. I asked to see the advertisement in question.

It was headed: A NEW HOLOCAUST.

That word.

I exploded in a rage about selfishness, self-involvement, the misuse of metaphor, disrespect for a word and a memory.

He looked at me indulgently. There I went, focusing on the wrong things again. "Well, I want to get people's attention," he explained.

"You have no right!"

Naturally, as it tends to do in such cases, this led to a discussion about whether I might be homophobic. I tried to explain that certain ideas can't be used to sell other ideas. The Holocaust shouldn't be brought out to cadge free office space.

There is difficulty using it as an occasion for literature, too, which is one of the starting points for the few great writings on the subject—the words of those who bore witness and were able to tell something. Yet despite queasiness, the event is continually present, surely for all Jews—when we make love; when our children are born; when we try to reckon with the Jewish idea that salvation is on earth, not in heaven, and in the works of humankind, which the idea of God has helped to make possible.

Our troubles with both the word and the deed, the idea and the memory, are now fixed in our lives forever, and in the lives of those who come after us.

At age near ninety, my cousin in Paris is still practicing medicine. Surely one of the reasons for his present survival is his will —he is the last of a line but for his son, now the only representatives in Europe of an extended family. In cheerful lunches at his apartment, avenue de la Bastille, we joke about wine and cheese, America and France, the quirks of our relatives, and the shadow is there in the teasing, too. When a converted Jew became the cardinal of Paris, he said, "The chief rabbi of France is Sephardic, but at least the cardinal is Ashkenazic." When the French government released Arab terrorists, played that pro-Arab game of oil and resentment which de Gaulle inaugurated at the end of his life, he turned somber about the nation that he had loved as an adopted child adores his new parents. "The reason the Arabs don't have magic carpets anymore," he said, "is that they don't need them. They just ask a Frenchman to lie down and they can ride on his back."

Each time, during my years of visiting France, he asks the old questions about our family in the United States, most of whom he has never met, with a greedy need for connection with something that endures. He is amused by my mother's pride that the two survivors from our family in Europe were both doctors. Perhaps there was a lesson there for me, she used to hint.

When the son of old Dr. Waynberger, who became a distinguished cardiologist, married a young woman from one of the ancient Sephardic families that had been among "the pope's Jews" in Avignon, I recognized the pride and relief of his mother and father. The line would not stop. Surely now it would not stop.

The idea of humanity seems to be a guest thought that we entertain because we love our parents, our children, perhaps our husbands, wives, lovers. The German woman I met at Big Sur was tormented by the imagination of continuity, the line backward and forward in time, a father who fell away from her, leaving traces she did not dare follow. She is a psychoanalyst who wonders if her father was a criminal, a coward, a time-server, a man crazed by horrors, or merely a father unsustained in troubles by the thought of his child. The miracle of biology fashioned her—she is an intelligent and beautiful woman—and she chose a profession that is all about continuity, although she possesses only scraps of a past and she cannot accept them. Without a past we can participate in, we're not sure we can hold on to the idea of humanity. Our own reality is blurred. For most of us in this part of the century, humanity is not more than a guest idea.

For a Jew, the idea persists. One of the survivors I met in Paris in 1949 had written a book in tribute to the murdered Jewish artists. I don't remember his name, I couldn't read Yiddish, but I sat with him as we looked at the photographs and illustrations and he translated the biographies printed on facing pages.

There was a dedication. I wondered which of his family, which of the artists, he would remember in this way. I asked him to translate it. He explained, "In the camp, one of them said to me, You Jews will be remembered. We are forgotten."

His book in memory of the murdered Jewish artists is dedicated to the Gypsies.

Protecting the Dead

FRANCINE PROSE

Whenever I write a sentence of this I feel the dead enter the room. I feel them crowding behind me to peer over my shoulder, to read what I have written, to grumble and complain. The theme of the dead's conversation is that I know nothing about it. There is no argument about this—certainly not from me.

I write a few more sentences, each intended to keep the dead from misinterpreting the last, and then I write more, explicating these, and my essay branches endlessly like some fantastic fairy-tale tree on which, as the dead watch without particular interest, I am quite free to hang myself. I rush immediately to explain to the dead that I mean only figuratively. Every metaphor confronts me with my ignorance of the fact.

But isn't that what we hope for from the dead—that we no longer have to explain? We'd like to believe that they understand or at least no longer care. But not these dead, not these. These dead are ours to take care of, and oh, the protectiveness! We imagine that we can cause them further injustice and pain; the prospect is humbling and frightening. We believe we owe it to these dead to keep them in living memory; we feel this is important, although their death is painful to write about and is never greeted by anyone as welcome news. Worse are the moments we even doubt the purpose of this record-keeping, this witness-bearing; we wonder if memory has any sway over how anyone acts.

What's hardest to imagine are the numbers of the dead. My study could hold thirty at most, standing, rush-hour style. That would leave five million, nine hundred and ninety-nine thousand, nine hundred and seventy to wait on the stairs and through the hall and out the door through the yard and to the road. If the dead stood single file along the side of the road, I could go down and get in my car and drive slowly past them forever. If the dead are massed in the fields—how much land would they cover? I think of crowds I've been part of, crowds I've seen filmed from above, waves of people coming and coming—nothing close to 6 million. Nor do I *want* to imagine: the actual faces, the children.

Two nights after I write this, I am watching television. My husband flips through the channels and stops at a documentary about a group of now-elderly Hungarian concentration-camp survivors who return to the camps as tourists.

On the screen a woman says, "My mother and father and sister died here." She is a little homely, she wears eyeglasses and a scarf, she says this as if it were a simple fact. Then she says something I don't quite catch about finding her parents' shoes.

I say to my husband, "I don't want to see this."

"You're writing about it," he says.

The room is dark, it is warm in my bed. It is late, I am half asleep. "I don't want to see it," I say.

All I know firsthand about the Holocaust is how I learned to perceive it—how I envisioned it as a child, and how my sense of it changed and later changed again. My personal idea of the Holocaust is, it goes without saying, an infinitely small corner of the subject, hardly worth exploring, a contribution to the literature not worth making except in the hope of its touching on something slightly larger. When I think about the Holocaust, of how my view of it shifted, it seems to me to suggest something about how we apprehend suffering, how the suffering of others becomes part of our consciousness, part of how we perceive the world, how the pain of others is, in turn, an object of curiosity, indifference, envy, titillation, and may finally become real to us, almost as real as our own pain. I am interested in the growth of our senses of empathy and of evil, of history, possibility, memory, and obligation.

I am watching another film, again on television—not the film about the Hungarian tourists, but a documentary about (among other things) how the legacy of the Holocaust affects young Germans today. The filmmaker, the daughter of a Dachau survivor, asks the granddaughter of a Dachau kommandant: how is it possible that her grandfather—by all accounts a good man, a loving man, kind to his family—could pat his grandchildren on the head and go off to his daily work?

Waiting for the granddaughter's reply, I find I am holding my breath. For this is the central question, the question that all my thoughts about the Holocaust keep running into like a wall: the question of how it could happen. At issue here is nothing less than the mystery of evil, the genesis of morality, of empathy, the civilizing power of knowledge and of love. To consider this is to fear that all my concern with moral education and the ability to apprehend and empathize with others' suffering is finally beside the point.

The granddaughter has been crying; her nose and eyes are red. She says she does not understand, though she has tried and tried. She says: Could two souls inhabit one body, maybe something, something like that?

For a long time the Holocaust had for me an aura of the voluptuous. It seems perhaps incredible and certainly perverse to say that about an unspeakable horror. Part of this was simply the product of childish misapprehension, the synesthetic blurring that causes children to confuse what they hear with the circumstances in which they hear it. I learned about the Holocaust as children hear of a storm when their own house is unthreatened. They hear: It is windy and unsafe outside. They hear: We are fortunate—inside it is warm. Like many American Jewish children, I felt that had I been born in another place at another time, I too would have been killed, and this astonishing idea—that there existed people who would kill me just for being me—gave me a sense of vulnerability and especially of evil. (Not long ago I read in an essay about New Age religion that its sunny oversimplifications betray the lack of a sense of evil, and it occurred to me that this sense was always fully developed in me.)

But the knowledge that one might be dead if some alternate self had lived in another place is not useful information to the child, first because the child has quite a concrete sense of self, and also because the self finally balks when asked to imagine not being itself. This idea of lucky, narrow escape and its concomitant terrors meant less to me than what I sensed intuitively when my mother and father spoke of the Holocaust: that this was something dark, mysterious, forbidden, tragic—at once terrible and exciting.

And so the Holocaust for me became invested with an air of the romantic. It was terrible and glamorous, dark-toned and nostalgic, a black-and-white or sepia film in which it was always raining. I knew that it was serious—my parents made that clear —a subject for adult discussion that ended suddenly with warning looks over the children's heads. Emotionally it was highly charged, but historically abstract. I was born in Brooklyn, two years after the war. No one in our family—not one person we knew—had been killed.

There was a building not far from our house in which war refugees lived—the poorest apartment house on the poorest block, on the ragged Flatbush Avenue edge of prosperous Ditmas Park. The entire block for me was charged with mystery and fascination. Walking past, I used to stare into the hallways, at the tile floors and landlord-green walls; to look was to stand on the edge of a pit I could jump into if I wanted. In summers the refugees sat on the stoops and in folding chairs. A kid named Armand lived there, he was in our third grade; we all knew he was different from us, but I can't now remember how. I refused to connect these people with the Holocaust I imagined, the Romeo and Juliet Holocaust of *The Diary of Anne Frank*.

I cannot remember how old I was when I first read Anne Frank's diary. Perhaps I was nine or ten. I read it from cover to cover and went back and read it again. For years I reread it every few months till I knew my favorite parts by heart. These were not the passages other people cherished, those expressions of strength and courage and unwarranted faith in humanity. Rather they were the sections that dealt with Anne's romance with Peter Van Daan. For me the book was the story of a girl who had a love affair and a girl who died, and in retrospect I am not sure I knew the difference; it is never so easy to confuse sex and death as when we are young and have had no experience of either. For me the unfolding drama of Anne's infatuation with Peter was inextricably connected with what I knew of her subsequent fate, and something in me saw this confluence as extremely attractive. I think that I would have been willing to suffer the death if I could have had the romance.

This is what I mean by voluptuousness, this connection of tragedy with pleasure and abandon, at an age when what we secretly feel about suffering is that we don't have enough, when whether a life is tragic or comic means less than that it is dramatic. This longing to drown in some warm ocean of (imagined) suffering is part of childhood anad adolescence. Young Werther and Adolphe and even Holden Caulfield are taught, when they are taught at all, like amusing period pieces instead of accurate renderings of periods in all our lives.

Late childhood, adolescence—one way to know you were alive was to stick yourself with a pin. The Holocaust was and still is an extremely sharp pin, with which even adults can stick themselves, although for different reasons. I was glad that no one in our family had died in the Holocaust, but having no real experience of a family member dying, I also felt slightly cheated: to have suffered even a minor loss would have made my connection with history much more firsthand and authentic.

At that age I resembled the famous photograph of Anne Frank, and I would stare at her picture for hours till I felt it was my own. It gave me a kind of half-scary, half-pleasurable chill, and as I look at it now, I can recapture some of that sensation: that peculiar, heady mix of melancholy and exaltation. I knew something about the Holocaust, and why the Franks and the

Van Daans were forced to hide in that attic. I knew the number
—six million—knew of the camps and the images: the barbed
wire, the striped suits, the shaved skulls, the sunken eyes.

I can't remember precisely how I first heard about the Holocaust, but I somehow suspect that my earliest knowledge was
connected to an early form of sexuality, to being shown snapshots of my father as a handsome young soldier in the Philip-
pines, and being told the reasons why he'd risked his life in the
war. My father was brave, he did what he had to do. Hitler was
killing the Jews. It took only childish logic to make history come
full circle: My father had joined the army to save Anne Frank.

The lesson I was meant to learn was that we were fortunate,
but that we must never take our good fortune for granted, because this could happen to us. Another Holocaust could happen
anywhere—even here, where you might least expect it. This was
the history of the Jews.

I have spoken of the Holocaust as a pin with which to stick
yourself, and it functioned this way, I think, for my parents, who
very much saw themselves as Jewish, although they'd left their
immigrant parents' neighborhoods, stopped keeping kosher or
going to shul. They were in many ways religious people, though
—both doctors—they considered themselves modern and scientific and thought it quaint and a little absurd to imagine a God
in a heaven. But when they felt in danger of assimilating too far,
they'd stick themselves with that pin of the Holocaust and, punctured, fall back on the comfort (comfort, characteristically, born
of uneasiness) of their Jewish identity.

I don't mean to imply that the idea of the Holocaust was for
them—as it was for me, as a child—an instrument of sensation.
They were too wise, too experienced for that, and could no more
view it that way than I can at my age now. Both were gifted with
great reservoirs of compassion; both found it painful that anyone
should suffer pain. In telling us about the Holocaust, they were
saying what fortunate children need to hear: the fact that they
are lucky, that fortune should bring a sense of responsibility
toward those less fortunate, that elsewhere and at other times
there is and has been great injustice, and finally that this reality
should be immanent to us all.

Also, I suppose, they were offering the Holocaust to me as a pin to use as they did, to remind ourselves of our Jewishness. But children, by nature, reject those pins—that is, when they come from their parents. The things that parents worry about, and want us to worry about! I didn't believe it could happen in this country, that storm troopers would ever march into our house in Brooklyn. I thought my parents slightly backward for thinking so, just as they'd thought their parents backward for their Old World ideas. Children want to distance themselves from disaster, to disassociate themselves from the embarrassment and the shame of death.

Not only did I believe it couldn't happen here, I believed you could outsmart death if you were clever enough. I took (and I think my father did, too) a certain pride in the fact that my great-grandparents brought their families from Russia after the 1905 pogroms. They saw what was coming—saw it and got out. The victims of the Holocaust could have been our brothers, our aunts and cousins, or in the case of Anne Frank, our sister, our double. But ultimately they were not our family, not our dead; they were, in some crucial way, entirely different from us.

This perception of difference was confirmed when I met my first *real* Holocaust survivors, that is, the first whose lives seemed to match the romance I had in mind. These were friends of my parents, a married couple—like my parents, both doctors. I met them around the same time I was compulsively rereading *Anne Frank*. European, sophisticated, multilingual, extremely hand-some (Ingrid Bergman, Charles Boyer), they were the living embodiments of the Holocaust I'd envisioned. My parents told us their story, with respect and a certain pride, because they recognized it as a story with so much narrative power that some might even rub off and cling like glitter to the teller. It is enno-bling just to know people whose lives have been touched and narrowly saved by history and great drama.

So we learned how they were hidden by Polish peasants, how her mother had been lost in the camps and found after the war, how he had wanted to be a concert pianist—afterward he never played. This may not have been their story at all—but it's what I remember hearing. And mostly what I remember was how glamorous it sounded, how romantic, dramatic—how much like the Holocaust movie I had dreamed up in my head.

I was, as they say, a sensitive child, compassionate, easily hurt, neither stupid nor unfeeling; what I want to make clear is that I was never unaware that all this involved real suffering, suffering on a scale that I found nearly impossible to imagine—and still do. But the knowledge was abstract for me, distanced; only much later did it become what I would call "real."

What interests me now is what such knowledge means, the complex epistemology of how a protected American child comes to apprehend it: how the knowledge of the Holocaust—and of suffering in general—is romanticized, sentimentalized, glamorized, personalized, abstracted, denied, internalized, and finally, if not understood, then seen, insofar as possible, without the blinders of sentiment and confusion.

The other side of voluptuousness is curiosity and indifference—the ways in which the self steps back and watches itself and the world. Distance is what allows us to look at the photographs, to confront the violation, the nakedness of the dead. There is much that is pornographic about photographs of disastrous death, some connection beyond their obvious power to fascinate and shock. Something private and secret is happening here—but we are allowed to look. The precondition of looking at death is to stand back, to distance one's self; it is easier than imagining that this could happen to us.

Some years ago in a library, in a city far from my home, I found a stack of magazines from India; this was just after Bhopal and the bloody Sikh-Hindu riots. I remember staring, hypnotized, at the legions of the dead, the dead of Bhopal laid out in rows, the Sikhs left strewn about. What made me keep looking was partly horrific interest, partly the recognition that I was free to look; I remember fearing that someone would come in and catch me. It might as well have been conventional pornography.

I'm sure that this mixture of distance, horror, pity, curiosity, and titillation is how I first saw pictures of the Holocaust dead. I remember seeing them in *Life* magazine—though this is a vague memory and may not be true. But I do recall that pull of fascination, of seduction, that fear I might keep looking and never be able to stop. Only still photographs exert this power; in film the editing does the turning away for you; the moving eye of the camera intercedes and breaks the spell.

In college I went with my boyfriend to see the movie *Night and Fog*. I remember that it left me feeling heavy-hearted, slightly queasy, and also irritated with my boyfriend, who was not Jewish and could not have experienced it as I did. But how did I experience it? I was able to watch it through, to detach myself on some level that is no longer available to me.

One summer, when I was in high school, I went fishing for the first time. I drove with a friend to the North Shore of Long Island, and there, from a bridge, we caught blowfish. That day they were so plentiful that we just had to lower our hooks in the bay. Blowfish are remarkably sweet-tasting, but their most unusual quality reveals itself in death. Taken from the water, they puff up like bladders and bounce like balls on the ground.

I watched this happen again and again with interest and indifference as, heady with our own success and a kind of primal acquisitiveness, we went on catching fish. We caught a bucketful, then another, and continued fishing until we had caught more than I and my friend and our families could possibly eat. I can't remember what our mothers did with what was left over. My point is not that we went fishing but that we took more than we needed, and it never occurred to us that what we were taking was life.

It was in every other way an uneventful day, one I had wholly forgotten until, in preparation for this essay, I began thinking about the ways, the stages in which suffering comes to seem real. I was trying to remember if I had ever knowingly caused real suffering or simply known of and done nothing to stop it. Discounting romantic suffering, and the torments I visited on my brother as a child, my conscience was mostly clear—except for that one day, fishing.

Clearly no meaningful analogy can be drawn between killing a few dozen fish and causing the deaths of millions of people. It is absurd to even distantly connect irresponsible fishing with being a Dachau kommandant. Yet what struck me was that, even for a day, I had been able to suppress my awareness that I was causing death and pain. And I know I could not do that now. It is hard for me to believe that the person I know as myself could have spent a day watching living creatures die for no reason. But it happened twenty-five years ago, whoever that person was.

Now, when the television channels flip by and land on the documentary about the elderly survivors, it is so difficult for me to watch that, even though it relates to what I am writing, I refuse to see it. I know that afterward I will stay awake. I will not be able to sleep.

Everything has changed. The other documentary—this the one by and about the young Canadian woman, the daughter of the Dachau survivor, who visits Germany, and along the way interviews the granddaughter of the Dachau kommandant—is impossible not to watch. It asks the essential, crucial questions, questions about evil, about compassion, about the apparent presence and absence of a moral sense. These are precisely the questions that I want to hear asked and answered.

The filmmaker was born in 1947, the year of my birth. She was born in Germany, two years after her father's release from Dachau. She asks the kommandant's granddaughter how it is possible that a man who is kind to his grandchildren could go to his job, day after day, the job of killing Jews.

When the filmmaker asks this, I—as I've said—hardly breathe. For me it is the question that everything keeps breaking on, like waves pounding and pounding the same unyielding rock. This question is tied to all I have been thinking about empathy and morality, the ways in which suffering stops seeming abstract, glamorous, distanced, until others become so real to us that we could no more hurt their children than our own.

The granddaughter has been crying; now her eyes fill with tears. She is a pretty woman, though she does not look like someone who has found much peace. She says she has tried to understand. She says she does not understand. She points at her head and shrugs and smiles a tight, embarrassed smile. She asks, It is possible that two souls could exist in one body?

Interspersed with the interviews is footage of the camps and the war: two young men with the faces of skulls, an old woman being humiliated, pushed around on a street. I think I see something being hooked roughly behind the old woman's shoulder, a bayonet or just an umbrella. But this is just an impression, because I am not really looking. A grown woman, the mother of children, I am hiding my eyes like a child.

For me, the knowledge that the suffering and the evil of the Holocaust were real (by which I mean not Hollywood, not glamorous) had to exist before I could understand—not in the automatic way we understand the gravity of important historical events but with personal conviction—that the issues the Holocaust raises are the most important there are. Everything turns on the question of how the kommandant could take his granddaugher on his lap and the next day order the killing of children. The hope is: If this could be understood, it could somehow be changed.

I think of these questions obsessively, though I often try not to. I will not go to see *Shoah*. Some years ago, when I read D. M. Thomas's *The White Hotel*, I skipped the chapter about Babi Yar. When a Holocaust film is on television—the one about the elderly Hungarian woman finding her parents' shoes—I ask my husband to keep switching channels. I say that I have enough of those pictures in my head. I don't want or need any more.

But the pictures are always present. Whenever I talk about history, the Holocaust is there. It is part of what I mean when I tell students to study history. When I tell them to take fewer writing workshops and more history courses, I mean the Holocaust, I mean the Middle Ages, I mean the empires and the wars and the shifting alliances through time and all over the world. I mean a sense of perspective; I would not want them to get out of school with an undeveloped sense of evil.

Clearly it is possible to live without scenes from Leni Riefenstahl flashing intermittently through one's mind, images of mass rallies, roaring crowds, Hitler's mad-puppet rhetoric—but it is not possible for me. So many things recall these images—the rhetoric of certain politicians and preachers, the flag-waving and chanting on "The Morton Downey, Jr. Show." It would certainly be more pleasant not to have these images in my head, but wanting that is like wishing for a different eye color, a different body, a different past.

Three years ago I agreed to co-translate, from the Polish, *A Scrap of Time,* a book of stories about the Holocaust by a Polish Israeli writer named Ida Fink. After I agreed, I had many second thoughts, mostly about my reluctance to have "more of those pictures in my head." But often, as I worked on the book, it occurred to me that one of the things that art can do is to seduce us into hearing bad news, news we would rather not hear. The intensity of Ida Fink's short stories and something unique in their voice—a voice at once absolutely soft-spoken and absolutely urgent, totally accessible and yet charged throughout with that "strangeness" we recognize as art—were powerful and extremely moving and seductive enough to make me willing to work that closely with their painful (more painful for being quiet and exquisitely rendered) subject matter.

I found the work—the freedom to tinker with language, with the meaning and usage and cadence of words—enormously satisfying. But at times it was *very* hard work, winter afternoons when I worked on the couch, wrapped in a blanket, and the sentences I pushed word by word toward greater clarity and grace evoked a world of fear and sorrow that seemed suddenly so immediate that I felt as if it were some sorrow in my *own* life, one I was familiar with and which refused to disappear, and I'd feel unhappy, then weepy, then tired, and I'd close my eyes and fall asleep till my children came home from school.

One story, in particular, I could barely get through. I'd finish a sentence and then put the manuscript down and fall asleep and later try again, and again find myself nodding off into that borderline narcolepsy through which the panicky desire to flee becomes the heavy, compelling urge to escape into sleep.

In this story, a man and a woman wake to hear the rumbling of the trucks that will take them to the camps. While they wait, they talk about the possibility of saving their small daughter, the futility of hiding, their doubts about having brought the child into the world they find themselves in. Before long they are rounded up and set out marching, the father carrying the child.

In a rush of pure instinct, the father puts down the child and tells her to run, run to safety; the child runs and is shot. The father must march on bearing her body.

In 1978, when our first son was born, we named him after Bruno Schulz—a great genius, a Polish Jewish writer shot, almost on a whim, by an S.S. officer. I had read all of Schulz's work, starting with *Street of Crocodiles,* then his *Sanitorium Under the Sign of the Hourglass.* Reading Schulz, I felt that powerful admiration, that near-euphoria one feels in the presence of a master, a feeling not entirely unlike the emotions of falling in love. I read everything of his I could find—that is, his two books —and what little about him I could discover. When I think now of his unfinished novel, *The Messiah,* lost in the Holocaust, when I think that if not for the war, Schulz might still be alive, and who knows what he'd have written in the years since then—I feel a surge of what by now I've learned to recognize as real grief, adult grief.

Now our son Bruno is fishing. Our younger son, Leon, watches. We have all talked, a little solemnly, about not catching anything we won't eat. I am not crazy about the idea of my son fishing, but he enjoys it, and I tell myself that he probably won't catch anything anyway. In fact he catches a bluegill, bony and too small, but colored—blue and orange and silver—like some tropical fish. As my husband removes the hook from its mouth to throw it back in the water, our younger son bursts into tears. "It's so beautiful," he keeps saying.

Some people (Chekhov immediately comes to mind) seem born with profound empathic imaginations, others develop a moral sense when they are still children; they learn, without confusion and misinterpretation, what their well-intentioned parents are trying so hard to teach them. Others—the evidence of the Holocaust would suggest—never come to that knowledge, or else some monstrous parallel "moral" sense grows inside them and emerges at some later age, freakish and grotesque.

I learned very early not to do harm, but it took longer till I understood that those who are harmed bleed just as I do, that suffering is not glamorous, that death is only death. The lesson of the Holocaust was not that we were fortunate. I could not imagine the victims as me, born at the wrong place and time. In fact what I had to see clearly was that they were *not* me. The lesson (which other children, I am sure, learned faster) was that the pain and terror that the Holocaust victims suffered was precisely the same pain and terror we would have suffered in their situation—if we could imagine their situation.

Certain paths to knowledge are faintly embarrassing. I am acutely aware of the smarminess, the sentimentality of saying I knew nothing about empathy until I had children. I know how soft-headed this sounds, this claim to some mysterioso maternal knowledge, although one might ask why. I can think of other experiences that are commonly accepted, without shame or question, as revelatory and illuminating—warfare, illness, even travel. No one would question the premise that a bad auto accident or trip to China could change your life, but it seems somehow murky and suspect to say that about the experience of seeing a life come out of yours, one you love more than your own.

I do not mean to generalize or suggest that this is how anyone else might (or might want to) learn to apprehend the world directly. Mother Teresa has no children; many Nazi war criminals did. All I am saying is that this is what happened to me, that after my children were born I noticed a drastic decrease in my threshold for pain (that is, for the pain of others) and a parallel increase in my uneasiness and impatience with how little I actively do to relieve what others are suffering. I worry about what I read in the Americas Watch and Amnesty International newsletters, reports of the brutalized and disappeared, and I worry that I may be guilty of what Dickens called telescopic philanthropy: caring more about people in distant lands than the homeless on my own doorstep and the people I come in contact with—supermarket checkers, students, other drivers on the road—and whom I mistreat through exhaustion and carelessness.

I remember very clearly, though it was years ago, reading, in a review of a novel, a description of a German soldier killing a child in front of its mother. How many times this must have happened, how many times I must have read similar descriptions, yet by then my sons had been born, and I could not stop thinking of it. I kept imagining what it would be like to see one's child killed—how could you go on living? The way I felt when I contemplated this was entirely different from the way I used to imagine being Anne Frank, the way I used to think of the sufferings of Holocaust victims, the way that, as a child, I used to lie awake and think how my parents might someday die. There had been a kind of voluptuousness in that, a terror I used for sensation, to cause myself pain. But in the years that had passed since then, my father had died, and I'd learned that pain was sharper and deeper than the chasm of grief I'd imagined jumping into as a child. Real pain could not be tried out, tried on, explored like a tongue in a sore tooth; real pain sneaked up and seized you and shook you when you least expected it. And gradually I realized that something profound had changed, that suffering no longer seemed to me abstract, romantic, desirable, or voluptuous, but rather ugly, terrifying, deeply moving, and entirely real.

Of course the birth of true compassion need not come through the bearing of children, or the experience of loss, but—for those come to empathy late—from any experience that ties one to life, that makes one see it as precious and fragile. Once one has had that strong sense of life, apprehended it directly, one realizes the magnitude of what it means to destroy it. But once again everything founders on that Dachau kommandant. He had children, he lost parents, he went off and did his work.

That this should happen is finally such a mystery that even the man's granddaughter falls back on the language of religion: Is it possible that two souls could inhabit one body? The question of how the father of children could order the killing of children is one you can think about forever, meditate on till you're dizzy, like some nightmarish Zen koan.

This question could, if you let it, infect everything, paralyze every action—including, I should say, the art of writing this. Because if love or loss, if direct emotional experience cannot confer empathy and morality, what can we expect historical knowledge to do? Pol Pot is well educated; probably he knew all about the Holocaust, and apparently that didn't stop him from staging one of his own.

The second half of the stories in *A Scrap of Time* concerns memory and its importance. In one story, set years after the war, a Jewish couple visits the Polish farmhouse in which they hid in a tiny bunker throughout the war. Out of gratitude they have financed the remodeling of the farmhouse, which, they now see, includes a roomy hiding place so—as the Polish couple proudly tells them—the Jewish couple will be more comfortable should they need to be hidden again. In another story, a young Jewish woman, a survivor, leaves her American fiancé, who, wanting to love and save her, urges her to change her name and forget her painful memories. The irony is that while we were working on the translation, my cotranslator kept looking in modern German dictionaries for the meanings of words in Nazi officialese—terms for specific army ranks, types of roundups, and "actions." And what she kept finding was that the words no longer existed; no definitions were listed for *ordnungdienst* or *aufseherin*.

The notion that memory and testimony are a moral and spiritual obligation goes beyond the question of what we expect it to accomplish. One burdensome by-product of a sense of evil is that some things seem wrong. There are terrible sins of omission. It is wrong not to say: The Holocaust happened, it was not glamorous or romantic. And it seems inexcusable to act as if no one will be changed by hearing this, no one will be saved, evil cannot be struggled against, it is part of human nature, the Dachau kommandant went to work—why bother then to discuss it, better to just let it drop. Such views are not only incorrect, but cowardly and dangerously close to the evil they so coolly acknowledge.

Whenever I hear anyone using metaphors of the barnyard to describe human behavior, I have learned to steel myself for something suspect to come. But once again I ask the dead to forgive me because I want to be very clear. What I have come to, when I think about the necessity of action in the face of some possibly ineradicable strain of evil, is this: if you put a flock of chickens in the barnyard, sooner or later they will start pecking the weakest chicken. This is the mystery of cruelty and evil. But to know this is no reason not to try to stop it, not to try to save the chicken from being pecked. I have come to believe that the chicken *will* be pecked and that I could not live in this world without saying: Look, that chicken is being pecked. Stop, stop pecking that chicken.

Because when you no longer say it, no longer feel the responsibility to say that it has happened and is happening, the words in which to say these things mysteriously disappear, and soon no one is saying them. It is important not to let the words vanish, to remember, to keep repeating: The Holocaust happened. It was not glamorous or romantic. It was not abstract. Six million men, women, and children died horribly, and the very impossibility of imagining so much needless, cruel death is precisely the reason why we must keep pushing ourselves to imagine.

My Debt to Elie Wiesel and Primo Levi

ALFRED KAZIN

In 1960 I came to know Elie Wiesel through a review I had written of his first book, *Night*. Wiesel was then thirty-two, earned his living as a correspondent at the United Nations for an Israeli paper belonging to a religious party, and lived in a single room on the upper reaches of Riverside Drive. I remember that he signed his first letter "Eliezer," his Hebrew name. When I met him, he seemed to me diffident but awesome, a figure still visibly suffering the atrocities he had experienced in Auschwitz and Buchenwald but holding himself together with a certain strain. But awesome was the word. He personified the Holocaust as no one else in New York did.

Sheltered lives indeed! Nothing had happened to *me* during the war except some very rich experiences in Britain, where I lectured for the Office of War Information on American litera-ture and spent most of my time preparing a report for the Rocke-feller Foundation on the revolutionary discussion programs organized in the British army and in factories to boost morale after Dunkirk. My only distress came from the excessively strong drink with which British officers, all in fun, liked to ply American

---

115

guests. Although a spectator at the war, and far removed from the daily, hourly massacre of my fellow Jews in occupied Europe, I had been as aware as anyone could be, in print, of what I had always known would happen to Jews after Hitler was given power in 1933. I came from a working-class Socialist background, had known from 1934 on of the first concentration camps in Germany for German Socialists and oppositionists. In 1943, as a young literary editor on *The New Republic,* I wrote an impassioned article on the suicide in London of Shmuel Ziegelboim, who represented the Jewish Labor Bund in the Polish cabinet-in-exile, and had taken his life in an effort to rouse the world's attention to the slaughter of his people. In his letter to the world Ziegelboim wrote:

> I cannot be silent—I cannot live—while remnants of the Jewish people of Poland, of whom I am a representative, are perishing. My comrades in the Warsaw ghetto took weapons in their hands on that last heroic impulse. It was not my destiny to die there together with them, but I belong to them, and in their mass graves. By my death I wish to express my strongest protest against the inactivity with which the world is looking on and permitting the extermination of my people.

In April 1945 I had read the unforgettable report in the London *Times* of the discovery of Belsen by a stray British medical detachment. "It is my duty to report something beyond the imagination of mankind," began the article, which went on to list 40,000 sick, starving, and dying prisoners, over 10,000 corpses stacked in piles. I was still in England when the Parliamentary Commission that had gone out to Auschwitz reported its findings. The crematoria had a total capacity of 5,500,000 during the time they functioned. Auschwitz was worse than Majdanek, Treblinka, and other annihilation camps. Theses were published on the experiments performed on human beings. Seven tons of women's hair were found ready for dispatch to Germany. Human teeth, from which gold fillings had been extracted, were piled several feet high. There were 100,000 children's suits of clothes.

Long after it had been admitted by left-wing intellectuals in New York that Nazism was not a pro-capitalist conspiracy, the "mystery of iniquity," as Herman Melville called it, left everyone

I knew in New York essentially dumbfounded but still anxious to press their theories upon the world. While the occasional survivor of the camps I met after the war had no explanation to offer, brilliant refugees like Hannah Arendt lived and wrote in an atmosphere altogether obsessed with Nazism. Hannah, who impressed me as deeply as she did many Jewish and non-Jewish writers, had turned from metaphysics to political philosophy. She made her reputation with her first book in English, *The Origins of Totalitarianism* (I helped with the English), which outraged some true believers still by identifying Nazism entirely with Communism, but liberated literary intellectuals on both sides of the Atlantic by its moral passion and its contempt for authoritarianism of every description.

Still, all this was theory. Even at the end of the war, when I sat in a newsreel theater in Piccadilly looking at the first films of newly liberated Belsen, I knew myself to be far removed from the actuality of what had haunted me virtually since boyhood. And the response around me to those films was not calculated to make me feel any closer. On the screen (as I wrote in my book *Starting Out in the Thirties)* sticks in black-and-white prison garb leaned on a wire, staring dreamily at the camera; other sticks shuffled about or sat vaguely on the ground, next to an enormous pile of bodies, stacked up like cordwood, from which protruded legs, arms, heads. A few guards were collected sullenly in a corner, and for a moment a British army bulldozer was shown digging an enormous hole in the ground. Then the sticks would come back on the screen, hanging on the wire, looking at us.

It was unbearable. People coughed in embarrassment, and in embarrassment many laughed.

Wiesel and his book *Night* were totally out of my experience. Not only had he been deported to Auschwitz when he was a teenager, had seen his mother taken away immediately on the railway platform and his father murdered—his book was inflamed with a religious urgency and despair, of some profound outcry against the Jewish God, that seemed to me mystically ancestral. This was something I knew only from the spiritual vehemence accredited to the Hasidim. Everything about *Night* spoke of "religion," not least the preface by the French Catholic novelist François Mauriac, bespeaking his anguish as a Christian at Wiesel's testimony in person as well as in his book. Mauriac described young Wiesel as "a Lazarus risen from the dead," and as if recalling Nietzsche's dictum "God is dead," expressed his compassionate understanding of why a boy in Auschwitz should have thought that "God is dead, the God of love, of gentleness, of comfort, the God of Abraham, of Isaac, of Jacob, has vanished forevermore, beneath the gaze of this child, to the smoke of a human holocaust exacted by Race, the most voracious of all idols."

Mauriac's preface was written with a charity and intellectual passion by no means characteristic of French Catholics on the subject of Jews. Many Catholic intellectuals were viciously anti-Dreyfus in the last century and were enthusiastic about Vichy and its support of the Nazi proscription of the Jews. As the French critic Sainte-Beuve said, "In France we remain Catholics long after we have ceased to be Christians." So Mauriac's preface was particularly moving in response to Wiesel's anguish as a Jew.

This anguish seemed to be the heart and center of *Night*. This first of Wiesel's books, translated into French from the Yiddish, was also clearly influenced by Sartre's and Camus's existentialism; Wiesel was at the Sorbonne after his liberation and would write his future books in French. The infusion of existentialism into what Wiesel seemed to be presenting as a Hasid's rebellion certainly made for extraordinary intensity. Although I did not fully know it at the time, it was to Wiesel's "religious" intensity that I was responding. I found it salutary in its very despair.

Growing up in an entirely Jewish milieu whose most active faith, at least in my family, was a naively credulous socialism (in my case this did not survive the war), I had long been bored by so much enclosed Jewishness and found no illumination in Judaism proper. Nor was I easily impressed by the ostentatiously learned Jews, whether observant or not, who seemed to me lacking in religious fire. I was strong on Jewish solidarity, especially as my knowledge of the Holocaust developed. When it came to matters of faith I had a horror of public piety and depended on my own reading of the Bible and on certain incomparable mo-

ments of illumination in my favorite poets, novelists, philosophers—and composers.

So a certain religious frustration in me responded to Wiesel
precisely because of the rebellion he experienced in Auschwitz. I
was, as I remain, always on the side of those (like Isaiah) who
find God hidden. Very hidden. As T. S. Eliot was to say of
Tennyson's "In Memoriam," it is the poet's "doubt" that makes
the poem "religious." Kafka in his conversations with Gustav
Janouch, a Prague Gentile: "He who has faith cannot talk about
it. He who has no faith should not talk about it."

Wiesel was still a boy when the war ended for him. He had
lived at Auschwitz with the constant odor of burning flesh; he
had seen starving men, in the cattle cars transporting them from
one camp to another, fighting to the death over pieces of bread
negligently tossed them by German civilians. There were details
in his book that could be read only with fresh astonishment at
the unflagging cruelty of the Nazis and the peculiarly sadistic
frivolity of those who directed the factories of death. Wiesel
must have been among the very first to describe the infamous
Dr. Mengele, who quickly "selected" those who were to be
gassed from the terror-stricken masses walking and stumbling
before him. Mengele, said Wiesel, would motion people to death
with a conductor's baton!

There was one particular scene, the thematic center of the
book for me, that was to make *Night* stand out among other
camp memoirs. A young boy, after days of being tortured in an
attempt to make him reveal where a Dutch prisoner had hidden
arms, was put up on the gallows to be hanged. His body was
too light and so he kept strangling in front of the prisoners, who
had been forced to watch the execution and who were marched
past the gallows. As they went by, Wiesel heard a man asking,
"Where is God now?" And Wiesel heard himself thinking, "Here
He is—He is hanging there on this gallows."

I was more than "moved" by this account. I felt it was bringing me home—to something at the heart of the age-old Jewish
experience: an intimacy with God so deep-rooted and familiar
that it could rail against Him in a bitterness more eloquent of
faith than all ritual practice of faith. I had never been impressed

by what I saw of Judaism as minute obedience and certainly not by the curses poured out in the Passover Haggadah against aliens and idolaters outside the light. The despair Wiesel experienced seemed to me very possible, very true, precious in its individual authenticity of feeling. To me at least, it suggested that, in addition to all the suffering and humiliation inflicted by the Nazis, the final outcome for the survivors could be an absolute emptiness of soul, the blackness of "night" indeed. This also is the torpor that Aharon Applefeld describes in *The Immortal Bartfuss,* for all the new life in Israel.

In the first days of Hitler's campaign against the Jews I heard a rabbi in the great synagogue on Stone Avenue in the Brownsville section of Brooklyn explain that the Jews were being punished for their sins. What lifted Wiesel's book above the many accounts of the Holocaust was the pain of this *sudden* loss of faith by an intensely religious young Jew, still a boy, who grew up among Orthodox believers in Sziget, Transylvania. My knowledge of such things was obviously limited, but I was somehow convinced by Wiesel's cry before the gallows that no one of his background had left behind him so moving a record of religious crisis. Of course this is not so. Wiesel's literary gift had come through the translation into English of a French text translated from Yiddish.

What made the book compelling was its presentation of a world that remained unreal, unbearable, seemingly fictitious for all its terrible reality. Nazism did indeed create a fiction-world, as Hannah Arendt demonstrated in *The Origins of Totalitarianism.* But Wiesel's personal experience of this satisfied as a human document. It brought one back to the blank, secular universe we all know, but in terms that belonged more to the nineteenth-century crisis of faith that Orthodox Jews could still live in—witness that extraordinary novel of religious guilt, Israel Joshua Singer's *Yoshe Kalb.* The story of Job, which may not derive from a Jewish work, remains the most universally understood part of the Bible. Young Wiesel's embittered interrogation of Providence united, as it were, Job's ever-human cries against God to the most terrible event in the history of the Jews. It brought back that peculiarly scolding closeness to God that I had often seen quoted in past texts but that was peculiarly applicable to

Auschwitz. So Wiesel became, as it were, "my" Holocaust. I certainly knew it only from books.

Wiesel soon became a charming friend. I liked him for playing recordings of Red Army bands. When French students broke out in revolt like their contemporaries at Columbia and Harvard, Wiesel was radiant quoting his favorite slogans on Paris walls—*"L'imagination au pouvoir!"* A bachelor still, he expressed himself wistfully on the subject of women, professed himself astonished by the openness with which American Jewish writers were describing the sexual life. I explained that these writers—some of them of Orthodox background like Saul Bellow—were astonishing themselves too, now that so many of us were divorced.

With his European good manners and a sort of anxious civility, an accent positively reassuring in his fluent English, he articulated every word so carefully, it was not always a solemn experience to be with Elie, although nothing that came up about the war could be taken lightly. As we sat in Riverside Park watching young families on parade, Wiesel's dramatically tortured face, his martyred thinness, the deliberateness of his speech, were all the more striking because he suffered violent headaches. I felt very humble. He looked as if he had taken into himself the whole cruelty of what Churchill had called "the worst episode in human history."

Then things began to slide; I thought of him as a survivor, was not prepared to see him become such a professional survivor. My astonishment at his celebrity did not please him. He was increasingly swept, by the very demand of the madly achieving but Holocaust-shaken Jewish community, into their favorite surrogate. For the many Jews who like me had experienced nothing of the horror, Elie Wiesel became the very embodiment of the Holocaust. He did not seem to shirk the role; his very bearing in public, his sorrowful but irresistible eloquence, suggested that he was still living—as he was certainly still writing—the hallucinations of Auschwitz.

Wiesel's increasing magnetism for a great body of American Jews was of course not matched by his fellow writers. Isaac Bashevis Singer scoffed at his novels; Hannah Arendt put him down as a publicity-seeker; an Israeli novelist said bitterly of him: "The Holocaust—and me." An Israeli philosopher was to describe him in print as a master of kitsch. The novels and "testimonies" of Jewish life everywhere won the highest literary prizes in France; I thought synthetic the hysterically "religious" atmosphere he built up in his books. He once said to me, without the slightest rue, "I am not a novelist," and even said it with a certain pride. In the Jewish tradition, he explained, it was more important to bear witness, to speak for the people, than to write "stories."

What bothered me in Wiesel's sudden emergence as a Jewish sage was a certain sleight-of-hand he performed on the stage of the 92nd Street Y. Sitting behind a table on the platform as if addressing a class, talking in the gravest possible tones to enchanted audiences that often included Catholic priests and nuns, he made the wonderful Jewish texts he spoke from, spoke *for,* a rally of Jewishness. Wiesel's extraordinary quality as a platform presence lay in his ability to fuse personality, voice, text into the most expressive myth. Here was the Jew taken from the fire. Here was the ageless Jewish truth come round again in the person of *the* survivor. The ceremony was irresistible. Above all, it was "spiritual," as of course Jews know themselves to be.

Nor was this power exerted on Jews alone. I once heard a Catholic philosopher say in a lecture, "The Jews not only created a God, but a God who *spoke* to them!" Wiesel seemed to speak for the God of Israel to religious Christians who had stopped crediting Jews with belief. I once spent a year at Notre Dame as a visiting professor and discovered that Wiesel's lectures there had totally captivated the Catholic community. They had come to think of him as the most religiously exemplary figure outside of Catholicism itself—writer, evangel out of Auschwitz, almost a saint.

So who was I to wonder if the young rebel against God, who had virtually denied God in Auschwitz, could be reconciled with the platform idol who gave such rhetorical assurances of the Jewish tradition to secularized middle-class audiences? America was certainly a powerful solvent. The Jews, the most conspicuously successful, prominent group in America, and also packing a powerful wallop politically, needed something to bind them

back to the sacred. And had found their image of it in the Holocaust, not least as personified in Elie Wiesel.

For me, however, the Holocaust had not and never will have
religious significance. It ws not a "sacrifice" but a massacre most
unspeakable, an annihilation of millions that sought to wipe out
millions more, a whole people. The Holocaust was just the worst
that humanity could show. On the other hand, it was my need
to follow the fate of my people, if only through books, films,
documents, that had led me to Wiesel in the first place, as it was
his religious extremity that had made his Auschwitz so particularly real to me. Alas, I had to conclude that Wiesel was a powerful myth-maker about his relation to God, with himself as the
bearer of the myth. The more I learned about him, the more I
pursued the vast literature about Auschwitz, the less surprised I
would have been to learn that the episode of the boy struggling
on the rope had never happened.

Still, the Jews—in history—constitute such an extraordinary
example of a religious community that I can well understand
how the attempted extinction of *this people as a whole* brings up
questions of divine providence. As a Jew, I have been asking
such questions all my life, if only to come to the conclusion that
Lincoln came to about the meaning—and the horrors—of the
Civil War. "The Almighty has His own purposes." And just as I
was moved by the boy Wiesel in *Night* for imagining God Himself on the gallows (Wiesel did imagine this, whether in Auschwitz or not), so I admire another writer-survivor of Auschwitz,
Primo Levi, for remaining an old-fashioned rationalist. As a student at the University of Turin before the war, Levi said he
encountered all sorts of "trashy" ideas, the chief of these being
—in the context of fascism!—"the supposed superiority of spirit
over matter." If I once related to the Holocaust through Elie
Wiesel, I have learned over the years that Primo Levi is a far
more trustworthy witness and indeed, as Italian literary opinion
has come to admit, one of the two greatest (with Italo Calvino)
postwar writers Italy has produced.

I write of Levi in sorrow. His supposed suicide in 1987 was
such a shock to me that even now I feel some mistake was made

in reporting what actually happened. Though he was deeply troubled by family problems, it is possible that with Levi, as with the greatest Jewish poet of the Holocaust, Paul Celan, the camp experience finally came to its full horror in his mind only years after the liberation. And perhaps his proud intransigent rationalism rooted in his professional training as a chemist—this saved his life in Auschwitz—could not, after all, stave off the final indignity of the camp experience. In any event, Levi's was a scientific intelligence so controlled even in his ten months in Auschwitz that after the war, recounting the questions addressed to him from all over the world about how he had survived, he admitted: "I had begun describing my experiences there, on the spot, in that German laboratory laden with freezing cold."

This was a man who could write of Auschwitz, and this right after the war:

> I believe in reason and discussion as the supreme instruments of progress. Thus, when describing the tragic world of Auschwitz, I have deliberately assumed the calm and sober language of the witness, not the lamenting tones of the victim or the irate voice of someone who seeks revenge. I thought that my account would be more credible and useful the more it appeared objective, the less it sounded overly sentimental; only in this way does a witness in matters of justice perform his task, which is that of preparing the ground for the judge. The judges are my readers.

In 1985 Levi returned to Auschwitz "in the role of a tourist," accompanying a group of students and professors from Florence, as well as some other survivors of the camps. His visit was recorded on film by the Union of Jewish Italian Communities. It is extraordinary to see and hear the slight, sprite-like Levi recall with such directness and precision his life in the camps, the mental bruises he still gets from hearing rough Polish voices—

> I traveled in these places as a lost, misplaced person, searching for a center, for someone to take me in, and truly it was a desolate landscape. . . . To see a car in a freight train has a violent, evoking effect on me. . . . Having traveled for five days in a sealed box car is an experience one doesn't forget. . . . Then as now the entrance into Polish cities—this is a mining country and even individual houses are heated by coal—gives out a sharp smell which is the smell of the Lager, of Poland. . . . Back then we hadn't seen people,

we had only seen the jailers of the Lager and their collaborators, who for the great part were Polish, Jews, Christians. . . .

There were forty-five of us in a small, a very small car. . . . we could barely sit, there wasn't room enough to lie down . . . they had told us to bring food, foolishly we hadn't brought water, no one had told us, and we suffered from a terrifying thirst even though it was winter. . . . The temperature was below zero and our breath would freeze on the bolts and we would compete scraping off the frost, full of mist as it was, to have a few drops with which to wet our lips. . . . And the baby in the car cried from morning to night because his mother had no milk left. . . . The children and their mothers would be killed right away. . . . Out of the six hundred and fifty on the train, forty-five died the same evening we arrived. . . . Or the next. . . .

As a writer Levi was so insistent upon clarity, speaking directly to the reader, that he could say, "It is not by chance that the two least decipherable poets writing in German, Georg Trakl and Paul Celan, both died as suicides. . . . Their common destiny makes one think about the obscurity of their poetry as a pre-suicide, a not-wanting-to-be, a flight from the world, of which the intentional death was the crown."

Ironic words, yet it is difficult if not impossible to think of Levi as a pre-suicide, a not-wanting-to-be, a flight from the world. Quite apart from the lucidity and restraint with which he described some terrible events in *If This Be a Man* (the original title of *Survival in Auschwitz*), and then the wry, comic touches he gave in the sequel (*The Truce* or *The Reprieve* as it is variously called) to the Russians who took him to Russia when they liberated Auschwitz. Levi not long before his death seemed excited and happy. He told Philip Roth about the origins of his novel *If Not Now, When?* (about Yiddish-speaking partisans) that after "so much plain or disguised autobiography" he was going to dare becoming a "full-fledged novelist." In *If Not Now, When?* he wanted to write "a story of hope," to "assault the usual stereotypes of the Jew, to be the first Italian writer to describe the Yiddish world."

In any event Levi, working as a chemist in the IG Farben laboratories at Auschwitz for not quite a year, did not experience the full horrors that others did. Nor was he there with his family and deprived of them, Wiesel's terrible experience. It must be further remembered that Levi wrote in his native language. There is something utterly reassuring about the tone and style of Levi's writing, especially when any question of "divine providence" comes up. In *If This Be a Man* Levi at one point quotes to a fellow prisoner the great lines from Canto 26 of Dante's *Inferno*, which describes Ulysses's ship going down, "as pleased Another," because it has transgressed the limits of the known world by crossing the Pillars of Hercules into the Atlantic. Levi then adds:

> I keep Pikolo back, it is vitally necessary and urgent that he listen, that he understand this "as pleased Another" before it is too late; tomorrow he or I might be dead, or we might never see each other again. I must tell him, I must explain to him about the Middle Ages, *about the so human and so necessary and yet unexpected anachronism, but still more, something gigantic that I myself have only just seen, in a flash of intuition, perhaps the reason for our fate, for our being here today* [my italics].

On January 18, 1945, the Germans left Auschwitz, taking with them those still able to "march." Levi: "Today I think that if for no other reason than that an Auschwitz existed, no one in our age should speak of Providence. But without doubt in that hour the memory of biblical salvations in times of extreme adversity passed through all our minds."

Levi felt that he owed it to his conscience to report events and people exactly. He was not sparing of the opportunism and corruption among the prisoners. No one is likely to forget "Henri." "Here he is again, intent on his hunt and his struggle; hard and distant, enclosed in armour, the enemy of all, inhumanly cunning and incomprehensible like the Serpent in Genesis."

What is it to search to the depths the very *look* of people continuously inflicted, living every second under the gun? In this respect Levi in Auschwitz is already the future novelist, whether he knows it or not; he wishes above all to report what his own eyes have seen, and nothing else. In a strange way he would extend this even to his German boss at the lab, and not only because working there saved his life.

Pascal says that the more intelligence a man has the more he finds in other people. That is Levi, and his intelligence is of the kind that still stares life in the face even in those moments of extreme emotion that crush the heart. Take the great passage describing the Russians entering Auschwitz. I once saw a Russian documentary on this subject, and it was clear that the soldiers knocking down the gates with the butts of their rifles and entering as "deliverers" had done several takes before the film's director was satisfied. Here, by contrast, is Levi on the Russians:

> They did not greet us, nor did they smile; they seemed oppressed not only by compassion but by a confused restraint, which sealed their lips and bound their eyes to the funereal scene. It was that shame we knew so well, the shame that had drowned us after the selections, and every time we had to watch, or submit to, some outrage: the shame the Germans did not know, that the just man experiences at another man's crime; the feeling of guilt that such a crime should exist, that it should have been introduced irrevocably into the world of things that exist, and that his will for good should have proved too weak or null, and should not have availed in defence.

Reading that for the first time, I realized with a start what made this passage so strange in the many books I had read about what David Rousset called the "concentration-camp universe." The sense of shame that a Jew could feel about the human race at Auschwitz bespoke a reflectiveness, an old-fashioned philosophical intelligence in a situation that caused some of the best minds to become hysterical. Theodor Adorno: It would be barbaric to write poetry after Auschwitz. Hannah Arendt: "the banality of evil," by which she meant that the evil-doers were banal, empty, did not *think* of what they were doing, had become as banal as the rest of us, who do not commit such crimes only because we do not commit ourselves to anything.

Compare Levi's further meditation as the Germans left Auschwitz, taking the supposedly healthy with them and leaving the others to be cared for, and not just physically, by those who were still erect. Like Levi. His deepest concern at this moment?

> So for us even the hour of liberty rang out grave and muffled, and filled our souls with joy and yet with a painful sense of pudency, so that we should have liked to wash our consciences and our memories clean from the foulness that lay upon them; and also with anguish, because we felt that this should never happen, that

now nothing could ever happen good and pure enough to rub out our past, and that the scars of the outrage would remain within us for ever, and in the memories of those who saw it, and in the places where it occurred and in the stories that we should tell of it. Because, and this is the awful privilege of our generation and of my people, no one better than us has ever been able to grasp the incurable nature of the offence, that spreads like a contagion. It is foolish to think that human justice can eradicate it. It is an inexhaustible fount of evil; it breaks the body and the spirit of the submerged, it stifles them and renders them abject; it returns as ignominy upon the oppressors, it perpetuates itself as hatred among the survivors, and swarms around in a thousand ways, against the will of all, as a thirst for revenge, as a moral capitulation, as denial, as weariness, as renunciation.

Loftiness is not a word one uses about many writers nowadays. As Levi foresaw, we have become the victims of what we hate. The memory of Nazism has become imperishable, even for the Germans dragged kicking and screaming into the light of truth. But it has also poisoned the century for everyone. Levi is so "elevated," stern, and above all faithful to the natural reflectiveness of a mind at peace with itself, that one is astonished, one is endlessly grateful, that anything like this could have occurred to a man in and out of Auschwitz. For once, the old-fashioned belief that virtue is a kind of intelligence seems as real as the fact that, for our technological age, intelligence is the only virtue. Which, da capo, makes it all the more bitter to think that such a man is no longer among the living.

ANNE ROIPHE

For an American Jew, one born under purple mountains' majesty, this thing called Holocaust is not a neutral disaster, like the pillaging of villages by Genghis Khan, or the forced march of Indians across the Montana trails, or the sacking of Rome, or the battlefields of Antietam and Gallipoli. It is not even like the Stalin years in the Gulag or the self-genocide of the Cambodians. It is a thing that happened not to oneself and yet almost to oneself, so close that one can feel the breath of the dead on one's back, the moment when the car almost crashed and you turned the wheel just in time, the moment when the beam fell from the construction site and you had just turned the corner and were saved, the moment when death was looking for you and found someone else. Here is the hook, the horn of the dilemma, here is the tragedy we cannot place on the shelf with the others, in our heads where we understand history is cruel, nature is vicious, and life is temporary and without mercy. At the same time here is a tragedy that we cannot, we American Jews, claim as our own, because our bodies, our brothers and sisters, our parents, our streets that we played on, our memories are clear of threat, threat to our own particular heart's beating, to our own particular legs moving, to our own souls churning out traces in the dust. Nevertheless, here is a tragedy that we American Jews feel strangely strongly completely belongs to us too. How we manage this oddity, how we live with our history, what we make of it in the future, this will be on our hands, this will be our responsibility. Nothing about this is easy or clear or without anger, or shame, or without dangers of self-enhancing, self-protection, grandiosity.

I was in camp in Maine on VJ Day in 1945. I was nine years old. In Maine the night air was cold, cold blowing through the pines, cold on the dirt paths to the cabins, cold on the tennis courts, and cold on the baseball field where I was a pitcher for the junior team. We heard the news sitting in the main bunkhouse, on a floor covered with bear rugs, wearing our blue sweaters with our nametapes sewed in the back, assembled by the head counselor because something that would change our lives was coming that night over the radio. The radio, a brown box in the shape of a house in the Alps, sat on a table in front of the large screen that on other occasions showed us Charlie Chan and Batman and the Red Cross film about what to do if while swimming one's arms and legs got tangled in underwater weeds. A fire was blazing in the big brick hearth, over which a moose-head with its huge antlers was mounted. We heard the announcement, we heard the wild cheering on 42nd Street. It was over at last. The bonds we had saved for, stamp by stamp, the scarves we had knitted for soldiers overseas, the silver foil we had rolled into balls and brought into school, had all done their job: the enemy was gone; the world was at peace. The camp was for Jewish girls. The head counselor was Jewish. She turned off the radio and said, We will have a moment of silence for the Jews of Europe who have died, all of them have died, the mothers, the fathers, the children, have died, been killed by the Nazis. We had of course heard it before, when the reports of VE Day came through. We had heard it before in the rumors that passed above our heads at the dinner table. They are killing them all, the grandmothers too and all the babies. Why, we would say. They don't like Jews, the adults replied, they shrugged, they hushed up the conversation, they changed their story, who knew for sure what was happening so far away. We knew it was true because the adults were ashen and tight-lipped, because the adults changed the subject if we asked questions, because the Jews had been killed before: in Egypt, in Jerusalem, in Spain, in Portugal, in Russia on the slopes where most of our grandparents came from, in Poland when the Bolsheviks and the Royalists chased each other back and forth, the Jews were the people who lay crushed under wagon wheels when the fighting was over. Although we were Americans born of American parents or parents who pretended that they had learned English with their mother's milk, we knew the word "pogrom." We knew that there was something fated in the Jewish condition, something we were to consider each Passover as if it had all happened to us, the waters parting, the pharaoh and his soldiers chasing and the slavery that arrived before Krupp, before the idea that work shall make you free. About pharaohs we already knew, about Jewish peril we knew, and we knew something else, which occurred to us that night in camp, a place where camp meant maple syrup on pancakes and jacks played on bunk floors, we knew that being Jewish was a matter that transcended nationality, that united beyond other loyalties, that made us one with a line that had been sacrificed on too many altars, that survived because each of us, none of us wicked children daring to say what has this to do with me, knew that we counted too, in the dash across time to a safe place, in the wait for the Messiah, in the danger that didn't spare children just because they meant no one harm. That night in Maine the northern lights, like a white mist, spread across the distant horizon, the stars were brilliant overhead. Orion, the Big Dipper, the Little Dipper hung above the camp, the pine needles sticky with sap, the infant pinecones brown on the ground, the birch bark that had peeled from the trunks of the trees, all blew in the wind, the wind that rustled across the archery field and raised whitecaps down on the lake. Here in America, in pioneer country where we learned how to canoe like the Indians, how to light a fire in the forest without a match like Davy Crockett, how to tell north from south by looking at the moss on the trees like scouts for George Washington's army. Here we were very far from Europe, where the Jews had been killed, and yet as we sat in a circle and sang the camp song a kinship burned with those on other shores, a kinship that made the marshmallows toasting in the fire seem like a pagan rite that had nothing to do with the self. We breathed on borrowed time on this globe, we were here only because someone went west instead of east, someone had made the correct wager a generation ago.

The counselors were crying with joy, boyfriends coming home, peace forever after, a world made secure for the generations to come. They jumped up and down and kissed one another. Campers and counselors together were celebrating the end of the war, having a party with cupcakes and milk in the kitchen. Some of us went straight to bed, where under the covers on our cots we thought of the death of the Jews and were frightened, unreasonably frightened, considering that the enemy had been defeated, once and for all, vanquished. But even a child could tell, without yet knowing the full story, or the names of Dachau, Treblinka, and Auschwitz, without having read *Anne Frank* or seen the pictures that *Life* magazine would soon be printing, without knowing that Hiroshima and Nagasaki were names that would one day make our own children shudder, without knowing that an A-bomb had left shadows of people on the ground and had incinerated a city leaving trails of leukemia and yards of human skin broiling with radiation, we knew that a past so gruesome did not promise well for the future. The next day I pitched a two-hitter, my team won, and I was presented with a team letter to sew on my sweater. This I wrote home to my mother. About VJ Day my letter said nothing. The words were not there.

In the next years the full reports came clear. Clear even to children who still believed in their own immortality, to children who, like Anne Frank, were willing to make the mistake of believing in the basic goodness of humankind. But the facts of the disaster clearest in the pictures that my mother hid on a high shelf and that I pulled down and in turn hid under my bed, were quickly submerged in the immediacy of things, things like school, like one's jealousy of one's brother, like the loss of a best friend, like the invitation to a birthday party that was never received. World events, tragedy, even those that ring like bells of warning, seemed distant from the world of the moment, where, during Friday night dances at our Jewish country club, the lights on the patio swung pink and blue in Chinese lanterns and I went to dancing school with boys who wore white gloves and could hardly speak unless you encouraged them with questions about baseball.

There was a new menace in the world that had taken the place of the Nazis and this we all understood was the Commies. They didn't single out the Jews for extermination but they were after America, all that we held dear. They were everywhere trying to subvert the purity of democracy. Commie, Pinko, goddamn he has such a Jewish name, said my father about a former friend who had been named in a list. The dead were dead. They were hardly mentioned. That suited us children just fine. Who wanted to walk around chained to a past on which 6 million bodies were strung. But Israel, or Palestine, now that was another matter. Here was a moment for heroism, for courage against the British, for courage against the Arabs, for standing tall, for thinking boldly, for making speeches about justice and history. The nightmares that ended in camps with skeletons and striped pajamas faded before these wonderful new images of Jews on tanks, Jews with fighter airplanes, Jews addressing the United Nations. One could forget the dead, the millions of dead and the chill of fear that they brought. One could chase away images of boxcars and crematoria with magic words like Golda and Ben-Gurion, and send money to plant a tree. Once again we had bonds. My uncle gave me two. I planted a tree in the name of my best friend, who had moved to St. Louis. What child would be wicked or foolish enough to say what has this to do with me?

But it's not so easy, this crossing of personal life with the major events of one's time. The personal, of course, is so much more vivid, so much more immediate, and the pain of one's own history is never matched with the whole, except perhaps in saints, which is what makes them saints, and Jews don't have saints because we are so familiar with disaster that we have difficulty in adding romantic gloss to the reality of suffering. When I was twelve my friend Packy Sonnenschein, who had been catcher when I was pitcher on the team, who had an album of horse pictures just like mine, and who was my colleague in dropping water bombs out of our Manhattan apartments on doormen and nursemaids who stood, inviting targets, below, my friend Packy's father died. He was an orthopedic surgeon who worked half time in a hospital in Harlem. He believed in caring for all people and he had dinner with his wife and his children and sometimes I had stayed for supper and he talked to us about his patients and their lives and what he could do to make them easier. He kissed his daughter on the forehead and he patted his son on the shoulder. He died suddenly of a heart attack.

Now my own father was interested in making money. He did not serve the poor or any other creature. He was not so fond of his family and yelled at his wife and looked through his children as if they were ghosts in someone else's horror story. He left the house each morning in his immaculate suit with his monogrammed handkerchief, with his eyes as blank as stone and his teeth clenched tight. His heart was fine and he lived. My friend Packy's father had died and this was a puzzle that needed to be solved. Here in my personal immediate world was clear, irrefutable evidence that Who shall live and Who shall die was not based on past performance or on moral considerations. Here was God who had demonstrated to me what I must have already known, but had not allowed myself to see, that goodness was no protection, that human pain had no moral point, that God if He was all-powerful was careless, and that reward and punishment could be neither avoided nor evoked by attention to the rules. The prophets were wishful thinkers. The universe was directed by mysteries never revealed or perhaps it spun in random arcs: good and bad, loving-kindness, were these all human inventions? This rudiment of struggle with matters of good and evil and their manifestations on earth seems childlike now, and why not, these were thoughts of a child whose body was moving into ripeness but whose mind still plodded with small steps. On the other hand, discovery of all the fine works of others who have faced down the problem of why the apple was eaten, of why the forbidden tree grew in the Garden of Eden, of why death, of why injustice, of why God's infrequent mercy and man's implacable fury (or is it the other way around), knowing the language of discourse has not brought an answer. The questions that stirred in my mind when Dr. Sonnenschein died grew as I did, bigger and more troublesome. With this thought about Dr. Sonnenschein and my father, the Holocaust came back into mind.

What kind of God would allow this to happen to His chosen people and what kind of justice existed and if the Jews had died in such numbers in such a way for nothing, like Dr. Sonnenschein, carried off in his forty-fifth year, then what was the point. I became the wicked child, what has this all to do with me.

That year, Yom Kippur, two months before my thirteenth birthday, I refused to enter the synagogue with my mother. I refused to fast. I stood on the steps and glared at the congregation as they entered. I was wearing my new suit, the one that was too warm for the season, the way all High Holiday clothes are always for the season to come and never for the season that is, and I stamped my foot still in its shiny patent leather shoe at God, whom I informed had lost me. How could I go into the synagogue and beg forgiveness for sins when none of my errors, misjudgments, evil thoughts, had resulted in even one death, whereas God, who might just not exist, in which case what were the Jews doing following this covenant right to the ovens, had permitted the death of so many, including of course one innocent Dr. Sonneschein, whose fate had nothing to do with the Holocaust but had nevertheless opened up the entire question of guilt, God or man's. On the steps of the synagogue, underneath the blue awning, as the doors opened and closed, I thought of my mother, whose repentance the Lord demanded. My mother, whose eyes were often swollen from tears, whose marriage offered a feast of humiliation, had begged me, "Come in and sit next to me, you don't have to believe what you're saying, just stand and sit down like everyone else." "Hypocrite," I called her and waited for a whirlwind to chide me. Later, I thought, "Rescue her, God, and I'll repent too." The year of my puberty God became the God of the Holocaust for me and this was because of Dr. Sonnenschein.

If there are problems of logic in this it can't be helped. If scholars and philosophers would provide wisdom that would reconcile God with the crimes of this century, would even reconcile God with the cry of Dostoyevski's dying child, they have not yet convinced me, proved their case beyond a reasonable doubt. Answers I have heard, yes, wishful answers that insist that you leave unknown things that you know. Truths may be coming, another generation may find them, some mysteries may be better left alone, but I remain as I did on that Yom Kippur of Dr. Sonnenschein's death, caught up in anger at a God whose actions have called His existence into question and made a mockery of the deaths, martyrdoms intended and unintended in His name. The comfort of the Kaddish rings hollow when the source of the pain and the source of the peace may be the same. Now it is true that I may have been angry at my father and not at God the Father and confused them one with the other. It is true that rebellion is the seed of growth and that I was growing and it is true that all those thoughts might have been exactly the same if there had been no Holocaust, but there had been and the deaths of the 6 million became a fact that settled itself into my mind, gathering to it all kinds of private pains.

I became and remained a wicked child who would no longer claim connection to the past. I belonged to humanity in general, in toto, and I no longer thought, Is this good for the Jews or bad for the Jews, I thought only of mankind broiling in pain, driven by instincts toward destruction, driven to hate and to conquer and to suffer. I loved Gandhi as much as Ben-Gurion and when folks talked about boycotting Volkswagen I spoke of the will to murder that rose in Cain's heart, and Cain was an ancestor of mine just as Goebbels would be somebody's grandfather. I grew up and listened to Sartre, who said that nothingness was the peanut butter and and jelly of space. I married a non-Jewish man who followed Wittgenstein into designs of logic that brought cold smiles to the lips. Why did I marry a man who wasn't Jewish? I wish I could report that love swept me off my feet as the songs of the day promised, but that would be a simplification or perhaps a lie. The same forces that led so many Jewish men to seek out a gentile woman, the lady with the smell of America in her blond hair, in the free swing of her long legs, and a history of Pilgrims and prairies that rested somewhere behind her blue eyes, led me to look for a Yankee, a man whose revolution had occurred in 1776, not 1917, a man whose people seemed in control, admired, dignified, successful, independent, and who spoke only one language and who didn't have a Diaspora full of words for enemy. Shakespeare and Dickens, Emerson and Thoreau, I wanted a man who didn't need to study the tradition because he was the tradition. This search for the other, the stranger, has been told by Jewish American male writers over and over. Some of us, although female, were also looking for sex and marriage in forbidden places, places that seemed to promise safety for the next generation, that proposed to wipe out the pictures of the cattlecars heading east. This turn against the Jewish male, who seemed to me unromantic, probably unable to defend me or my children if once again the enemies marched in the streets, was only possible because assimilation, moving into the mainstream of America, leaving Jewish culture behind, leaving Jewish religion behind, was the quick of the historical moment, a huge wave that picked many of us up and carried us off and dumped us on rocky shores. Did the Holocaust have a role in this or would it have happened the same way without it? It's not easy to tell but I know that the Holocaust, which at that time (the late fifties) was not something we talked about, not something to dwell on, to learn about, to understand, but sat like an undigested lump, a piece of mourning that could never be acknowledged and yet would not go away, lay heavy, hidden at the center of my thoughts. The Holocaust must have influenced us all. I did not want my children bound with Isaac on some altar of my ancestor's choosing. I did not want to feel like a victim, like an outsider, like a person whose jokes always needed translating, whose suitcases should always be packed, whose passport and identity papers should be ready. I did not want to be Jewish because Jewish and victim became confused in my mind. Why say this now when I no longer hold this vision of history, this opinion of myself or my people? I write it here because it was so. Because it partially explains why I married the man I did and because if individual personal mistakes are made they are made because we are part, each of us, of an historical experience, and how I saw things then, how some Jewish men and some Jewish women misused romance then, these were not completely separated from what we thought of the Holocaust and how it cast its shadow over our most protected lives. There is something else. It is possible that if my father had been a better man, a more involved Jew, if I had been able to admire him and love him, I would never have lost my connection to the Jewish people. All that seems certain today is that the appeal of the American dominant culture, the fear of being a victim, mingled with my personal story and affected my sexual attractions and my marital choice.

This matter of Jewishness that I intended to leave behind me proved more deeply rooted in my being than I had anticipated. In 1957 I went with the man I married to Germany. He had won an Adenauer fellowship in philosophy. I believed that one should read Ezra Pound and Céline because they were good writers. I believed that religion was the opium of the poor and the creation of man in his terror. We lived in Munich on the top floor of a grand house on Bavariaring and looked out on the field where the masses of Hitler's supporters had rallied, goose-stepped and waved flags and listened to speeches. As the weather got cold I wrote my name each day on the windowpane. I am here, my name said, and all of you are gone. We ate dinner in the best restaurant in town, our American dollars made us afflu-ent well beyond our real station in life. The restaurant was in the Hotel Vier Jahreszeiten right in the room where Hitler's Munich headquarters had been. I wrote my name on the windowpane in the hotel lobby. I threw up in the ladies' room and thought it was the food. One day my landlady invited me for tea. In her dining room, the table was so polished it shone and the teacups had edelweiss trailing in patterns and the napkins were embroi-dered with buttercups. The widow poured from a silver teapot and asked me if I was really an American. She had spent time in Boston before the war and somehow she thought I was not really an American. But I am I said and then I noticed above the sideboard, bordered in black, with black ribbons over two framed photographs, two sons, handsome and young, each killed in the war, each wearing the uniform of the S.S. I am a Jewish woman, I said to her, and stood up to go. I thought so, she said, and passed me my tea and that was all that happened. Except that I knew that I was not just a member of mankind, not just a bundle of Freudian instincts some good and some bad, but that out in the world, a few miles from Dachau, where the economic wonder was taking place beneath my window, I was a Jewish woman and bore a rage that could not be contained by sorrow for the widow who had lost both her sons. I could find no pity for her.

A week or so later I was in our apartment alone, when I

heard steps on the stairs, booted steps, heavy and thunderous. There was a pounding on my door and when I opened it a man in a black leather outfit stood there. I fainted at his feet. As I recovered, I saw with half-opened eyes my landlady hovering over, cooing and waving a handkerchief above my nose, and the young man who was clearly just my age and complicit only by genealogy in the events of the war, was assuring me that he meant no harm, he was only trying to deliver a letter, a special delivery letter from my mother, who wanted to wish me a happy twenty-second birthday and let me know that she had shipped my winter coat the week before. After that I looked at the green-grocer, the conductor on the train, the professor at the university, the mothers whose children played in the park, and I wanted to tell all of them I was Jewish. I felt for them no human kindness, or kinship. Mankind may be capable of equal cruelty, and Jews, if they had power—and this was before the thesis could be tested—might also abuse their sticks and their guns, but none of this theorizing mattered to me anymore. I was a Jewish woman who had, although my God might have been less effective than He ought, remembered at last that this had happened to me as if I had passed out of Egypt and eaten the bread of affliction in the dry desert of wandering times. I went to Dachau with my husband and some American friends. They were appalled and stunned. They were decent people all of them, filled with a horror at what man had done to man, and they went on to talk about the massacres of Indians by the British and the bombing of Dresden and the smithereens of Nagasaki and the Manchurian ditches and the Gulags that were Russian, how many millions had died there, sixteen or fifty, the numbers reeled about. But as I listened to them, I withdrew. I turned silent. I was not one of them, I was not my husband's wife. I was not a friend to my friends. I was with the dead in Dachau, the dead who wore tallith and the dead who spoke languages I did not know, and the dead who were merchants and the dead who were rabbis and the dead who, I had to admit, had nothing to do with me and my American life but who nevertheless had everything to do with me and my anger, and my raw grief told me that it was not the same to me as all of human cruelty and that while my husband could talk of slavery on the plantations and enforced prostitution in Hong Kong I was connected in some profound and unshakable way to the Final Solution. I was, as I told them, and they looked at me amazed, a Jew who might have been killed. My husband, whose logic had won him some prizes, pointed out that I might also have been born a Muslim in Tunis or an Inca in the highlands of Peru as easily as a Jew in Poland sent off in the boxcars to die in the crematoria. Logic has nothing to do with it. The truth is one of another order, where reason is confounded with emotion and the soul of a Jewish woman belongs with the fate of her people and that is that.

My marriage dissolved. Not because of Jewish matters, although those were a part of the troubles between us, but because I had married without knowing myself; the safe harbor I was seeking proved an illusion. I married again, this time a Jewish man who was a psychoanalyst, a man trained to look through choices to the darker motives that swim like so many piranha through our unconscious rivers. I now wanted a Jewish man, one who understood that family was creation and that skeptical as we remained, closer perhaps to Spinoza than to the Rambam, we nevertheless were Jews, whose memories, personal, collective, and projective, were familiar. We were lovers who did not need the excitement of being strangers.

Years later we were in Israel and of course we went to Yad Vashem and we walked through together and the rage we felt, the sorrow we felt, was not new but it was fierce and we touched each again and again, our children are safe, we are here. We felt uncomforted by the path of the Righteous Gentiles. Each single name reminded us of the multiple unrighteous. Later in the sun by the Red Sea we saw the miracles of tomatoes growing and irrigation lines dripping through the desert. My husband thought for a moment that he should have been a doctor who traveled from kibbutz to moshav bringing antibiotics in his black bag. We thought we might better have used our lives had we moved in time to join the return to the land. When we travel to Europe we look for the absent Jews, we visit their synagogues, the ones abandoned in 1492 and the ones burned in 1940. When we think of our children's future we take nothing for granted. They must learn that the ditches can be dug again and that the stake through the heart of anti-Semitism will never find its mark.

The Holocaust has convinced us that progress, goodness, reason are always in jeopardy and that the worst may happen and the human drives for destruction, for dominance, and for death can erupt again at any point. These thoughts do not make us harmonious, joyful souls. We believe, truly believe, that the end of everything is possible and this we have taught our children. Hope but be vigilant. Hope but have no illusions. Don't be surprised at the demon within others or the one within yourself. Once I wanted to be an American with a clear look in my eye, a kind of piercing eye that saw all the way to the Pacific, looking over cornfields and smokestacks, and believed in the Bill of Rights and the Constitution and the "Battle Hymn of the Republic" for which it stands, but for a Jew that vision, today at least, is always clouded with words like *Einsatz* group, stuff, Zyklon B, and every Jew shares a knowledge of the human soul almost too bitter to be borne.

Here in these stories, not very startling, typical, I suppose, of an American Jewish girl, especially one who ran around in black leotards and sandals and wanted to sit in the café that had been host to Oscar Wilde in his troubles, who wanted to visit the home of André Gide, who had erotic dreams about Rimbaud, who would have died for a glimpse of Simone de Beauvoir, and who thought that art and psychoanalysis were the only truths that had not yet deceived, fallen in pieces, or crumbled in the hand. These stories of a naive postwar girlhood still reveal our impossible and even treacherous position.

How central to Jewish identity is the Holocaust and how central do we wish it to be? A religion or a people that is bound together only by a disaster will surely dissolve in time as the disaster recedes and the emotional connection fades and dies with those who have lived through it or in its immediate aftershock. The richness and vitality of the moral and liturgical tradition, the learning of Talmud, and the retelling in each generation of the history, a mystical concoction of politics, theology, and morality, need reason for being beyond catastrophe. This richness of Jewish learning and tradition was missing from my childhood and its absence made it easy for me, even necessary for me, to rush away from the Jewish people, to look for security and connection somewhere else. Today we know how important it is that we nurture the full Jewish experience. We see how dangerous it is to rely on disaster to keep the people together, but it is hard to find a perspective for the Holocaust, one that does not overburden the Jewish people and one that does not diminish or deny the experience. We are still under the sky of the Holocaust and it is hard for us not to feel stunned by the particular history of the twentieth century, not to feel loyal to those who died, not to feel fear, even paranoia, as we look at the world around us, a fear that stems from the facts of the Holocaust. It is true that after the Holocaust assimilation that was well on its way, with Reform synagogues all but erasing the traditions of Yavneh and Jews intermarrying and rushing off to melt their bones in the stew of America, has been slowed. It is harder for any Jew who carries the pictures of train tracks in his head to turn his back on the people. That's what my story of my time in Munich is about. Post-Holocaust Jews must know that assimilation brought no safety and that adopting the ways of the stranger was at least a four-generation matter if one hoped to hide from the enemy. This information, this fact of our history, has made the Holocaust a central matter to Jews; not only our anger holds us there, but our judgments about our safety, our commitment to Israel. The Holocaust has left us with the justified conviction that the rest of the world is a malignancy that may invade us without notice or reason. We can make pronouncements about what the role of the Holocaust should be in Jewish life, we can have wishes and visions of course, but the reality is that the Holocaust has made Jewish existence simultaneously more perilous, as Jews question the covenant and the value of chosenness, and more binding, as Jews feel a sacred connection to those who died, to their mores, their vanished towns, their hopes for their children, to the lost languages and the ancient prayers. It cannot be decided by edict, the Holocaust should be this or that percentage of Jewish identity. It will evolve as it will, regardless of what is best or what is right. In a few more generations we can see if the Holocaust fades into the line of Jewish history as a prelude to a rebuilding of Jerusalem, a sorrow before a time of cultural invention and creativity, or if it remains as the moment when God publicly forsook His people. But for us who witnessed or almost witnessed, who came close to being murdered, if only in imagination, if not in fact, we remain staring at the Holocaust, knowing that it reverberates into all the corners of our lives. We try not to be too cynical or too swayed by paranoia in the afterglow of the ovens. When in the fifties there was talk of the bombs falling and the world ending, I believed it. Not out of any particular apocalyptic leanings, but because the ferocity of man, the capacity to turn technology against life, the push toward violence and destruction, had shown us that the enlightenment was only a chimera, a wishful dream that made more painful the inevitable awakening. It was clear that reason directed history with no more success than the worship of golden calves or the obeying of the laws of kashruth. We now know ourselves to be an endangered species, and this vision, at least as Jews have received it, did not come because of the invention of the nuclear bomb. The dreadful announcement was made by the Holocaust.

What right as an American, safe in my bed, do I have to feel so affected by the Holocaust? No right at all. Yet imagination is not always dutiful, will not always stay in its proper place. I never thought of myself as anything but wicked when I renounced my connection with the Jewish past. I had no other vocabulary for such a condition. Later when I was older and became a simple child, I realized that the Holocaust lived in its special way, its dark and terrible way inside my thoughts, because it was as if it had happened to me; I had believed the words and this is what had made me Jewish. These words have remained in my head as absolute truths even while all the other tenets of Jewish thought were bathed in the waters of philosophy, comparative theology, and the other advantages of modern education. Today the Holocaust is everywhere, museums, memorials, a giant library. My capacity to respond has been dulled. I do not grieve as actively as I did some years back, but the fury remains, a dark coal at the center. How could they? At bottom, when all is said, my simple question remains, How was it possible, how could they? Could I? Hypocrite, I say to myself, what is it you believe? It is time to forgive God, to take up the covenant again, I say, stand up and sit down with the others. But I don't and I do. Child, I say to myself, let it go. But I don't, Jews can't. American Jews can't either.

Blue Skies

LESLIE EPSTEIN

I was born in 1938, in May, the same month Germans began mass deportations of Jews to Dachau. Germans? Jews? Dachau? I saw the light in Los Angeles, and for all I know the nurses in St. Vincent's wore the starched headgear of nuns. One of my earliest memories has to do with that sort of mix-up. I must have been four at the time, maybe five, and was sitting with my playmates around the edge of the Holmby Avenue pond, waiting for tadpoles to turn into frogs. The topic for the day seemed to be religion. At any rate, one of these contemporaries turned to me and said, "What are you?" Here was a stumper. All of the possible answers—a boy, a human, a first-grader— were common knowledge. While I stalled and stammered, one of the others took over:

"I know what I am! I'm a Catholic!"

That rang a bell. A historical tolling. Over a half-century before, and close to a century ago now, my grandfather had stood in line at Ellis Island, wondering how he could translate the family name—Shabilian, one way, Chablian if you're in the fancy mood—into acceptable English. Just in front an immigrant was declaring, *Mine name it is Epstein!* My grandfather, no dummy, piped up, "Epstein! That's my name, too!" Now, on the far side of the continent, his grandson provided the echo:

"Catholic! That's it! That's what I am!"

I must nonetheless have had my doubts, which I brought home that night. That's when I first heard the odd-sounding words, *Jewish, Jew.* "It's what you are," my mother informed me. "Tell your friends tomorrow."

The next afternoon, while the pollywogs battered their blunt heads against the stones of the pond, that is what I blithely proceeded to do. I do not think that, forty-five years later, I exaggerate the whirlwind of mockery and scorn that erupted about me. I can hear the laughter, see the pointing fingers, still. What horrified my companions, and thrilled them, too, was not so much the news that I was a Jew—surely they knew no more about the meaning of the word than I—as the fact that I had dared to switch sides at all. "Religion changer!" That was the cry. "He changed his religion!" *Vanderbilt*: what if the gentleman, the greenhorn, ahead of my grandfather had said that magic name? Or Astor? Or Belmont even? What then?

From that day to this, the word *Jew,* especially in the mouth of a gentile, has remained for me highly charged, with the ability to deliver something like an electric shock—rather the way the touch of a sacred totem might be dangerous to a Trobriand Islander, or the image of God forbidden, awesome, to the devout of my own tribe. The irony is, I doubt whether, through the first decade of my life, I heard the word mentioned within my family at all. In this my parents, the son and daughter of Yiddish-speaking immigrants, were not atypical. The second generation, emancipated, educated, was as often as not hell-bent on sparing the third the kind of orthodox regime they had had to undergo themselves. Still, I imagine the situation of my brother and myself lies beyond the norm. For we were brought up less in the faith of our, than that of the founding, fathers: that is to say, as deists, children of the Enlightenment, worshipers before the idol of FDR.

This minimifidianism sprang in part from the fact that our parents had settled in California while still in their twenties. Eastern shrubs in western climes. More decisive, I think, was the reason they'd made the move. Phil, my father, followed his identical twin brother, Julie, to Hollywood, where both began (and Julie yet continues) distinguished screenwriting careers. Now, the figure of the Jew, on celluloid, had undergone any number of vicissitudes (the best book on the subject is Patricia Erens' *The Jew in American Cinema*); but by the advent of the talkies, particularly with *The Jazz Singer* and *Abie's Irish Rose,* the puddle in the melting pot, the stuffing in the American dream, had pretty much taken on, at least insofar as the Jews were concerned, permanent shape. In the latter film, for instance, Abie Levy and Rosemary Murphy have to undergo three different marriage ceremonies, Episcopal, Jewish, and Catholic. As Erens points out, the title that introduces World War One reads like this:

> So in they went to that baptism of fire and thunder—Catholics, Hebrews, Protestants alike . . . Newsboys and college boys—aristocrats and immigrants—all classes—all creeds—all Americans.

Moreover, one can easily determine, by the treatment of the descending generations in this film, from the bearded, accented, and quite money-minded grandparents on, the ingredients for this Yankle stew: acculturation, assimilation, intermarriage; followed by blondness, blandness, and final effacement. These last three traits are meant always to apply to the third generation. Thus, *Abie's Irish Rose* comes to a close with the birth of something like a genetic miracle—twins: Patrick, the lad; the girl, Rebecca. The movies rarely deviated from this recipe, which Erens calls "the tradition of casting Jewish actors as parents and Gentile-looking actors as their children."

The point I am making is that my brother Ricky and I were firmly in that tradition, too. Do not think for a moment that my father and uncle were not proud of their own Jewishness or that Hank Greenberg and Sid Luckman were not figures followed with special attentiveness in the Holmby Hills. Indeed, Julie and Phil wrote the script not only for *Casablanca* (whose first word is "refugees"), but for what I believe is the *only* wartime film that dealt with domestic anti-Semitism. That, of course, is *Mr. Skeffington,* about which the Office of War Information complained, "This portrayal on the screen of prejudice against the representative of an American minority group is extremely ill-advised." Moreover, it should be pointed out that Jews of a certain stripe —the American Jewish Committee, for instance, or the Anti-Defamation League—have, from the days of Griffith's *Intolerance* through *Gentleman's Agreement* and beyond, been no less zealous than government bureaucrats in trying to expunge the image of the Jew from the screen. Ostrich-ism, not ostracism.

In this atmosphere, is it surprising that the real-life children of the film community should suffer the same fate as the Rebeccas and Patricks their parents had created? That my brother and I should, in a sense, be acted by, or inhabited by, gentiles? Or that, since the word *Jew* had been banished from American popular culture from the beginning to the end of World War Two ("If you bring out a Jew in film, you're in trouble": Louis B. Mayer), it might for the duration disappear from the households of those engaged on that particular front? Remember, the success of *The Jazz Singer,* whose theme was the repudiation of anything resembling ethnicity, turned Warner Bros. into a major studio: the Epstein twins had been writing for Jack ("See that you get a good clean-cut American type for Jacobs") Warner pretty much from the start of their careers. How could Julie and Phil, busily creating the American dream in a film like *Yankee Doodle Dandy* (don't look for their names, they gave the credit to a needy friend), not allow their own children to become part of that great national audience of upturned, white, anonymous faces? Would not we, no less than Paul Muni (né Weisenfreund) or Edward G. Robinson (Manny Goldenberg of yore) or John Garfield (another Julie—Garfinkle) become transformed? "People are gonna find out you're a Jew sooner or later," said Warner to Garfield, though it was meet that all who toiled in his domain heed the advice: "But better later."

Meanwhile, the lives of the deists went on. The great ceremony of the year was Christmas. I never lit a Hanukkah candle in my life until, mumbling the words of a phonetic prayer, I held the match for my own daughter, my own twin boys. The Hanukkah miracle is pretty small potatoes compared to the star in the heavens, the wise men and their gifts, the manger filled with awestruck animals, and finally the birth of the little halo-headed fellow before whom all fall to their knees. Rest assured that when all this was acted out for me, year after year, by the students of the public schools of California (I may well have donned a beard myself, and gripped what might have been a shepherd's crook or wise man's staff: either that, or I am once again adopting the guise—*that's what I am!*—of my friends), the J-word was never mentioned.

What most sticks in my mind, however, is the Christmas trees: giant firs, mighty spruces, whose stars—emblematic of the supernova over Bethlehem—grazed our eleven-foot ceilings. There were red balls and silver cataracts of tinsel and strings of winking lights—all strung by the black maid and butler the previous night. Mary and Arthur were there the next morning, too: she, to receive her woolen sweater; he, his briar pipe. Of course my brother and I were frantic with greed, whipped up by weeks of unintelligible hymns (*myrrh,* for instance, or *roundyon* from "Silent Night," or the Three Kings' *orientare*), by the mesmerizing lights and smell of the tree itself, and the sea of packages beneath it—and perhaps above all by the prospect of the rarest of all Epstein phenomena: the sight of our parents, in dressing gowns, with coffee cups, downstairs before the UCLA chimes struck noon.

Hold on to your hats: there was Easter, too. Not a celebration. No ham dinner. No parade. But there was no lack of symbols of rebirth and resurrection: the ones we dyed in pale pastels, the ones we hid under the cushions of the couch, or others, pure chocolate, that we gobbled down. The eggs I remember best were large enough to have been laid by dinosaurs, covered with frosted sugar, with a window at the smaller end. Through this we could see a sylvan scene: bunnies in the grass, squirrels in the trees, and birds suspended in a sky as perpetually blue as the one that arched over the city of the angels. Aside from Christmas and Easter, there were ordinary Sundays, when it was my habit to lie late in bed, listening to the radio. More than once, twisting the dial between a boy's piping voice, "I'm Buster Brown! I live in a Shoe! *Arf! Arf!* That's my dog, Tye(?): he lives in there, too!" and the genie's growl, "Hold on tight, little master!" I'd linger at a gospel station. At which point Mary would appear at my bedroom door. "That's right," she'd declare, with a broad smile.

"You going to be blessed!" She was at least more subtle than the all-American rabbi in *Abie's Irish Rose,* whose words to a dying soldier the sharp-eyed Ms. Erens quotes as follows:

> Have no fear, my son. We travel many roads, but we all come at last to the Father.

Make no mistake. Muni Weisenfreund turning into Paul Muni is one thing. Saul of Tarsus becoming St. Paul is quite another. Everyone knows what happened after the local priest gave his Easter sermon. Those were not chocolate eggs the peasants of Europe went hunting for five hundred years. The Jews who were rounded up the month I was born would have gone free, just as the millions who were soon to be gassed in ovens or shot at the edge of ditches would have been spared if Constantine the Great—*religion changer!*—had not seen a flaming cross in the sky: that is, if Christianity had remained, as I dearly wish it had, a minor sect, instead of becoming major heresy. Nonetheless, those performances at Brentwood and Canyon Elementary had done their work. How appealing to a child those dumb donkeys! Those cows of papier-mâché! The mumbo jumbo of *inexcelsisdeo!* Few films have moved me as deeply as Pasolini's *Gospel According to St. Matthew,* which I sat through twice in a row, weeping at the figure of Jesus, the babe in the grade-school manger, broken now on the cross.

Inconceivable that the whole of World War Two could go by without leaving a trace. Nor did it. But the truth is that for us, in California, in sunshine, the conflict was more a matter of Japanese than Germans and Jews. I doubt very much whether I noticed when the Orientals in nursery school and kindergarten disappeared. Almost certainly I paid no heed when the same fate befell the old gardener who smoothed our flower beds with his bamboo rake. Odds are I was too distracted by the exciting talk of submarines off the coast or of bombs falling by parachute over Seattle.

There was never any question that the threat to us would come, as it already had at Pearl Harbor, from the Pacific. I can still remember the barrage balloons, like plump brown eggs, tied off the local beaches. My brother—aged what? three? four?—

saw them from the end of Santa Monica Pier, and began to whimper. A trick of perspective, the sharp sea air, the taut lines gathered on buoys or barges, made it seem that these fat blimps, a mile offshore, were streetcorner balloons. "Want one! Want one!" Ricky cried, stamping his feet, throwing himself onto the planks of the dock. For the loss of this toy he would not be consoled.

Throughout the house on Holmby, half-smoked cigarettes, my mother's Chesterfields, bobbed in the waters of the toilet bowls. Sitting ducks, they were, for my stream of urine, which would sooner or later burst the zigzagging hulls, sending thousands of tiny brown crewmen over the side, to drown next to their floundering transports. Even after the war, when we moved to a yet larger house on San Remo Drive, my fantasies remained fixed upon the Far East. And on nautical warfare. We'd purchased a surplus life raft, yellow rubber on the sides, blue on the bottom, which was initially, thrillingly, inflated by yanking a lever on a tube of gas. In this vessel, on the smooth waters of our swimming pool, I floated for hours. Through the windless afternoon. Under a pitiless sun. The downed airman. With a metal mirror, also surplus, I signaled every passing plane whose silhouette did not resemble that of a Zero. Through the taut rubber, the slap-slap of the wavelets, I listened for approaching sharks. *Rain*, I prayed. *Oh, God: send rain!*

Naturally my imaginative life was shaped by the movies. The jump from the cartoon festivals I attended each Saturday at the Bruin theater to the war films showing everywhere else seemed a normal progression, just as the cartoons themselves were an innate part of the animism of a child's world. If a discarded pair of pants could become, in the dim light of one's bedroom, a slumbering crocodile, or a breeze in the curtain a masked intruder, then there was little to wonder at when barnyard animals, creatures of instinct much like ourselves, began to dress up, sing like Jiminy Cricket, or scheme for a piece of cheese. Also: murder each other, poleax their enemies, chop them to smithereens, or flatten them, under the wheel of a steamroller, as thin as a dime. All victims, it seemed, had nine lives. No death was unresurrected. It was this, I suppose, along with the white-hat, black-hat morality of the westerns, with their thousands of expendable Indians, that eased the transition to *Winged Victory* and *Pride of the Marines*. Now the enemy were mowed down like ducks, or blown, as Tom was by Jerry and Jerry by Tom, sky high. *Yankee Doodle Mouse*. 1943.

The early immersion in cartoons may help explain why, since I probably saw as many movies about the war in Europe as I did about the fighting in Asia, my attention remained firmly fixed upon the Pacific Theater. The Germans in movies were simply too adult, real smoothies like Conrad Veidt, witty, cunning, prone to understatement and reserve. Even the Prussian stereotypes, the smooth-shaved head, curled lip, and glinting monocle of a Preminger or Von Stroheim, possessed a kind of refined sadism worlds removed from the clear-cut cruelty of a mouse handing a cat a sizzling bomb.

There were no problems of reticence in the movies that dealt with the war in the Pacific. Here the violence was full bore. More crucial, the enemy, like the Indians, were a different race—no, almost a different species, like the talking animals we already knew. Indeed, when these short, comical characters—yellow-skinned, buck-toothed, bespectacled—did speak, they had something of the stammer of Porky, or Woody's cackle, or the juicy lisp of Daffy Duck. Thus the most forceful images of war remained, for me, those of death marches, jungle patrols, palm trees bent under withering fire, and kamikaze pilots with blank faces and free-flowing scarves.

What made these images pleasurable was the certainty that nothing I saw was real. I was, remember, a Hollywood child. Towering over the lot at Twentieth Century–Fox was a huge outdoor sky, painted so much like the real one, white clouds against a background of startling blue, that whenever we drove by I had to look twice to see which was which. The decisive moment came when I visited a sound lot, probably at Warners, where a pilot, one of our boys, was trapped inside his burning plane. A cross section of the fuselage rested on saw-horses; the actor's legs protruded beneath it, standing firm on the floor. Also on the floor, flat on their backs, were two civilians, one with a flame-throwing torch, the other with a plain wooden stick. *Ac-*

tion! shouted the director. At once the pilot began to beat on the inside of his cockpit. The torch shot gobs of fire in front of the white linen background. And the fellow with the stick banged at the fuselage, so that, bucking, shaking, it seemed about to break apart. Finally the pilot managed to pry off his canopy and thrust his head into the wind machine's gale. *Cut!*

The ambiguity of both that Magritte sky and desperate scene, which took most of the afternoon to shoot (and which, with all its wind, flame, courage, and terror, seemed to be missing when I saw the completed film—was it *Dive Bomber?*—a year later); indeed the tranquil unreality of the war itself: all that concluded one afternoon at Holmby Park. What I remember is my father running pell-mell down the avenue, snatching me off the playground swing, and then dashing back up the hill toward our house. "The war is over!" he shouted. Either that or, "The president is dead!" I have a scar, hardly visible now, under my lip, from the time I fell off that very swing. Possibly it's that catastrophe I recall—the same sense of urgency, the same excitement, the elation at flying along in my father's arms—and not Roosevelt's death or the bomb-burst that brought the war to an end.

Not long afterward we moved to the house with the swimming pool. Already my missing schoolmates were starting to return. So did our gardener: or one like him, arriving like a comical fireman in an old truck covered with hoses and ladders and tools. He tended lawns set with cork trees and fig vines and eucalyptus. The property was surrounded by lemon groves, which perfumed the air and filled it, two or three times a year, with canary-colored light. We weren't the first movie people in the neighborhood: Joseph Cotton's place was catercorner, on Montana, and a block or two over, toward Amalfi, were Linda Darnell, Lou Costello, and Virginia Bruce. Down the hill, our school bus made a loop into Mandeville Canyon to drop off the son of Robert Mitchum. Not the first film folk, then: but among the first Jews. For when the former owner of our house, Mary Astor, changed her name, it wasn't from Manny or Muni, but from the proper Lucille. The gentile who disguised himself as Phil Green in *Gentleman's Agreement* was none other than our neighbor Gregory Peck. The closest we came to a refugee was the sight of Thomas Mann, walking his dog along San Remo Drive. The Epsteins were the pioneers.

That meant my friends had such names as Warren and Sandy and Tim and John. We used to build forts together, ride our bikes through the polo fields, and use our Whammos to shoot blue jays and pepper the cars on Sunset Boulevard with the hard round pellets that grew on the stands of cypress above. We also camped out on each other's lawns. The smear of stars in the Milky Way is the prime text for deists. All is order, beauty, design. The ticking of the master clock. Yet our gaze, once we closed the flap of our pup tents, was lower. In the new sport of masturbation one kept score by palpable results. A drop. A dollop. At one such tourney, the champion posed in our flashlight beams, his member bent at the angle of a fly rod fighting a trout. At precisely the midway point in twentieth-century America, the rest of us, the slow pokes, saw that something was amiss. Uncircumcised. Here was a rip, a rent, in the universal design. From this common sight I drew a skewed lesson. I may have been in the immediate majority, hygienic as any in the crowd. Yet I knew as gospel that the one who had been torn from the true course of nature was not he, the victor, our pubescent pal, but I.

Which is to say that, over time, we discovered differences. This was palmy Pacific Palisades: no crosses were burned on lawns, no swastikas scratched on lampposts. In our half-wilderness—polo ponies in the fields below, and, above, hills covered with yucca, prowled by bobcats—there were not even lamps. Why, quail sang in our hedges and stood on the lawns! The bus for Ralph Waldo Emerson Junior High School picked us up at a vacant lot on Sunset near Amalfi. Wheat seemed to be growing in it, and fiddleheads that tasted like licorice. One morning I arrived to find that the usual allegiances had shifted. My friends greeted me by throwing clods of dirt, sending me back to the wrong side of the boulevard. Their cry was "Kike! Go home! Kike! Kike!"

Now this was not, in the words of the old transcendentalist, the shot heard round the world. Certainly the incident was a far cry from the kind of warfare the Epstein boys had engaged in, circa 1921, on the Lower East Side. There, you had to battle your way, against the Irish, against the Italians, just to get to the end of the block. On the other hand, while my schoolmates had never learned Emerson's pretty rhyme—

> Nor knowest thou what argument
> Thy life to thy neighbor's creed has lent—

Once a year farflung branches of the family gathered for the Passover Seder at my grandfather's house in Santa Monica—a time warp away, hyperspace distant, from Bialystok. "Say, der!" we called it, gazing with some dismay at these strange, gawky relations, mole-covered, all thumbs. The only cousins who counted were Jimmy and Lizzie, who, since they were Julie's children, and Julie and Phil—bald from their college days, two eggs in a carton, peas in a pod—were identical twins, were therefore my genetic half-brother and -sister. Jim (later a starter at Stanford) and I made a point of throwing the football around the backyard and bowling over the pale kinfolk as if they had been candlepins. During the ceremony itself, which droned on forever, Jim and I would sit at the far end of the table, arm wrestling amid the lit candles, the bowls of hot soup, the plates of (here is a title for a novel or a memoir like this) *Bitter Herbs*. The empty chair, we were told, the untouched glass of wine, were not for yet more distant cousins, missing in Europe, unheard from since the start of the war, but for Elijah, who was fed by ravens and departed the earth in a chariot of fire.

That was the extent of my religious knowledge. Not once had I set foot in a synagogue or been exposed to so much as a page of the Bible. I knew more about gospel music—*You going to be blessed*—and Christmas hymns—*Glo-or-i-a-a, or-or-i-a-a, or-or-i-a-a, oria!*—than I did about the songs concerning grasshoppers and boils that my relatives chanted while thrusting their fingers into the sweet red wine. Bar mitzvahed? Perish the thought! Yet the idea must have occurred to someone because, for perhaps three weeks in a row, I found myself in a Sunday school class of glum Jews whose dogma was so Reform in nature as to hardly differ from that of Franklin and Jefferson and the other founders. About this trial I remember little. Bad food, for one thing. And a distinctly dubious rabbi. My fellow sufferers seemed unlikely to be interested either in the fortunes of the Hollywood Stars—not the film colony, but our triple-A franchise—or in pup tent pleasures. Before I left, or, more likely, was asked to leave (the issue being my habit of roller-skating between the pews of the temple), I did pick up the fragment, the refrain, of one new song: *Zoom-golly-golly-golly,* so went the nonsense syllables, *Zoom-golly-golly!* Then I zoomed off myself, on my eight little wheels, back to the rhapsodies of secular life: *Sha-boom!* and *Gee (love that girl),* by the Four Crows.

"I got ice cream! Every flavor! Chocolate! Coffee! Vanilla! Strawberry! Lamb chop!" That speech, from a little Cub Scout play, was the first line I can remember writing. I suppose it was in the cards I would try my hand at the craft. Phil and Julie, unique among studio employees, did their writing at home. Once, Jack Warner cracked down about this, pointing out that their contract called for them to be at work on the lot by 9:00 A.M., just as bank presidents had to. "Then tell a bank president to finish the script," said one or the other of the twins, and drove off the premises. It wasn't long before Warner had another such fit, demanding that the boys, as they were habitually called, show up at the stipulated hour. They did, and at the end of the day sent over the typescript. The next morning Warner called them in and began to shout about how this was the worst scene he'd read in his life. "How is this possible?" asked the first twin. Concluded the second, "It was written at nine." So it was that I'd often lie upstairs, on the carpet, outside the closed library door. From the other side I'd hear a muffled voice—maybe Julie's: *yattita-yattita-yattita,* it would declaim, with rising inflection; then another voice, let's say Phil's, would respond, *yattita-yattita-*yattita*!* Then both would break out together, indistinguishably, in their crystal-shattering laugh. It seemed an attractive way to live one's life.

Still and all I don't think I wrote a story until my first year at University High. Its subject matter is the point of this memoir. What I remember, more than three and a half decades later, is a public plaza, a milling crowd, a feeling of excitement, anticipation. There is, in the description of the square, the clothing, the mustachioed faces, something of a South American flavor. The snatches of dialogue, while not Spanish, must have been accented somehow. Buenos Aires, then. There was no real plot, only the waiting, the crush of numbers, the electric expectation.

Finally, when the tension was as great as a fourteen-year-old could make it, that is, when all the upturned faces had turned in the direction of the tall brick building, when all eyes were focused upon the high balcony that jutted out over the square, the closed doors of the palace open. A small figure, unprepossessing, clean-shaven save for his mustache, and dressed in plain uniform, moves into the open. A sudden hush falls over the crowd. The man, not young, aged in fact sixty-three, steps forward. He leans over the balcony's wrought-iron rail. Then, suddenly, he stands upright and raises his right hand in the air. A great wave of sound, long suppressed, breaks from the crowd. It is half a sigh, half a shout. *"Viva!"* That is the cry. *"Viva,* Hitler!"

Where on earth, or at any rate in California, with its blue skies, from which the sun shone in winter at much the same angle it did in July, did this vision of evil incarnate come from? Had I, after all, noted something hidden, unspoken in those wartime films? Or heard a few whispered remarks around the Seder table? Or seen, in newspapers, a blurred early image of what would later become such familiar photos: bulldozers at work on piles of bodies; heaps of spectacles, sheared hair, shoes; wraithlike figures in striped pajamas; the lamp shades, the ovens, the showers, the ditches? The answer is no. Rather, an answer of yes would be superfluous here. The truth is I had always known —in the same way that one knows, from childhood on, the laws of gravitation. What goes up must come down. From childhood? I might have been born with an innate grasp of the fate of the Jews. What a person learns later, the facts of physics, the formulas about the mass of objects and the square of their distance, only confirms what he carries within like the weight of his bones. Hints, hushings, inflections, a glance: these pass from Jew to Jew, and from child to child, by a kind of psychic osmosis. So it was that history passed molecule by molecule through the membrane that held me apart from my fellows, and apart from a world long suppressed, long denied.

That's not the end of the story. Indeed, there was a second piece of fiction written for that same freshman class. The time, the present: that is, 1953. The place: the American Southwest. We see an old man, a prospector perhaps, a desert rat, dragging his way across the alkali flats. He pulls his burro behind him.

The plot, hazily remembered, involves the way he had tricked everyone into thinking he had left the area, when in fact he had no intention of quitting the spot. It may be that he was about to make his big strike. Or might have remained from cussedness alone. In any case the ending goes something like this. As the man and beast turn eastward, away from the setting sun, the sky lights up in a fireball, which grows larger and larger, lighting up the white sand, the tall cacti, the quartz hills, brighter than any day.

I mention this tale not because its subject, like that of its companion piece, was, for the frosh squad, so portentous, but because it indicates that in matters of war and peace my gaze was still out over the Pacific. How could it be anywhere else? The year before we had exploded a hydrogen bomb on the atoll of Eniwetok, and now the Russians had replied in kind. The weapon that had leveled Hiroshima and had killed a hundred thousand Japanese served as a mere trigger, a kind of spark, for these giant explosions. The very air, it was thought, might catch fire. At University High we drilled for the moment the bomb would fall. There were three levels of strategy. The first, which assumed we had something like an hour's notice, involved a brisk march through the hallways and down the stairs to the fallout shelter in the boys' locker room. Not much different than a fire drill, really, except that instead of milling ouside we waited for the all clear with our backs against the green metal doors. An imminent attack was indicated by a pattern of bells. The teacher lowered the blinds against flying glass while the students filed into the hall: silent, we were, in the dim light, the endless corridors. But the maneuver we practiced over and over occurred when there was to be no warning at all. A student might be in the middle of a recitation, *Tomorrow and tomorrow and tomorrow* from *Macbeth,* when suddenly, from nowhere, the teacher would bark out the word, "Drop!" There would be a rustle, a rumble —falling books, falling bodies, a flutter of paper—as we hurled ourselves under our desks. We tucked our heads into our laps and clutched our knees, like the little crustaceans, the tightly coiled sowbugs, we unearthed from our lawns. The main thing, the great thing, was not to look out the windows. The light would blind us. It would fry the whites of our eyes.

Silent in the hallways, silent in the nation at large. Dumb-struck. Numb. This is how my brother and I entered the fifties. Ricky had already taken the measure of this world: He knew an illusion, the veil of maya, when he saw one. Hence he drew inward, toward the realm of the spirit. That is to say, he drifted yet farther toward the East—specifically toward the gardens and incense clouds and priests of Vedanta. I must not neglect to say that Ricky's sudden, but lifelong, interest in karma, the way one's actions determine his destiny in past and future incarnations, the hope of rebirth on a higher plane, the dream of final release from the endless round of being—that all this was surely precipitated by the death of our father in 1952.

Even then we did not enter a synagogue. What rabbi could hope to match the vision of nirvana preached by the followers of Vivekananda? Or compete with the scenes—Alec Guinness scrambling down the Eiffel Tower, clutching his ill-gotten gains —in the movie we attended instead of the funeral? A comedy, no less. There might be an echo, in our laughter that afternoon, of the afternoons at the Bruin. No death, to a child, is irrevoca-ble. Cartoon critters pop up living and beathing. Why not our father, in the guise of his identical twin? Retake. Double expo-sure. Remember, though, that at the end of *The Lavender Hill Mob* Guinness is punished for his thievery and led off in chains. The doctrine of karma is no less strict than the Hollywood Pro-duction Code. Our crime, those hours distracted, the glee, may yet lead to a lower form of existence—as Republicans, say, or even reptiles—in the incarnation to come.

I cannot say whether Ricky was aware of the Holocaust, or, if he was, whether the knowledge had anything to do with his withdrawal. I do think that what little the country had discov-ered—in newsreels, mostly—about the destruction of the Jews of Europe, and the consequent erasure of those same mental traces, may have had no small part to play in the symptoms of paranoia, the deep, dumb shock, that characterized the decade. I do not mean to say the national hysteria had more to do with denial of the Holocaust than apprehension about the role of the Soviet Union in Europe and its testing of the same kinds of weapons we had already used. But those quick glimpses on the Movietone screen were not altogether ineradicable. That they left a mark could be determined from the kinds of comments people allowed themselves at the time. "How could these things happen in *Germany?*" was the most common remark. "So clean. So enlightened. So civilized." Now we know better. It was the very modernity of German culture, its mastery of technology and the means of mass communication, that made it, with its glorification of violence, its infatuation with death, not our century's aberration, but its paradigm. Hence the chill that fell over the land. All the values of modern life had been given an ironic twist, a mocking echo. Belief in cleanliness? Here were bars of human soap. The quest for light? Here were lamp shades of human skin. What we feared in the fifties was not only communism, it was ourselves.

Speak for yourself! Very well. After my quick start in the freshman year at high school, I too withdrew. That is to say, I did not write any more stories, or playlets, or imaginative prose of any kind, until my undergraduate years in New Haven were drawing to a close. Why not? While the answer is complex, I think it fair to state that in the course of the decade I was, all unwittingly, willy-nilly, coming to a decision: when I was ready to write, it would be as a Jew; or, better, when I was a Jew, I would be ready to write. There was, however, a long way to go.

Among the newsreel pictures in my own mental gallery— wasn't there a crowing rooster in the old Pathé titles, much like the roaring lion in MGM's?—are shots of crowds dancing about piles of burning books and young, grinning soldiers cutting the beards of learned men. These images, together with what I soon read about the music the Nazis banned from their concert halls and the paintings they mocked in their Exhibition of Degenerate Art, convinced me that the war against the Jews was in some measure a war against the nature of the Jewish mind. Absurd, I know, to claim that by exterminating the Jews the Germans were in fact attempting to eliminate Jewish art: but it is far from senseless to claim that the oppressors had come to identify the Jews with some quality of imagination, and in creating a world without one they were attempting to confirm that it was possible to live without the other.

In a sense the Third Reich had no choice. An aesthetic of blood and kitsch must, by its very nature, try to undo that embodied in Abraham and Isaac: that is, imaginative reenactment, the metaphorical power of words, the inseparable link between act and consequence, and the symbolic prohibition of human sacrifice. Specifically, what fascism repudiates in the ancient tale is the power of faith, the recognition of limits, and trust in the word of God. Enter the Jews. It was they who took the greatest imaginative leap of all, that of comprehending, out of nothingness, an empty whirlwind, the glare of a burning bush, the "I am that I am." In spite of much backsliding, in spite of having been warned by a jealous God (in a commandment they have rebelled against ever since) not to make likenesses, this people has continued that "repetition in the finite mind of the eternal act of creation" that Coleridge defined as the essence of imagination. In an age when such faith was no longer tenable, when the supreme fiction, which is *that we matter*, became a rebuke to the countervailing belief, which was *that everything is possible*, then those finite minds, with their dream of the infinite, had to be eliminated.

These are the thoughts, or half-thoughts, I entertain now. The lesson I drew at the time, however, was little more than the proven adage: hard to be a Jew. And dangerous, as well. Hence I joined the ranks of the silent, the stunned. Once, in the mid-fifties, traveling back to California for summer vacation, I found myself on a New Orleans bus. A pleasant-looking lady leaned forward from the seat behind. "See that? See him there?" she asked, pointing out the window to where a motorcycle policeman sat on his machine, hidden behind a billboard. I nodded. The belle of the South lowered her voice. "The Jews put him there!" Now I knew how Gregory Peck felt, but—the Jew as gentile, not the gentile as Jew—in reverse. He had a swell speech for the occasion. I held my peace. A smile sufficed, and a nod.

Nonetheless, the ground beneath my feet was shifting. For one thing I had wheels. The friends with whom I cruised Hollywood Boulevard in the latest model of the Buick turned out—to my surprise: no, to my shock—to have names like Alan and Robbie and David and Dick. Similarly, the books I was reading, and the stories in *The New Yorker,* were written by fellows like Norman and Saul and Bernard and, soon enough, Philip. Not to mention J.D. I saw new kinds of movies: *Night and Fog, The*

Diary of Anne Frank, and, best of all, Renoir's *La Régle du Jeu*.

Still, beneath the calm surface, however, much was in turmoil. The symptom was this: no matter what situation I found myself in, I moved to the verge, the very edge. More to the point, having already been thrown out of the Jewish temple, I proceeded to get myself banished from the citadels of Christendom. First was the Webb School, where I'd been sent, with several gross other products of broken or unhappy homes, two years after my father's death. *With the cross of Jeee-suus,* these were the words I mouthed in compulsory chapel, *going on beeeforrre!*

"What's this?" asked one of the preppies as the turnips were plopped on his plate.

"The week's profit," sweetly said I.

Gone. Rusticated. Dismissed. Expelled. In the land of the goyim, however, what is done may, through contrition, repentance, and a good deal of breast-beating, be undone. The suspension lasted only three days. Perhaps my goal was not so much to draw the wrath of the Christians as to bask in their forgiveness. Better a prodigal son than no son at all. A more likely explanation is that, at loose ends, in limbo, I was pushing myself toward becoming that marginal figure the wisecracking Jew.

This pattern continued when I went to college in the cold, cloudy East, I met a different cast of characters. My instructions from Uncle Julie were as follows: when in New Haven buy an overcoat at Fenn-Feinstein; when in New York, eat the free rolls at Ratner's. There I was, a freshman again, at Second Avenue and Fifth. My coat, three sizes too large, was reddish-brown, with hairs sticking out of the lining. On my head, a snappy hat. Round my neck a Lux et Veritas tie. After studying the menu I raised a finger to the waiter. "I'm not electric," he said, hobbling by. A quarter of an hour later a second old man shuffled over.

"What's this *ma-ma-li-ga?*" I inquired.

Said he: "Not for you."

At about the same time I first met my maternal grandparents, who lived off the Boardwalk in Atlantic City. What drew me to them, through the last half of the fifties, and into the sixties too, was the way the aged couple clung together, whereas my own family had always gone their separate ways. A dead cigar in his lips, Herman would bicycle through the streets of the black ghetto, collecting rent. Our favorite restaurant—Clara, bedridden, was not to know—was a place that fried up forbidden crab cakes. Once I was at their shabby flat watching the evening news. "Nixon!" Herman said, grabbing his nose. "P! U!"

The waiter was right. Not for me. Not yet. It was still the era of the deaf and dumb. What I saw, first, was an upside-down world where the old men with white rags on their arms were the aristocrats, the kings; and, second, an aged couple, squatting by an alien ocean, with whom I felt more at ease, more myself, than when I had splashed in the waves of the blue Pacific.

At Yale, where the quota for those of the Mosaic persuasion was 10½ percent. One afternoon, toward the end of my junior year, I was standing on High Street when the mayor came out of Fenn-Feinstein and stepped into the barbershop next door. "What's the mayor doing?" asked my current straight man, as his honor emerged from the doorway and moved toward the entrance to Barrie Shoes.

"Wednesday. Two P.M.," I replied, not quite sotto voce. "Collection time."

We were, remember, still in the fifties. Thus the next thing I knew I had been thrust up against the side of a car, told to hand over my wallet and be at the dean's office the next morning by ten A.M. By eleven, I was no longer a Son of Eli. Historians may yet come to note that this injustice, together with the response it provoked, represented the true birth pangs of the counterculture. I did not, as demanded, return to California. I spent a pleasant fortnight in nearby Hamden, strolling to the campus each evening to be interviewed by various senior societies, Manuscript, Elihu, Scroll & Key. Meanwhile, enough of a flap had developed—beginning with mimeographed notes on bulletin boards and ending with an interesting call from the New Haven *Register*—to bring about my reinstatement. Thus did the balance of power between the student and administrative bodies begin to tip. Some years later, when I returned to the drama school, the quota had been abandoned, Bobby Seale was camped on the New Haven green, and the knock on the Elihu door was answered by—her blouse unbuttoned, a babe at her breast—a coed. *Après moi, le déluge.*

Oxford, or "Oggsford," as my coreligionist Meyer Wolf-sheim is made, in *The Great Gatsby,* to call it "one of the most famous colleges in the world": Oxford proved a tougher nut to crack. What do you do with people who, when asked to pass the salt, say, "Sorry!"? My boorish crowd used to hang out in the taverns and try, with comments on the weather and the bangers and the temperature of the beer, to drive the locals out. The low point (or pinnacle, depending) of this campaign occurred in the dining hall of my college, Merton (a place so stuck-in-the-mud that its library, as old as Bologna's, turned down the gift of T. S. Eliot's manuscripts because he was not yet dead). Let me paint the scene. On the floor is a series of long tables, upon which sit pots of marmalade made from the very oranges Rich-ard the Lionhearted sent back from Seville. Huddled on long benches are the undergraduates, shoveling down peas and gruel. On a platform, perpendicular to the masses, the dons are drawn up at high table. The crystal, the flatware, shine. The chef, a Frenchman, has made a *poulet en papiette.* Even down in the pit, we can hear the puff of the little paper bags as they are punctured by the professors' tines. Time for the savory. The dons tilt back their heads, dangling asparagus spears over their open mouths. But what's this? A stir on the floor? Where the Americans sit? In the Jewry? Indeed, at the moment, friend Fried, out of New Jersey, is about to be sconced.

> *Sconce,* says the O.E.D. *At Oxford, a fine of a tankard of ale or the like, imposed by undergraduates on one of their number for some breach of customary rule when dining in hall.*

The first infraction, 1650, was for "absence from prayers." Fried's folly, however, was making a serious remark, since the aforesaid rule forbade any conversation about one's studies, about politics, or about anything that might be construed as an idea. That left the girls at St. Hilda's and cricket. No sooner had Fried made his point about Marxist dialectics than a gleeful cack-le broke out among the Brits. Instantly a waiter appeared, sport-ing the usual bloodshot cheeks and bushy mustache. In his arms he held the foaming chalice that untold numbers of Merton men —including, surely, the animated Eliot—had raised to their lips. Fried, deep in his argument, paid no mind. The ruddy waiter—

in his white apron he looked the kosher butcher—tapped him on the shoulder and held up, with a grin and a wink, the tankard. Fried whirled round.

"What am I supposed to do with this?" he asked, as if unaware that custom dictated he drink down the contents and order an equal portion for all those at table. "Shove it up your ass?"

Immense silence. Everything—the dons with their buttery spears, the students balancing peas on their knives, the thunderstruck waiter—was as frozen, as still, as the twelfth-century fly caught in the marmalade amber. Then, as if a howitzer had been fired, a sudden recoil. The students shrank away on every side, their hands to their mouths. "Oh!" they cried. "Oh, God!" Meanwhile Fried had turned back to his interlocutor, out of California, and together they resumed their argument about the merits of Marx and Freud, a sort of mental arm wrestling not much different from that at the end of the Seder table.

Clearly if Fried was not rusticated for this, I had my work cut out for me. To make a long story short, I found myself on the telephone with the head of my department, Dame Helen Gardner. I fear that in so many words I told her that she ought to deposit her Anglo-Saxon riddles and Middle English charms (how to get honey from honeybees, for example, or cows out of bogs) where my compatriot had suggested placing the tankard of ale. Then, having resigned the major, I packed my bags, determined to leave the university at the start of the next term.

The two best things about an Oxford education are the length of the vacations and the relative proximity of the Mediterranean Sea. I'd already been to Greece, Spain, Italy, and southern France. Now, on a broken-down freighter, the *Athenai*, I chugged right across the greasy gray waters. Easy enough in the lurching bowels of this vessel to imagine that you were your own grandparents, storm-tossed, debating whether it was permitted to survive on a scrap of pork. Never mind that this journey lasted only two days, and that the welcoming landmark was not the Statue of Liberty but the golden dome of the Bahai temple, high above the harbor at Haifa.

What happened to me in Israel was at once common enough and most bizarre. Instantaneously, virtually on the docks, the wall between myself and the world, that membrane, dissolved. Before my eyes hustled Jewish porters, policemen, soldiers and sharpies and sellers of pretzels. Osmosis cannot take place, nor can one live on the margin, or be expelled, when there are Jews in solution inside and out. The idea that I had grown up with— that the very word *Jew* was awesome, sacred, terrible, not to be thought of, never mentioned—became ludicrous on these shores swarming with the usual run of big shots and bums. What made Israel so appealing to many Jews like me (and so repugnant to the zealots of Crown Heights and the Mea Shaarim) was the promise of the ordinary, the prospect of the mundane. Only in the Holy Land could the Jews escape being a holy people.

The impact of that part of my trip (the fact that I now kept track of Sandy Koufax on his way to mowing down 269 of the goyim) was altogether banal. But there were stranger, eerier forces at work, and they involved the history of the Germans and Jews. Of course I visited the memorial at Yad Vashem and the smaller museum, with its cases of torn scrolls and striped pajamas, on Mount Zion. At the center of everything, dominating each day, was the spectacle of a well-guarded German, Eichmann, pleading for his life before a court of his former victims. What was odd about these things was that I saw them in the company of someone who belonged to the last generation of Germans to feel, if not guilt, then more than a twinge of shame. This was Katrin, an architect from Munich, whom I had met aboard the *Athenai*. Everything you need to know about her background may be inferred from the fact that the name on her passport read *Karen* and had been changed by her parents to avoid what became, in the Third Reich, the most fashionable Aryan moniker.

Our relationship ("Don't tell Clara" was Herman's reaction upon hearing the news) lasted five years. When it ended I met— and was eventually to marry—a young woman who had also been a passenger on the *Athenai*, just one week later than Katrin and I. That we had both suffered seasickness on that old Greek tub and had quite likely rubbed elbows in one museum or the other was but one of a series of near misses. Here was an image in a slightly flawed mirror: an identical twin herself, and not the offspring of identical twins; a mother dead in childhood instead of a father; years on the beaches of Florida instead of California; Christmas celebrated, but without servants, the carols, the trees.

All this had to be sorted out in the future. At present fate had more tricks in store. My plans to leave Oxford were suddenly abandoned when Khrushchev put up the Berlin Wall. Waiting for me in England was a letter from my draft board stating that I would be inducted the moment I set foot on native soil. "Agriculture": that was the first degree-granting program listed in the university bulletin, which I'd dashed the mile to the Bodleian to read in only a little over the landmark 3:59:4 that Roger Bannister, my fellow Oxonian, had set a few years before. *Better boot camp*, I decided. *Better Berlin*. The bulletin's second entry was "Anthropology." The wise guy set out to talk his way back into yet another institution of learning. *Dip. Anthro. Oxon* reads my laconic degree.

But it was the beast in man I studied, while pretending to solve the kinship system among the Nuer. Nor was it the wall in Berlin that occupied me, but the one the Berliners had erected in the streets of Warsaw. In brief, I spent my second year in Oxford reading everything I could about the Holocaust. And when I wasn't reading, I was writing. The subject, at last, was myself.

This story, my first as an adult, was called "The Bad Jew," and in it the title character—a cool Californian, aloof from the faith of his fathers, unmoved by the traces of the Holocaust he sees about him—is nursed through an illness by two aged survivors. While recovering, he comes across a long letter from one child in a death camp to another. The key passage deals with the time the letter writer, Jacob, gave way to despair and attempted to smother himself beneath a pile of dirt in Bergen-Belsen. He is foiled, first, by the sensation of an earthworm moving up his leg, and then by the fear that the slightest movement on his part will crush that little creature. The right thing to do, he realizes, both for himself and the Jews, is simply to wait. At this point a shift occurs in the tone of the story. The burden of irony, of detachment, is shifted from my alter ego to the survivor, the mother of the dead Jacob. The crisis takes place when, on a bus trip across the desert, she turns in disgust from a group of dark-skinned Sephardim and says to the hero, "*Shvartzers!* Look at them!

Shvartzers!" The Angeleno, while no angel, is no longer the bad Jew.

I am going to close where I began, in the sunshine, by the Pacific. I owe this much to that city and those climes: if I had grown up there as a Jewish child, that is, if there had been nothing to search for, no vacuum to fill, I would never have become a Jewish adult. I returned immediately after completing my degree at Oxford, to spend a year at UCLA. Ricky and I lived in an empty flat on Fountain Avenue. I moved off when he burned his incense, and he stayed away when he knew I was writing. The year sped quickly by. I was jogging with a friend, my old pal Alan, when the Cuban missile crisis was at its worst: no way to fast-talk my way out of that one. Koufax, I noted, was on his way to winning twenty-five games and striking out three hundred and six. Marilyn Monroe died, and so did Pope John.

Adolf Eichmann, of course, had already been hanged. In the course of that year the work that affected me most was Hannah Arendt's account of his trial. What so angered her critics—her claim that the Jewish leadership in Europe had been so compromised, so woeful, that the Jews themselves would have been better off with no self-government at all, and had merely run—seemed to me then, as it does now, so obvious as to be almost a truism. How on earth could things have been worse? The second half of her thesis, concerning the banality of the *Obersturmbannführer,* and of evil in general, was not welcome news either. Clearly her readers, Jews and gentiles, were more comfortable thinking of Eichmann and Himmler and Goebbels and the rest as either subhuman, or superhuman, monsters, beasts, and psychopaths, not as human beings much like themselves. What struck me most about her argument—that evil was a kind of thoughtlessness, a shallowness, an inability to realize what one is doing, a remoteness from reality, and, above all, a denial of one's connectedness to others—was how much it resembled a defect, and perhaps a disease, of imagination.

That malady, whose symptom, a stunned silence, was as prevalent in the early sixties as in the fifties, could only be healed by the writers and poets whose special responsibility was to show the world what those plain men had done. As Arendt maintained, only those who have the imagination to recognize what they share with the force of evil—in her words, "the shame of being human . . . the inescapable guilt of the human race"—can fight against it. And only that fight, it seemed to me, that fearlessness, could give meaning to the suffering of the Jewish people and, in that narrow sense, bring the millions of dead back to life.

Grandiose thoughts, granted. I cannot claim to have entertained them, or worked them through, at the time. But it was partly under Arendt's spell that I spent the academic year writing a play. It doesn't take a prophet to guess the subject. An Ivy Leaguer, first initial L., falls in love with a German heroine, first initial K. In spite of some humor ("An American Jew is someone who thinks a shiksa is an electric razor"), this is a tortured piece of work, haunted ("I have the feeling, when I think of Europe, of what happened here, that I ought to be dead") by the destruction of the Jews. Somehow, it won a large prize, the Samuel Goldwyn Award, and persuaded Yale to let me in yet again— this time to the School of Drama.

Here, if you so desire, is our Hollywood ending. The award ceremony drew many loose ends together, completing a kind of cycle. Goldwyn (né Goldfish) was the producer of one of my father's last films. Uncle Julie was in the audience. So was his ten-year-old son, Philip, named for his identical twin. Jimmy and Liz, grown-up, were in the auditorium, too. Alfred Hitchcock, for the Christians, gave a speech and handed over the prize. Thus did the film industry, which had played such a large role in making my childhood Judenrein, now bestow upon me—and for a play so Jewish it would make *Abie's Irish Rose* look like a crowd-pleaser at Oberammergau—its imprimatur.

Still, there were no happy endings. Katrin was in Munich, recovering from a recurrence of tuberculosis she had contracted during the war. I was already preparing for my trip to the East. Little did I know I would not return—at least not for more than a few days at a time—to the West Coast again. "Include me out" —that is not just a wacky Goldwynism. It is a description, canny to the point of genius, of the lives that Jews lived on the screen, and beneath the white clouds and peacock blue of the painted sky.

II

The Dark Thread
in the Weave

MARGE PIERCY

In the summer of 1941, on my father's two-week vacation from Westinghouse, we drove from Detroit to Florida in our two-door brown Hudson. It was a hot July. We stayed in what used to be called tourist homes—a far cry from the bed-and-breakfasts of today, more like overnight rooming houses, catering to salesmen in the field, men looking for work, families traveling on the cheap. It was not the first trip my family had taken. My father repaired and installed heavy machinery all over Michigan and often we went with him. Several times a year we visited my mother's family in Cleveland or my father's in Pennsylvania. The year before we had taken a ferry to the Upper Peninsula and rented a little cabin with an outhouse near Lake Superior. But this was the longest trip we had ever taken. I was to start kindergarten in the fall, and I was told that in future we could not run off with my father so freely.

Etched in my memory are the words I learned that day we reached Miami, new words, exotic words. I learned the word "coral," explained to me because we passed through Coral Gables, "hurricane"—and what I see is a stucco wall on which the mark of the high storm tide had marked itself, perhaps ten feet above where the water ought to be—and the Pan Am Clippers taking off for Lisbon. My mother stressed to me as we walked barefoot alongside the bay carrying our shoes carefully by the straps that "Over there," and she pointed where the clippers were droning off, Jews like us were being killed. I strained to see, imagining that if I were as tall as my mother (she was four feet ten exactly but seemed tall to me when I was six), I would be able to see what was happening on the other side of the water.

It was a world of catastrophes I grasped that day, starting with the Portuguese men-of-war washed up on the beach dying; if I touched them, I would suffer horribly, I was told. They would sting me to death. The high-water mark on the stucco wall marked still-visible damage from the fury of the hurricane. This was all grafted onto the frightening information that "they" were killing people like us in the place where the big planes went. This is encapsulated in a poem called "Unbuttoning" from which these lines come:

> *This [button] from a coral dress she wore*
> *the day she taught me that word,*
> *summer '41, in Florida:*
> *"Watch the clipper ships take off*
> *for Europe. Soon war will come to us.*
>
> *"They will not rise so peacefully*
> *for years. Over there they're*
> *killing us and nobody cares.*
> *Remember always. Coral is built*
> *of bodies of the dead piled up."*

from *My Mother's Body*

My mother and grandmother were both storytellers. Each of them was always telling me a different version of the same story, and my mother would say, And don't forget it, don't let your head be like a sieve that everything goes through the holes; and my grandmother would say, *Sha! Herst sich tsu. Gedeynk!* and the tale would begin. My childhood was full of admonitions to remember, which apparently worked at least a good percentage of the time.

My adored grandmother lived with my Aunt Ruth in Cleveland. Aunt Ruth was the youngest of my mother's sisters and was midway in age between me and my mother, who had had me when she was forty-four. Aunt Ruth worked for the Navy during the war. She was a smart, brash, athletic woman who had been deprived of the education she should have had because she had to go to work straight from high school. My mother's family were working-class Jews all but for one uncle who had married a woman with money, had passed for gentile, had more than the rest of us put together times ten, and who had killed himself some years after the war. My grandmother kept kosher (and thus so did Aunt Ruth). Every summer when my grandmother came to us and shared my room, which was not entirely mine and my bed which usually was, we ate differently and to my childhood judgment better than we ate other times. It was a time when my grandmother told me all the stories my mother usually told, entirely differently. It was a time for refighting all family battles, rearguing old choices. It was also a time for discussing in low intense mutters what was going on Over There, where my grandmother and my dead grandfather came from, Lithuania in her case, the Soviet Union in his, back when it was czarist Russia and he escaped with a price on his head.

I must have said something silly, probably about, Why didn't the people of my grandmother's village just leave, because I remember being lectured by both of them about the war and what was known of the camps—and it is ridiculous to imagine that the camps were not known about. It was not that working-class Jews in Detroit or Cleveland knew a lot about what was going on, but the information that Jews were being rounded up, put in camps, and that many were being killed was certainly something we knew. For one thing, the Jewish papers were full of stories and occasionally photographs that had been smuggled out. I cannot remember a time when the Kol Nidre did not carry connotations of terrible destruction and murder. There were occasional small stories in the regular press, but it wasn't big news. To none of us was the extent of the massacre conceivable (nor is it still), but that Jews were being killed in large numbers was certainly known. I was given the impression that being Jewish was a dangerous dramatic destiny, an ancient and hazardous treasure being handed on to me. We followed the war with a particular edge on our anxiety.

My father was not Jewish and did not believe these stories. He had no religion at all and prided himself on his rationalism. At some point around twenty, he had read Herbert Spencer (he rarely read books, so it must have made a tremendous impression for him to go through it all) and that had given him what philosophy of life he had. He compared the stories and rumors of death camps with scare stories from World War One that turned out to be propagandistic inventions: the kaiser's soldiers bayoneting Belgian babies. His opinions on Jews carried no weight with my mother or the rest of my relatives, but to avoid argument, they generally talked when he was out of the house. Since my mother was backed up by my grandmother, I generally believed her, but even if I had not been inclined to, after all, it turned out that the emotional women were correct and my rational and skeptical father was wrong.

Although we played at war constantly in the vacant lots of my Detroit neighborhood, my imagination was fired most vividly by resistance fighters. When my father was sent to Baltimore, our landlady had some kind of connection with Czech exiles. We went with her to a rally in support of Czech resistance that filled my head with images of heroic fighters, mixed in my head with folk dancing and the releasing of hundreds of pigeons whose feathers had been dusted with red and blue besides their own white. When I wanted dreams of glory, I imagined taking part in guerrilla warfare in some unspecified mountains in some vague distant country.

I can remember the early newsreels from the liberation of the camps and the photographs in *Life*. By that age, I had experienced considerable ordinary everyday anti-Semitism. Nothing life threatening, nothing particularly savage or serious: mostly just hostile jokes, an awareness of housing covenants that prevented Jews along with Blacks and the occasional Chinese or Japanese American from buying into most neighborhoods, the hate tracts that the worker-preachers distributed, the rant of Father Coughlin pouring from radio after radio in the blocks around our home. It was a matter of an occasional fight in the schoolyard or the alley; the routine use of phrases like "dirty

Jew," "He tried to jew me down," "loud kikes." But that casual chipping at one's ego, one's sense of security, one's comfort level with others made it easier to believe such small kicks and pricks could escalate into something truly frightening.

When I was growing up, anti-Semitism was not only legal; it was widespread and almost pervasive. It impacted on me every time I filled out a form or an application. Every form tended to ask religion, whether you were at a new school, trying for a scholarship, applying for a job typing or waitressing or working a switchboard. It was easy to imagine such information being turned against you. Sometime around the middle of the war, my mother was seized by a vehement paranoia and kept hissing at me whenever she was confronted by a form, "Say Protestant. Write down Protestant. It doesn't mean anything, you don't have to believe anything to be a Protestant, but they can't come after you. It doesn't do any harm." From the time I was twelve until some time in college, when she relinquished that particular head-in-the-sand routine, we quarreled constantly about it. My grandmother and my Aunt Ruth were of course on my side.

It was not that I made a simple transition from the casual anti-Semitism of daily life to the distant massacres. It was rather that being regularly insulted and occasionally knocked about gave me a sense of being apart, being obviously different in some way that I did connect with those rumored disasters.

I cannot remember a time before I knew Jews were in terrible danger over *there,* somewhere east of us, east of Cleveland too, somewhere where my family had lived when Grandma was a girl. Could it, will it, might it happen here was an ongoing discussion and argument among those three most important women in my life. My mother, who was the least open and the least faithful in the practice of her religion, the only one who did not live in a Jewish neighborhood, had also the darkest view of what might happen to us all.

Thus when I stress remembering the first newsreels, it was not in the context of discovering that mass murder existed. It was that these paranoid discussions, this odd dark cloud of pain and whispered disaster that had hung over my entire childhood, were suddenly resolved from amorphous threat to specific skeletons, those rags of flesh with immense eyes, the bodies heaped for the bulldozer like a run of smelts dumped out of a net. The worst imaginings and the most fantastic scenarios of my dramatic mother and my *bubbe* with her tales of pogroms were not only validated but surpassed on the movie screen, where I usually saw Gene Autry catch bad men or Mickey Mouse dance. I learned that paranoia is often inadequate to the realities of life in our times, but definitely superior to reason as a means of grasping what is going on. This was not the worst preparation for being a writer whose work has a politically conscious dimension.

I loved my grandmother dearly. She was the most loving, the most affectionate person in my world. She had not been the mother of my own mother's dreams. In fact she had tried to abort my mother because they were so desperately poor when my mother was conceived. My mother was the third girl and was given a boy's name, Bert, an American name, by my grandfather, who was so furious at getting yet another girl he would not give her a proper name, although her Hebrew name was of course feminine. Then my grandmother gave birth to six boys in a row, but never mind. The damage was done. My mother kept trying ineffectually to please her father and kept resenting her mother, and their war never really ended.

But I was the oldest child of the next generation (except for my brother, whose energies went into being ultra-American and who fled her) and I got the lion's share of my *bubbe*'s unjudging ungrudging irresponsible and incomparably rich love. My grandmother was observant as my mother was not, and my earliest memories of the rituals of Judaism are inseparable from the scent of her clothes and her body and her kitchen. I did not resent the *mehitzeh* as a little girl, for I thought of it as a refuge where I could hide among my *bubbe* and her cronies and be petted. By the time my grandmother died, I was at war with the rabbi who prayed over her; I could not stand the position of women in Orthodoxy, but I never said that to her.

Of the generation of my mother, only my Aunt Ruth was observant. Most of the children married non-Jews. My grandmother saw her children melting away from their own identity. After the war ended, Hannah began to try to find out what had happened to her family in Lithuania. I don't know if it was June of 1945 or of 1946 when she heard, but I suspect it was probably 1946. That would make me ten. Certainly she had given up her little apartment in the Jewish neighborhood in Cleveland and had taken her cat Blackie (who is one of the only real characters, along with William and Elizebeth Friedman, in *Gone to Soldiers*) to the suburb of South Euclid, where she moved in with Aunt Ruth. I remember the dining-room table and Hannah giving that great cry of grief. It took me a while to understand that she was mourning, not one death (I could grasp that for by that point in my childhood I had been to a baker's dozen of funerals and as many telegrams of death had come to the doors of friends in the neighborhood), but the death of an entire family, a village, a society.

All the people she remembered, her cousins, her girlfriends with whom she had gone down to the river to wash clothes and to bathe, with whom she had gone to the *mikva*, with whom she had shared secrets and stories, everyone she had known when she was growing up in a shtetl where her father was a poor rabbi, all were gone, everyone was dead. That was a shock to her life. She never stopped mourning those dead. It was a world gone, she said, a *ganzeh velt*, an entire world vanished forever.

What she contemplated as she mourned was the death of a people. She feared that there would soon be no more Jews, that the little light handed down from generation to generation over thousands of years and sheltered with so many bodies would go out. I made her a promise that afternoon which I view as one of the first commitments of my real, my adult life. If I have sometimes contemplated that promise with irony, I have never been tempted to let it go. I told her that I would always be Jewish, that I would never turn away or back away from that identity.

My grandmother took some little comfort in my ten-year-old promises, but I doubt she took my word seriously. She was used to children's broken promises. But she did remember, for she reminded me of that vow when I was first job hunting and fighting with my mother about what to write down on applications. But I did not forget. It is not a vow from which I have ever imagined myself released. It is at the core of my identity.

My religious instruction came through my childhood from

my mother and my grandmother. Although my father had no religion, active Jewishness made him uncomfortable, and my mother was a passionate assimilationist. She thought you should attempt to blend in, to act like "they" did, for safety's sake. If she had been middle class and we lived in a Jewish neighborhood, she would undoubtedly have been comfortable with a Reform synagogue, but she didn't drive and her Judaism came over the radio mostly. The Jewish holidays belonged to my grandmother; observance if we were at home was always somewhat muted and it was much better to be in Cleveland. I plotted from middle childhood on that I would observe the holidays fully, as Grandmother did.

I was still in grade school when I saw a movie about the birth of Israel. It was called *A Sword in the Desert*. I have never heard of it again, but it was immensely important to me at age ten or twelve or whatever I was when I saw it, for here were Jews as fighters instead of as victims. Here were Jews carving out a place that would belong to them. It excited me and formed the germ of fantasies for some years.

In high school I used to hang out a lot in the main public library, on Woodward in Detroit. One day in the card catalogue room I got into a conversation with an Israeli woman. It was 1952, and my grandmother Hannah had recently died. I was sixteen, rebellious, bored, alienated, a lone radical writing Walt Whitman imitations. She was twenty-two and studying to be an engineer. She had been a soldier; she had fought. Unlike the present Israeli army, in the early years women did fight, and she had a kind of confidence I was used to in men but had never encountered in a woman. I was smitten. Jews could fight, Jews could be powerful. A Jewish woman need not be a victim.

I never saw her after that day but for months I talked of going to Israel to a kibbutz. Had I been more assimilated into Jewish organizations in Detroit, I probably would have gone, but as it was, I won a scholarship to the University of Michigan, the first person in my family to attend college, and all my passion and all my efforts went into making that happen: arguing with my reluctant parents, working various jobs to save the money for dormitory expenses and books.

When I was seventeen, I went away to Ann Arbor to college, where I began to explore my religion, my identity as a Jew as I could not at home. Nonetheless, in college I learned little about the Holocaust. Student culture was more interested in possible nuclear wipeout, and we spoke about Hiroshima, not of Auschwitz or Sobibor. I was glad to be around other Jews. I went out occasionally with gentiles, but most of my lovers and my more casual dates and partners were Jewish. Their families interested me, in how they were like, but also how extremely different they were from, my own family.

Very few of my fellow students came from poor or working-class Jewish families. Often they had what was to me the quaint notion that all Jews in the United States were middle class. Some of the girls from Reform families had had bat mitzvahs, which I had never heard of. I was jealous; I still am. Most of the Jews at college had grown up in Jewish neighborhoods or in New York; perhaps they felt less vulnerable as Jews. I became very much a lox-and-bagels Jew. At this time I would have described my Jewishness as cultural. Yet always working in me under everything was that old dark knowledge of what had happened, the old promise, the old sense of something that must be carried forward and somehow made new.

Part of the fantasy life of every Jewish child who grew up when I did has to be not wish fulfillment but self-torture: How would I have behaved? Would I have resisted? Would I have betrayed? Would I have been sent at once to the gas chambers or would I have been worked to death? Experimented upon? Would I have been one of the tiny remnant of survivors? How would I have borne such twisted and nasty testing, years of unremittant starvation and torture? Yet for all that I must have thought of this hundreds if not thousands of times, I only recall two conversations on the subject in all of my college years. Both were tentative and somehow embarrassed.

My last semester in Ann Arbor, I began seeing an exchange student, a French Jew whom I married in September. He had a degree in nuclear physics from Physique et Chemie but had come to the States for a Ph.D. in particle physics, studying first at Ann Arbor and later in Chicago. When we went home to his family in Paris and later while we traveled around Europe and met others in his extended family, I was struck how many nationalities and how many passports were represented.

> *A gaggle of fierce insistent speakers of ten*
> *languages had different passports mother*
> *from son, brother from sister, had four*
> *passports all forged, kept passports*
> *from gone countries (Transylvania, Bohemia,*
> *old despotisms fading like Victorian wallpaper),*
> *were used to sewing contraband into coat*
> *linings. I smuggled for them across two borders.*
> *Their wars were old ones.*
> *Mine was just starting.*

from "The Ram's Horn Sounding," *Available Light*

Originally Polish Jews on both sides, all of Michel's grandparents had migrated to Germany, where both his parents had been born and educated as professionals. Both had been doctors before they married. They fled to France soon after Hitler took power, where their sons were born. France had passed laws to prevent immigrants—particularly the Jews fleeing Germany—from entering the professions, so they had to work as shopkeepers. Michel described to me the terror of the "rafles" through his ten-year-old eyes, his mother seizing the children and running through a gap in the police line and escaping, fleeing from town to town, hiding in the woods, tearing up their French passports so they would not be returned to France.

His immediate family had had what they called "a good war." They had to enter Switzerland illegally. Once in, his parents were interned in a Swiss camp and my husband was placed with a Swiss family, who insisted he go to church and observe Christianity. The Swiss kept many Jews alive, but reluctantly, and they were careful not to make the experience pleasant. My husband felt rejected by his parents (why was his little brother allowed to stay with them in the camp?), miserable and lonely.

When I met his family, they were part of a tight and affectionate group of friends who had survived the war, some in Switzerland, others underground, abroad, or in the Resistance.

It was in Paris I first learned of the Jewish Resistance, that it had existed, that its casualties had been huge, but that it had been important and extremely active. I heard stories of Jews who had carried out the many actions available to those who sought them out with courage and imagination: Jews who had published clandestine papers carrying news of Allied victories and encouragement to resist, those who had forged papers to enable Jews or escaped prisoners of war to blend into the population or move through the country in hopes of escaping, those who had led children or adults over the heavily patrolled borders into Spain or into Switzerland, those who had committed sabotage or operated illegal radios, those who had helped free prisoners, those who had taken part in armed actions or bombings, those who had taken to the mountains as Maquis, the French guerrilla fighters, who I was astonished to learn (only because the images I had been presented with up to then had been of passive victims) had included Jewish armed groups.

Those Jews living in Paris had a battered tough joie de vivre that I admired immensely. They were close, trusting in each other, warm with each other. They knew each of them how they could rely upon the others. They knew what they were made of. At the same time, the roll call of the dead was enormous, this brother, that grandmother, this cousin, that best friend.

I went with Michel to the Tomb of the Unknown Jew in Paris. The documents of the Holocaust made it real to me in a factual way, turning nightmare into bureaucratic process, the artifacts of daily life and daily death. Michel and I were not together long, but what I learned from my French in-laws and their friends and acquaintances remained with me. It made that mythical fascist apparatus of death something that happened to real people, something that threatened people I loved, people I slept with or ate with at the breakfast table, people I fought with over what material to buy for curtains, or how much to spend for a present. I understood how one could be living a private family-centered life just concentrating on children and friends and the rent and doing one's daily work well, while the machinery of the State revved up to steal from a person their food, their home, their work, their friends and relatives, their parents and children: life itself. I would never be able to assume a private life can remain so, that it is possible to ignore the public policy of the country in which one lives—or its neighbors. It made me aware too how fragile are the plans by which we define our future lives: we will marry next year, we will have two children, we will buy a house in the country, and our children will go to this or that university. Maybe. Maybe we will be dust, nameless dead whose graves leak poison into the water table in second-growth forests.

I think the Holocaust made me feel that being political is a necessity and that only fools and the very naive permit themselves the luxury of remaining aloof from the political process. I am not someone who adores meetings, who loves the organizational work that carries groups forward, but I have spent a fair amount of my life engaged in this toil, partially because of carrying with me that sense of it being something a whole and sane person must take the time and energy to carry out.

Of course in marrying Michel I was marrying the European Jewish experience of World War Two and the Holocaust, just as I was marrying French culture, history, and the French left, all in one poor unfortunate *zhlub*. It was a type of bad faith, a romanticism run amok, a silly collision of cultural imperatives at war with each other. Neither of us had the faintest idea who we were actually marrying until well after the fact, but never mind. My next teacher was a landlady, in whose rooming house I lived in Chicago when I was dead broke, working a secretarial job, and in the process of getting my divorce. On her arm were the fabled numbers. She had managed to buy a slum house with toilets in the hall, usually out of commission, infested by mice and, as I discovered one morning when I heard a clunking noise and saw one waddle past my bed with a mousetrap stuck around one leg, extremely large brown rats. My landlady reminded me of the ghosts in the *Aeneid*, which I was teaching in a world literature course for which I was paid three hundred dollars a semester: greedy wan creatures who flit toward a sacrifice to drink the blood that will momentarily give them life. My landlady had been twisted by huge pain into a creature of greed and want and bleating fears that drove her half crazy. She would fix nothing. If I attempted to confront her about the toilets or the vermin, she would tell me I had not suffered and who was I to complain, and I would retreat muttering but chastened, my guilt clattering after me like the trap on the rat's leg.

In the years I was active in the antiwar movement and the New Left, most of the Jews I met were cultural Jews. Usually they were anti-Zionist, which always caused me trouble. I often disagree with particular Israeli policies, but I never, never doubt Israel's right to exist and to be a nation. I do not want to live in a world where Israel does not exist.

Further, the New Left had little patience with Judaism. Most of the Jews had some sense of a cultural identity but little else. They tended to be far more tolerant of the Christianity of the Catholic left, of the religiosity of the Quakers, of Buddhism, than of Judaism. As a religion, it seemed to embarrass many of them. The Holocaust usually figured as a basis for comparisons for something the government was doing that was wrong, bloody, genocidal. During this period I was less observant than before or after. In the community mostly of Jews in which I lived and worked, people monitored each other's choices and habits rather severely. If I had lit Sabbath candles or gone to services, it would have been a matter of causing much acrimonious discussion. I did not resume many of the weekly or holiday practices until I left New York.

I don't remember a time I did not imagine I would have to confront World War Two in my writing. I cannot remember back past the intention to write such a novel. However, it was not until 1980 that I began—seriously, actively—to carry out the research preliminary to beginning such a project. I found myself swamped very quickly, and the need to stay on top of that research material was one of the primary motives that drove me to begin working on a personal computer so that I could handle the immense amount of data I was collecting.

When I first began to work on the ten characters in the novel, to create each of them as a voice, a milieu, a point of view moving through the war, I thought I would deal with the camps only through the experiences of the twins. Naomi, who has been sent to the United States through an exit visa that will cover only one child, is separated from her twin, Rivka. Rivka is arrested with her mother, Chava, during the grand rafle of July 1942. They are confined in the Vel d'Hiv without food and water for eight days. They are then sent to Drancy, outside Paris. From Drancy in December 1942, they are shipped to Auschwitz. From there they are moved to Dora/Nordhausen, where they work in the hollowed-out mountain building rocket parts. Chava is worked to death. Rivka survives until the death marches. While trying to escape, she is set upon by dogs and then shot.

We see Rivka through Naomi's mind. As occurs with some twins, they are linked. It was a quasi-surrealistic device for dealing with the camps. Everything that Rivka experiences is based in what happened, but Naomi often cannot understand what Rivka is going through and interprets it as best she can. It was my original intention to deal with the camps only through this second-level reality. I was not sure I was capable of doing justice to what had happened.

But as I worked through the story of Jacqueline, their older sister, I came to realize I had to deal directly with Auschwitz through her. I tried for almost a year to avoid writing those scenes, but, in terms of Jacqueline and in terms of the novel, I could not escape the necessity.

By this time I had read perhaps two hundred memoirs by survivors and perhaps another hundred interviews. Those buildings, that low sky, that city of the slaves had taken on an almost hallucinogenic reality to me. I could close my eyes and see it step by step. I was immersed in it and it rotted my ability to sleep; at the same time, of course, I had only to open my eyes and see pine trees and my amiable computer with a cat sitting on top blinking at me. I have never written anything more difficult. I think the chapter had power from the beginning draft, but it required so many drafts I can no longer recall whether I wrote it through twenty-four or twenty-seven times. No writer can ever be "satisfied" with such a re-creation, such an attempt to make the reader understand as much as you yourself have been able to grasp, but I could not have felt right about *Gone to Soldiers* without that chapter.

My on-site research was severely limited by my inability to get a grant to do it. I paid for the trip to Europe out of my own pocket, and my pockets got rather empty during the four years of the actual writing. Just before my husband, Ira Wood, and I went over, I had the good luck to be introduced by Ruth Linden of the Holocaust Oral History Project to Regine Barshak, who was one of the few survivors of Drancy, the camp outside Paris. Regine Barshak is an attractive, vital energetic woman who attributes her survival to her mother, who managed to get her out of Drancy before the mother herself was shipped off to Auschwitz. She is a forceful speaker, a tremendous resource for Holocaust memorial projects. Interviewing her just before I went to Paris and to Drancy made the accounts that I had read much more meaningful.

Getting to Drancy turned out to be more difficult than I had anticipated. I had rather hazy directions and I could find Drancy, an industrial suburb, on any map of Paris and environs. I knew the train left from the Gare du Nord. Now the Paris Métro is extremely well marked, but with suburban commuter trains, the assumption is that if you use them, you know them; and if you don't know them, you have no reason to use them. We took a wrong train to the wrong destination before we got the right train to Drancy.

Once we were there, nothing was solved. It should be said that my French while rusty always comes back after a couple of days in France, and I was speaking pretty decent French at this point. I would not like to have to defend a thesis in French, but I can conduct an interview and chat away.

I asked the men at the ticket counter what bus I would take to get to the Memorial for the Deported. They said they had never heard of it. I said it was at the Housing Projects. They said buses were none of their business, that they were only required to give information about trains. Then they would not answer further questions.

Outside I asked people at the various bus stops. At least six or seven buses took off in various directions from the train station, and we had no idea which to get on. It was hot.

The Housing Project at Drancy

Trains without signs flee through Paris.
Wrong trains. The wrong station.
The world as microwave oven, burning from within.

We arrive. Drancy looks like Inkster,
Gary, the farther reaches of Newark.

In the station they won't give directions.
C'est pas notre affaire. We don't deal with that.
Outside five buses limp in five directions
into the hot plain drugged with exhaust.
Nobody ever heard of the camp. They turn away.

Out on the bridge, over marshaling yards:
Here Jews were stuffed into cars nailed shut.
Here children too young to know their names
were counted like so many shoes
as they begged the French police hemming them in,

Take me to the bathroom, please, please,
before I wet myself. Mother, I have been so good,
and it is so very dark. Dear concierge,
I am writing to you as everyone else
is dead now and they are taking me away.

Yes, to the land children named Pitchepois,
giant's skull land grimmer than Hansel came to.
On the bridge I saw an old bald workman
staring down and I told myself desperately,
He is a communist and will answer me.

I asked him where the camp was, now a housing
project. He asked, Why do you want to know?
I had that one ready. No talk of novels, research.
My aunt was there. Oh, in that case,
he pointed to distant towers. You want that bus.

Where we descended the bus, Never heard of it.
Eyes that won't look. Then a woman asked that
same question, Why do you want to know?
A housing project crammed with mothers.
The guard towers are torn down and lindens grow.

In flats now with heat and plumbing, not eighty
but one family lives. Pain still rises,
the groaning of machinery deep underfoot.

---

*Crimes ignored sink into the soil like PCBs
and enter the bones of children.*

from *Available Light*

I knew he was a Communist because he had a red flag on his lapel, and yes, he said, these were in fact the marshaling yards where the deportees had been loaded into boxcars and the cars nailed shut. We were standing on the bridge when he came along. I was in despair, for we had to leave Paris early the next morning and I had to, had to go to Drancy. I was arguing with my husband about whether there was any point just taking one bus after another, when the balding man came along and saved the day.

The monument itself, when we finally got there, is powerful. I sat on a bench among the welfare mothers and wept. Drancy had been supposed to be a housing project, but its construction had been interrupted by the outbreak of war. The buildings were standing, but incomplete, without water or electricity, when the Jews were brought there and penned up, as many as could be forced into a room. Guard towers were erected. Between the moderately tall buildings a sea of mud stretched, fouled with human waste. Now it is grass and linden trees.

In Toulouse I found the building on what is now a posh shopping and office block where Gestapo headquarters had been located. I found neighborhoods where the Jewish resistants of the novel might have lived and met. Then we went into the mountains of Lacaune, where Jewish Maquis had been based.

Lacaune is not much of a tourist area. It's poor country, beautiful in a low-key way that reminded me of Exmoor. The rocks look like the sheep and the sheep look like the rocks. Prehistoric remains abound, as they do in Devon. It is not exactly as it was then because reforestation is covering many of the low mountains with a monoculture of future lumber. We had no trouble finding the sites of several of the Maquis strongholds. The villages are poor, dark gray, the older houses slabbed with slate for shingles. Many of the villagers are Protestants, which makes them also a minority in a Catholic culture.

From Lacaune, we went just south to the Montagne Noir. The descriptions I had read were so precise I was able to navigate in the rented car through the maze of timber roads up into the area where there had been a battle in which many Jewish fighters had been killed and others captured. Since this battle figures in *Gone to Soldiers,* I wanted to find the place. We did, and there was the little monument to prove us right. As we walked in those noble woods of hemlock and beech, it seemed to me I could hear the rumble of tank treads in the distant sound of the timber trucks.

> *To die here*
> *under hemlock's dark drooping boughs, better I think*
>
> *than shoved into the showers of gas to croak like roaches*
> *too packed in to flail in the intense slow pain*
> *as the minutes like lava cooling petrified the jammed*
> *bodies into living rock, basalt pillars whose fingers*
>
> *gouged grooves in cement. Yes, better to drop in the high*
> *clean air and let your blood soak into the rich leaf mold.*
> *Better to get off one good shot. Better to remember trains*
> *derailed, turntables wrecked with plastique, raids*
>
> *on the munitions dump. Better to die with a gun*
> *in your hand you chose to pick up and had time to shoot.*
> *Dying you pass out of choice. The others come, put up*
> *a monument decorated with crosses, no mogen davids.*

from "On Black Mountain," *Available Light*

Constantly I had a sense of walking among the dead as I moved over the map of a war that had ended forty years before. It is not that I believe in ghosts, but that to me time seems not entirely linear, so that at moments different times touch and you feel something now gone.

As I was researching the American political scene during that war, I was shocked to discover how little President Roosevelt really did for Jews, how few the United States would let in, how adamant Congress and the State Department were that mere extinction was not a sufficient reason to ease immigration quotas for people whom nobody wanted. I had been raised to a reverence for Franklin Roosevelt bordering on idolatry. My father, who became a Nixon Republican in his later years, would always use a voice that quavered with feeling when he spoke of Roosevelt. My mother felt he had saved our family from hunger. She had considered him a friend of the Jews. I am glad I never shared the results of my reading with her, for she would have been hurt in a personal way, as if betrayed by a blood relative.

Working on *Gone to Soldiers* and the death of my mother, a year saying Kaddish for her, engaged me actively with Judaism again, made me want to create and experience a religion I could give myself to without turning off any part of my mind or my experience. I became interested in Reconstruction and active in attempting to create prayers and rituals that would work for people somewhat like myself. I had to be actively a full Jew again but with my entire being, my history, my intelligence, my knowledge and aesthetics. This is an ongoing preoccupation.

My grandmother was Orthodox, as I have said. She prayed mostly in Yiddish and in prayers she had been taught. My mother seemed to have a highly personal relationship with G-d. He was definitely masculine, as mine has never been, and could be moved by beseeching, could be bargained with, perhaps bribed, certainly coaxed and flattered. Make it not be so, she would urge; from the time I reached puberty, I could never do that.

I find that I cannot imagine a world that contains both the Holocaust and a personal omnipotent G-d. I cannot, in times of fear of danger, pray to someone powerful to deliver me. I pray in order to align myself in tradition, in history, in my own community, in my own consciousness. I pray to clear my mind of petty greed and distractions and meanness. I pray in an attempt to abrade false consciousness. I pray to feel a unity with all beings. I pray to feel my oneness with the earth. I pray in order to cleanse and correct myself. But I cannot pray for something to happen or not to happen, not even when my life seems to or does in fact depend on it.

I simply cannot imagine that any petition of mine, rising, would have any impact on something that would not be moved by the anguish of several million pious and fervid Jews or the cries of babies thrown living into the fire. I leave it to those more theologically gifted than myself to craft explanations or those athletes of faith who can believe because it is impossible. I can't.

I experience holiness. I feel it, it comes through me when I write. I feel it in the attempt to live justly, wisely. I feel it in the necessity to forgive and to ask forgiveness that sanctifies the New Year. I feel it when I am properly aligned with other living beings and with the earth. There are holy places and unholy places that speak to us when we walk upon them. The Shekinah is vivid and real and she comes into the mind and body; she brings the Sabbath if we only pay attention and clear ourselves to prepare.

It is impossible for me not to recognize to what an extent the Holocaust has shaped my religious beliefs. I am nervous about people using the Holocaust freely as a basis of comparison or as metaphor. It seems to me to go with a desire usually to deny the extent of the horror and the loss. But genocide is an old habit of our species, and the Holocaust is an extreme of something many societies including our own resort to when dealing with minorities experienced as in the way, unassimilatable, dangerous in some real or invented manner, turned into devil people.

When I was twelve, I was befriended by an older man, a storyteller who was a Wyandot Indian. His people had once owned the land on which my parents had just purchased a little summer cottage about an hour out of Detroit. There was almost nothing left of his tribe, their language or culture. I remember learning to count in Wyandot as a kind of tribute to him and his kindness. I used to run away into the woods—there was a state forest then across the weedy little pond where the cottage stood —and Thomas was full of information about plants, animals, the trails, who had made them, and why. He died around the time I stopped going out to the cottage; from my fifteenth summer, I was always working to earn money I hoped would take me away to college, but he was important to me because of his kindness, because of his storytelling, because I was moved by his isolation, his being one of the last of his kind.

When I read accounts of the massacres of Indian tribes, like the Sand Creek massacre, where even the babies were bayoneted, I recognize on a small scale what Hitler had had his willing bureaucracy carry out in the millions with assembly-line efficiency. We as a species are capable of such I/Them dichotomizing, such civilized savagery, such organized sadism, and as a writer, I have to enter and embody that death-loving part of our collective and individual psyches. But I also believe in people's enormous ability to open up, to give, to grow, to shine and stretch and make incredible beauty in the beautiful world we inherit and often abuse. The moral and ultimate issues are pressing in on us as we write, as we think, as we act.

I become nervous when the Holocaust becomes a metaphor appropriated for anybody's suffering or other people's favorite causes. At a recent invitation to my *havurah* to share a Holocaust memorial day service with local clergy, the Catholic priest tried to insist that abortion should be included in the commemorative ceremony.

At the same time, there is a sickness that finds Nazis sexy, swastikas a titillating emblem to wear or draw or display. In a society that confounds sex and violence and finds violence fascinating to watch on the screen and to imagine and sometimes to inflict on others, goyish sexual fantasies mess around with images of concentration camps. Mostly the Holocaust as it happened in reality is of interest only to us. Jews need to keep memory alive because others are already denying that it actually happened, are turning it into a rhetorical condemnation of any policy or action that has bloody consequences, making it a blur that evokes nothing more than a yawn. Sometimes others act as if we had possession of some powerful moral issue that we are usurping or controlling, and they want to pry it from us.

Knowledge of the Holocaust is knowledge of the darkest secret, the worst obscenity about being human. It is a sore that cannot heal, a pit that swallows light. Yet survivors triumphed by surviving, and Jews exist. In survival and in resistance, I find strength I stretch to imagine. It gives even more of an importance to reshaping and revitalizing Judaism than it might otherwise have had, or had not for generations that did not grow up into the sense of it as one of the boundaries of human existence.

The Stone That Weeps

JULIUS LESTER

1

It is a summer day, any summer day, 1944. I stare into memory but I see no pictures of what I did on any of those days that summer. I suppose I did what any five-year-old does. And whatever that is, there was less of it for a five-year-old black child in Kansas City, Kansas, in 1944.

It is a summer day, any summer day, 1944. I do not know there is a place called Europe and that all across the continent five-year-old Jewish children are being murdered.

I could not have known. I was only five. Somehow that does not matter. If knowledge is limited to that which we have experienced personally, we are all named Narcissus.

But knowledge is not synonymous with the subjective. Knowledge and experience also include the impersonal—an airplane crashes halfway around the world and tears fill my eyes because someone's child was on that plane—and because I am a parent, I do not have to know the name of the child to feel the grief of a parent. (The bell always tolls for me if I am listening for it.)

During the first six years of my life, I did not know that something was being done to me on the bodies of Jewish children. Now I know that I am alive and so many are not who should be.

Though I was only a child, I am struck by guilt. Perhaps it is because, after Auschwitz, innocence is not possible. I am alive. So many are not who should be; innocence can be no more. I cannot permit myself the charming irresponsibility of thinking that it should be otherwise. I cannot permit myself to assume that because I am black, because I am a Jew that, by definition, I belong with those who involuntarily went to heaven through the chimneys of crematoria. To be innocent is to believe that because I am a Jew, because I am black, I am, by definition, victim and am therefore exempt from being executioner.

Thus, my guilt has two faces: I am alive because I happened to be born black in the United States rather than Jewish in Europe, and because I am alive I am guilty to the extent that I deceive myself into believing the victim cannot also be executioner. I am guilty to the extent that I look at the Holocaust and insist on my innocence, for to be innocent is to deceive myself about what it means to be human.

2

I cannot remember when I first became aware of the Holocaust. I suppose it was the fall of 1957, the beginning of my sophomore year at Fisk University in Nashville, Tennessee. Rhoda Miller, a classmate, thrust a book at me and said imperiously, "Read this."

The book was *Exodus* by Leon Uris. I do not remember one scene from the novel and I refuse to go to my bookshelf, take down my copy, and leaf through its pages to see if any memories come back after thirty-one years.

For me the Holocaust is not contained in or embodied by specific images created by passages in books or remembered from still photographs or films. It is more pervasive than that.

I read *Exodus* by Leon Uris, and at age eighteen, I was transformed. It is similar to that experience one has after being married a certain number of years or after the birth of a child. You know that you had a life before you were married, before you had this particular child, but you cannot remember what that life was or how you could have thought it had meaning. Most odd are those times you turn to your wife and say, "Remember when we saw such and such a movie," and she doesn't remember and you persist, recalling the restaurant where you ate, and she still recalls nothing. Suddenly you remember. You saw the movie before you met she who now sits across from you and, in fact, you were with whatever her name was that night. So fully has your life been absorbed into marriage that your wife's presence has infiltrated and claimed periods of your biography that are not hers.

Does it really matter, then, when I or anyone first encountered the Holocaust? Whatever life we had is swallowed whole and ingested by the metaphor of Auschwitz. It is as if it was always there, as if I knew about it from the instant of conception and the first word I spoke was not "Moma" but "Auschwitz." That is not objective reality, of course, but that was how it felt that autumn of my sophomore year and feeling is a reality that forces the objective to conform to its needs.

It is my junior year, spring 1959. I am attending San Diego State College (California) for a semester, and among my three roommates is a Palestinian named Khalid Tuck-Tuck.

I am assigned the top bunk over his lower one and perhaps it is for this reason that Tuck and I are supposed to be friends. But very quickly I know that I do not want to be his friend. He is obsessed by Jews, and at least once a day something makes him angry and he blames the Jews. Often he talks about the orange trees around his family's home in Jaffa and how beautiful they were until the Jews came and kicked his family out, and then he cries.

It is an act I soon weary of and I try to ignore him. One day, in the midst of one of his tirades against Jews, I hear him say, "I wish Hitler had finished what he started."

I am not aware that I am humming until Tuck screams at me, "I hate that song!"

I listen. I am humming "Hava Nagila," which I have heard at a local coffee shop. I hum it louder, and the next thing I know,

Tuck's hands are around my throat. Our roommates pull him off me.

Oddly, he and I are close friends after that. But he never talks about Jews around me; I never hum "Hava Nagila" around him.

The following spring I find myself approaching the moment of graduation with no idea of what I want to do with my life. On the first Sunday in June, I will be granted my B.A. in English and exhorted to go forth and conquer the world. All I want is to know who I am.

It is a month or two before that fateful Sunday. I am sitting in the International Student Center listening to a short, stocky woman with a European accent talk about some girl named Anne Frank.

Dr. Rosey Poole is Dutch and Anne Frank was a Dutch Jewish girl who wrote a diary that Dr. Poole has translated. Although Dr. Poole is not a Jew, she was part of the Dutch Resistance and her parents were murdered by the Nazis.

As I listen to her talk about a child hiding in an attic, my imagination topples from its perch as if it were a boulder on a mountainside dislodged by unseen stresses from the earth's core. I understand her accented words, but they don't make sense. I don't know how to live with the knowledge of such evil and such suffering.

A few days later I sit on the side porch of Robert Hayden's house. He is a poet and teaches creative writing, Victorian literature, and early-twentieth-century American literature. "What did you think of Rosey Poole's talk?" he asks me.

What am I supposed to say? It was good? I enjoyed it? "It's hard to believe," I say finally.

"We think we know something about suffering," he says, referring to black people. "We don't know what suffering means." His protruding eyes peer at me intently through the thick lenses of his glasses as he lights his pipe and puffs at it strenuously until the tobacco glows red. "Well, that's not entirely true. Maybe it's a problem of language." He chuckles. "But that's always the problem, isn't it?" There is a long silence. "Maybe I'm not comfortable using the same word 'suffering' to describe what we have gone through and what the Jews went through. Do you know what I mean?"

I did. I had ridden at the backs of buses all my life, had read signs telling me where I could and could not eat, what doors I could and could not go through, what water fountains I could and could not drink from. I had been trained by my parents not to look at white women. Then I thought about living in an attic and gas chambers and furnaces into which human beings were shoveled like waste paper.

"I'm not saying that Jews have suffered more. How can you measure what a human being suffers? But there is a difference, and we need a word to make that difference clear." He chuckles. "Are you still sure you want to be a writer? That's what writing is, you know. Finding the right word."

I would like to be the one to find the right word, to find that word which would crush people and make them understand what it was like to be a Jew in Europe during those years. But is there a word strong enough to hold naked bodies stacked in hills beneath a sunny sky? Being forced to ride at the back of a bus is not in the same realm of experience.

But Jews had to wear yellow Stars of David on their clothes to be identified as Jews. My star is my skin color. Yet I am alive. Anne Frank is not.

We sit on his side porch relaxing in the languid and heavy beauty of spring in Nashville, Tennessee. We sit and we talk about Jews being killed in Europe and I begin to feel unreal. The city of Nashville is undergoing a revolution and I am not part of it.

Since February students from Fisk and the other black colleges have been demonstrating to desegregate the lunch counters and restaurants downtown. I have not sat-in at one lunch counter and I am ashamed.

Why do I rage over and mourn for murdered European Jews as I never have for my own people? I want to ask Mr. Hayden but I am afraid that he will not understand the question any more than I do.

I still do not understand, but what is it I think should be understood? Is it so strange and unusual and out of the ordinary for a young black to feel that the Holocaust was an experience on such a scale that it requires a response exceeding any you would give to your own people?

Ah! There's the rub. We are taught in America to care for our own first and most. We are taught that the other guy's problems are his problems. Take care of your own and don't worry about anybody else.

So, I felt guilty because, compared to Anne Frank, I was fortunate. Despite segregation, despite racism, despite all the negative experiences that would come to me because I was black, I was alive and so many my age were not who should have been. Was I forbidden to mourn for them because all my sorrow and grief were supposed to be reserved for those who were black like me?

But I could not help myself. So many my age were dead who should not have been and, except for an accident of birth, I could have been one of them.

3

When Rabbi Hanina the Great came up from Babylon, he wanted to know when he reached Israel, so he picked up stones as he walked, weighing them in his hands. As long as they were light, he said, "I have not yet arrived in Israel." Eventually, the stones were heavy in his hands and he said, "These can only be the stones of the land of Israel." And he kissed them and quoted: "For your servants have desired its stones."

I used to think of my soul as a bird with broad wings that could hold the tiniest wisp of wind. But I was young then, a Peter Pan in danger of disappearing behind the third star to the left as I went toward an eternal morning of perpetual promise.

Now I am older, and I know better: My soul is a stone, broken from that mountain of pain which my ancestor, the Old African, knew when he felt the rough boards of the slave ship beneath his shackled feet, when he looked for the last time at the landscape of the African coast and knew he would never see it again. (When I go to Africa and lift the stones, will I know when I come to the land from which the Old African was stolen?)

My soul is a stone—black, with a texture as rough as

scars that never healed, as heavy as sobbing that can never be quieted.

But how does one lift a stone that weeps? You can't, not until you open your ears and listen to the crying.

Inside me there is a crying that wails hysterically as I remember a childhood destroyed by fear. I remember the violence hurling itself at me every time I rode a bus and could not understand why I was not "good" enough to sit anywhere I wanted to. I remember not knowing why I was not "good" enough to eat at a lunch counter or restaurant, and why, at gas stations, there was a separate rest room for "colored," and sometimes it was the field of weeds behind a pile of old tires. I remember that survival meant never looking a white man in the eye, never looking a white woman anywhere, and always saying "Yes, sir" and "Yes, ma'am."

But I also remember another pain. Yet how can I remember that which did not happen to me? Why does it feel as if I remember Auschwitz when my body does not carry memories of its mud, when my nostrils did not inhale the odor of burning flesh, when my eyes have not seen the glow of the crematoria against the night?

Could it be that memory is not only sensory and that I am not only I?

The summer of 1961 I moved to New York City and my first job was as a counselor at a camp in the Catskills. I did not know that the camp was what would be considered a progressive Jewish one, meaning that the majority of the campers were the sons and daughters of Jews who had grown up listening to Paul Robeson and Pete Seeger, Jews for whom union songs and Woody Guthrie songs were liturgical chants.

Within a week I am calling people meshuga, referring to the camp food as *trayf,* and muttering *oy gevalt* under my breath. I fall in love with another counselor, a large-eyed Jewish girl with long dark hair, who tells me stories about her grandparents fleeing Russia and invites me into her childhood through borscht, bagels, lox, sour cream and herring, and gefilte fish.

At night I sit in the camp dining room with the campers, playing my guitar and singing spirituals and songs from the civil rights movement, which is little more than a year old. They sing

Jewish and Israeli songs. I don't know or understand the words, but the melodies sound familiar, and instinctively I seem to know the odd intervals with which they proceed. The simplest Israeli song—*"Shalom Chaverim,"* or "Every Man 'Neath His Vine and Fig Tree"—brings tears to my eyes as spirituals never have.

Perhaps that is when I first see myself standing in a synogogue singing Kol Nidre. The centuries of black suffering merge with the millennia of Jewish suffering as my voice weaves the two into a seamless oneness that is the suffering and at the same time is the only appropriate and adequate response to it.

The following spring I sit in Manhattan's Riverside Park every evening and watch bearded men walk by in black hats, black suits, and white shirts without ties. They are Hasidim. No one has told me but I know that is who they are. I stare at the older ones and imagine I see the blue-stenciled numbers on their forearms, and as I stare, unconsciously I rub my forearm. It is my suffering and theirs I want to avenge and give voice to—for them and for me.

I am obsessed by the desire to be a cantor, and sometimes when I walk past a synagogue, I think I hear melodies of pain and beauty rising toward heaven.

I did not understand how that could be. But why was it necessary to understand myself? It was enough to live what had come to me to be lived.

What came was the omnipresent subliminal awareness that 6 million Jews had been murdered, not on some day in the backwash of history. No, they were murdered while I played and while I slept, while my cousin, Dorothy, was teaching the four- and five-year-old me to read and play the piano. It did not make sense that in one part of the world a little boy could be sitting in a library choosing books he wanted to read, while elsewhere in the world, at the same moment, a little boy was being murdered. But once I knew that, I could not think of my childhood without also thinking about those other little boys. I didn't dare do otherwise.

My childhood could be true only to the extent that my memory of it included remembering that which had happened to me though I had not seen it, smelled it, or even known.

How do you lift a stone that weeps?
You reach down and pick it up.

4

It is important to remember that which did not happen to me. I do that by using that most amazing of human faculties—imagination, that ability to experience another in myself, to experience another as myself.

As a human, I am more than I have experienced directly. If this were not so, literature, poetry, film, drama, etc., would not communicate to anyone except their creators. If I were no more than *my* experience, I could not communicate with anyone else, or they with me. Imagination is the wings of the soul, carrying me from the singularity of personal existence across the void of Time and Space to alight in that realm where each of us is the other and God is One.

But we seldom give imagination a place in our reflections on history and ourselves. We seldom include it as integral to history, ignoring that the Nazis did what they did to the Jews because of whom they *imagined* Jews to be.

When I confront the Holocaust I use the faculty of imagination because my mind is incapable of understanding death on the scale of the infinite. Imagination is the only faculty that can bring comfort, and comfort can be found only in choosing to live with the images of a suffering so vast that to cry would sound like raucous laughter.

So the Holocaust becomes a macabre scenic backdrop in my life, a presence which becomes a companion.

It is summer 1970. I get into the first cab waiting at the curb outside the terminal at La Guardia, give the driver the address of my apartment in Manhattan, and slump into the corner of the backseat. I notice the driver looking more at me through the rearview mirror than at the cars that he is passing with reckless confidence.

"It's you!" the cabbie finally proclaims, grinning.

That was a statement fraught with philosophical peril.

"It's you!" he repeats. "Remember me?"

I lean forward, puzzled, and look at him. After a moment I

recognize him as the same cabbie who has taken me from La Guardia into Manhattan twice in the past year. To get the same cabbie more than once in New York is almost impossible; three times deserves a story in the *Daily News*.

"How've you been?" he wants to know after we finish exclaiming over the coincidence.

"Fine," I say politely. I ask about him, hoping he will respond with equal insincerity and then leave me alone.

"You're a writer, right?" he says after a long pause.

I know what's coming: He's had a very interesting life and he knows that it would be a best-seller if he could only find somebody to write it up, and if I help him the two of us could make a lot of money, etc., etc., etc.

"I've got a problem. Maybe you can help me." There is another long pause. "I just got a letter from this cousin of mine." He stops. He opens his mouth several times but no words come. Finally, in a gesture of desperation, he takes his right hand from the steering wheel and bends his arm back at me. I look at the numbers stenciled in blue on his forearm. "You know?"

"I know," I respond quietly.

He puts his hand back on the wheel, and the words come rapidly now. "My problem is this. I just got this letter from my cousin in Israel. She's the daughter of my mother's sister. But the problem is that for the past twenty-five years I thought everybody in my family was dead. Then last week I get this letter from her. She'd thought everybody in the family was dead, too, but somehow she heard that maybe I was alive and she got an address and wrote." He stops. "It's such a shock, you know. So, I thought since you're a writer, you could tell me what to write to her."

I slump back into the seat, my eyes shut against not only the pain and sorrow of it all, but my own impotence before the enormity of his request and the numbers on his wrist. Doesn't he see that I am black? Hasn't he read that blacks and Jews aren't allies anymore? Why ask me? And so what if I'm a writer? Only God knows what one ghost should say to another.

"Were you happy to hear from her?" I hear myself ask after a long silence.

"Oh, yes! It's a shock, but I'm very happy."

"Well, maybe that's what you should write. Tell her how happy you are."

He thinks for a moment, then looks at me through the mirror. He is smiling and nodding his head. "Thank you. That's what I'll do."

We say nothing else. I've flown into La Guardia many times since, but have never seen him again. I wonder now if he was real or if he was an angel who descended from an ash-filled sky.

There are memories, important memories I cannot assign years to. Why is that? Is it because an evil as enormous as the Holocaust had to have happened outside time, because history would be destroyed if it had to contain and understand such evil? Or is it that I am too small to contain evil of such breadth and therefore my contacts with the Holocaust remove me from dailiness and put me into an eternal present in which there can never be a tomorrow because the sun can neither rise nor set?

It is some time during the early 1970s. One evening I am turning the channels on the television set looking for something that will entertain me and allow me to forget enervating dailiness for a while.

"Sighet," the voice on the television says. It is a quiet, compelling voice and I do not know who or what Sighet is, but I am entranced by the sound of the word and the sound of the voice saying it. I sit down to watch, at least long enough to have my curiosity about Sighet satisfied.

Sighet is the name of a town in Eastern Europe and the narrator of the film is a Jew, a survivor, who has returned to Sighet for the first time since he was transported from there to Auschwitz in 1944.

I missed the beginning of the film and do not know who possesses that voice so filled with sorrow that my soul feels itself to be in the presence of a suffering for which there is no comfort.

When the credits are run at the end of the film, I learn to whom the voice belongs: Elie Wiesel.

In the summer of 1974, I teach summer school at Mercer College in Macon, Georgia. Most of the students in my ethnic literature course are elementary and junior high school teachers, black and white women going to school to get master's degrees in education. Why did I include *A Jew Today* by Elie Wiesel on the reading list? I do not know. I do not recall how I taught the book, what I said about it, or what they said about it. I only remember the feeling that it was important that I include something about Jews and the Holocaust in the course because I didn't want my students to think that ethnic literature meant only blacks, Hispanics, and Native Americans.

5

Winter–spring 1979.

I am on sabbatical from the university. I am planning to use the time reading recent novels by black writers and revising my Contemporary Afro-American Novel course. One January evening I happen to pick up Raul Hilberg's *The Destruction of the European Jews* from the pile of unread books stacked beside my rocking chair.

I begin reading and I cannot stop. The more I read, the more depressed I am. A depression is a hollow in the land. Its root meaning is "to strike." That is how I feel. I have been struck so fearfully that I have fallen into a hollow in the land. I have been struck by grief and mourning for the 6 million murdered Jews.

Days pass. They are as heavy and silent as stones. I cook, and nag the children about their chores. I shop; I watch hockey games on television with my son. I take my pregnant wife to the doctor. There are no words inside me. Only images:

I am four or five years old and come downstairs one morning and notice that the clock has stopped. Moma tells me there was a "blackout" during the night. I know it has something to do with the war but I cannot imagine what.

I sit on the top step of the front porch of my aunt's house in Little Rock, Arkansas. I sit all day, watching army trucks and Jeeps and tanks and soldiers go past. I know there is a war somewhere, but what is a war and what does a tank do?

I remember ration books. I remember buying orange stamps in school and pasting them in a book and when the book is filled, I am given a war bond. I remember sitting in the kitchen, a plastic tube filled with margarine in my hand. It is white, but at the center is a yellow globule and I press the tube until the yellow globule breaks and I squeeze the tube until the yellow color spreads through the whiteness and the margarine becomes yellow like forsythia.

The war was funerals for young men in khaki-colored uniforms at Daddy's church, and a bronze bulletin board in the church vestibule onto which were etched the names of those killed, and little children at church on Father's Day, white flowers pinned to the lapels of their jackets or on the right shoulders of their dresses. Their fathers had died in the war and I was afraid of them.

I remember, also, my red tricycle, my doll with her blue pajamas, the pear tree in the yard whose green fruit gave me one of the worst stomachaches of my life. I remember gathering eggs in the mornings and the bantam rooster who beat me so thoroughly and so consistently that Daddy finally had to sell the chickens. But before that happened, I remember the Saturdays Daddy went into the chicken house, caught a chicken, and brought it out to the yard, and grabbing its head, he twirled his arm around and around, faster and faster until the chicken's body flew through space and landed in the dust where it flopped and ran with drunken steps, blood spurting from the hole where its head had been. Eventually, the headless chicken toppled over, twitching and flopping in the dust until death stilled its body. Daddy would give me the chicken's head and after Moma scalded off the feathers and cut the chicken up, she gave me the feet. I would sit with them in the narrow alleyway between the church and the parsonage, trying to imagine what it was like to be alive and then be dead.

What was it like to be a child and inhale gas? What was it like to stand before a pit at Babi Yar and watch others being shot, knowing that within seconds you, too, would be dead, tumbling into that pit? What was it like to have been that child whom an S.S. officer grabbed by its ankles and swung through the air in a swift arc against the side of a railroad car, the child's head and life shattering like a falling star?

Why was I alive?

Why were they dead?

I do not understand.

Chaim Kaplan, the Warsaw ghetto: "It is almost a mitzvah to dance. Every dance is a protest against our oppressors."

An anonymous Jew as he is being pushed into a cattle car, the Warsaw ghetto: "Jews, don't despair! Don't you realize that we are going to meet the Messiah? If I had some liquor, I'd drink a toast."

Words written on the wall of a cellar in Cologne, Germany, where Jews hid: "I believe in the sun when it is not shining. I believe in love even when feeling it not. I believe in God even when He is silent."

I do not understand.

The more I read, the greater my numbness as I witness Jews affirming God in the midst of their own negation.

Elie Wiesel: "They were pressed together so that they could hardly move or breathe. Suddenly an old rabbi exclaimed, 'Today is Simchat Torah. Have we forgotten what Jews are ordered to do on Simchat Torah?' Sombody had managed to smuggle a small *Sefer Torah* aboard the train. He handed it to the rabbi. And they began to sing, to sway, since they could not dance. And they went on singing and celebrating the Torah, all the while knowing that every motion of the train was bringing them closer to the end."

Hermann Graebe, eyewitness to a massacre of Jews in the Ukraine, 1942: "I watched a family of about eight persons, a man and woman, both about fifty, with their children of one, eight, and ten, and two grown-up daughters of about twenty to twenty-four. An old woman with snow-white hair was holding the one-year-old child in her arms and singing to it and tickling it. The child was cooing with delight. The couple were looking on with tears in their eyes. The father was holding the hand of a boy about ten years old and speaking to him softly; the boy was fighting his tears. The father pointed toward the sky, stroked his head and seemed to explain something to him. At that moment the S.S. man at the pit shouted something to his comrade. The latter counted off about twenty persons. Among them was the family I have mentioned."

Would I be able to hold the hand of one of my children and talk of life, directing the child's eyes to the clear blue sky so that he or she would not see the soldiers raise their rifles, so he or she would not see death? I do not know.

I awake each morning, tired. In the night I have wandered among naked bodies piled atop one another; I shovel bodies into ovens and I am the Jew closing the oven door and the Jew inside; I am smoke and flame spewing from smokestacks; I am particles of ash and soul seeking my burying place in cloud and sky.

One morning I awake and, with my eyes still closed, say to my wife, "Even God does not understand the Holocaust."

Another morning I awake and my lips are moving. I listen. I am trying to say *"Sh'ma Yisrael Adonai Elohenu Adonai Ehad."* At night those words resound in me and when I awake, they are the first words I hear from my lips.

I do not understand.

Some understanding comes in December 1981, when I decide to convert to Judaism. I, too, want to be one of those so in love with God that I would say the *Sh'ma* when facing death.

6

I like stones. I used to collect them. The last time I moved, however, I found myself carrying a box of stones up from the basement. So, I don't collect them anymore.

I don't need to, now that I know that my soul is a stone, impenetrable and eternal.

My soul became a stone when I realized that God needs us. God's fate is inseparable from our own, asserted Yaakov Yosef of Polnoy. God created everything by the Word, except us. Into us He breathed His own spirit. God is dependent on us to care for that portion of His spirit which is our birthright.

If that is so, and it is, then the evil within us is from God, too. But if God and I are convenanted, and we are, then He suffers, too—from His capacity for evil as well as mine. Only to the extent that I accept this suffering can I accept God. Only to the extent that I remember the suffering of others do I remember the capacity for evil which is mine because God breathed a soul into me.

To remember. That is the key. It is not an intellectual act. It is a commitment of being. The word comes from a root which means "to mourn." How amazing! To remember is to mourn. It is an essential way by which God is known to us and we are known to ourselves. There is an old Jewish saying: "Forgetfulness leads to exile; remembering leads to redemption."

And so I remember the survivor of Treblinka who returns after the war with a group to the now-deserted death camp. They peer into the craters made by bombs dropped at the end of the war, and peering into one crater, they see human bones protruding from the dirt.

Someone points and says, "These are bones from a child's leg!"

The survivor, this Jew who was one of only 40 Jews to survive where 1,200,000 were killed, rushes to the crater and pulls out the bone of a child's leg.

"There's still some flesh hanging from that leg!" someone exclaims.

The man takes a section of newspaper from someone in the group, wraps the bone in it, puts it in the breast pocket of his coat and hugs it to himself. "Perhaps," he said, "it's the foot of my little boy whom I brought here with me."

I remember and I mourn because God should've commanded the sun to stand still in the nave of the sky until humanity mourned.

I remember with the same intensity as the Jews of Psalm 137 remembered Jerusalem. It is believed that this psalm was written some time after the destruction of the first Temple and Jews were forced into the *galut* of Babylon. In the Midrash on Psalms, there is this story:

Among those carried away were the Levites, the musicians of the Temple. One evening in the midst of a large banquet, the tables laden with food and wine, the hall filled with dancing girls, King Nebuchadnezzar thought to heighten the evening's entertainment by having the Levites brought to him. He commanded them to play their instruments and sing the Lord's songs for him as they had done in the Temple. There was great applause and laughter from the Babylonians feasting themselves. When the laughter stopped and the hall was quiet, the Levites stood up and each man put his thumb in his mouth and broke it.

Remembering is not only to be carried on the scarlet wings of imagination through the void of Time and Space. Remembering is also the act of total and singular commitment to myself as the silence in which God dwells. Such a commitment might require me to break my thumb rather than forget you, O Jerusalem!

Such a commitment also requires me to know that remembering is not only composed of mourning and sorrow but there is another emotion, too—anger. Psalm 137 states it forcefully:

> *O, Babylon, Babylon the destroyer,*
> *A blessing on him*
> > *who repays you for all that you did to us!*
> *A blessing on him*
> > *who seizes your children and*
> > *dashes them against the rocks!*

There are times when anger, and yes, even hatred can be holy. Interestingly enough, another of the roots of the word remember is in the name of the Old Norse god Mimir, "a giant who guards the well of wisdom."

How often I feel within me an anger so enormous and so fierce that it feels like a giant that would devour me. Anger of such proportions is frightening and I fear that if I give in to it I will be seized by a giant who will plunge me deeper and deeper into some depth where I will drown. Suffering can be like this, too. But it is not a drowning that anger would lead me to. The giants of anger and suffering guard the well of wisdom.

To remember the Holocaust is not only to mourn; it is also to be enraged. It is to stand naked beneath the sky, shake my fist at heaven and demand that God bless "him who seizes your children and dashes them against the rocks!"

Just as it was not right or possible for the Jews in their Babylonian exile not to feel rage at the destruction of Jerusalem and the Temple, it is not right if I do not feel rage for the murders of those 6 million women, men, and children.

When I truly meet the giant guarding the well of wisdom,

when I allow myself the rage as well as the sorrow, the tears as well as the desire for vengeance—and the desire is not the same as the act—then, and only then, do I lower my bucket into the well of wisdom.

7

Rabbi Abbahu said: God mourned only over the heart of man, as one does who has made something bad, and knows that he has not made a good thing, and says. "What have I made?" So God said: "It was I who put the bad leaven in the dough, for the *yetzer* of the heart of man is evil from his youth." God grieved over man's heart.

That is the antidote to evil. I must grieve over the hearts of us all. I must grieve so loudly that my grief becomes a prayer. I must utter no words asking for forgiveness, but let my grief be the forgiveness. If God grieves over my heart for having created me with the *yetzer,* then I must grieve for God for having created the *yetzer*.

Evil is. That is the unmistakable message of the Holocaust. Look and see what evil is capable of. Evil is. Until I accept this, I cannot accept that I am human. I cannot accept God as God.

In the Mishnah Berakhot are these words:

> A man must recite a benediction for evil, just as he recites a benediction for good. For it is said: "And thou shalt love the Lord thy God with all thy heart, and with all thy soul, and with all thy might." "With all thy heart"—with thy two wills, with thy will to good and thy will to evil.

God is to be loved with the *yetzer ha-Ra,* too. I cannot truly love if I omit from that love my capacity for evil. If God loves me by His grief, then it is with my grief that I must love.

Isn't that what I am called to by the Holocaust—to love by grieving. I am not called to understand. I am not called to speculate on the concept of God after Auschwitz. I am not called to be rational in any way. I am called to remember, that is, to mourn and to grieve and to bring into my soul the evil that is.

This is the stone my soul is becoming. It is a stone that weeps. It is a stone that bleeds.

It is my offering to God

and

you.

In Every Generation:
A Meditation on the
Two Holocausts

LESLIE FIEDLER

For a long time now I have resisted all importunities to confront head-on in print the destruction by Hitler of 6 million Jews, what has come to be called, "the Holocaust." It is in part this intrinsically theological name for an essentially secular atrocity which has put me off. Not merely has it become an instant cliché, but by employing it (as how can I not?), I predetermine, as it were, my own attitudes and the response of my audience. Think how different those attitudes and that response would be if I were to use more secular sociological terms like "genocide"; or even the Nazis' mythological one, "The Final Solution."

Moreover, I have always been afraid that in dealing with that subject, I could not keep from seeming to suggest that I, who as an American was safely removed from the European catastrophe, insofar as I am at least allegedly Jewish, have been, in some sense, its victim. It is true, of course, that Hitler would have (whatever my own doubts about my identity) considered me a Jew; but this gives me, I am convinced, no right to exploit rhetorically, politically, philosophically, the ultimate misery of those alien others with whom he would have lumped me. At any rate, both my Jewishness and theirs remain for me even now not a given fact but an enigma, elevated by their fate as victims and mine as an unscathed survivor (perhaps to some degree a victimizer) if not quite to the level of a full theological Mystery, at least to that of a modest lower-case "mystery." It is, in any event, this minor mystery which I propose to explore in the subtheological meditation which follows: a meditation on not just one Holocaust but—for reasons which I hope will become clear before I am through—two.

Unlike many religious thinkers (though I speak their language, it should be understood that what for them is revealed truth is for me myth and metaphor), I do not consider the failed total destruction of European Jewry a *novum*—an event not merely monstrous but unprecedented, unique, and, therefore, incomprehensible, ineffable. It seems to me in retrospect disconcertingly predictable: an occurrence or, better perhaps, re-occurrence in history of what already existed out of historical time; which is to say, an event that had long since become a myth, the key myth, indeed, of Jewish existence.

My maternal grandfather, who had before he was quite full grown fled the Eastern European world of pogroms and the threat of pogroms, when asked what was happening in the world, would usually answer (at least so I remember it), "Nothing new. *M'hargert yidd'n*. They're killing Jews. What else?" The first time I heard it, I was left wondering whether it was some strange kind of adult joke at which, if I lived so long, I would be able someday to laugh. But it no longer seemed a joke of any kind when at age seven or eight I found myself reenacting in fact that myth of our history. I was then a student in a suburban New Jersey grade school, where my brother and I constituted half of the total Jewish enrollment. We felt ourselves, therefore, interlopers in a goyish institution, where, of course, all of our teachers were goyim and we had weekly school "chapels," at which we were expected to repeat *their* Lord's Prayer and, at the appropriate seasons, sing hymns celebrating the birth and the resurrection of *their* Christ.

All of this, however, had made me only a little uncomfortable, until one day in the schoolyard all hell broke loose. During recess and after class, when my fellow students gathered together to choose up sides for a game, more often than not they would end with Protestants on one side and Catholics on the other (for me it was a baffling distinction without a difference), then proceed to pummel each other in a kind of mock Holy War. On this occasion, however, for reasons I still don't understand, they noticed me slinking off alone, as I customarily did; and remembering that I was a Jew, which is to say, the legendary enemy of both, joined together to chase me all the way home, screaming, *"You killed our Christ."*

At that moment of sheer funk (I was sure that they meant really, *really* to kill me), I learned not only that my grandfather's joke was not a joke at all, but the reason why Christians had long slaughtered us in earnest: their myth of the Jews. But of course I did not yet know how to say this even to myself, much less my pursuers. If I had been able to find breath for anything but running, I would probably have shouted, "What, me killed your Christ? I wasn't even there." Certainly, I would not have had the chutzpah, even if I had the breath, to answer their charge of deicide with the defiant affirmation I was to hear years later on the streets of Jerusalem. It was in the midst of the turbulent sixties when a band of marching Israeli hippies cried aloud to watching tourists, including me, "We did so kill him. We did *so!*"

But after all, those marchers were at home in a world of their fellows; while I (as I realized first back then in New Jersey) was a stranger in a strange land, and would remain so to the day of my death. No matter that I could already read better the language of the land to which my forebears had fled, speak it better, write it better than my child persecutors, to whose ancestors it "belonged" as it did not to mine. As a matter of fact, this only made matters worse.

Perhaps it would have helped if I had been familiar with the Jewish countermyths explaining the hostility between us and the gentiles, myths invented before Jesus had claimed to be the Messiah and had been condemned by the High Priest of Israel as a blasphemer, then turned over to the dubious justice of Rome.

The key text is, of course, in the Haggadah for Pesach, repeated annually by all who consider themselves still Jews: ". . . for not one only hath risen up against us, but in every generation there are some who rise up against us; but the Most Holy blessed be he, hath delivered us out of their hands." "In every generation," the threat warns us, looking forward to Hitler and Muslim terror as well as backward to Haman and the pharaoh "who knew not Joseph."

But it is not the final word, being followed by a promise of deliverance, which reminds us that not merely did 6 million Jews die in the Holocaust, but millions escaped alive to tell the tale. It is, indeed, their survival and subsequent fate which is for me the true, the final mystery. Before returning to it, however, I feel obliged to wrestle with the question of *why* the threat of annihilation and the promise of redemption have continued to be the pattern of our history. Here, too, there is text suggesting an answer: the cryptic fifty-third chapter of Isaiah, in which the prophet imagines the kings of the gentiles confessing that only through the suffering which they inflict on God's faithful servant, Israel, can they themselves be saved: "Surely he hath borne our griefs, and carried our sorrows; yet we did esteem him stricken, smitten of God and afflicted. / But he was wounded for our transgression, he was chastised for our iniquities; the chastisement of our peace was upon him; and with his stripes we are healed."

It was not, however, until I was approaching middle age that I became aware of those texts and their relevance to my own fate as well as that of my people; which is to say, not until after the defeat of Hitler, the revelation of the full horror of the concentration camps, and the simultaneous loss of my earlier faith in socialism and the universal brotherhood of all mankind. I was a Communist of the Stalinist persuasion at age thirteen, a Trotskyist before I was twenty. My "Holy Books" therefore were not the Torah and Talmud, but the collected works of Marx, Engels, and Lenin, which seemed to me then to teach the True Way: not just a way to make a better world but a way to escape the limitations of my ancestral religion. To be sure, those limitations were not very onerous since neither my parents nor my grandparents observed the rules of kashruth, nor were they members

214

of any congregation. But they had nonetheless preserved intact in the New World the parochialism and xenophobia which had been concomitants of Old World Judaism.

Though my grandfather no longer recited the morning blessings in which he thanked his Creator for not having made him a goy, he taught me to sing, "*Oy, oy, oy,* shiker is ah goy . . . a drunkard is he and drink he must, because he is a gentile. . . ." Moreover, when I behaved intelligently, he told me, beaming, that I had a *yiddisher kopf* and when I acted stupidly, I was reproached for having a goyish head. For my grandmother, who kept none of her opinions secret, all gentiles were contemptible: the Irish, the Italian, and especially those from whose midst she had fled, the Poles, along with the *shvartzers,* the Negroes, who seemed to her their American equivalents. Even in the mouths of my native-born parents, the words shegetz and shiksa were epithets of contempt; and I was not surprised to discover that the root meaning of these standard words for a gentile male and female was "abomination." Small wonder, then, that the parents of my favorite high school teacher, a Jew, sat shivah for him when he married a shiksa, mourned for him as if he were dead.

To be sure, I was aware that such Jewish hatred and fear of their non-Jewish neighbors were reflexive, a reaction to generations of persecution in Eastern Europe—and that, of course, it was finally impotent as well, drawing not a single drop of gentile blood in return for the buckets of Jewish blood shed by the gentiles for so many generations. Yet it was, I knew, weakness rather than charity which had made my people in their long exile settle for calling upon their God to pour out His wrath on the goyim, instead of slaughtering them themselves as their ancestors had done, moving into the Promised Land.

In any event, I was convinced in those days that until such mutual recrimination and hostility ceased, until anti-Semitism and anti-anti-Semitism alike were ended, there could be no social peace. Nor would it cease, I believed, until the International Soviet had become the human race, until in a world without poverty, exploitation, and greed there were no longer Christians and Muslims, Hindus and Buddhists—and, yes, no longer Jews. Though I did not then go on record, in the thirties my response to a question about the future of American Jewry would doubtless have been much like that of Henry Roth, who wrote three decades later: ". . . I feel that to the great boons Jews have already conferred upon humanity, Jews in America might add this last and greatest one: of orienting themselves toward ceasing to be Jews."

Since one of the boons of the Jews to humanity to which Roth was referring was clearly Marxism, I felt that in abandoning Judaism in favor of socialism I was merely swapping an earlier, lesser Jewish faith for a later, greater one. After all, I assured myself, Marx had been ethnically Jewish; and from the start his doctrines had been especially appealing to his fellow Jews. Of this I became aware early on when my grandfather, wanting to teach me a little Yiddish, began by making me sound out in the *mama-loshen* the masthead slogan of the *Daily Forward: "Workers of the World Unite!"* My father, to be sure, was a violent anti-Marxist; but being as confirmed an atheist as he was an American patriot (he dreamed that I or my brother would make it into West Point), he brought me up reading Bob Ingersoll and Tom Paine, to whom organized religion was also anathema.

The mythological Hebrew texts, therefore, to which I alluded at the beginning of this meditation, were quite unknown to me until I was closing in on middle age and had become the father of three sons. It was at that point that, finding myself and them all the more "strangers in a strange land" in Missoula, Montana, I organized the first Seder I had ever attended: a communal celebration for a handful of Jewish exiles, most of them also teachers in the state university and, predictably enough, almost none of them married to Jewish wives. It was in that congregation, at any rate, that I first heard ringing in my ears (in my own voice and, of course, in English) the warning that "in every generation there are some who rise up against us. . . ." and began to puzzle out its meanings.

Even earlier I had begun to wrestle with the second key text, when, just after the end of World War Two, I spent a full semester in the Harvard Divinity School, studying the twelve mysterious verses that constitute that fifty-third chapter of Isaiah. I had gone there to learn Hebrew, but why, I was not really sure. I was motivated perhaps by a desire to rediscover—or more accurately, to invent for the first time—my Jewishness, though there was a certain irony in my attempting to do so in a Christian school, as there was also in my simultaneously joining a choral group preparing to sing Christmas carols on Beacon Hill. Or maybe what motivated me was shame at the fact that of all the languages I had been exposed to up to that point—some eight or nine, I guess—the only one I had failed to learn well was my own ancestral tongue.

I had actually been sent shortly before I turned thirteen (over my father's scandalized protests) to be prepared for bar mitzvah. But I stubbornly resisted learning Hebrew—spending most of my lesson time haranguing the rabbi who sought to instruct me about Jewish discrimination against Negroes in America and Arabs in Palestine; or trying to explain to him why all religions, including his own, were "the opium of the people." To all of this he would retort only that I read Hebrew "like a Cossack," which was, alas, true.

Indeed, I still read the Holy Tongue like a Cossack, even after the valiant efforts of Robert Pfeiffer, the eminent biblical scholar who was my teacher at Harvard, and who did his best to teach us "proper" pronunciation, insisting over and over (for the benefit of the few Jews in the class) that "Hebrew was not a dialect of Polish Yiddish." It was, in any case, pronunciation, grammar, and lexicography in which he believed. Of the mythic import of the text he said little except that it was *not,* as Christian theologians insisted, a prophecy of Christ's vicarious atonement for the sins of mankind and that the Suffering Servant was Israel —as should be clear to anyone who understood the tenses of the verbs.

But in what the myth of the Suffering Servant might mean after the rise and fall of Hitler, Professor Pfeiffer was not interested. I, however, *was,* having come begrudgingly and at long last to recognize the full scope and horror of the Holocaust, of which I had so long remained at least half-deliberately unaware. Before America's entry into World War Two, I had dismissed the skimpy, garbled newspaper accounts of the Nazi persecution and slaughter of European Jewry as propaganda: "atrocity stories," like those about the poor Belgians and the rabid Huns which had circulated during World War One—and intended, like those, to brainwash the exploited masses into supporting a conflict that would mean more profits for their exploiters and death for them.

Such imperialist wars, I continued to believe even after I had lost faith in Stalin's Soviet Union and had begun to entertain doubts about Marxism-Leninism itself, were the ultimate evil threatening humanity. I was therefore proud that during the thirties I had stood shoulder to shoulder with my fellow students at NYU, crying aloud the "Oxford Oath," which is to say, vowing that we would never support our own country in any war. Moreover, even as we shouted our resolve, we hoped, believed that, simultaneously, massed protesters were echoing our words, not only throughout our own country and those of our so-called allies, but even in those lands which a hypocritical FDR (promising peace, but plotting war) had labeled our "enemies." Really, however, we were convinced that the "enemy" was the ruling class of one's own country. That is why we sang over and over as we marched the streets of our cities and towns in the years between the Great Wars:

> *In seventeen we went to war,*
> *In seventeen we went to war,*
> *In seventeen we went to war,*
> *Didn't know what we were fighting for.*
> *Time to turn those guns the other way.*

So too we stubbornly resisted the argument that Hitler's planned extermination of the Jews made possible a moral distinction between the capitalist Third Reich (where, after all, multinational corporations like Krupp continued to prosper) and the rival capitalist powers, including our own. To grant this, we believed, was also to grant that our imperialist war against Hitler was a just one. It was a notion which most American Jews found it easier to believe than did their Jewish brethren in Russia, where anti-Semitism had long since become a weapon in Stalin's struggle for power; or in France, where the Dreyfus case was still a living memory; or even in England, where every schoolchild grew up haunted by the nightmare figures of Shylock and Fagin.

Consequently, those of us self-styled "revolutionaries" who

were also Jewish Americans considered it important to keep pointing out that the Jews were merely *one* target of Hitler's campaign of extermination, which also included gypsies, Poles, homosexuals, congenital malformations, Jehovah's Witnesses—and, especially, Communists. To contend otherwise, we felt, would be to play into the hands of the capitalist warmongers like those well-to-do *allrightniks* whom we had always despised: those former bootleggers and sweatshop owners who sought to prove that they were good Americans as well as good Jews by simultaneously launching Liberty Bond campaigns and raising money on behalf of Zionism. Which was worse, I would then have been hard put to say—their offensively blatant American patriotism or their equally egregious pledges of allegiance to a nation-state which did not yet exist.

Even after I had ceased to be a Marxist, their Zionism seemed to me especially offensive; since the last thing an already atomized world needed, I was convinced, was one more nation-state. Because of the blessing-curse of exile from their original homeland, the Jews, it seemed to me, had been peculiarly well suited to play a leading role in the inevitable progress toward a world without borders, flags, and ethnic divisions. The dream of a return to Zion, translated from the mystical to the political sphere, could, however, only eventuate in a society in which there would be not only Jewish statesmen and bureaucrats, but Jewish cops and soldiers—Jewish Cossacks, in short. That in turn would (as it needed no prophet returned from the grave to foresee) breed an answering nationalism in the Arab inhabitants of what was to them also the Holy Land, whom the new settlers would have to dispossess or displace. And to the ensuing Holy War, with mythic roots on both sides, there would be no end.

For a while, as the ensuing drama of terror and counterterror unfolded, I was tempted—following the Communist and Trot-skyist line—to side in that struggle with the Arabs, who pre-ferred (like the American Indians, with whom I could not help identifying them) poverty, disorganization, even tyranny under a regime of their coreligionists, to prosperity, law and order, and a modicum of democracy under the auspices of colonizers whose technology, culture, and myths were utterly alien to their own. But I have ended by crying out—without ever ceasing to wish that the remnant of Israel in the Middle East survive and flourish —a curse on both your houses, though, of course, I would prefer to wish on both the blessing of universal brotherhood.

Clearly this has not come to pass in the land of Israel, or indeed anywhere in the world, and it does not seem likely to come to pass in the foreseeable future. Yet it has not been easy for me to confess that I, who in the first quarter century of my life was sure that (if I lived so long) I would live to see a global ecumene without ethnic distinction, have instead lived long enough to see, as I prepare to begin my fourth quarter of a century, a world which atomizes rather than unites: a congeries of self-imposed ghettoes, in which the chief sources of political dynamism are particularism, parochialism, and sectarianism.

Perhaps I surmised all this (though I did not yet have the words to say it to myself) as early as 1942, when I enlisted in the war that I had so long anticipated with fear and loathing. Let me be clear. I was not drafted but volunteered, though I was at that point married, with a first child and a second well on the way; and I kept volunteering until I finally ended up at Iwo Jima, in the midst of what not only I came to think of as the mythological culmination of that bloody conflict. But *why?* is the question I can still not answer.

I was prompted not, I think, by an indifference bred of despair after my discovery that the world had turned out so utterly different from what I had expected. Nor did I act as I did because, as I sometimes told those who asked, I could not endure refusing pusillanimously to share the key experience of my generation. Perhaps it was only that I wanted to escape from what I had begun to feel as the restrictions of premature maturity. Or maybe I just wanted to learn another language, and the program promised not only to make me a commissioned officer in the navy but to teach me Japanese. This would, however, take me to the remote Pacific—which is to say, at the farthest possible remove from the threatened Jews in Europe. It was there, at any rate, I finally found myself, listening to reports of what was happening on the other side of the world as if they were events on another planet. Though I *did* listen to those reports in Honolulu, on Guam, and in China, I could not help wishing—I feel obliged to confess—for the defeat of our own expeditionary forces and those of our Russian allies, unable to forget what I had learned too well in my years of Marxist indoctrination: that it was the defeat of the Russians in World War One which had helped make possible the first successful socialist revolution.

I did not, of course—like the defeated soldiers of the czar—turn my guns the other way: since, without ever having fired a gun in any direction, I ended up as one of the victorious. When, therefore, I found myself at the war's end, helmeted and in full battle gear, marching down the streets of a "liberated" Chinese city, I felt like some Hollywood version of conquering Nazis entering Paris. So, too, grilling terrified and filthy POWs, I seemed to myself more like an S.S. interrogator than a Jew boy from Newark, New Jersey, trapped in a war in which he did not believe; but never so more than when, flanked by a pair of offensively trim commanding officers, I helped capture an alleged "war criminal": a pudgy Japanese businessman who (quite like, I could not help thinking, a Jew trying to pass as a gentile to escape the gas chambers) had disguised himself as a Chinese. He had castrated a coolie, we learned from a "reliable informant," and had buried in his backyard "a treasure in gold coins." But there was, it turned out, no treasure of any kind, which led me to suspect that the mutilated coolie might have been a fiction as well.

I went therefore to the prison to which my "war criminal" had been taken to ask whether there might have been some mistake, and I was told that the "mistake" was mine; that no such person had ever been incarcerated, or indeed existed at all. It is an incident I have never forgotten, though; quite as if, indeed, he had really never existed, I cannot recall his face. What has continued to haunt my dreams ever since, however, is the painted face of the little girl (his adopted "daughter," he assured us, as my Chinese companions smirked) into whose hands he thrust a farewell gift, breaking temporarily from our grasp, as she kept screaming his name—which I have also forgotten. Another scene from a wartime propaganda film, in which I am once more hopelessly miscast.

Small wonder that long before I was finally shipped home, I had come to identify with the Japanese rather than with my American comrades-in-arms, whom I had seen performing not only acts of valor, which put me to shame, but also atrocities: brutally beating disarmed prisoners, for instance, or stopping long enough under fire of their living enemies to extract with their bayonets the gold teeth of those already dying or dead. I never doubted for a moment that had I seen the Japanese as victors, I would have witnessed equally atrocious acts. But I encountered them only as victims: and as victims, all men, I came then to believe, are the "suffering servants" through whose stripes their victimizers are healed, that is, are—in the mythological sense—Jews.

Real Jews, however, were as rare on shipboard and the islands of the Pacific as they had been in Montana; but when I finally got to China—which is to say, when my long westward flight from my ancestral past had reached the ultimate East—I encountered, to my surprise, genuine Jewish refugees from European terror. They had not fled the Nazis, though, these loud-mouthed hustlers in tight-waisted sports jackets, with whom I chatted over Sunday morning bagels and tea at the Imperial Hotel in Tientsin. Nor were the more soberly garbed burghers-in-exile, like the soft-spoken old gent who invited me home to show off his dog who understood Yiddish and his Hebrew prayer book autographed by Eleanor Roosevelt.

It was the Bolshevik Revolution from which they had run in 1917 and were running still, side by side with goyim, to whom the new regime was equally threatening. But the goyish and Jewish expatriates in Tientsin had almost nothing to do with each other; the former socializing with their own kind in the White Russian Club (some of their rebellious children had already split off to form a Red one), while the latter forgathered in what they called, of course, the *Kunst,* which is to say, the Art Club.

The only art practiced there, however, was—as far as I could tell on a single visit—money changing. But after all, a Jew has to live, and what else was there to do for these stateless wanderers, except maybe peddle contraband on streetcorners or run on a shoestring some sleazy brothel-saloon. Nontheless, I could not despise or condescend to—much less, God forbid, pity—these *luftmenschen* without a past or future. Undefeated and undismayed, they were capable still of a kind of ironical acceptance of their fate, which made me feel childishly naive in my alternating fits of euphoria and despair.

I shall never forget, for instance, the time I made the mistake of saying "thank you" to one of them, after he had given me in exchange for a single U.S. dollar several thousand yuan, or whatever the local inflated currency was called. For an instant he regarded me in astonishment, then shrugging his shoulders and looking up at the heavens, shouted (in an accent which reminded me heartbreakingly of my grandfather's), "Look at him. He gives me good American money. I give him shitpaper, and he says thank you." At that point, I knew that I had still a goyish *kopf,* perhaps would never be a real Jew.

Nevertheless, quite as if I were one, I joined in conversations with those who were speaking about the persecution of "our people" by Russians and Ukrainians and Poles. As far as I can remember, however, we never talked about the atrocities inflicted by the Nazis on their fellows who had remained behind in the shtetl from which they had fled. Perhaps, once more like my grandfather, they could associate such murderous violence only with their traditional enemies, the Slavs, or maybe what was happening in a Europe in which they could no longer quite believe had remained for them as invisible and unreal as it was for me.

It became realer, however, once I had returned to America, where the full horror of the Holocaust was, I soon discovered, being relentlessly documented in print, on stage and screen, radio, and television. There was, therefore, no way in which I could avoid becoming aware not just of that horror but of the shame it triggered in me for having so long (deliberately? half deliberately?) remained unaware of it. My first response, though, to that belated awareness was not pity or terror, but rage: a blind rage directed at first not—consciously at least—at myself, but at all the people of Germany, living or dead. For a long while, I would scream at anyone who attempted, however innocently, to address me in German, "I do not speak the language of Hitler!" forgetting that it was also the language of Kafka, whose *The Castle* I had, at age seventeen, painfully read in the original, not knowing that it had already been translated into English.

That visceral, irrational anger was further exacerbated by the fact that a catastrophe which had been labeled in an instant cliché "unspeakable" was being not only spoken about everywhere, but packaged, hyped, and sold on the marketplace: Anne Frank's diary, for instance, becoming overnight a best-seller, and the Nuremberg trials translated almost immediately from the headlines to the movie screen. The motives of the publishers and producers were, quite obviously, crassly commercial, which was bad enough; but what prompted their paying audiences, both Jewish and gentile, was, I could not help feeling, something worse: on the one hand, a kind of sadomasochistic voyeurism, which they did not confess even to themselves; and on the other, a desire, which they have easily confessed, to assuage the guilt they suffered for their earlier blindness.

That covert relish of horror pornography I shared, as well as that guilt; plus the added shame of being, though a Jew, an unscathed survivor. Nonetheless, I stubbornly resisted seeing any of those films or reading any of those books, because, I told myself, the vicarious atonement they afforded was too easy, too cheap. I was afraid, moreover, that seeking in such secondhand fictions—only print on the pages or images on the screen, no matter how "true to life"—a substitute for the experience I had never really shared would make that experience for me not more but less "real." For similar reasons, I also refused to confront the killers of my people (of my family that had remained in Europe, I learned on my return, not a single member had survived) on their own home grounds.

Before the war, whenever I mentioned going to the Old Country, my grandfather would observe scornfully, "The dog returning to his vomit," and so I never had. But even when in the early fifties I did make the voyage back, eventually living in Europe for two years, I still did not venture into Germany or Poland. Some ten years later, however, convinced that my reluctance was foolishly perverse, I began lecturing and attending literary conferences in Münster and Würtzburg, Heidelberg and Berlin, finally even Munich, the very heart of Hitlerdom. Inevitably, I was asked by the German academics I encountered, their guilts obviously deeper than mine, "Why did we do it? Only we Germans could have done it, no?"; to which I was able to answer at that point, almost, almost believing it, "If you could have done it, *anyone* could."

In smugly, offensively prosperous Munich, however, my rage was kindled once more, so that crying out (as my ancestors had for generations), "Why do the wicked prosper?" I fled to nearby Dachau. It was not tearful compassion or nauseated revulsion I experienced, however, visiting my first and last concentration camp; only a sense of anticlimax, so nearly comical that I came close to laughing out loud. The spankingly trim barracks and gas chambers, I soon discovered, were not the originals, where real Jews had really bled and died; but a scrupulously reconstructed ersatz—like the restorations of bombed-out medieval churches at which I had gawked earlier. Finally, in the midst of giggling schoolchildren, shepherded by grimly serious teachers, and bored sightseers just off the bus, I felt myself not a pilgrim to a place of martyrdom but a tourist in some horrific Disneyland.

Consequently, I returned with actual relief to the Munich Conference on Post-Modernism from which I had been playing hooky; though once back, I endured the indignity, as I had everywhere in Germany, of being regarded not just as a representative American but as a token Jew. And why not, after all, since —however problematical my Jewishness may have seemed to me —it is as a Jewish American spokesman for the Jewish American Renaissance of the fifties and sixties that I have been invited to speak almost everywhere on the face of the globe over the past two or three decades. During those exhilarating years gentile readers in Italy and France, India, Japan and Korea, particularly the younger ones, had been reading Saul Bellow and Bernard Malamud, Allen Ginsberg and Philip Roth in preference to writers in their own languages—feeling somehow that they spoke more directly to them. And they called on critics like me to explain to them why—assuming of course that, like those writers, I was a Jew. Nor did I refuse to play that part.

But I have had a little more difficulty maintaining that role when those who call upon me to bear witness are Jewish themselves. The first time, for instance, that I ever visited Israel was as a participant in a symposium of Jewish writers, American and

Israeli; at the end of which David Ben-Gurion himself urged me to make aliyah. Not only was my life in exile inauthentic, unreal, the then prime minister told me, but "unless more Jews like you return," he went on to explain, "*they* will outnumber *us.*" It was clear that by "*they*" he meant the Sephardim, the black Jews, and by "*us,*" the Ashkenazim, the white ones. Never in my life have I felt less like a Jew, black or white. Nonetheless, I have gone back to Israel five or six times over the years since, only to leave each time further confused and dismayed.

On my latest visit, for example, without quite realizing that it was the Sabbath, I stood outside my hotel to watch Jerusalem turn golden under the setting sun and to smoke a farewell cigar in peaceful meditation. My peace did not last long, however; since almost instantly a group of ultra-Orthodox zealots gathered together across the road to scream Hebrew imprecations at my blasphemy; to which I screamed back, "Don't worship idols!"—unsure whether this made me more or less Jewish than they. In any case, they understood my English as little as I did their Hebrew, which made it all a sort of bad joke.

My other close encounter with the ultra-Orthodox, however, was no joke, good or bad, though it too exacerbated my life-long identity crisis. I had been invited in the early seventies to a private audience with the Lubavitcher rebbe, who, it was evident from the first, assumed that I was a Jew. Certainly, it was as a Jew that he gave me his message, which was "The house is burning. Save the children!" Nonetheless, when he went on to ask me for my name, I was confused enough to answer "Leslie Fiedler"; and only after he had shaken his head rather ruefully, did I confess that my Hebrew name was "Eliezar," my mother's in the same tongue "Leah"—that I was, therefore, as he understood reality, really, *really* Eliezar ben Leah. Under that name, at any rate, he promised to ask a blessing for me when he next talked to his predecessor, who had been dead for twenty years.

I was not churlish enough to say, though I could not help feeling, that I, Leslie Fiedler once more, believed in no blessings from beyond the grave; and that in any case I needed no such blessing, since I had already been blessed by the living: by the gentiles among whom I have made my career. Like him, they had assumed I was a Jew, and seeking to make amends for the

Holocaust, they have opened up to me—along with other Jewish Americans of my generation—academic posts and cultural distinctions, access to which had earlier been barred to those descended from the Killers of Christ. I have, that is to say, profited from a philo-Semitism as undiscriminating as the anti-Semitism in reaction to which it originated. And to make matters worse, I have shamelessly played the role in which I have been cast, becoming a literary Fiedler on the roof of academe.

But in what sense, though, am I really the representative Jew for which I have been taken, I have long asked myself, and ask myself still at age seventy-plus. "It's hard to be a Jew," my grandfather used to tell me; and from childhood on I have taken this to be an essential aspect of Jewish identity. For me, however, after that single scare of my childhood, it has all been only too easy. Ever since, anti-Semitism has been something I read about in the papers, what happens to someone else. Even in this negative sense, therefore, I can lay no claim to being really Jewish; and even less can I lay a positive one, being bereft of all *yiddishkeit* and almost entirely ignorant of rabbinic lore. What I know of the Five Books of Moses I know in King James English. Indeed, English is not just my *mama-loshen* but my *lashon-ha-kodish* as well. My Holy Books, though no longer *Das Kapital* and *What Is to Be Done?* as in my youth, or *The Waste Land* and *The Golden Bowl* as in my early manhood, are in my declining years not the Torah and Talmud but *Huckleberry Finn* and the Collected Plays of Shakespeare.

Moreover, I have never in my life put on *tefellin* or attached a mezuzah to the doorposts of my house. Nor have I ever joined a Jewish congregation or fraternal order. In this, to be sure, I am like my father and grandfather, who also rejected all outward signs and symbols of Jewish belonging. In fact, the only religiously observant member of my family whom I ever knew was my paternal great-grandfather, the first of my seed to have been buried in American soil. I had met him, however, only once or twice (neither of us understanding the language of the other) before his funeral, where an equally pious friend of his delivered —in their language, not mine—a graveside sermon which set the mourners to weeping and screaming.

What they were crying and screaming about, however, I did

not learn until much later, when an aunt interpreted for me. What Grandpa's friend had said, she explained, was that he had suffered the worst indignity a good Jewish father could endure, seeing some of his children die before him, and this was because he had permitted those doubly accursed children to abandon their ancestral faith in the heathen New World. That they had indeed abandoned that faith became ever more evident as the years passed. The funeral service, for instance, of my father's only brother, who had married not one but two shiksas, was held in a Methodist Church; and his son's sons do not even know that their ancestors are Jews. Small wonder then that the children and grandchildren of my brother, who has long since become a Lutheran, are similarly ignorant of their roots.

Moreover, not a single one of my own eight children has at the present moment a Jewish mate; nor, for that matter, do I. Most of those kids, it is true, still think of themselves as in some vestigial sense Jews. But of my six grandsons only three have been circumcised—and one of those primarily because such ritual wounding is a part of the ancestral traditions of his Ashanti father. In any case, there is no one to say Kaddish for me when I die. I am, in short, not just as I have long known, a minimal Jew—my Judaism approaching degree zero—but, as I have only recently become aware, a terminal one as well, the last of a four-thousand-year line. Yet whatever regrets I may feel, I cannot deny that I have wanted this, worked for it. From childhood on, I dreamed of a world without ethnic or religious divisions, though I knew that this meant a world without Jews.

What I did not suspect was that, ironically, in my lifetime half of that dream would begin to come true; reminding me of an aphorism of Goethe I should not have forgotten: "Be careful of what you wish for in your youth because you will get it in your old age." What I have lived to see is a world in which even as sectarianism and anti-Semitic violence flourish in certain gentile communities, an ever larger segment of Jewry is losing its ethnic identity. Such attrition through intermarriage and assimilation has not, of course, been confined only to my own family —or even just to the United States, in which we are far from atypical. It is evident wherever large numbers of Jews continue to live in exile: particularly, perhaps, in England and the Commonwealth nations, but also throughout Western Europe, South America, and the Soviet Union, where *refuseniks* are the exception rather than the rule.

But none of this excuses my own complicity in what those who deplore it most (those observant Jews who feel threatened and defensive) call with deliberate malice "the Silent Holocaust." That pejorative epithet I cannot help resenting, preferring neutral terms like "acculturation" or "assimilation"—even "apostasy." Finally, however, I must grant that the implicit comparison of the "Final Solution" which I have abetted to Hitler's is hyperbolic perhaps, but not entirely unjustified. Both propose, that is to say, an end to a separate Jewish identity, whether defined racially, religiously, or culturally.

To be sure, our "Holocaust" is not imposed from without by brute force but freely chosen. Moreover, it is not motivated by hatred (not even self-hatred, as is sometimes charged) but by love: a love of all humanity, including those who have long persecuted us. Finally, we unreconstructed assimilationists unlike the Nazis seek not to obliterate along with their bodies the very memory of the Jews, but rather to memorialize in honor the last choice of the Chosen People: their decision to cease to exist in their chosenness for the sake of a united mankind. Still in all, it cannot be denied that the future we have dreamed is, like that foreseen for the Thousand Year Reign, Judenrein. It is for this reason that I have found it impossible to reflect self-righteously on the Holocaust, which left me unscathed, without alluding uneasily to that other which has left me feeling like a Last Jew.

Nonetheless, Last Jew that I am, I cannot resist confessing in conclusion, that each autumn, though I do not, of course, go to shul, I dutifully observe the Fast of Yom Kippur. So, too, each winter, I light the lights of Hanukkah, more often than not beside an already lighted Christmas tree. And each spring, after dyeing Easter eggs, I gather my family together for a Passover Seder—crying out to the God in whom I do not think I believe, "Pour out your wrath upon the goyim. . . ." My children somehow do not ever ask me why, perhaps because they are sure they already know. If they did ask, however, I would say to them, as my grandfather said to me, sneaking off to some storefront synagogue on the High Holidays, "Not because I believe, but so you should remember."

I remember.

The Bough Breaks

LORE SEGAL

INTIMATIONS

"Ring a round o' rosies" sings our nursery rhyme, and it adds "ashes, ashes, we all fall down." Watch out for the hidden terror in the lullaby—

> *Rock a-bye baby*
> *in the treetop.*
> *When the wind blows*
> *the cradle will rock.*
> *When the bough breaks*
> *the cradle will fall*
> *Down will come baby*
> *cradle and all*

—the baby, the cradle, the bough, the whole tree comes down, and the mommy and daddy, the grandparents, and all the aunts and cousins, they all fall down. Ashes! Ashes!

I recall the family breakfast when my father refused to hear the preliminary creaking of that bough.

"Did you read this, Igo?" my Uncle Paul asked at dinner in the autumn of 1937. "Another speech and Hitler can put Austria in his pocket. I know the university; it's ninety per cent Nazi."

"A lot of Socialist propaganda," said my father.

My mother's brother Paul, who lived with us in Vienna and was twenty-six, a medical student, and generally avant-garde in his thinking, liked taking extreme positions in order to prick my father, who was forty-two and an accountant, to his predictable platitudes.

"You're talking about a handful of lunatics," said my father.

"We Jews are a remarkable people," Paul said. "Our neighbor tells us he's getting his gun out for us, and we sit watching him polish and load it and train it at our heads and we say, 'He doesn't really mean us.' "

"So what should we do? Go and hide in the cellar every time some raving lunatic in Germany makes a speech?"

"We should pack our rucksacks and get out of this country, that's what we should do," Paul said.

"And go to the jungle, I suppose, and live off coconuts. According to your brother, Franzi," my father said to my mother, "every time a raving lunatic in Germany makes a speech, we should go and live off coconuts in the jungle."

"Is it going to be war?" I asked my mother, aside. I had a sick feeling in my stomach. I knew about the First World War. I had a recurring nightmare about my mother and me sitting in a cellar with tennis rackets, repelling the bullets that kept coming in through a horizontal slit of window.

"No, no, no. Nothing like that," my mother said.

I tried to imagine some calamity but did not know how. My mother was ringing the bell for Poldi, the maid, to bring coffee. I decided there must not, there could not, be anything so horrible that we would have to pack and leave everything. I stopped listening to the grown-ups.

On the eighth of the following March, I had my tenth birthday. On the twelfth, Hitler took Austria.

from *Other People's Houses*, pp. 3–4

Shall we blame my father, who chose to quarrel with my Uncle Paul instead of packing our rucksacks? And how was it that Uncle Paul did not pack up and get out of the country while that was an option?

Remember Lot. It took three of the Lord's messengers to mobilize Lot. "If you have kinfolk in the city," they said to him, "sons-in-law or sons or daughters, get them out of town. Lot went out and said to his sons-in-law, Quick! Leave the city! The Lord is going to destroy it. Lot's sons-in-law thought he was joking." And what does Lot himself do? Does he hurry to pack his rucksack? The Book knows our human hearts. "When morning came, the angels of the Lord tried to hurry Lot and said, Quick, take your wife and the two daughters who live with you, or you will be destroyed. . . . Still Lot hung back, so the men took him by the hand and took the hands of his wife and his two daughters . . . and led them away and did not let go of them until they were outside the gates. . . ."

Reader, how quick will you or I be to look our next calamity in the eye? Here's an exercise for us: Regard the rucksack. Now look at all the stuff we can't pack into it—our backyard, our friendly old bed, and our brand-new tennis racket; the season ticket and our next year's vacation that is all paid up. Our savings, our promotion, and the annuity for our old age; the language in which we make our living and in which we understand ourselves and speak to our friends. We will have to leave our friends and our aunts and cousins and our mother and our father. Now, it seems to me, *after* we have imagined my father at that moment, in that situation, and have pitied him, I think that we must blame him. Nor did any messengers from the Lord come to take him by the hand.

My own childish denial was to think "it can't happen because that would be too terrible." I wonder if that familiar formulation comes as readily to the post-Auschwitz, the post-Hiroshima generation, which has historical evidence that the gun into the barrel of which we are staring can go off in our faces, and does.

ANSCHLUSS

Early in the morning after events of March 12 . . .

> my parents took me downstairs and we stood in a long line of people outside the bank at the corner; the bank did not open. All around us in the street were young men in strange, brand-new uniforms, saluting each other with right arms stretched forward. It was a clear, sunny March morning. Bright new flags were flying, but my parents hurried me . . . home. [p. 4]

At school the teacher

> announced that instead of poetry we would have an hour of handicrafts and would take down the pro-Austrian anti-German post-

ers . . . we had been made to paste and pin around the school room walls. . . . By the end of the week, the desks in our room had been rearranged so that the half-dozen Jewish children in the class could sit together in the rear with two empty rows between us and the Aryans in front. . . . [Then] the Jewish children . . . were assigned to a separate classroom. We knew very well that no teacher wanted to teach Jewish classes. . . . I remember the teacher who came into our . . . room. . . . She was a soft-faced, stout young woman and her eyes were red. We stood up to greet her with the awe of children in the presence of a grown-up who [is] crying. . . . [Then] the school had been cleared of Aryans and the Jewish children and teachers had been brought in to make ours the Jewish school for the district. [pp. 15–16]

By May, Poldi, the maid, had to leave our Jewish employ. My father was given a month's notice at the bank where he had worked as chief accountant for twelve years. A week later, an S.S. sergeant commandeered our . . . flat and all its furnishings, including my mother's . . . . piano. [p. 5]

FISCHAMEND

My mother and father and I moved out to Fischamend, a village some half hour from Vienna and not far from the Czechoslovak border, where my grandparents owned a house and haberdasher's shop. I loved Fischamend, especially after my Uncle Paul arrived from Vienna. His left ear was dangling. The Jewish students had got into a fight with the Nazis at the university and that was the end of Paul's medical career. One night there

appeared in the street outside the entrance of the shop, letters tall as a man, painted in white on the macadam: KAUFT NICHT BEIM JUDEN (Don't buy from the Jews).
"The local boys," my father said.
The following morning, the front of our house had "Jew" and dirty words written in red paint all over it. The bloody color was still wet and dripping down the stone when my grandfather went out to take the shutters down. He washed it off—the letters disappeared slowly but the color blotched the wall. [pp. 10 and 13]

It was perhaps a week later. My grandparents, my parents, Paul, and I were sitting in the room over the store.

"Pst!" said my father, who happened to be facing the south windows and saw the heads appearing above the sill. We looked around. There were heads in the two west windows, also. Beneath the second-story windows, a narrow corrugated-iron ledge jutted out over the lower floor like a little roof. Ladders had been put against the ledge, and boys and girls from the village, still in their uniforms, had climbed up and were sitting in our windows. They stayed all night. Now and then, one of the boys would swing his legs over the sill and step into the room with us. There were some books they didn't approve of, and possessions they did, and they carried everything portable away.

The next day, the shop remained closed. The family sat around the dining-room table. I remember sitting under the table, playing with their shoelaces and listening: It was clear that we must leave Fischamend. . . . The villagers stood in the street, throwing stones against the upstairs windows until they were all smashed. . . .

Around dusk, the S.S. boys came and took the three men to the police station next door. My mother and grandmother waited in the room where I slept, leaning out of the empty window frame. My bed was pushed against the inside wall and barricaded with a mattress. All night, even while I slept, it seems to me that I heard the two women's voices speaking softly in the darkness.

At some point, I was awake, and knew that the men were back. I don't know how I know that my father had been slapped and that his glasses had been knocked off and broken. I have a vivid and quite false memory of this brutality, as if I had been a witness. [pp. 18–19]

The Nazis gave us twenty-four hours to leave Fischamend and we returned to Vienna without a roof over our heads. My parents took me to the apartment of a schoolmate, Ditta Adler, and went to find themselves a place to live. Jewish apartments, in those days, were infinitely expandable to accommodate the newly homeless. By nightfall everybody had been stowed with friends or relations.

I remember it as a central worry during the terror of the next weeks that I didn't know my parents' address. My mind's eye had no information about the placement of the walls or the arrangement of the furniture of whatever place they might be in, so that I could not imagine them in any place. I think I doubted their being somewhere.

> I have been told that people who are hungry can talk of nothing but food. In 1938, in Vienna, Jews talked endlessly about ways of getting out of the country.
>
> The men went out mornings, as punctually as they had once

left for business, to make the rounds of the consulates. One day when I was off from school, I went with my father. He met a friend and stopped to talk. The friend said he had heard something was doing in the Swiss Consulate and he was going over to put his name on the list. I had caught sight of one of those small flat boxes that had recently been attached to houses at street corners, where, behind chicken wire, pages of the newspaper *Der Stürmer* were fixed open for the public to read. . . . I inched over and looked through the chicken wire. There was a picture of an old [Jewish] man with monstrous lips, and another of a very fat [Jewish] woman standing with her feet planted grossly wide apart, but I had no time to make anything of it before my father came and hustled me away. "Where are we going?" I said, embarrassed to have been caught peeping.

"To the Swiss Consulate," he said. "To put our names on a list."

When not sitting in the waiting rooms of consulates and embassies, everybody was going to the classes that had sprung up all over the city. Jewish professionals were scurrying to learn hand skills, to feed themselves and their families in countries whose languages they would not know. My father . . . learned machine knitting and leatherwork. The sad little purses and wallets he made turned up in our luggage for years. My mother learned large-quantity cooking. She took a course in massage. [pp. 20–21]

She practiced on me. Another day I went with my father to the American Consulate. The queue stretched down the stairs, out the door, down the street, and around the block. I remember a couple of downy-faced Hitler Youth watching from the other sidewalk. My father got our names put on the "American quota." The quota system limited the yearly number of immigrants to the United States according to the applicant's country of birth and the number of nationals from that country who had entered the United States in the year 1924. My grandparents' Hungarian number came through in 1950 and our Austrian number a year later. By that time we had emigrated to England, where my father died, thence to the Dominican Republic, where my Uncle Paul's pregnant young wife and my grandfather lie buried. By then, though we did not know it at the time, eleven of my grandmother's fourteen brothers and sisters and their spouses had been killed in the concentration camps.

KRISTALLNACHT

On November 10th, a Jew named Grüspan assassinated a minor Nazi official on a diplomatic mission to Paris. When the news reached Vienna in the afternoon, school was dismissed. We were told to go home by the back roads. The grown-ups sat beside the radio all afternoon. Toward evening, the doorbell rang, and outside stood an elderly neighbor from across the hall, and his wife, and an immense mahogany sideboard, which they were being made to move into our flat. A couple of uniformed Nazis stood along the banisters. They said to get on with the sideboard, there was more coming. In the course of that night, they forced the five Jewish families in the apartment house to move themselves and their households into our three-room, fifth-floor apartment. The rooms soon had the grotesque look of usual objects in unusual positions: chairs stacked high on wardrobes, a table upside down on the bed with china, books, and lamps between its legs. The wife of the elderly neighbor sat on a chair crying, in a thin voice, without intermission. The Nazis became playful. They had discovered the main switch and kept turning the lights off, sometimes for as long as half an hour, then off and on, and off and on. Into the middle of this walked my friend's mother's brother, hoping to hide out because his own apartment was being raided, but he was intercepted and taken away to a concentration camp. My friend's mother stood in the doorway and wept. All night, the heavy baroque furniture bumped on the stairs, and squeaked over the tiles of the hall. I sat down and howled for my mother. [p. 22]

The following day nobody went out. The children stayed home from school. I remember the open bed in the living room and a man who walked around in his pajamas. My memory cannot fill in the place where he must have had a face, but I see the pajamas. Every time the doorbell rang the man in the pajamas got quickly into the bed and made as if he were asleep. We children understood that he was meant to seem too ill for the Nazis to take him away. I remember my awe at the deception and my horror at the powerlessness of the grown-ups to prevent the world from walking into their apartment. I understood that world to be inimical and malicious and tried to picture my mother and my father out there, somewhere, in it. There is a line of Emily Dickinson's that describes a boy's perception that he is in the presence of the snake: zero at the bone. From Kristallnacht onward we lived with zero at the bone.

I remember the day drawing to an end. I sat on the sofa next to the man in pajamas, who was playing chess with a young boy. I looked toward the window where the November sky behind the gray apartment houses grayed imperceptibly into darkness. I remember yearning for the drama of a sunset, for a sign, an earnest of salvation. I remember imagining how on the far side of the world there were people sitting, this very moment, in rooms, on sofas, who were not imagining what was happening to us here.

EMIGRATION

When I read or remember a date between 1939 and 1945, say, of a wedding I attended, or a graduation, or an outing, or a movie I saw, there superimposes itself on the recollection of the event an attempt to imagine some particular anguish, some terror, some death that might, at that same moment, have been suffered, by my Onkel Max, on whose lap I used to sit, or his wife, fat, beautiful Tante Frieda, who had brought out her stereopticon when she saw me getting sleepy from the grown-ups' jokes and laughter at her Sunday afternoon get-togethers at her apartment in the days before Hitler.

In December 1938 my father heard of an experimental children's transport—a test to see if the Nazis would allow a trainload of six hundred Jewish children to cross the border. My mother has told me that she argued for my staying in Vienna—for our living or dying together. She says that the determination to send me to safety was my father's. She says that afterward, when they got home from the station, he went to bed and lay as stiff as a ramrod for two days. When my daughter, Beatrice, was ten years old I used to watch her walking across a room and imagine sending her to another country, with no address.

My father had come to pick me up from Ditta's and we took the tram to Vienna's chief temple. It had been burned out on Kristallnacht. What looked to me like thousands of children and their parents milled around the gutted ground floor where the men used to sit. The queue inched around the women's gallery and up the stairs. I heard my name called and my father and I stepped out of the line: My mother had a cousin who had a girlfriend who worked in the offices of the *Jüdische Kultus Gemeinde*—the Jewish Cultural Community. We were conducted into her office, where she processed my papers.

Yes, I wonder, once in a while, whose life I have usurped.

> In the streetcar going home, my father held my hand. He said, "So you will be going to England."
>
> I said, "All by myself?" and I remember clearly the sensation, as if my insides had been suddenly scooped away. At the same time I felt that this "going to England" had a brave sound.
>
> "Not all by yourself!" my father said. "There will be six hundred other children."
>
> "When am I going?" I asked.
>
> "Thursday," said my father. "The day after tomorrow."
>
> Then I felt the icy chill just below my chest where my insides had been.

I have a friend who was born in England. His American father died suddenly. The young widow sent the older, ten-year-old son, to his American grandmother. He and I discovered that we had used the same survival trick: Both of us had, in effect, said to ourselves, What a lark! I remember that

> . . . we got into a tram. Across the aisle there was another little Jewish girl with a rucksack and a suitcase, sitting between her parents. I tried to catch her eye in order to flirt up a new friend for myself, but she took no notice of me. She was crying. I said to my mother, "I'm not crying like that little girl."
>
> My mother said, "No, you are being very good, very brave. I'm proud how good you are being." [p. 29]

But I suspected myself then, and for decades to come, of being a species of monster.

> The assembly point was a huge empty lot behind the railway station in the outskirts of Vienna. I looked among the hundreds of children milling in the darkness for the girl who had cried in the tram, but I never saw her again, or . . . did not recognize her. . . . Someone came over to me and checked my papers and . . . hung a cardboard label with the number 152 strung on a shoelace around my neck and tied the corresponding numbers to my . . . rucksack. . . . I have no clear recollection of my father's being there—perhaps his head was too high and out of the circle of lights. I do remember his greatcoat standing next to my mother's black pony fur, but every time I looked toward them it was my

mother's tiny face, crumpled and feverish inside her fox collar, that I saw smiling steadily toward me.

We were arranged in a long column four deep, according to numbers. The rucksack was strapped on my back. There was a confusion of kissing parents—my father bending down, my mother's face burning against mine. . . . the line set in motion. . . . Panic-stricken, I looked to the right, but my mother was there . . . keeping at my side, and she was smiling so that it seemed a gay thing, like a joke we were having together. . . . The children behind me said, "Go on, move!" . . . We were passing through the great doors. I looked to my right; my mother . . . was nowhere to be seen. [pp. 29–30]

One hundred of the six hundred children on our transport that December 10, 1938, got out in Holland, where the German Occupation overtook them two years later.

I remember seeing them ranged on the platform—the smallest, who was four years old, in front, the big ones in back. . . . [p. 24]

The rest of us crossed the Channel to England.

Inside the ship . . . I had a neat cabin all to myself. I folded my dress and stockings with fanatical tidiness and brushed my teeth to appease my absent mother. . . . I lay between white sheets in a narrow bed . . . and prayed God to keep me from getting seasick and my parents from getting arrested. . . . A big Negro steward came in with a steaming cup, which he placed in a metal ring attached to the bedside table. . . . I searched my mind quickly for something . . . to say to keep him with me. I asked him if he thought I was going to get seasick. He said no, the thing was to lie down and go right to sleep and wake up on the other side of the Channel in the morning. And then he put the light out and said, "Remember now, you sleep now." [p. 34]

That was fifty years ago. Once—is it every few years?—I remember the big black man. I could tell that he could tell that I was scared. He talked with me. He leaned toward me and promised me I wouldn't throw up.

We were taken to a workers' summer camp at Dover Court on England's east coast that coldest winter in living memory. For days on end the snow drifted through the air inside the great glass-and-iron dining hall. They installed stoves. We sat around and waited for the English families who were to come and take us home with them. I wore my coat and mittens and executed my first intentional piece of "writing." It was a tear-jerking letter full of sunsets. I sent it to the addresses of a refugee committee that my father had given me, and my letter moved them to procure the job, the sponsor, and the visa that brought my parents to England, proving that bad literature makes things happen.

> One evening I was sitting by one of the stoves, writing a letter to my parents, when two English ladies came up to me. One of them carried a pad of paper, and she said, "How about this one?", and the other lady said, "All right." They smiled at me. They asked my name and age and I told them. They said I spoke English very nicely. I beamed. They asked me if I was Orthodox. I said yes. They were pleased. They said then would I like to come and live with a lovely Orthodox family in Liverpool. I said yes enthusiastically, and we all three beamed at one another. I asked the ladies if they would find a sponsor for my parents, and watched them exchange glances. One lady patted my head and said we would see. I said and could they get a sponsor for my grandparents and for my cousins Erica and Ilse, who had not been able to come on the children's transport like me. The ladies' smiles became strained. They said we would talk about it later.
>
> I finished my letter to my parents, saying that I was going to go and live with this lovely Orthodox family in Liverpool and would they please write and tell me what did "Orthodox" mean. [p. 46]

OTHER PEOPLE'S HOUSES

I was one of twenty little girls who were brought north for distribution to Liverpool families. I kept my eye on the large woman in a prickly fur coat and hoped she wouldn't pick me, but she did. I had to go with her to a big house with a lot of lights, and women running up and down the stairs. A little man sat by a fire in a square hole in the wall. He had tiny eyes behind the multiple rings of his thick glasses. He pulled out a footstool for me to sit on. He gave me a sixpence. I think Mr. Cohen and I made each other shy. The youngest of the Cohen daughters, sixteen-year-old Ruth, was a generous, clever, spirited girl driven out of all patience with her five dull sisters. I was amazed at the way she dared yell at her parents, but she took an interest in me and paid me attention. I was grateful and loved her.

And I did my second piece of writing: Here I was on that other side of the world for which I had yearned out of the window in Vienna, that gray dusk, the day after Kristallnacht, and it seemed to me that the people here were not properly imagining what was going on in Vienna and what might be happening to my parents.

I bought one of those old schoolbooks with purple covers and a white label with a red border in which English schoolchildren do their homework, and I filled it from front to back with my Hitler stories. It was my first experience of the writer's chronic grief that what was getting down on paper was not right, was not all that there was to say. As poor J. Alfred Prufrock puts it, "That is not it at all. That is not what I meant, at all," and so I added several sunsets. Ruth got someone to translate it into English. I observed with interest that it made Mrs. Cohen cry.

My parents arrived in Liverpool on my eleventh birthday en route to their job in the south. England was suffering a shortage of domestics and my mother and father came as a "married couple," that is to say, as cook and butler.

I visited them in the summer holidays, during which time the Cohens found an ailing aunt who needed their care and made it impossible to have me back. Wouldn't I perhaps like to stay with my parents in Kent?

I called my book *Other People's Houses*. Between my tenth year, when I came to England with the children's transport, until I went to the University of London at eighteen, I lived in five different families up and down England's class system and across its geography. Since the cook and butler could not have a live-in child, the Church Committee for Jewish Refugees found me a home in nearby Tonbridge. Mr. Gilham was a railroad stoker, a union man, and a Socialist. When the younger daughter, Marie, got a scholarship to the local private school, she turned it down as a betrayal of her class. When I got it I went and the Gilhams found a blind cousin who needed their care. The Refugee Committee placed me with the family of a munitions worker, whose name I do not remember. I remember that his wife had a bland round forehead and that the youngest boy set the bathroom curtains on fire. When they moved to the factory town of Croydon, I went to live with her parents, who were called Foster. The old man was a milkroundsman with a little cart and horse. Mrs. Foster had beautiful white hair. They lived in a sooty row house across from the railroad. You stepped up a clean white step into the parlor, behind which lay the kitchen, through which you passed into the yard, which the sons were digging up for a bomb shelter. There seemed to me an unusual number of young males, including one smart-ass evacuee from the blitz, which was raging over London. The young men shared the front bedroom, and I got the room in back which belonged to the elderly daughter, Ruby, who worked as a lady's maid across town; on her days off she had to sleep at the neighbor's.

THE WAR

Early in 1940 my father and Uncle Paul and all male German-speakers over sixteen had been interned on the Isle of Man. Now Kent was designated a "protected area" out of bounds to all "enemy aliens."

I was twelve. When my mother and I arrived in the ancient market town of Guildford in Surrey, I was throwing up. Between bouts, I lay on a bed in a narrow room at the head of a steep stair and my mother read me *David Copperfield* and the concept "writer" burst upon me and I knew that that's what I was going to be. Come to think of it, I had *been* writing since I was ten.

This was also the day when my father suffered a first and minor stroke. The authorities must have taken a look at him, figured what a nuisance a sick inmate would be in the camp and that he didn't look much of a threat to England's war effort, and they sent him "home." My father arrived in Guildford with our temporary address on a piece of paper. The policeman whom he approached for directions, arrested him for being out after curfew, took him to the police station, and booked him. Then he put my father in a police car and drove him to the house with the steep stairs. All night I kept waking from a nauseous sleep and saw my parents sitting together on the edge of the other bed, talking. I saw my father cry.

The Guildford Refugee Committee lady was called Miss Wallace. She found my father a job as a gardener where he gardened until his next stroke. She got my mother a job as a cook and took me home to live with her and her older companion, Miss Ellis, in a grand Victorian house with plum trees, gooseberry and currant bushes, a rockery, and a rose garden.

Do I sound snide about my foster families? The fact is that they were not particularly warm or imaginative or sympathetic. Except for Ruth Cohen in Liverpool and Miss Wallace in Guildford, I did not love them. They did not love me. The fact is, also, that I was not a particularly lovable child. I leveled a critical eye at my benefactors. At night I wet my bed. I'm astonished—I am moved—that all these people took me in, that they housed me, fed me, clothed me, and looked after me for as long as they could stand me. Needy children abound. How many of us will take a small prickly alien to live in our inmost home? I have not done so.

Miss Ellis and Miss Wallace kept me from my twelfth till my eighteenth year. Miss Wallace paid for my piano lessons. Miss Ellis bought me a green silk dress to wear evenings in the elegant drawing room. Here is a tableau in which I have described them:

> Miss W., whose girlhood was spent in Heidelberg, Germany, studying voice, sits at the piano giving us a little uneven Schubert until the 9 o'clock news. We cheer the number of Germans our boys have downed that day; Stalingrad is holding out. We sit reflected and miniaturized in the circular convex mirror that hangs over the fireplace—the two elderly Church of England spinsters in long velvet gowns, and the 13-year-old in skimpy green silk.
>
> We don't read—not in the evenings; it would be unsociable. Miss W. holds the old gray cat, Caro, on her gentle lap and embroiders hollyhocks along the border of a white linen bedspread.
>
> Miss E. is a harsh, aristocratic old woman, with a lump the size of a teaspoon on her scalp under the thin white hair. She looks like a female impersonator. She hires maids with illegitimate babies and plays with the babies and underpays the maids. Miss E. has sent me for her sewing box. She is cutting an old linen sheet into squares into which she stitches wads of cotton wool. Miss E. is sewing the Jewish refugee from Vienna a first set of sanitary napkins.

> *The New York Times*, "Hers" column, December 3, 1987

A CONCLUSION

When I came to New York in 1951 I went to the New School and took a class in "creative writing." I couldn't think of what to write about. My Holocaust experience, it seemed, was already public knowledge. I read it in the papers and saw it on the news in the movies. It was at a party that somebody asked me a question to which the answer was an account of the children's transport that had brought me to England. It was my first experience of the peculiar silence of a roomful of people listening to what you are telling them. And so I understood that I had a story to tell.

It took me six years to write *Other People's Houses*. I was at pains to draw no facile conclusions—and all conclusions seemed, and seem, facile. I want not to be able to trace the origin and processes by which the past produces the present. The novelist's mode suits me—I posit myself as protagonist in the autobiographical action.

Well, then, I'm a tough enough old bird, of the species survivor, naturalized not in North America so much as in New York, in Manhattan, on Riverside Drive. The place fits me. There are things that make me happy.

But I keep out of the movies. I've sat next to friends as they cozy themselves into that communal darkness and assume their pleasure in what I experience as an acutely disagreeable sensation of suspense. Could a chemist analyze the bloodstream and isolate an additive that produces anxiety? Even nice suspense disagrees with me and I don't buy lottery tickets. I experience the calamities of my life as a palpable relief from the perennial expectation of calamity.

Reader, you say that I describe your very symptom exactly? You say you're anxious too and you were born in Westchester ten years after Hitler croaked in his bunker? Anxiety, you say, is not the prerogative of the refugee? I should hope not. The novelist does not claim peculiarity or singularity of experience. On the contrary, I depend on you to put your fellow feeling at the service of what I write. But what I write will not be suspenseful. I shy away from the strong event that leads to strong event, guaranteeing you an absence of plot and myself that I'll not be a good read.

As a reader I'm fascinated by representations of the intimations of disaster: Giraudoux's *Tiger at the Gates* opens with the Greeks returning from battle. We sit in on the negotiations between Greeks and Trojans trying to prevent the Trojan War, which, as the curtain falls, is about to happen. As a child, in art class, I remember painting Cassandra with wide eyes and screaming mouth because she had no companion in her knowledge of the destruction at hand. Max Frisch's *The Firebugs* has us watch a man open the door to two flamboyantly sinister characters who will not allow him not to understand that they have come to burn his house down. They make him invite them inside; he settles them into his attic and hands them the matches.

And there is the moment in Exodus when the foremen return from their interview with Pharaoh.

> On that same day Pharaoh summoned his slave drivers and said, From this day on don't give them straw to make the bricks. Let them collect their own straw, but make sure they make the same number of bricks they made yesterday. Don't let them get away with less. . . .
>
> The slave drivers went out and said, Pharaoh says, From now on I will not give you straw. Go gather your own straw. . . . And they beat the Hebrew foremen and said, Why haven't you made your daily quota of bricks that you have always made before?
>
> The Hebrew foremen went to Pharaoh and cried, What are you doing? It's your own people who won't give us the straw to make the bricks, and then they tell us to make our daily quota and beat us. . . .
>
> Pharaoh said . . . Go, get back to work. you'll get no straw, and you'll make the same number of bricks as you made yesterday!
>
> And now the Hebrew foremen saw how things stood and that a bad time was coming.
>
> *The Book of Adam and Moses*, p. 66

My own exodus gave a strength that exacted a price. Cut yourself off, at ten years old, from feelings that can't otherwise be mastered and it takes decades to become reattached.

Shall I claim that that's what makes me such an inappropriate and inefficient mourner? When my father died in 1945 it was a bleak October, a rough wind. I walked onto the Downs back of

Miss Ellis's house looking for tears that did not come till 1968, when David, my American husband, insisted—against my own wishes—that I owed myself a return to my childhood. I cried the whole week in Vienna. I cried at *Lulu* in the Staats Oper; I cried at dinner at the Hotel Sacher, where a man played the theme from *The Third Man* on a sentimental zither. "This is silly," I kept saying. "I'm not even feeling particularly sad," but I kept crying. David blew me the saliva bubbles with which he used to amuse our two children and made me laugh and then I cried. All through the Austrian Alps I cried and I cried and I cried. We had hired a car. David, who could look at the outside of an inn and know whether the wine would be good, would say, "Let's stay here," but I said, "Let's go on to St. Gilgen. There was a lovely lake where we spent my father's last vacation the summer before Hitler. There was a green house with a steep hill on the right." We drove to St. Gilgen and stayed in a chalet with flood-lit ivy and ate gray roast beef with the kind of gravy I remember from the Lyon House in postwar London.

I got up in the morning while David slept and went to look for the green house with the steep field. I remembered the contour of the mountain in back like a man with one shoulder higher than the other. But there was no lake. I turned around and walked in the other direction until a brand-new six-lane highway laid itself across my path. There were so many houses! Some fields were steeper than others. Mountains humped. Could the lake I remembered have been in Mallnitz, a different summer? And so my father continued dead.

And would that chemist be able to identify the cause of my sometimes inappropriate happiness—of euphoria. Is that, too, a displacement?

My Uncle Paul and I have compared the sense of double vision—the superimposition upon some present comfort of the images that have been or that might have been. I think we don't entirely settle into our good fortunes. My mother used regularly to visit her mother's youngest sister, Tante Poldi, in a nursing home in Queens. Tante Poldi died in her nineties and left my mother a couple of thousand dollars which were put in a savings bank. When the monthly statement comes, my mother says, "They have made a mistake," and goes down to the bank, lines up at the counter, and asks the officer to verify her account. The officer calls up the account on the computer; the account is correct. My mother comes home and says, "It's a mistake. I have made withdrawals. I *can't* have this much in the bank."

My mother is perfectly sophisticated and understands about interest. It is her past and her nerves that cannot accommodate the happiness of solvency.

I think I'm a latter-day Manichaean: I know the devil exists because I have seen his works and have been their victim. I have also seen goodness muddling alongside in Jew and in Christian and have been its beneficiary.

Politically I'm addicted to argumentation: I urge the Palestinian cause to my friends on the right, because they refuse to imagine it. I argue the Israeli case to my leftist friends because that's what *they* are refusing to imagine. Each believes I belong to the other side. I keep urging them to imagine each other.

It is the Kristallnacht in my head that so engrains everything I mean I've only lately diagnosed its presence. Let Ecclesiastes speak for me:

> And again I looked and saw all the oppressions that are done under the sun. I saw the tears of those who are oppressed, and that they have no comforter; power is on the side of the oppressor, but they have no comforter.
> Therefore I say that the dead, who have already died, do better than the living who are still alive.
> Yes, and better than both are they who have never been born and have not seen the evil business that is done under the sun.

This speaks to me and says that it is my business to imagine the oppressions that are done under the sun, particularly those which I am in a position to perpetrate.

As a writer it says that my business is to imagine you and to make you know me.

"In Childhood Begin Responsibilities . . ."

ALAN LELCHUK

At the age of thirteen, according to our tradition, one makes the transition to manhood and responsibility, but for me, maybe it happened five years earlier. I was eight, sitting in my Sholem Aleichem school in Brownsville, and I had been cutting up, as usual, when the Lehrer, Chaver Goichberg, had had enough. Growing red-faced with fury, he threw down his green *Geshichte* and came toward me. I trenched down in my seat, behind my small school desk. Finding my wrists, he began shaking and twisting me, declaring, "Enough now! You will not disrupt this classroom anymore, *fahrshtey?!*" As he twisted me this way and that, I caught sight of something curious on his wrist, what I suppose I had first taken to be a tattoo of sorts: little blue numbers. In my pain and confusion, those little blue numbers, five as I recall, registered in my consciousness, and I promised myself to find out what they signified. My teacher continued, "*Nu,* do you hear me? Decide now, whether you're going to behave," and here he gave me a sudden schlepp, "or whether you want to get right out of here now, and stay out!"

Although I nodded weakly, in blurry pain, I didn't really

hate him for embarrassing and hurting me because, inwardly, I respected and liked him, and knew that he felt the same way toward me. And we both knew that I could be a problem, a troublemaker. But as I sat in that dark basement shaking, trying, I think, to entice a noble sympathy from pretty chedermates Pesha and Golda, I wondered about those blue numbers, and promised myself to find out about them later on.

That night, over dinner, I asked my parents. My mother, usually a realist, waved her hand and shrugged and asked if I wanted the tender neck of the chicken. So I asked my father, who, using both knife and fork European-style, finished his bite and wiped his lips before answering.

"Goichberg was in a camp," he explained, "a concentration camp."

Now I knew about the prisoner-of-war camps of the Nazis and Japanese, but not this sort. "What are those?"

"Camps where the Nazis killed Jews," he explained, but when I asked him to continue, my mother said, "Not now, yeah? Not over dinner, please."

So afterward, in the small living room, I pursued the conversation and listened closely, though couldn't understand clearly, my father's words of explanation. That was the first time that I heard directly about those camps, and Hitler's solution. Oh, I had known vaguely earlier on, during the war—when I followed the Allies via Gabriel Heatter on the radio and *The New York Times*'s maps and stories sitting on Father's lap—that the Nazis were our enemies, that they hated the Jewish people especially. But until that day and night in 1948, I didn't really know what the Holocaust was.

Before sleeping, I pictured again those little blue numbers on my Lehrer's wrist, and tried to see him in one of those camps, along with all the other Jews from Poland, Russia, Germany, France, Holland. It was very difficult. I just couldn't figure out *how* they had killed all those people, or exactly *why*. Startled by that strange news and by my own lack of comprehension, I turned, I imagine, back to my own world, of the Dodgers and Jackie Robinson, and focused my fury on the open prejudice shown against him by the white players. That situation, that fierceness, that blue number, 42, I understood well.

In the ensuing days and weeks, I felt as if it were up to me to keep that secret about my Hebrew teacher, and I did. I suppose it also influenced my behavior, because Chaver Goichberg commended me for my improvement in class at one point. Of course I couldn't quite keep that up and was back to my usual antics by the end of the month. But when he came after me again, angry and red-faced, I felt strangely satisfied this time, rather happy that he was evincing such anger. I couldn't quite believe, or imagine perhaps, that this tall, firm, passionate man, whose prematurely white hair flew in a storm around his head when he blew his top, had, just a few years ago, been subjected to Nazi degradations. (Did his unclothed body, I wondered, show more signs like the wrist numbers?)

Although he couldn't know it, I grew closer to him because of my inside knowledge. I began to feel somewhat protective of him, despite my own shenanigans. It didn't hurt matters that I was a good student when I wanted to be, reading the short stories of Mendele and Peretz, Sholem Aleichem and I. J. and I. B. Singer, and giving book reports aloud in my somewhat fluent spoken Yiddish. Or knowing certain strands of Jewish history. Or playing the various Friday afternoon games with zeal and humor. So what if, taking breaks from my scholarly side, I cut up a bit and he had to scold me, at times severely?

Protective, I said, both inwardly and outwardly, let's say, as though I were his practical and spiritual bodyguard here in the New World.

For example, when the foolish parents of my friends mocked Goichberg and the Sholem Aleichem school for being Communist propaganda—since it was a creation of the Polish Bund, a socialist organization, and concentrated on Yiddish culture in the first three years rather than Hebrew and Torah—I stuck up for him and the school vehemently. (No matter that their sons felt bullied and brutalized at the local Talmud Torah school, and grew up considering Jewish culture as a vile obligation at best, a "greenhorn" intrusion at worst.) But in defending Chaver, I was not willing to inform the morons of what he had gone through, come through. Why should I let them have the easy way out, cheap sympathy?

I also sought to help him out when our classroom was hit by

those random attacks at the cheder's windows by the local gentile toughs. Standing at the first basement window, which overlooked Lehrer's large wooden desk and the front student desks, the teasing teenagers would rattle the window, throw objects at it, gesture, and shout obscenities. At first Chaver would ignore them, and proceed, but when they got out of hand, he'd brandish his fist, throw down his book, and race across the basement and outside, in pursuit. Well, after I knew about those blue numbers, I'd follow him outside, some five paces behind, into the garage driveway between brick homes. Usually, the "hard" guys would hustle away immediately, sighting the red-faced teacher storming after them, hair and tie flying. But one time they stayed put, the leader standing with his hands on his hips, four or five pals nearby, waiting to test the waters. Goichberg went right up the the leering tough, who started to wield a garrison belt only to have his arm bent back swiftly by Chaver, who ordered, "Drop it, son! C-o-m-e on!" Just then I saw one of his comrades suddenly cock his arm, and I yelled, "Duck!" as a stone went flying past the teacher. He simply shook his head, in dismay, and suddenly lunged at the boy, capturing his arm, and holding his face close, advised carefully, "If you ever try that again, ever dare to pick up a stone and throw it, you'll be sorry, very sorry, you, and your bully-pals," a declaration of such sure, quiet solemnity that it stunned me as well as that boy. (In later years I found that shock of fear in the opening pages of *Great Expectations,* where the criminal Magwitch rises from the marshes to terrify Pip.)

Walking back toward the basement, he put his arm around me and patted my shoulder, making me feel like a partner. I swelled, I'm sure. And that night, lying in bed and using all my invention-time before sleep, I enlarged my small gesture into the heroic leadership of a rebellion in one of those camps, armed with a pocketful of sharp stones and a stolen kitchen knife, and starting with an ambush of the Nazi commandant in his rooms.

I stayed in Jewish school for five years, until graduation, mainly because of Chaver Goichberg. But I never discussed with him those blue numbers or my secret knowledge; nor did he ever bring it up with me or with the class, which impressed me. Suffering, the brute stuff, was to be borne silently, was the message as I understood it from Lehrer. That forceful man was, to me, for some half-dozen crucial years, part teacher, part friend, part hero. (Nor did I ever know, until adulthood, that Goichberg was also a published Yiddish poet, of some prominence.)

And years later, I found myself protecting him yet again, with creative sympathies. In my early short stories, Chaver came back to play sympathetic roles, once as a cuckolded husband, victimized by the licentious father of one of his cheder students; another time, as the maligned teacher harassed by a community of stupid Jewish merchants and superpatriots. Even more, he came to play an interesting personal role as a sort of counter-father to the real one I portrayed in my fiction, a figure at once more just, more sympathetic, more compelling than the real one. But curiously enough, never once did I mention what I knew about his Holocaust past, as though that dark past were out-of-bounds for me as a writer, a private pact not to be disclosed without his permission. In my teacher's case, *his* real-life horror was to be honored even in *my* imaginative working life.

In childhood too, I learned about the killing of Jews in another way, through my father. After his own father had had his head lopped off in his village home by a marauding Cossack who, during a pogrom, wanted his money, my father had left Russia (1915–16), with the aid of his large family, to make his fortune in America and to return one day. He kept up a steady correspondence with that family, writing in Russian on thin sheets of lined paper, once a month at least, and receiving mail frequently. In about 1941–42, he received word that his youngest brother had been killed, possibly on the war front. But it wasn't entirely clear that the Nazis had killed him, rather than some anti-Semitic Russians. At four or five years old, I couldn't quite fathom what was being said, implied. "You mean the Nazi soldiers shot him, Papa?" I asked. He nodded, half smiling feebly. "The Nazis, or some Russian peasants." I must have looked bewildered, not understanding how nonsoldiers could kill you, and he replied, "Some Russians don't like Jews, sonny boy. So *ver veis?* Who knows?"

Somehow, somewhere, sometime, in my boy's consciousness, the grim sum was figured: first, his father, my would-have-been grandfather, murdered by a Cossack, and the family and home broken up in the same pogrom; and second, his young brother, my would-have-been uncle, killed maybe by peasants. Add to that the layers I learned later, the numbers murdered in the streets and camps. Over here, in America, a small Jewish boy was following the Dodgers and listening to "The Shadow" and "The Green Hornet" and playing boxball on the sidewalk, while, over there, in Europe, the game was the killing of Jews. Such was history. It was hard to take all that in, like hearing a bizarre tale filled with violent actions and characters, but confusing in its full meaning.

I was in my late twenties, teaching at a university outside Boston, when I wrote a long piece—my only piece—of Holocaust fiction. My version was not directly connected with Europe, however; it was set at home, in New York. Nowadays, when I reread my novella, "Final Solution in Manhattan," I am aghast at its innocence, stressed by several key choices and resolutions, bemused by its collage of strangeness. I find it hard to believe that I wrote it and interested that I then tucked it away, out of memory, away from print. Where did it come from, I ask, what were its deepest roots, sources?

Its immediate jumping-off ground, I can see, was the Eichmann trial in Israel, and a young Jewish writer in the Diaspora trying to figure out his own responses. Beneath that existed other layers, diverse and complex, mingling uneasily, begun in childhood, nurtured in adolescence, involving innocence and vengeance, justice and eroticism, mystery and irresolution.

The story concerns a young boy on the eve of his bar mitzvah who lives in Manhattan with his mostly secular parents—including a determinedly anti-ethnic universalist (Jewish) professor father and sister. The time is the 1950s and the setting is the Upper West Side. At the Broadway supermarket where young Marc Shuler works after school, two things occur that set the plot in motion. The first is his budding romance with an older woman, a lovely Jewish widow to whom he makes grocery deliveries. The second is the arrival of a somewhat mysterious stranger, a middle-aged man with a paunch and a history.

It turns out that ex-Nazi Hans Lenzner has been kidnapped from Argentina by a group of American Jewish vigilantes, including Holocaust survivors, and transported to New York, for an "experimental" punishment. This entails employment in Yerna's Market, working under and living amid West Side Jews, under the careful surveillance of a Jewish guard (and bodyguard, with blue numbers on his wrist). Well, Lenzner, a quiet, civilized, broken creature, and young Marc gradually become friendly, discussing various things, including Yiddish literature (which Lenzner has taken to read extensively) and, at one point, the Holocaust. When asked about it, Lenzner acknowledges his (functionary's) role in the genocide, stating his guilt and sorrow evenly, with Marc having to come to terms with this civilized man confessing to his part in those infamous crimes. The boy's confusion and ambivalence are compounded and heated when a relationship appears to be developing between Lenzner and Lily Hurwitz, Marc's widow friend. When Marc finally decides, impulsively, while at work in the market, to assassinate Lenzner, he believes it is because of that erotic betrayal, though Lenzner believes otherwise, when facing the boy and understanding his fate in Yerna's basement. Afterward, when the local Jewish community discovers the facts of the murder, it celebrates the boy's act and protects him from the outside, official law. From these events, inevitably, Marc Shuler has a nervous breakdown and is sent to upstate New York; eventually he recovers and goes on with his life. The tale itself is told in retrospect, years later, when the boy is grown up and settled into a routine life of husband and graduate student.

Looking back now upon that young writer and his peculiar mix of materials, his odd protagonists and naturalistic-surreal world, I'm struck by how methodically this story of confusion and breakdown proceeds and how pressing is the force of the Holocaust question. The improbability of certain characters and incidents, and the underlying framework of hyperbole, pale in significance, it seems to me, next to the urgency of the basic theme that comes through. There is a kind of absorbing, even driving, need pulsing in that young writer, to try to imagine a live German who has been a Nazi and to put him in a familiar setting of native streets and American Jews. In other words, an attempt to demystify the mythic enemy and to bring that grisly history a little nearer to home.

Moreover, the problem of punishment for a crime beyond boundaries is attacked here with some vigor, as well as innocence. It reflects, I believe, the young Jewish writer's unease with, lack of belief in, the simple system of justice implemented by the Israeli courts. Finally, the essential, unyielding question of *why,* is looked at, if not answered, in the story. "Final Solution in Manhattan" strikes me as an attempt at rendering a boy's confused version of justice, a native Jewish writer's uncertain vision of European horror. Clearly the imagination of the young Diaspora writer has been gripped by the European *shoah* and has tried to come to terms, some emotional and intellectual terms, with the materials formed by his adult knowledge and childhood memories.

For different reasons, the young writer decided not to publish his story. Considering that gesture now, by itself, I think that reluctance was right. All the more so, though, in light of the survivors who have written genuine literature from it, like Borowski, Appelfeld, Levi, (Jorge) Semprun, (Ilona) Karmel, and the many misguided interlopers, Christian and Jewish, who have embarrassed themselves by attempting to imagine it.

Was it before or after my novella that I met Hanna R, an art teacher in her late fifties who lived near me in Cambridge and who presented me with another angle of the situation? I forget now. In any case, I was having a tea in her apartment one late afternoon, and we got to talking about her student art days in Poland. As the afternoon sun slanted across the meager carpet of the living room, I began to listen with rapt attention as an ordinary life of a Warsaw art student turned into Holocaust horror. With reticence and embarrassment—"You don't really want to hear about this, do you?"—she related the grisly facts of life in Majdanek and Auschwitz while I drank my tea and gazed at the pastoral drawings on the wall. If that room was beginning to spin from that history, my brain rotated even faster when she asked, almost deferentially, if I cared to see her "uniform" from the camp? In a daze, I said yes, not knowing what else to say.

From her hall closet, she brought out a gray prison uniform, with black stripes and sewn yellow star, and held it up to her trim form, like a model showing a dress. "My souvenir." She half smiled, weakly, a handsome woman with remarkably smooth skin and light brown hair. Something was at my throat, and I found it hard to talk or swallow. I nodded. She sat down, holding on to the top absentmindedly, and went on talking about living there, surviving there, while watching her good friends starve slowly or get gassed. She spoke matter-of-factly while she smoked, crossed her legs, as though talking about a few months away in a strange, rather unpleasant place.

I listened, and stared, took note of the lace doily and graceful reading lamp, and tried to absorb words whose meaning stretched beyond my comprehension. I listened. And gradually, to my surprise, my listening and my interest seemed to be somewhat consoling to her, if that's the right word. At one point, she said, "I don't get to tell this story too often here, you know," and she stirred the sugar in her refilled teacup, a perfect Victorian lady narrating her ancient, haunting tale, hoping not to bore the accidental listener too very much.

I was feeling as though I had been watching a six-hour play, perhaps O'Neill, in a foreign language, some of which I understood, some not. About nine o'clock, I realized we hadn't had any dinner, and I urged us out to a local Greek restaurant. And sitting there, at the Parthenon, with my familiar waiter smiling at me and regular customers eating, chatting, tinkling wineglasses, ordinary reality began to seep back into my life, sweet and easy America back into my soul. So palpably had Hanna and her gray horror tale entered my head and nervous system.

The living presence of a survivor on *home ground,* the physical incarnation of a ghostly tale, had assaulted my senses. Suddenly the Holocaust was real again, death and its gaseous smells were alive, and I felt innocent, childlike innocence. And guilty, somehow. And angry, too. And helpless. Six hours with the Polish woman had been like six hours of combat, in the trenches, I thought that night and felt the next few days, and I didn't wish to protect myself from either the bolt from history or the waves of feeling. Periodically, then, I found myself walking past her apartment, glancing at her curtains, and allowing the news to send tremors through me again. And even saw the messenger herself on several more occasions, feeling as though I were meeting a visitor from a faraway place, a specter, one who, interestingly enough, made me feel much less certain of my solid self, my self-image.

The Polish woman, and her "uniform," had made me question myself, and my relation to her, to her/our history. She, and it, frightened me.

How, why?

Was I somehow . . . implicated? Responsible?

Had I been somehow part of the betrayal, in some crazy way?

From Hanna the Polish woman and her talk (and my self-questioning) stunning to the Polish writer Borowski and stunning literary/scenes was a natural bridge, it seems to me now.

I began reading Tadeusz Borowski sometime around then, in the late sixties or early seventies, and was riveted by what I found there. For Borowski, first of all, is a genuine writer, not a "mere" witness to the awful events who then wrote about them. That meant, for me, that it is not the events themselves that are the chief concern of the writer, but the voice narrating those events, the eye and ear registering the odors and sounds and words, the sensibility searching for subtle moral distinctions to make (amidst the larger, simpler one), the storyteller always on the lookout to carve a coherent story out of the daily debris. In other words, Borowski takes Auschwitz for his turf in the same way that Bellow takes Chicago, Dickens takes bleak London streets, or Faulkner takes the poor rural South. A place where human beings are killed every day is no different as your context, your background texture, Borowski implies, as a place where people take elevators or taxis, go to barbershops or work in factories, make real-estate deals or argue in law courts. You work with the material at hand, period.

Borowski proceeds, in *This Way for the Gas, Ladies and Gentlemen,* to show that routines of life go on, even there; that character is character, even there; that stories still turn on greed, jealousy, desire, chance, even in the camps. Not high rhetoric, but telling detail; not easy sentimentality, but earned sympathy;

not divine suffering, but human longing. By taking careful note of the everyday details, from shaving and smoking to remembering and fantasizing, Borowski reveals camp life to be a partially understandable territory. By focusing on conflicts in character and human turns of plot and surprises of landscape (a makeshift soccer field or brothel), he creates real literature—rather than sociology or religion—out of hell.

And by turning Dante upside down, showing hell as a live, concrete fact of recent history, not grand metaphor of medieval philosophy, Borowski makes realistic the apparently surrealistic. And instructs me, an American boy, that the Nazis were real too, could think and act rationally, might even show small acts of kindness, on their self-created stage of torture and killing. The Greatest Theater of Murder ever concocted was a production of real human beings, Germans (called Nazis) from all walks of life; and the chosen victim was the Chosen People. Meanwhile the spectators were citizens and governments from all nations, who looked on or looked away, depending, but did not seek to help. Interesting, all that, coming from a Polish Catholic writer, not a Jew. I appreciated that.

(In the same way that, a decade later, I was to appreciate another book of stunning truth by a non-Jew about the Holocaust, this one about American responsibility, David Wyman's *The Abandonment of the Jews*.)

For me, a literary fellow, it was not surprising that it took a literary book to press my nose to the windows of that theater, and to keep me pressed there. I read Borowski once, then read him again and decided to teach him, in my university classes, and I've taught him wherever I've been, Brandeis, Amherst, Haifa, Dartmouth. I do it as a kind of multiple service, for Borowski, a great writer; for the students, to make them literary witnesses; for myself, to keep a pact, I think; for the dead, to remember them. It is a service wherein admiration mingles with a weird sense of duty, literary pleasure with moral debt. For me, it acts as a kind of Bible, to be read, studied, commented upon, referred to.

(Not surprisingly, it takes a while for students to bear down and face the Borowski reality of life in the camps. Expecting Death and Heroism up front, they get instead smaller cruelties, smaller decisions; expecting sermony rhetoric and portentous statement about the Large Evil, they have to learn to make do with the excruciating presentation of everyday details, and more details, the stuff of art. Perhaps especially disturbing is the dissonances of humanized faces within the dehumanized context, from a Nazi captain worried about his cigarette lighter in the midst of a death command, to a prisoner worrying about the even surface of the soccer field while thousands are lined up for the gas chambers. And the professor too needs to bear down to teach such a class, or at least I do, trying to balance literary points with history lessons, deflationary remarks with inflationary knowledge.)

On home ground then, in my thirties, a living Polish Jewish survivor and dead Polish Catholic writer hooked me to the mat of the Holocaust.

I was invited to Israel in November 1976 and stayed for three months in Mishkenot Sha'Ananim, the artists' residence in Jerusalem. It was the first time I had been in the country, and I came as an interested tourist, not a devoted Zionist or religious believer. During that short stay, I got hooked by the place and stayed on in an apartment for another six weeks, just to make sure that it was the country and not the glamorous residence that compelled me. In the next decade, I was to return at least a half-dozen times, including a full year in 1986 as Fulbright writer-in-residence at Haifa University. It has become for me a second home, at the same time that it remains a foreign place.

For an American Jew, Israel is a country of the familiar and the exotic, of faces and habits known, and customs and people absolutely foreign. A country where you first really learn about the ancient traditions of Sephardic Jewry, and see the dark-skinned Jews (from places like Yemen and Iraq, Ethiopia and Iran), alongside the pale faces of the more familiar Ashkenazi Jews. It is also very much a nation that wears its Holocaust memory on its sleeve, by means of monuments (like Yad Vashem) and annual memorials (who can forget the stunning siren calling everyone to a halt, cars to stand still, with drivers outside, on the Day of Remembrance?) and museums everywhere (like the small kibbutz in the north that houses a museum of drawings and paintings from the camps, and features one of Israel's best painters, Kupferman, himself a kibbutznik and survivor, whose dark abstract paintings are filled with haunting images and feelings). And it is impossible to escape the survivors themselves. These run the gamut, intellectual and kiosk vendor, doctor and bus driver, farmer and writer, knesset member and army general. These figures float throughout the society, specters of memory wandering amidst the younger, firmer sabras and Diaspora innocents. Once they brush you with their presence and fantastic tales, you find yourself recruited. Into the service of memory, and the witnessing army of bewilderment, questioning, anger.

Consider Daniel F, a sophisticated French intellectual and historian by profession. A slim, darkly handsome man of about fifty who wears black turtlenecks and could easily star in movies, Daniel was originally a Czech boy secretly deposited by his parents in a Catholic seminary in Paris in order to be saved from the Vichy government or the Nazis. Thinking himself an orphan, he grew up wanting to be a priest, only to discover in teenage his Jewish heritage. Shocked back into his Jewishness, he chose to come to Israel to fulfill his adult life, rather than priesthood in France.

Gradually I came to see in this complicated man the subtle consequences of his early dislocations. What I took to be an elusive figure was in fact an elusive identity, unsure of itself, shadowy, furtive. A man who lived in permanent exile, with himself, with countries. You felt with Dan that Israel was a stopover place only; no wonder he spent half the year outside, teaching here, wandering there. In Israel he looked like a European outsider, too refined for rough-and-tumble Sabra living, too elegant for the informal Israeli style. Yet, in America, for example, he looked and acted like an absolute Jew, cosmopolitan, yes, but decidedly Jewish. Because of his exotic early years, Dan was the displaced person par excellence, a figure forever on the run, even from himself. A fine protagonist for a modern novel, to be sure, whose existential elusiveness had its origins in social reality, not fashionable metaphors.

Haim B was a small, middle-aged man, with wire-rimmed eyeglasses, round head, and broad smile when it appeared. An obscure writer when I first met him, he too had been displaced; he had wandered alone as a boy in Eastern Europe while his parents had been taken by the Nazis. Coming to Israel at age eleven or so, he had grown up on his own and was marked by instinctive terror of the outside world, fear and distrust of gentiles. His intimacy with Jews and Jewish soil was at once deep, personal, and religious. At times he would take my hand and say, "Alan, why don't you come here and live with us? Do! You'll see how different it is, from just visiting! You know the truth? I love Jews! And so do you," his face shining, "I can see it!"

For me, Haim's love, like his fear, seemed to be as authentic as it was childlike, an earned, cultivated emotion. And through him, as through a fine prism, the Holocaust was refracted, in rays that touched and penetrated me.

Solomon R was my friend's father, a Hungarian refugee about seventy, who still worked as an accountant in Tel Aviv. He was a stocky, tactiturn man who had survived Auschwitz but had lost, there and in Budapest in 1943–44, the rest of his family, brothers, sisters, and parents. He lived with his wife in a small plain apartment in an older part of the city, and we sometimes met there on Shabbat evenings, along with his daughter and son-in-law, to enjoy his wife's famous dishes of chicken or beef paprika, and apple strudel, Hungarian (dry) style. Rich food, good talk, easy humor, with Solomon usually nodding and smiling, a rather timid man saying little. When we spoke about America, however, where he had never visited, and I showed a few pictures of my country place in New Hampshire, he perked up like a boy envisioning Disneyland. It was a sudden spark in an otherwise ordinary soul.

When my friend Judith brought him and his wife up to visit us, in the summer of 1982, he was clearly more alert and talkative and humorous than he had been in Israel. He seemed inordinately keen on the simple, ordinary items of my home and country life. One evening, for example, while I barbecued pieces of chicken in the Weber grill on the porch, he stood right alongside me and took a surprising interest in the variety of ways the Weber could grill, bake, and roast, raising the lid up and back to check the smoke differential and playing with the adjustable air vents below, as though it were a complex engine. Next, in better broken English than I knew he had commanded, he asked about the birds flying back and forth by the two maples in the front yard, and I identified the two species, the barn swallows swooping and the yellow-breasted grosbeaks in their family routine. "Grosbeaks?" he wondered, and I handed him the binoculars for closer inspection. He shook his head, his eyes twinkling, and he uttered, "It's wonderful to have your own birds, come and go, yes?" I nodded. "Free of charge, too, yes?" he played with the idiom, beaming. "Live free or die," he teased the New Hampshire license plate logo. "I think I'd like to live free in your New Hampshire for a while in my life." He took my arm and gave it a little squeeze, a confirmation of his punning.

Two afternoons later he took an especial interest in my wood stacking, helping me collect some idle kindling and adjusting a pile for aesthetic balance. He asked, "You split this?" I said yes. "May I try?" "Sure." I found the smaller eighteen-inch splitting maul, took him to the sawed-off tree trunk, and whacked a few pieces, showing him the wrist action. He tried it, missing the first and barely tapping the second. "You're being too timid," I offered. "Really come down on it." This time he hit it right on, with a klop, and it flew into two pieces. You'd have thought he had just split the atom, the smile and "aha!" were so emphatic. He now tried a half log of red oak, and again he had success. Picking up two of the pieces, he inspected and sniffed them, uttering a slow *"Geshmecht,"* and asked if he might take a few pieces home with him, as "souvenirs." Why not? I smiled and, at his prodding, went on to talk about the differences in the wood, both in drying-out periods and heating powers, distinguishing for him among the ash, birch, maple, oak, and hornbeam.

Afterward, Judith said to me, "I haven't seen him this excited in years."

And nine months later, when I visited him in Tel Aviv, the split birch and oak pieces were stacked prominently in his living room. "The oak is still drying, of course," he explained. Naturally, there was no fireplace in sight.

In the camps he had been a hero, his daughter and I learned later. During one of the Gatherings of Survivors held annually in Israel, a long story in the Hebrew newspaper contained a photograph of her father, alongside three Hungarians he had saved, a middle-aged pair of twins and their mother in formal dresses, hats, and suits. It seemed that he was one of the chief saviors during the Hungarian deportation in 1944, and afterward, in the Bergen-Belsen concentration camp, risking his life time and time again to keep alive Jews, especially the children and mothers. The three in the picture hadn't seen him since the forties; the twins, youngsters then, returning from the United States for this reunion, found him by means of the special survivor file that had been set up. All that Judith had ever known was that he had been in the Holocaust, nothing more, since he had never said a word about the matter.

The dull accountant, my New Hampshire *redelman,* Judith's ordinary father, had developed another life, another face, and another will, during the rage, and that transformation had gone unnoticed, unremarked, for the past forty years.

Returning to Israel has come to mean for me, implicitly, returning to those faces and pasts. And others that resembled them, from the tragic years. I find myself there listening a little more closely to the random stories of the people I encounter, whether in Jerusalem living rooms, buses, *sheruts,* kibbutzim, waiting rooms. I know that every third or fourth soul has a Holocaust history, or family, and I feel, I guess, that it has become a kind of subtle moral duty for me, a lucky Jewish innocent, to hear them out. It is a curious scale or ledger, to be sure, to be balanced out, by me, a native son who was saved by the luck of geography; a curious strand perhaps in the anatomy of responsibility that has come to fall across me like a shadow in that sunny land by the Mediterranean. But it is not a debt that I feel as a burden, oddly, but rather, as a shadow of consolation, a kind of coded reward. Something akin to following along with Chaver Goichberg to face the young bullies when I was a boy of eight in cheder, knowing that I was of little practical use, but feeling good about the partnership.

It's that idea of partnership, that tacit contract with recent illicit history, if you will, that has attracted and interested me in my returns. A history that I experience, in Israel especially, as my history, too, no matter how unfamiliar the notion or unpleasant the sensation. Mingling with survivors, or survivors' children, has become a kind of habit, maybe even a developed gene; one that is primed with as much ambiguity as necessity. So I return to Israel regularly, for periods of three or four months at least, and tell myself that I'm there to see friends, talk literature, enjoy the weather, play tennis, and walk the streets of the German Colony, Baka, Rehavia, or attend the new cinematheque. All of which is true enough, reason enough. Privately, though, I sense another motive, another climate, drawing me there, one that needs no announcement or explanation, one that would indeed sound melodramatic and pretentious if stated aloud, even to myself.

In Etty Hillesum's remarkable diaries, published posthumously as *An Interrupted Life,* she writes this, from the camp in Westerbork, Holland, on August 24, 1943:

> I have told you often enough that no words and images are adequate to describe nights like these. But still I must try to convey something of it to you. One always has the feeling here of being the ears and eyes of a piece of Jewish history, but there is also the need sometimes to be a still, small voice. We must keep one another in touch with everything that happens in the various outposts of this world, each one contributing his little piece of stone to the great mosaic that will take place once the war is over. [pp. 207–208]

This young, talented Dutch Jewish woman, who died a few months later, at twenty-nine, in Auschwitz (November 30, 1943), puts the matter well, I think. The matter of partnership, connection, mosaic. If she, and others like her, provide the original witnessing voice, we the living provide another continuing piece of the history with our eyes and ears, and our voice. Their lives then—and deaths, too—would seem to be beamed, across the generations, to ours; we continue the signals; we are the latest outposts, listening and registering outposts. Our task would seem to be to keep the frequency of Holocaust memory clear and strong, despite the distracting noises and intentional or accidental blackouts. It is not so easy a task, really, and each one of us must choose his or her way of keeping that signal alive.

In childhood, there were also the pleasures, and for me a great one was baseball. I played it, watched it, worshipped the players and favorite teams, and digested the information and stories daily, so that it became like second nature to me. Well, my old Robinson and Reese, Mays and Mantle, Rizzuto and DiMaggio, have become, by the thrust of history and my transformation of interest, other names, other players. A kind of shadow lineup. For me now, it's Borowski and Karmel, Levi and Hillesum, Semprun and Bettelheim, Orlev and Appelfeld, Wiesel and Yaoz-Kest, Ringelbloom and Friedlander, Hilberg and Bauer, Ophuls and Lanzmann. That is the lineup I follow now with interest, with scorecard repetitions, with a fan's rectitude. And in their company I feel something like a beginner again, a beginner wandering in an adult's nightmarish realm.

The Anecdotal Holocaust

E. M. BRONER

In the fairy tale, the Snow Queen breaks a mirror that slivers vision and chills the heart of those whom the sharp pieces enter. We artists who work in metaphor have the mirror of the Holocaust that infuses our work, disturbs our vision.

1

A groom and bride step on the wineglasses and shatter them under the *chupah*. A stem rolls free of the napkin. I stare and hear the sound of rock exploding against glass in shop and *shul* and parlor window.

Crystal will never be the same since Kristallnacht. At night, when stars blink, I think there will be the tinkling sound of their shattering.

A busboy in a restaurant, in clearing the table, drops a tray of china and glassware. The restaurant stills. A few customers, largely Jewish, applaud for luck, for Jews have learned to applaud breakage.

I see the young person sweeping the shards, the slivers into the dustpan as the manager glowers nearby. He has endangered his job. The busboy is usually Oriental, Filipino, or Hispanic. He blushes and his skin burns hot.

This is an anecdote, an incident in the daily life that does not leave me.

Can an event like the Holocaust, which hardly touched me, have so altered me?

I once interviewed the labor leader Victor Reuther, one of the founders of the United Auto Workers. There were assassination attempts against his brother and himself. Walter's arm was shattered in one; Victor's eye shattered by gunshot through the window in another. Victor says he cannot stand near a window, look out of a window, have a window to his side or back.

And at night, in his sleep, he runs.

Windows, apertures become openings through which weaponry can be fired.

Attacks leave us running by night and by day.

2

Lists have become part of my psyche. To "list" is to tilt, and I feel a swaying, an altering of stance and posture.

That's because of something that may have happened.

My father, peace be with him, was a Jewish scholar and journalist. He co-authored *The Jews Come to America,* a pioneering work when it came out in the thirties.

During World War Two he worked on both the Hearst newspaper *The Detroit Times* and the English-language *Detroit Jewish Chronicle.* He was always typing, two fingers on each hand flying.

Throughout my growing up, my father was planning, setting up, laying out a series of independent newspapers, some commercial, some idealistic. I seem to remember a trade publication, *Beer and Bar,* which he planned with a sophisticated friend who was always compared in appearance to the movie star William Powell. Appearance or not, the trade magazine never made *its* appearance.

He edited the first labor newspaper in Michigan and wrote

speeches and even clad Democratic party candidates sympathetic to labor. John Dingle, Senior, ran for Congress in a shabby suit, and my dad not only put the words into his mouth but also the suit on his back. His son has, since, been a long-time congress-man.

He was, in his diminutive size and modest manner, a man who influenced opinion.

So that may be why I have this memory.

My father was either sent or given a book. How it arrived I do not remember. Our friendly mailman would have commented on a package, as he did on the postcards I received. This was a special book though cheaply compiled, the pages pulp, for in wartime there was no fine paper for printing. The inside was in some primitive reproductive method, not quite mimeograph or ditto, but something like that. The cover of the book may have been black or dark gray, a cardboard cover. The title, I believe, was not on the cover, but inside: *The Belsen Black Book.*

Books of this type, like samizdat, were passed around, sent to men of influence, statesmen, politicians, journalists. My father receives one, maybe at the *Detroit Jewish Chronicle,* maybe to alert the public, to arouse protest among the Jews. It would not have been sent to him at the *Times,* for the Hearst chain carried a pro-Nazi foreign correspondent and tilted toward fascist Germany.

Detroit, although called "Bastion of Industry" or "Mighty Detroit, the Munitions Capital," was pro-Nazi even before the Nazis. Henry Ford was forced to turn his plant into an aircraft-producing plant. His photo, after all, decorated the walls of Adolf Hitler, who had in the twenties received copies of Ford's anti-Semitic *The Dearborn Independent.*

Gerald L. K. Smith lectured from church halls in my city. Father Coughlin's voice came over the radio as mellifluous as the carillons of his Shrine of the Little Flower in Ferndale, outside of Detroit. He warned us all of the International Conspiracy of the Jew. Pelley's Silver Shirts flourished, as did the Black Legion, which, despite its name, was antiblack, anti-Semitic, and mostly antiunion. The Hearst paper catered to that crowd and their easy anti-Semitism.

My dad would kid, "I've gone from bad to Hearst."

Did the sender of the book know Detroit, where Jews would

buy neither Ford nor Hearst? Did the sender think that Dad's name on the masthead as editor of the *Chronicle* gave him special power? The Jewish community in Detroit was really outside of political influence, for no Jew had yet been elected to citywide office or appointed to a judgeship.

How did the book arrive? Did someone furtively hand it to my father? Was it accompanied by a desperate note? "Time is running out. There will be none of us left in all of Europe."

My dad's shirt pocket was pencil-marked, his face always lead-smeared. He was head writer and copy editor and out-state editor, and layout for the *Times* during the day, and by night, he wrote features, news, and editorials for the *Chronicle*.

There is my dad, not much taller than I, though I am a child. He is weeping (surely he was weeping) and the pencil marks on his face are smearing.

He is looking down at the lists of names. Someone must have copied these names carefully from the German clerk who entered them into his book. There is entrance and departure, as if they were passengers embarking on a ship. The names may have been in chronological order. They may have been alphabetized according to year. My memory is tactile, the gluey taste of pulp, the rough feel of cardboard, the long track of lists.

In the kitchen, perhaps at the porcelain enamel table, Dad is turning the pages and his tears pucker the paper.

"I don't know," he says, "what we can do."

I want to interview my father on the accuracy of this my memory, but my dad, who did so much interviewing in his life, died about a year ago.

His last interview was in the Jacuzzi at his retirement village, Leisure World, in southern California. He is talking to his neighbors, asking them questions about their origins, work, lives, families. He stays longer than the bell warning that five minutes have passed, and he becomes wrinkled in the steamy heat, pale white, like kreplach in chicken soup.

"Old people," my dad tells me, "are interested in two things, schnapps and talking."

While the Jacuzzi users talk, the women with rubber flowers on their bathing caps, the men careful not to wet their eyeglasses with the hearing aid in the earpiece, they are intruded upon by an energetic younger man, aggressing with belly and bristling beard, talking, interrupting. When he leaves, my dad says, "Those sixties, they get away with everything."

He, in his mid-eighties, got away.

So I cannot interview him, but I ask my mother.

"Did Dad ever show you the *Belsen Black Book?* Did this happen?"

"No," my mother says. "It did not."

"When did Dad find out?" I ask. "After all, he was working on all those newspapers."

"He found out when everybody else found out," says Mom. "And he had a guilt complex about it. He felt terrible, as did we all, that he hadn't known."

"I'm sure he knew," I say.

Mother shakes her head. "If he had known, he would have done something."

I ask my brother, Jay, born after the war.

"I was not told this," my brother says, "and he always talked history to me."

If I cannot remember the feel or texture of a story, it may not be a story.

But I remember the lists, looking down the lists, the printing of the names sometimes broken, a letter incomplete, a name fading. Perhaps there were misspellings, as if the list were hurriedly transcribed.

It was my first book of lists.

Years later I was at an artist's colony off the coast of Georgia, one of the Sea Islands. On the wall of the mansion were pages from the log of a slave ship, with name, age, price.

The man who purchased the island had floated a raft downriver with the supplies for the great house, had also mounted, framed, and hung this listing of captives: babies free; cripples, half-price; the old at a bargain.

No one has their African name, but nicknames: Peg Leg, Aunty, Big Boy, Buck. There was no effort to sell babies with mothers, men or women with their lovers.

The owner of this island was also a great white hunter. He had mounted animal heads in his two-story living room, and, in the evening, the guests of the colony watched a grainy, speeded-up film of the hunter in pith helmet and rifle. On the wall, along with the broken families, was the head of a rhino, bristling at us from the balcony, as we gathered around the fireplace for warmth and camaraderie.

I came, in my life, upon another list. This I found when cleaning out the garage and attic of a newly purchased home. Others had this house before us. In the attic we discovered the leavings of a World War Two bombardier, his K ration cans wormy, his aviator's jacket moth-eaten. We also discovered aerial bombing maps of Germany and the Soviet Union, the latter the source of much commentary.

Some owner left penciled markings on the doorjamb, documenting the growth of the children in the house.

Another owner altered the structure of the downstairs when he became stricken with a paralyzing disease. The kitchen became smaller and a downstairs bathroom was added. The living room was made smaller and the rest used for a library for the studious owner. And each owner either paved over the back lawn or tried to make something grow under the shade of the large oak tree.

I was clearing the garage and making space for myself. There I found a moldy book with listings, names of women, sometimes connected to men—a father, for instance, and sometimes sex of baby. It was the log of a kindly Jewish doctor who aborted the young unmarried women in his tight little community. He hid the evidence but for himself he kept a careful record.

There is the listing of the Martyrology at the High Holy Days. One kinesthetically feels flayed, burned alive, sees the words of the Torah aflame and cries out.

Was our past to enflame our future?

3

Could one avoid the future? Could one seek one's fortune? This obsessed me.

I was only sixteen, a graduate from high school, about to enter college, and for this summer, I went to seek my fortune in New York.

In those days there was a penny arcade where Lincoln Center

now stands. It was easy then to get a job. My first job was as an Esquire Shoe Shine Girl, until I began to understand that it was not only the shoe the men wanted polished.

I was hired at the penny arcade, first as a barker, then as a turtle seller. These were tiny land turtles, and as an extra inducement to buy, I would pretend to paint messages on their shells: "To the Boys in the Tenth Precinct in Buffalo from Matt."

But the summer was ending, that heady summer of first love and the requisite first heartbreak, of innocence, and, in those strict and proper days, innocence retained. I wondered what would happen to me in the fall.

Across from the turtle concession was the photo concession and the fortune-teller's booth.

The fortune-teller fascinated me, the model with moving parts encapsulated in a glass bubble. The customer inserted a quarter, the fortune-teller's eyes would roll, the head turn, the arm reach out and put the card into the slot with weight and fortune. (The figure in the movie *Big* was no exaggeration.) All summer that Gypsy-clad woman slowly, slowly moved her head with its kerchief, moved her silky arm, selected a card, and fed it into the slot. The citizens from Queens and Brooklyn, from Washington Heights and the Lower East Side, had their futures foretold.

With September there is a thinning of the crowd, a lull at the turtle concession.

I get change for a dollar from the photo concession, which specializes in quarters. The proprietor is a round-faced, sweet young Jewish woman, whose boyfriend is at the front. Every week I send off photos to my parents, stiff as a ticket, to let my folks know with documentation that their daughter is self-employed and recognizable. This time I want not photo but foretelling. The photo concessionaire watches. I nervously insert my quarter. The head moves slowly, the eyes look downward at the hands, the arm reaches for a card. It falls through the slot. On one side is my weight. I was skinny enough at sixteen. On the side for the fortune, the card is blank.

I show Photo. "It's a mistake," she says. "Try again."

I rush back to write a "Hi" on a turtle and to box it and mail it, in the days before animal rights. I take my second quarter to the fortune-teller. I stand on the scale, though I know my weight. My height has changed until this, my sixteenth year, but the fat is still missing from what could be the decorative parts of my body.

The Gypsy woman turns her head, rolls her eyes, looks seriously at her hands before selecting the card. The card is dropped through the slot. The fortune side is blank.

"What does this mean?" I ask Photo.

"It may not mean anything," says the proprietor with a slight frown, "but try again."

The store is empty. Nobody is buying at the candy counter, no couples are giggling in the photo booth, no out-of-town visitor is ordering turtles.

My turtles are doing their usual trick, climbing on one another's backs in a great column. Those on the bottom will have their shells cracked. A week ago, a deformed lot of turtles arrived, heads tilted, mouths to the sides, eyes uneven. I sold them anyway, boxed and mailed them, and my boss gave me a bonus. I would easily have a job this autumn.

So, I left those little creatures with the cartography of some secret world etched on their backs and approached the lady again.

My fingers were sweaty; the quarter kept slipping out of my palm and onto the aisleway. I finally inserted the quarter and activated the machine.

I half expected, this third time, for the woman to speed up, her kerchief to fly off, her tongue to stick out at me, her eyes to bulge, her hands to hit against the glass enclosure. But with the same patience, deliberation, and composure she had exhibited all summer, she sent me my card.

Photo looked at the blank future.

"Get out of town," she said. "There's nothing for you here."

She was right.

I returned to Detroit, enrolled at the university, met my love and future partner.

So, some fortunes come in avoidance, in flight and departure.

4

It was a year of Holocaust films or conferences.

Women Surviving the Holocaust is a conference put together by Joan Miriam Ringelheim and Esther Katz and taking place at Stern College in Manhattan. I tell the driver the destination.

"What's happening there?" he asks.

"The Holocaust," I say.

"That still playing?" he asks.

At the conference I hear the voices of ghetto fighters, of fighters in the woods and in the camps.

I hear the phrase "the extraordinary ordinary" in dealing with the daily efforts in the Warsaw ghetto to feed and to educate the citizenry. The mother of the speaker, Vladka Meed, had divided and secreted the food; the speaker, then a young girl, educated those younger, while the grandmother stood on guard outside, for education was forbidden.

"Those daily acts of courage," the speaker characterized them.

I learned that the figures were not all in about the deaths. Women may have survived better in the camps by sharing with one another and by replacing each other's losses.

"Your sister is gone, now I am your sister," would be told to one recently bereaved.

The women stood close to one another in the morning lineup to shore up those debilitated, feverish, about to collapse.

"We made a family for each other," speakers said, "and family does not let go so easily."

I had a friend who spoke movingly:

> My name is Mira Mammermesh and my place of origin is Lodz. . . . My mother died of hunger in the Lodz ghetto. My father was with the last transport from the Lodz ghetto and was liquidated, I think, on the last day of the war. . . . I left my native place at the ripe age of 13 or 14. . . . I had engineered . . . a way to get away from Lodz which distressed my mother. . . . So they made my older brother, who was 18, my guardian or chaperone. . . .
>
> On the day we were leaving, my mother stood at the door very distressed, crying that she would never see us again. She knew it.

For years I have never been able to purge myself of this image of a mother who had no power to stop her children; she lost her maternal power. [*Proceedings of the Conference, Women Surviving the Holocaust,* edited by Esther Katz and Joan Miriam Ringelheim, 1983]

Mira asks herself, if she had been a better daughter, would she have also perished?

In 1987, Mira Mammermesh won a prestigious documentary award from BBC for her South African film, *Maids and Madams.* When she heard them call out her name, she rose and said, "Mama, this is for you."

We try to please even those in the grave. We can never please them sufficiently.

I learned that more women than men may have been killed, for every woman carrying a child was sent to her death.

And I learned that blond women could more easily escape and that women who sewed would find employment even in a camp.

I was a curly-haired Mediterranean type, clumsy at the sewing machine at Durfee Junior High, where every girl had to take Sewing and Cooking. I got low marks in Home Economics and Sex Education. (In Sex Ed I forgot the "r" in "menstruation" and failed the semester's spelling test.) I would not so easily have survived.

We measure ourselves against the dead.

"It was surely an accident that I lived," I heard the survivors say again and again.

It was purely accidental and geographic that I lived.

5

Does one become sentimental, emotion warmed over, seeing again and again the photos? There is the schoolchild in short pants, hands in the air, Magen David on his chest. Does one automatically tear at the reduction of it all: the single baby shoe at Yad Vashem? And one is fascinated, intrigued, horrified by the traveling exhibition of Anne Frank and Her Times, with that slender, smiling, straight-haired child, her eyes mischievous or thoughtful.

It has become either sentimentality or Greek tragedy, knowing the fate that will befall, the final decree, yet resisting that knowledge.

The photos imprint themselves. I, a woman, feel all the more fragile, seeing the women with bundles, woman as refugee. What did they select—a blanket, a pot, a child's change of clothing, a heavy coat? I have always asked myself—not, "If there's a fire, what would I take?" but, "If there's the Holocaust"—would I take the dogs and the manuscripts?

Recently my youngest daughter suffered an auto accident and was concussed.

The doctor said to her, "The accident will be imprinted on your neurological system."

That collision still makes her shoulders and head ache, her neck stiff. The memory of the impact still causes her to shudder.

Those photos of the past find themselves under my eyelids, floating up in my dreams under the fluttering lids, which open to release them.

What did the Holocaust cause? Pregnancy. I carried babies to make up for the losses. I wrote a one-act play recently, *Letters to My Television Past,* in which the narrator explains about that generation having babies. "We had one for each of the million lost, so I had six million babies."

The air around me is permanently hazy.

The past summer the air in New York was smoky.

"It's from the forest fire at Yellowstone National Park," the weather forecaster said.

The smoke takes shape. There are clouds, gates, refugees. The smoke and ashes from another time still clog the nostrils. One's outer garments are covered with ash.

6

I could not spell the word for a long time, just as I would spell out, "I pledge legions to the flag." I wrote it *hollow-cost*. That was not the word on which I lost the grade spelling bee. It was *angel*. It seems I cannot spell words of bleeding, burning, or soaring.

I have listened attentively to the telling of escape stories from friends, relatives, writers, as if, somehow, it were my own escape.

Jerusalem writer Aharon Appelfeld once told us of escaping from the Nazis eastward into Russia.

"There was always a Jew, ragged, black-coated, like a scarecrow, against the light sky, against the snow. If I joined him, if there were two of us, we would both be lost."

Aharon was being offered the fruits of his first would-be translator. "Is this good English?" he asked and read to us: " 'A smile cracked across her face like an egg.' "

"No," we said. "It isn't good anything."

He has been translated, appreciated much since then.

I am aware of fleeing figures, of a smile cracking across a face.

I, who am in many ways profligate of time, energy, even affection, have been made by the Holocaust into a thrifty, saving person. I cannot bear people going to waste. I cannot bear the shamed, exhausted, defeated faces in the doorways of my streets, the tales of the subway tellers. I cannot bear the man on the corner of Sixth Avenue and my block who pulls up his cardboard mattress next to the black plastic garbage bags. I have seen rats gnawing through plastic to garbage, through flesh to bone, before I shook him awake.

This is a hollow time in the nation, in my city. Within it, I try to keep on feeling. It is a time of a different courtesy—the shoving body, conversation as curse, the unseeing eyes of the passersby, but I have to remember my history. I search for origins within each of these sidewalk sleepers. The man on his cardboard mattress is returned to his past. He is smooth-faced, with thumb in mouth, his receiving blanket puffed like egg whites.

7

I went across the country in 1984 for an art magazine, seeking the direction of women's art.

I found in galleries, performance pieces, on the field, in storefronts that women were engaged in what I came to call "Reseeding the Garden."

In their images, wood was being restored to burned-out forests, fish to the ocean, blue to the sky. There was flood, fire, devastation, but then, it seemed to me, in literature, art, and political action, there was the need to commemorate, to mourn, to make tombstones (Women's Pentagon Action), and, also, to replace. It was the opposite of nihilism, not in the direction of minimalism but a maximal feeling of power and energy expanding to save the earth.

Women in England at Greenham Common climbed on top of missile sites on New Year's Eve, to dance in the year. They were gnomish in cap and blocky jacket as they tread upon the snow-covered phallic missile, joy cavorting on death.

Among the women's actions, art was both declaration and decoration: tapestries, weavings, photos, and flowers stuck into fences in England and, also, in Seneca Falls, New York, from where the missiles were shipped to Greenham Common.

The women in Greenham Common were like refugees, setting up pup tents, homemade blanket shelters, makeshift boards so they could survive the years of British winters.

One performance artist, Helene Aylon, did a Save the Earth project, starting out in San Francisco and heading to New York for the U.N. Disarmament Conference. In San Francisco health workers put on prayer shawls and said *El Mole Rachamim,* a prayer for pity, for the earth was in mortal danger. The women climbed into a truck, painted white with red letters, Earth Ambulance, and set out to get soil samples from every nuclear research facility and plutonium plant located in every state in the nation. The samples were deposited in pillowcases, and along the route, women met them with their own messages upon pillowcases, for the women of the land were having a nightmarish time of it, their sleep disturbed with fears of imminent destruction. These pillowcases, a mile or so in length, were displayed on a clothesline at Seneca Falls, our outdoor laundry fluttering for all to see.

We have learned from our grandmothers about domestic decoration, doily upon slipcover, rug upon linoleum, about the need for decoration. It is the art of replacement and cover-up.

It is the making of the ordinary surprising and amazing to ourselves, for under each layer something else exists. Perhaps that chintz on the couch covers velvet; perhaps under the linoleum is an oak parquet floor.

We have learned, from great loss, to call out names.

It is not surprising that the Vietnam War Memorial called out names and was designed by a woman and that women's art, that of memorial, is upon it—a photo, flag, rose, letter.

Or that the AIDS Quilt Project takes lessons from the domestic art of women, the collage of our lives.

Perhaps we romanticize our search for the lost, our history, our lineage, those vanished along the way. But in each of us, in our art, we find a way to replace.

The Holocaust has made us search for documentation, external, internal, that tells us our lives are actual and continuous, that we have lineage: biblical, historical, literary, and biological.

We hope that our lives are not consumable, although the fire, smoke, and ash have burned in every Jewish hearth and darkened our abodes.

8

I have a friend, a psychology professor at the University of Michigan, Rafe Ezekiel.

Ezekiel is a social psychologist whose field of study is the current anti-Semite, neo-Nazi, Aryan nation, KKK. He often places himself in danger in their midst. Sometimes, when he's about to join them, he nervously kids, "I'm off to see the Wizard, the Grand Wizard."

He has been threatened. On the other hand, he's been consulted by them as to their legal rights, for they fear police invasion and perhaps death at the hands of the cops. Then they call Rafe and ask him to stay the night with them to discourage violence from the law. It is all too twisted for me.

They are revisionist historians. The Holocaust never happened.

"Why," I ask Rafe, "do you go to these people?"

He is publishing a book about them, *Hitler's Step-Children* (Viking), full of observation, indignation, even compassion.

They are peripheral, Rafe explains, ill-educated, ill-treated, abused as children, under- or unemployed. They are the boundaries, the borders of life. Their greatest fear is of disappearing. Hence, they must deny the disappearance of a whole people.

There cannot be a real disappearance. It has to be fake or they themselves, unrepresented anywhere, without any influence, would be made, in the new grammar, "to be disappeared."

9

Did I as a child see my name on the list of the *Black Book?* Did I think my parents would flee without me?

10

As a small child in Evansville, Indiana, on the Kentucky border, I would accompany my dad on his stories.

I held his hand as he went down the corridor of Death Row to interview a murderer. The convict may have touched my curly hair. "Shirley Temple," he might have told my dad.

My dad looked more like Charlie Chaplin, small mustache, curly hair, bouncy walk.

"He's not a murderer," I informed my dad.

My father never told me when the man was executed. Could it have been possible that none of this happened?

In Evansville I went on other stories with my dad, or sometimes he sent my mother out on assignment. We would go to the Tent of Meeting when Billy Sunday came to Evansville. The tent, with sawdust sprinkled in the aisles, housed most of the townfolk.

I was three but remember Billy Sunday picking up his chair and threatening with it. "I'll not let you get me, Satan!" he cried, and with the other hand, like Clyde Beatty, the lion tamer, he whipped Satan away.

Then came the call, "Who will fight off Satan? Who will hit the Sawdust Trail?"

All one would need was a chair, a whip, and a loud voice.

"I will!" I call out and slip alway and run down the aisle. My mother is in pursuit. She clutches the hem of my short dress.

"Satan's not after you," my mother assures me.

I never knew whether he was or wasn't. Nor did I ever again have such a chance to fight him off.

Once I went with my parents to Indianapolis for the Indianapolis Speedway. My dad was an all-around reporter, court, city, sometimes even sent to cover sports. He always loved sports. At the University of Michigan he had to sell his football tickets for food. The crowd would roar outside as the Wolverines played, and Dad would stand their listening to the music, to the roaring. I have never seen Dad salute the flag, but when "Hail to the Victors Valiant" plays, my dad rises and places his hand over his heart.

So there he was, a young reporter with a literate wife and a baby daughter, and we were off to the races. We had press-box seats. The cars whirred around the track. I stood up screaming and waving my bonnet. Then, directly in front of us, a car burst into flame and exploded.

I have never learned to drive in all my life.

Fire and flame and smoke have that effect on me.

There was not just fire in Indiana, and the Klan, and the early fascist organizations that flowered in the Midwest, but there was also the Flood, as if Genesis were being repeated, sin and destruction, *Hamas* and *Tashmad*.

The river overflowed its banks, flooded the park where I played, came pouring down the street.

That did not cause our departure. Something else did.

My dad had worked for a tricity newspaper on his first job in Moline, Illinois. Came the High Holy Days, Dad requested time off. He was refused. He took the time anyway. He was fired. This became quite a well-known case in those parts.

In Evansville, Indiana, Dad was on layout, front-page makeup the day the Italian anarchists Sacco and Vanzetti were executed. Dad ordered a black border around the front page. He was fired.

We left Indiana for Michigan.

Hirings and firings. He was not hired for newspaper work for some decades after that. During the depression he was even hired as a janitor to dust the judges' chambers in the courthouse.

Mother weeps when she remembers, twists the wedding ring that has grown into her finger.

"It's all right, dear," Dad said. "They were such interesting men, those judges, and we would sit and have long talks."

11

The Holocaust is too large, too inflammatory.

It makes us forget all the pogroms, Kishinev; all the cries and burnings are insignificant in comparison.

We became protective, possessive. We squat, clutching our bundles, protecting our belongings. We become, in memory and action, once again the refugee.

We hold conferences on that annihilation, but exclude the Armenians and the Gypsies and certainly the homosexuals.

We are possessive of our suffering.

On the other hand, we are also ashamed, so ashamed our character has altered.

We are not now a gentle people, scholars, students, facing east, learning.

We are like the rest of the world. We read that each year one rises up against us and once again we are saved. And we worry, what if God slips up one year?

So we must become eternally vigilant, become vigilantes ourselves.

We interpret everything through that horror and we update the villains. Black people are bringing the next Holocaust; Palestinians will massacre us. Smoke rises from the forests of Eretz Israel.

And we, in the New World, have smoke in our eyes.

12

Perhaps without the Holocaust, I would have been a different shape, another size.

October 1987, I was invited to participate in Woman-Church. Five thousand Roman Catholic women religious showed up, took over the streets of downtown Cincinnati, chanting, "We are the church," for they are often the only representatives in the ghetto, Central America, in places of starvation and devastation.

And marching with them, though these women are only a minority in their church, a tiny percentage, I wondered how it must feel to represent in America a religious body so many millions strong, instead of those hoppy, nervous, noisy Jews.

One can cast a shadow by just going out of doors.

We have to recast our shadows over and over again.

Resistance to
the Holocaust

PHILLIP LOPATE

When I was small, a few years after World
War Two had ended, my mother would drag me around Brooklyn to visit some of the newly arrived refugees; they were a
novelty. We would sit in somebody's kitchen and she would talk
with these women for hours (usually in Yiddish, which I didn't
understand), to find out what it was like. After we left, she would
say in a hushed voice, "Did you see the number on her arm? She
was in a concentration camp!" I didn't understand why my
mother was so thrilled, almost erotically excited, when she spoke
these words, but her melodramatic demand that I be impressed
started to annoy me. I had only to hear about those lurid arm
numbers to experience an obstinately neutral reaction and begin
digging in my heels. Maybe I was picking up some of her own
ambivalence; beneath my mother's sympathetic sighs, I sensed a
little distaste for these victims. Years later she confessed that,
when the camp survivors first started coming into her candy
store, they were the most difficult customers to please; they had
—and here she paused, realizing how insensitive her appraisal

might sound, given their tragic backgrounds—a "chip on their shoulders."

Actually, I was touched by her honesty; just because someone has suffered a lot doesn't mean you have to like them, has always been my motto. I used to go into a neighborhood hardware store run by a concentration camp survivor with thick wire-framed glasses, whom I did like but whose superior bitterness gave all transactions an air of mistrust. Once I heard this proprietor say after he had thrown a customer out of his store: "What can he do, kill me? I already died in Auschwitz." This advantage of the living dead over the rest of us seemed unfair.

But I am getting ahead of myself. I want to return to that moment when my mother and I were leaving some poor woman's kitchen and I froze at the demand for my compassionate awe. Let me try to explain by way of anecdote. I once heard of a very liberal Jewish couple whose child would scream whenever she saw a black person. The parents were distressed that their little girl might be learning racist attitudes from somewhere, so they went to a child therapist and asked his advice. After questioning the little girl alone and learning nothing, the doctor suggested that he go for an outing with the family so that he might observe them in an everyday setting. As they were walking along the street, he noticed that whenever a black person approached the mother would unconsciously tighten the grip on her daughter's hand and the girl would, naturally, cry out. In my case, whenever my mother uttered those magical words "She was in a concentration camp!" the music on our emotional soundtrack got turned up so loud that I went resolutely numb. Maybe this is the seed of that puzzling resistance I have felt toward the Holocaust all my life.

Before I give the wrong impression, let me interject that I am not one of those revisionist nuts who deny that the Nazis systematically exterminated millions of Jews. On the contrary, I'm convinced that they committed an enormous and unforgivable evil, about which I would feel presumptuous adding my two cents of literary grief or working myself into an empathic lather through the mechanics of writerly imagination. I was not there, I am not the one who should be listened to in this matter, I cannot bear witness. It is not my intent to speak at all about the atrocities of the Nazi era, but only about the rhetorical, cultural, political, and religious uses to which the disaster has been put since then. Of these, at least, I do have some experience.

When I was growing up, we never spoke of a Holocaust; we said "concentration camps," "the gas chambers," "six million Jews," "what the Nazis did." It might seem an improvement over these awkward phrases to use a single, streamlined term. And yet to put any label on that phenomenal range of suffering serves to restrict, to conventionalize, to tame. As soon as the term "Holocaust" entered common circulation, around the mid-sixties, it made me uncomfortable. It had a self-important, strutting air— a vulgarly neologistic ring, combined with a self-conscious archaic sound, straining as it did for a Miltonic biblical solemnity that brought to mind such quaint cousins as Armageddon, Behemoth, and Leviathan.

Then, too, one instantly saw that the term was part of a polemic and that it sounded more comfortable in certain speakers' mouths than others; the Holocaustians used it like a club to smash back their opponents. Lucy S. Dawidowicz states, "The Holocaust is the term that Jews themselves have chosen to describe their fate during World War II." I would amend that to say "some Jews" or "official Jewry"; but in any case, it is one of those public relations substitutions, like *African American* for black or *Intifida* for Palestinian troubles, which one ethnic group tries to compel the rest of the world to use as a token of political respect. In my own mind I continue to distinguish, ever so slightly, between the disaster visited on the Jews and "the Holocaust." Sometimes it almost seems that "the Holocaust" is a corporation headed by Elie Wiesel, who defends his patents with articles in the Arts and Leisure section of the Sunday *New York Times*.

"Shoah" carries over the same problems as the term "Holocaust," only in Hebrew. Both "Shoah" and "the Holocaust" share the same self-dramatizing theological ambition to portray the historic suffering of the Jews during World War Two as a sort of cosmic storm rending the heavens. What disturbs me finally is the exclusivity of the singular usage, *the* Holocaust, which seems to cut the event off from all others and to diminish, if not demean, the mass slaughters of other people—or, for that matter, previous tragedies in Jewish history. But more on these topics later.

We need to consider first the struggle for control of the Holocaust analogy. All my life, the *reductio ad Hitler* argument has been applied to almost every controversy. If it is not always clear what constitutes moral action, it is certain that each controversial path can be accused of initiating a slide that leads straight to Hitler. Euthanasia? Smacks of the Third Reich. Abortion? Federal payments make it "possible for genocidal programs as were practiced in Nazi Germany," according to Senator Orin Hatch. Letting the Ku Klux Klan march? An invitation to Weimar chaos. Forbidding the march? Censorship; as bad as Goebbels. The devil can quote scripture and the Holocaust, it would appear. We see in the Middle East today how both Israelis and Palestinians compare the other side to Nazis. The Hitler/Holocaust analogy dead-ends all intelligent discourse, by intruding a stridently shrill note that forces the mind to withdraw. To challenge that demagogic minefield of pure self-righteousness from an ironic distance almost ensures being misunderstood. The image of the Holocaust is too overbearing, too hot to tolerate subtle distinctions. In its life as a rhetorical figure, the Holocaust is a bully.

The Holocaust analogy has the curious double property of being both amazingly plastic—able to be applied to almost any issue—and fantastically rigid, since we are constantly being told that the Holocaust is incomparable, in a class by itself, *sui generis,* must not in any way be mixed up with other human problems or diluted by foreign substances.

When President Jimmy Carter made a speech commemorating all those liquidated by the Nazis, which he put at a figure of 11 million, the eminent Holocaust scholar Yehuda Bauer accused Carter and his adviser Simon Wiesenthal of trying to "de-Judaize" the Holocaust. "The Wiesenthal-Carter definition appears to reflect a certain paradoxical 'envy' on the part of non-Jewish groups directed at the Jewish experience of the Holocaust. This itself would appear to be an unconscious reflection of anti-Semitic attitudes . . ." warned Bauer. We Jews own the Holocaust; all others get your cotton-picking hands off.

"How dare they equate using napalm in Vietnam or even dropping the bomb on Hiroshima with the Holocaust?" one often hears. The underlying sense is: "How dare they equate anything with the Holocaust?" The Holocaust is a jealous God; thou shalt draw no parallels to it.

The problem is that drawing parallels and analogies is an incorrigibly natural human activity. I too find it deeply offensive and distasteful when flippant comparisons to Nazi genocide are made. But on the other hand, it does not seem to me unreasonable to regard the Holocaust as the outer limit of a continuum of state-sanctioned cruelty, other points along the spectrum of which might include the French torture of Algerians, Idi Amin's liquidations, My Lai and other Vietnam massacres, the slaughter of the Armenians, Pol Pot. I realize it may appear that I am blurring important distinctions among a genocide, a massacre, and other horrors; but I am not asserting that any of these atrocities was as *bad* as the Holocaust (whatever *that* means), only that the human stuff, the decisions and brutal enactments that followed, may have had much in common. I find it curious for people to speak of the murder of 6 million Jews as a "mystery" and the murder of several million Cambodians as perhaps a more run-of-the-mill open-and-shut affair. The truth is, unfortunately, that there are few things less mysterious and unique in the history of the world than genocide.

It is true that the Holocaust was singular in its hideous anti-Semitism, which made the mere fact of being a Jew ground for death. But as the historian Irving Louis Horowitz argues in his essay "The Exclusivity of Collective Death": "To emphasize distinctions between peoples by arguing for the uniqueness of anti-Semitism is a profound mistake; it reduces any possibility of a unified political and human posture on the meaning of genocide or the Holocaust. . . . Insistence upon separatism, that the crime was Jewish existence and that this makes the Jewish situation different from any other slaughter, whatever its roots, contains a dangerous element of mystification."

A good deal of suspicion and touchiness reside around this issue of maintaining the Holocaust's privileged status in the pantheon of genocides. It is not enough that the Holocaust was dreadful, it must be seen as *uniquely* dreadful. Indeed, the catastrophe of the Jews under Hitler is sometimes spoken of as an event so special as to sever history in two—breaking the back of history, in effect. "Holocaust stands alone in time as an aberration within history," states Menachem Rosensaft. And Elie Wiesel writes that "the universe of concentration camps, by its design, lies outside if not beyond history. Its vocabulary belongs to it alone." What surprises me is the degree to which such an apocalyptic, religious-mythological reading of historical events has come to be accepted by the culture at large—unless people are just paying lip service to the charms of an intimidating rhetoric.

In attempting, for instance, to resolve the recent "historian's dispute" in West Germany, President Richard von Weizsäcker declared: "Auschwitz remains unique. It was perpetrated by Germans in the name of Germany. This truth is immutable and will not be forgotten." *The New York Times's* reporter Serge Schmemann goes on to report (October 22, 1988): "Speaking to a congress of West German historians in Bamberg, Mr. von Weizsäcker rejected the attempts by some historians to compare the systematic murder of Jews in Nazi Germany to mass killings elsewhere—like those in Cambodia under Pol Pot or in Stalin's purges—or to seek external explanations for it. Such approaches have been assailed by other historians as attempts to frame the German crime in 'relative' terms."

Mr. von Weizsäcker has been rightly praised for his integrity and statesmanship in this matter—and yet I can't help thinking that he has also engaged in a certain amount of magically placating incantatory language: unique, immutable, never forget, antirelativism. I would have thought that a relativistic perspective was part of the discipline of competent modern historians. Not that history writing is ever entirely value-free or objective; but attempting to situate an era in a larger context still seems closer to normal historical methods than expecting historians to believe there is such a thing as an absolute historical event or an absolute evil. There seems to be a fear that, if we admit there are similarities between the Nazis' war against the Jews and other genocidal atrocities, we will be letting the Germans off the hook. On the contrary, we will be placing them on the same hook with other heinous criminals. And we will be asserting that the forces in history and human nature that brought about the death camps are not necessarily a fluke, so—be on guard.

Yehuda Bauer has astutely observed that "If what happened to the Jews was unique, then it took place outside of history, it becomes a mysterious event, an upside-down miracle, so to speak, an event of religious significance in the sense that it is not man-made as that term is normally understood. . . . If what happens to the Jews is unique, then by definition it doesn't concern us, beyond our pity and commiseration for the victims. If the Holocaust is not a universal problem, then why should a public school system in Philadelphia, New York or Timbuktu teach it? Well, the answer is that there is no uniqueness, not even of a unique event. Anything that happens once, can happen again: not quite in the same way, perhaps, but in an equivalent form."

Let us look at some of the cold figures on genocide in this century. According to Roger W. Smith, in *Genocide and the Modern Age*: "Turkey destroyed the lives of a million or more Armenians; Nazi Germany destroyed 6 million Jews, but it is often forgotten that it went on to murder other groups as well, so that a reasonable estimate for the total number of victims, apart from war deaths, is 16 million; Pakistan slaughtered 3 million Bengalis; Cambodia brought about the death of 3 million persons; and the Soviet Union first destroyed 20 million peasants in the 1930s and then went on to take hundreds of thousands of other lives in the 1940s with its assaults on various nationality groups suspected of disloyalty." These numbers may be somewhat high. Barbara Harff, who provides both lower and upper estimates in the same book, rounds out the picture with other twentieth-century genocides: Nigeria's extermination of 2 to 3 million Ibos; the Indonesian slaughter of supposed Communists, 200,000–500,000; the Indonesian action in East Timor, 60,000–100,000; Idi Amin's murder of fellow Ugandans, 500,000; the Tutsis' massacre of 100,000–200,000 Hutus in Burundi; Sudanese against the Southern Sudanese, 500,000; and so on.

The position that the Jewish Holocaust was unique tends to rest on the following arguments: (1) scale—the largest number of deaths extracted from one single group; (2) technology—the mechanization of death factories; (3) bureaucracy—the involvement of the state apparatus at previously unheard-of levels; (4) intent—the express purpose being to annihilate every last member of the Jewish people. Thus it is argued that, although Hitler killed many, many Poles, he still intended to use the majority of Poles as slave laborers. Some scholars counter that it was Hitler's goal also to eliminate the entire Gypsy population; others dispute this claim. The fact that one's group was not targeted for extermination *in toto* is a serious distinction, but hardly much consolation to the Gypsies, homosexuals, radicals, Poles, Slavs, etc., whom the Nazis did wipe out.

Alan Rosenberg asserts that the uniqueness of the Holocaust lies above all in "the Nazi abuse of science and technology, the application of bureaucratic techniques, principles of managerial efficiency and 'cost-benefit' analysis." This assessment, with its obvious implications for the present, dovetails with Adorno's and Horkheimer's philosophical argument that the systematic, orderly, "Germanic," if you will, manner in which the killings were carried out shows the ultimately debased heritage of Western Enlightenment reason. Certainly much of our abiding fascination with the Holocaust rests on its dystopian, nightmarish use of rational, mechanized procedures. But I wonder how much of the importance we ascribe to these factors represents the narcissistic preoccupations of our Western technological society. Does it really matter so much if millions are gassed according to Eichmann's timetables, rather than slowly, crudely starved to death as in Stalin's regime, or marched around by ragged teenage Khmer Rouge soldiers and then beheaded or clubbed? Does the family mourning the loved one hacked to pieces by a spontaneous mob of Indonesian vigilantes care that much about abuses of science and technology? Does neatness count, finally, so damn much? (And what about the tragic fiasco—not genocide, true, but equally fatal—of the Great Leap Forward during the 1959–60 famine in China, when "anywhere between 16.4 to 29.5 million extra people died during the leap, because of the leap," according to Harvard political scientist Roderick MacFarquhar.)

I find it hard to escape the conclusion that those piles of other victims are not so significant to us North Americans as Jewish corpses. Is it simply because they are Third World people of color? How much is social class itself a factor? In so many books and movies about the Holocaust, I sense that I am being asked to feel a particular pathos in the rounding up of gentle, scholarly, middle-class, civilized people and packing them into cattle cars, as though the liquidation of illiterate peasants would not be so poignant. The now-familiar newsreel shot of Asian populations fleeing a slaughter with their meager possessions in handcarts still reads to us as a catastrophe involving "masses," while the images of Jews lined up in their fedoras and overcoats tug at our hearts precisely because we see the line as composed of individuals. Our very notion of individuality is historically connected with the middle class; on top of that, Jews have often stood for individuality in modern culture, by virtue of their outsider status and commitment to mind and artistic cultivation. I am by no means saying that all the Jews who died in the camps were bourgeois (on the contrary, the majority were poor religious peasants); I am suggesting that, since the bulk of the narratives focus on middle-class victims swept up in the slaughter, this may help account for why the murder of European Jews plays on our sympathies so much more profoundly in this culture than the annihilation of Bengalis, East Timorese, or Ibos. The most obvious explanation may be demographic: There are many more Jews in the United States than there are Ibos or Bengalis.

"What's wrong with you?" I hear certain Jewish readers ask. "Are you not closer to your own dead than to those others? It's understandable for blacks to care more about slavery than about the Holocaust, or Armenians to mourn more for their massacred than for ours. But why do you, a Jew, insist on speaking as if these others mattered the same as our own flesh and blood killed in the gas chambers?" I don't know; I must be lacking in tribal feeling. When it comes to mass murder, I can see no difference between their casualties and ours.

That we must continue to come to terms with the Holocaust is obvious. The question is: What forms will these commemorations or confrontations take? And addressed to whom? And who will be allowed to speak? And what is the permissible range of discourse?

There exists at present the urgent sense that we must keep up the pressure of commemorating the Holocaust to counteract the poisons of the extremist "revisionist" historians, like Robert Faurisson. To be truthful, I don't believe that the Faurissons and their ilk, who deny that a mass extermination of Jews ever took place, pose a serious threat to altering the world's perception of the historical record. They are the lunatic fringe, which we will always have with us. It makes sense to be vigilant about them, but not so paranoid as to exaggerate their real persuasional powers.

As for the more moderate revisionist historians—such as Andreas Hillgruber, who has tried to link the collapse of the eastern front with the death camps' greater activity or to propose that many German soldiers were heroically doing their duty— their views may set our teeth on edge with their insensitive tone or alarm us with their usefulness to the far right. But the greater threat they pose to the purity of our outrage is that some of what they say could hold a grain of truth. Is it reasonable to deny that some German soldiers in World War Two may have been decent men victimized by the situation? Are we to divide the guilt by battalions—determine, as many are wont to do, that an ordinary German foot soldier may not have been entirely vicious, but that anyone in the S.S. was a sadistic criminal? I can well imagine a kid who didn't know better getting swept up in the mood of the day and joining the S.S. out of idealism. (One may scoff at the seeming oxymoron, Nazi idealist, yet every political movement generates its youthful idealists.)

I know of no event in recent years that has so united educated people in incredulous disgust as President Reagan's visit to the military cemetery in Bitburg, West Germany. At the time, glad to heap scorn on a president I despised, I heartily joined the chorus, although with a slight inner uneasiness that I was too cowardly to express. Now, thinking it over, I would say that it may not have been such a dastardly thing for the visiting president of a victorious nation to lay a wreath on the tomb of his defeated enemy's soldiers. The gesture contains a certain old-fashioned Homeric nobility. *But don't you understand? There were S.S. troops buried in that cemetery! Reagan was "signaling" the neofascists that all is forgiven.* Yes, yes, I remember that argument. To be fair to Reagan, he has also made tributes to the Holocaust. So what was really being objected to was appearances. We could not allow any reconciliation to appear to cloud the distinction between victims and culprits, radical good and radical evil, even if was perfectly obvious to all of us that Reagan was not condoning Nazism. The Holocaust has become a public issue around which Jews must Save Face, must spot anti-Semitism and decry it even when we know that the substance underneath is rather different.

A similar reaction occurred recently when the speaker of the West German parliament, Philipp Jenninger, made a speech in which he tried to show how the Germans were taken in by Hitler. In attempting to re-create the psychology of the typical German fascinated by Hitler's air of success, his irony was misunderstood—in some cases intentionally so by his political opponents—and he was forced to resign. Jenninger, a longtime supporter of Israel, was taken to task for saying honest things at the wrong time and, specifically, for quoting from Nazi speeches and reports without systematic, repudiating interruptions. Yet how is it possible to understand this complex historical phenomenon of the Holocaust without reexamining the Nazi point of view? What sort of intellectual grasp can we have of a historical situation if it is presented only from the standpoint of the horrors inflicted on the victims?

The "sensitivity" quotient operating around the Holocaust has begun to preclude any public discourse that goes beyond expressions of mourning and remorse. And even within that constricted discourse, how greedily we watch for signs of imbalance. Will the pope single out sufficiently the tragedy of the Jews in his remarks about World War Two? If not, Jewish organizations are quick to get on his case. There is something so testy, so vain, so divalike about this insistence that we always get top billing in any rite of mourning. Must every official statement that does not mention the Jews first among the dead be treated as an ominous sign of forgetting? Even if it were true that a certain resentment against the Jews, an incipient form of anti-Semitism, was lurking behind these official wordings or omissions, the result of all our monitoring and suspicious rebuttal is only to leave the impression of a Jewish lobby seeking to control like a puppeteer the language of politicians and popes.

Whenever I see in the newspaper a story about the opening of yet another memorial or museum dedicated to the Holocaust, complete with photograph of distinguished backers surrounding a cornerstone or architectural model, my stomach gets nervous. What I need to figure for myself is how much this discomfit derives from legitimate doubts and how much it is simply the old fear of making ourselves too visible, drawing too much attention to Jewish things in a world that will never be anything but anti-Semitic. I would like to think, naturally, that there is more to it than cowardice. All right, then, what could possibly be wrong with a Holocaust memorial?

We will start with an obtuse response: I just don't get why both New York City and Washington, D.C., should have to have Holocaust memorial museums. Or why every major city in the United States seems to be commemorating this European tragedy in some way or another. An Israeli poet on a reading tour through the States was taken into the basement of a synagogue in Ohio and proudly shown the congregation's memorial to the six million dead: a torch meant to remain eternally lit. The poet muttered under his breath: *"Shoah flambé."* In Israel they can joke about these matters. Holocaust monuments seem to me primarily a sign of ethnic muscle-flexing, proof that the local Jewish community has attained enough financial and political clout to erect such a tribute to their losses.

In the past, monuments commemorated victories and glory; they were a striving for immortality in the eyes of the polis. But with the very survival of the planet in doubt, eroding our confidence in a future public realm, and in light of our disenchantment with the whole ideal of glory after Vietnam and Watergate, a patriotic equestrian monument raised at this moment would seem embarrassing. Myself, I can easily live without more cannons and generals on pedestals. On the other hand, the dethroning of glory has brought about a tendency to erect monuments to shame and historical nightmare. These monuments have an air of making the visitor feel bad, at the same time retaining a decorously remote and abstract air—all the more so when they are removed geographically from the ground of pain. Auschwitz is one thing: The historical preservation of the death camps in situ makes perfect sense. But it is quite another to allocate the bottom part of a new luxury apartment tower in Lower Manhattan to a Holocaust museum, for which the developer will receive the usual tax abatement.

Snobbish as this may sound, I view museums as primarily places for the exhibition and contemplation of interesting objects. Institutions like Yad Vashem (the Holocaust Heroes and Martyrs Museum) and the Museum of the Diaspora in Israel, which have few artifacts—consisting mainly of slide shows, blown-up photographs, and accompanying wall texts—are, in my view, essentially propaganda factories, designed to manipulate the visitor through a precise emotional experience. They are like a Tunnel of Horrors or a Disneyland park devoted to Jewish suffering. The success of the exhibit depends entirely on entering a properly preprogrammed state and allowing one's buttons to be pushed.

A woman I know, the child of camp survivors, had grown up with tales of Hitler and Buchenwald at every meal. Finally she got to visit Yad Vashem. She was so bursting with emotion, so ready to be wiped out by the experience that, shortly after entering, she saw a lampshade and thought, "Oh my God, that could be my uncle Morty!" and ran in tears from the museum. Her companion caught up with her to try to calm her down. "But, Hilda," he said, "those lampshades are part of the exhibit showing a typical Jewish scholar's study, before the Holocaust even began."

In my own visit to Yad Vashem, I was part of a group of Jewish American academics who thought it so "heavy" that I didn't dare open my mouth. Some of the exhibits were undeniably interesting, but it was not an overwhelming experience for me; rather, I was disturbed by what seemed a theatrically partisan misuse of historical methods. I also found it hard to summon the six million dead in the face of such ennobling strain. The grounds were a sort of monument park filled with sentimental-expressionist statuary. Our tour guide explained that the steel pillar symbolized a smokestack as well as a ladder of transcendence. All this artistic symbolism talk reminded me of the remark of an Israeli friend: "If bad sculpture could be turned into food, then Israel could feed the world."

Yad Vashem's memorial hall did have a bleak architectural

elegance of stone and concrete; but the fire (another "eternal flame") was upstaged by an ugly black organic relief, symbolizing charred bones, I suppose. Someone in my group produced a mimeographed poem, which we read aloud. It was all about the flame being a symbol for the slaughter, of eternal memory, of oppression—a list of pious abstractions clunkily metered and redundant. Why did the poem have to be so bad? I found myself thinking. It is at that level of kitsch doggerel that I start to rebel.

Will the above seem the ravings of a finicky aesthete? I apologize. But remember that it *is* an aesthetic problem we are talking about, this attempt to make an effective presentation of a massive event. The dead of Auschwitz are not buried in Yad Vashem; believe me, I am not insulting their memories; Yad Vashem is the product of us the living and as such is subject to our dispassionate scrutiny and criticism. To project religious awe onto this recently built tourist attraction is idolatry, pure and simple.

In a brilliant essay called "The Kitsch of Israel," which appeared in the *New York Review of Books,* Avishai Margalit wrote:

> Israel's shrine of kitsch is not, as may have been expected, the Wailing Wall, but a place that should have been furthest away from any trace of kitsch: Yad Vashem, the memorial for the Holocaust. A "children's room" has been dedicated there recently. . . . The real significance of this room is not in its commemoration of the single most horrible event in the history of mankind—the systematic murder of two million children, Jewish and Gypsies, for being what they were and not for anything they had done. The children's room, rather, is meant to deliver a message to the visiting foreign statesman, who is rushed to Yad Vashem even before he has had time to leave off his luggage at his hotel, that all of us here in Israel are these children and that Hitler-Arafat is after us. This is the message for internal consumption as well. Talking of the PLO in the same tone as one talks of Auschwitz is an important element in turning the Holocaust into kitsch.

Another method of Holocaust remembrance takes the form of educational instruction in grade school. The pedagogic problem I have with these Holocaust study units is that they are usually parachuted into the classroom with very little connection to anything else in the curriculum. As someone who worked in elementary and secondary schools for twelve years, I've had many occasions to see how the latest concession to each ethnic lobbying group—be it Puerto Rican Week, Black History Month, or Holocaust Week—was greeted by the students as a gimmick, not to be taken seriously. I remember the morning that the local Holocaust curriculum person came into a fourth-grade classroom at P.S. 75 and in her sweet, solemn voice began describing the horrors of a concentration camp. The children listened with resentful politeness, distracted not necessarily because the subject matter was unsuitable for their age group, but because any subject matter introduced in so artificial a manner, with so little relation to their other studies, would be treated as an intrusion.

I realize it may be asking a lot, but we should be attempting to teach the Holocaust within a broader context, as part of an invigorated, general strengthening of historical studies. Why isolate Hitler completely from Bismarck, Kaiser Wilhelm, Adenauer, Stalin? Why teach children about Buchenwald and not other genocides? The Holocaust becomes their first, sometimes their exclusive, official school instruction on death and evil. Of course kids daily see war and gore on the six o'clock news, but in school we seem to want them to encounter the horrors of mass killing solely through presentations about the fate of the Jews. It is almost as if we Jews wanted to monopolize suffering, to appropriate death as our own. But as Irving Louis Horowitz points out, while Judaism as a way of life is special, there is no "special nature of Jewish dying. Dying is a universal property of many peoples, cultures and nations."

I cannot help but see this extermination pride as another variant of the Covenant: This time the Chosen People have been chosen for extraordinary suffering. As such, the Holocaust seems simply another opportunity for Jewish chauvinism. I grew up in Williamsburgh, Brooklyn, surrounded by this chauvinistic tendency, which expressed itself as an insecure need to boast about Jewish achievements in every field, the other side of which was a contempt for the non-Jews, the gentiles, who were characterized as less intelligent, less human, less cultured, humorous, spicy, warmhearted, etc. All my life I've tried to guard against the full force of this damaging tribal smugness, to protect myself from the weakening lies of group *amour-propre* (not that I don't succumb regularly to my own form of it).

"Secularization," Hannah Arendt has written, " . . . engendered a very real Jewish chauvinism, if by chauvinism we understand the perverted nationalism in which (in the words of Chesterton) 'the individual himself is the thing to be worshipped; the individual is his own ideal and even his own idol.' From now on, the old concept of chosenness was no longer the essence of Judaism; it was instead the essence of Jewishness."

There are reasons other than chauvinism why Jews might be loath to surrender the role of the chief victim. It affords us an edge, a sort of privileged nation status in the moral honor roll, such as the Native American Indians have enjoyed for some time. Following Hitler's defeat, Jews had a short grace period in world opinion, pitied as we were and valued as an endangered species. Given the world's tendency to distort and demonize Jews in the past, it would almost seem as though there were no middle ground: either continue to fight for persecuted, good-victim status or else watch the pendulum swing the opposite way, to where we would be regarded as exceptionally wicked. But in my opinion, there must be a middle ground, and it is worth fighting for. In the meantime, is it not possible for us to have a little more compassion for the other victimized peoples of this century and not insist quite so much that our wounds bleed more fiercely?

Theodor Adorno once made an intentionally provocative statement to the effect that one can't have lyric poetry after Auschwitz. Much as I respect Adorno, I am inclined to ask, a bit faux-naively: Why not? Are we to infer, regarding all the beautiful poetry that has been written since 1945, that these postwar poets were insensitive to some higher tact? Alexander Kluge, the German filmmaker, has explained what Adorno really meant by this remark: Any art from now on which does not take Auschwitz into account will be not worthy as art. This is one of those large intimidating pronouncements to which one gives assent in public while secretly harboring doubts. Art is a vast arena; must it all and always come to terms with the death camps, important as they are? How hoggish, this Holocaust, to insist on putting its stamp on all creative activity.

On the other hand, reams have been written arguing that you *can't* make art out of the Holocaust. Elie Wiesel once declared, "Art and Auschwitz are antithetical." Perhaps people would like to believe that there is some preserve, some domain that ought to be protected from the artist's greedy hands. Actually, a whole body of splendid art about the tragedy of the Jews under the Nazis has been made. One thinks right away of Primo Levi's books, the poems of Paul Celan and Nelly Sachs, Tadeusz Kantor's theatrical pieces, films like Resnais's *Night and Fog,* Ophuls's *The Sorrow and the Pity* and *Hotel Terminus,* Losey's *Mister Klein,* Corti's trilogy *Where To and Back. . . .* Maybe not a lot, true, but then not much great art came out of the debacle of World War One. We should not forget that 99 percent of all art-making attempts are failures, regardless of subject matter.

It has also been argued that the enormity of the Nazis' crimes against the Jews calls for an aesthetic approach of an entirely different order than the traditional mimetic response. This seems to me nothing more than a polemic in favor of certain avant-garde or antinaturalist techniques, hitched arbitrarily to the Holocaust. Yes, Paul Celan's cryptic, abstract poems are powerful approaches to the concentration camps, but so are Primo Levi's direct, lucid accounts. I would not like to think that every stage piece about the Holocaust must perforce follow the stripped, ritualized strategies of Grotowski's or Kantor's theatrical works —effective as these may be by themselves—out of some deluded idea that a straight naturalistic approach would desecrate the 6 million dead.

Art has its own laws, and even so devastating an event as the Holocaust may not significantly change them. For all its virtues, the longueurs, repetitions, and failures of sympathy in Claude Lanzmann's *Shoah* are not exonerated, no matter what its apologists may argue, by the seriousness of the subject matter, as though an audience must be put through over eight hours of an exhaustingly uneven movie to convince it of the reality of the Holocaust. A tighter film would have accomplished the same and been a stronger work of art. Lanzmann might reply that he is indifferent to the claims of art compared to those of the Holocaust; unfortunately, you can't play the game of art and not play it at the same time.

What is usually meant by the statement that the Holocaust is unsuitable for artistic treatment is that it is too vast and terrible to be used merely as a metaphor or backdrop. Certainly I understand the impatience of serious people with the parade of shallow movie melodramas and television docudramas that invoke the milieu of Nazi Germany as a sort of narrative frisson. Indeed, where would the contemporary European art film be without the Holocaust? As a plot device it is second only to infidelity. For the fractured European film market, the trauma of World War Two is perhaps the only unifying historical experience to which narratives can appeal commercially. Yet the mediocrity of such "prestige" movies as Truffaut's *The Last Metro,* Visconti's *The Damned,* Zanussi's *Somewhere in the Night,* Malle's *Lucien Lacombe,* De Sica's *The Garden of the Finzi Continis,* Szabo's *Hanussen,* among others, illustrates the degree to which—even for talented directors—the Nazi terror has ossified into a stale genre, a ritualized parade of costumes and sentimental conventions, utterly lacking in the authentic texture of personally observed detail. Now we have the Third Reich as dress-up: all those red flags with swastikas, those jeeps and jackboots suddenly flashing in key-lit night scenes, the tinkle of broken glass—accoutrements that seem considerably less menacing in technicolor, by the way, than they used to in black and white. We have endless variations of the *Cabaret* plot, as characters flounder in frivolous, "decadent" sexual confusion before the evil Nazis announce themselves at midpoint and restore order and narrative suspense in one blow. The Gestapo represents the principle of Fate rescuing the story from its aimlessness—a screenwriter's best friend. The Jewish protagonists are pulled, at first unknowingly, into that funnel of history, then gradually learn that there is something larger than their personal discontents. Meanwhile, the Christian characters sort themselves into betrayers and noble selfless neighbors, thanks to the litmus test of the Holocaust plot; and the audience readies itself for that last purgative scene, the lineup before the trains. . . .

To enumerate the clichés is not to agree with the viewpoint that no art can be made about the Holocaust. Quite the contary; it is only to demand that the artist go beyond a sentimental, generic approach to the subject and find a more complex, detailed, personal, and original path.

I have a former student, Bella, whose father was always trying to get her to see Resnais's *Night and Fog,* an admittedly fine film about the death camps. The father believed that we must all deal in one way or another with the Holocaust, and his way, as befit an educated man, was to read as many books and to see as many films on the subject as possible. This approach he urged on his daughter. But Bella did not want to see *Night and Fog.* As a child she had had many phobias, and even after she had outgrown them, there was something about the way her father talked up the film that made her leery. He would try to get her to meet him at a movie theater where it was showing. He kept saying, "But you owe it to *them* to see it." Them: the ghosts, the 6 million.

Bella refused. Since that time she has moved to Israel and is leading, in her own way, a good Jewish life.

What are our obligations to *them?* Whatever they may be, no living person can tell us.

While I also read books or see movies on the Holocaust, I do it more out of a sense of cultural curiosity and desire to learn about history than a religious debt to the victims. I am not convinced that learning history means trying to put oneself emotionally through the experience—or blaming oneself if one is not feeling enough.

I am trying to put my finger on a problem regarding empathy. A Jewish educator recently wrote that we must find a way to make our young people "feel more anguishingly the memory of the dead." But the effort to project oneself into the Holocaust, to "undergo" for a few minutes what others have suffered in the transport trains and the camps, to take that anguish into oneself, seems—except in rare cases—foredoomed. That way generally lies tourism and self-pity. It is hard enough in psychoanalysis to retrieve affectively one's own past, one's actual memories; to expect to relive with emotion invented memories seems overly demanding. Or gimmicky: like those black history courses for administrators that made the students crawl along the floor "chained" to each other to give them an existential feel for conditions in the hold of a slave ship.

False knowledge. Borrowed mysticism. By blackmailing ourselves into thinking that we must put ourselves through a taste of Auschwitz, we are imitating unconsciously the Christian mystics who tried to experience in their own flesh the torments of Christ on the cross. But this has never been part of the Jewish religion, this gluttony for empathic suffering. Though Jewish rabbis and sages have been killed for their faith, and their deaths recorded and passed down, Judaism has fought shy in the past of establishing a hagiography based on martyrdom. Why are we doing it now?

In certain ways, the Jewish American sacramentalizing of the Holocaust seems an unconscious borrowing of Christian theology. That one tragic event should be viewed as standing outside, above history, and its uniqueness defended and proclaimed, seems very much like the Passion of Christ. Indeed, in a recent book, *The Crucifixion of the Jews,* Christian theologian Franklin H. Littell has argued that the true crucifixion *was* the Holocaust, not the death of Jesus on the cross, and that the subsequent establishment of the State of Israel was the resurrection. Littell asks: "Was Jesus a false Messiah? . . . Is the Jewish people, after all and in spite of two millennia of Christian calumny, the true Suffering Servant promised in Isaiah?" And John Cardinal O'Connor of New York wrote: "To say to the Jews, 'Forget the Holocaust,' is to say to Christians, 'Forget the Crucifixion.' There is a sacramentality about the Holocaust for Jews all around the world. It constitutes a mystery, by definition beyond their understanding—and ours." Complimentary as all this may sound, it worries me because it shows how easily Judaism can be Christianized—or at least co-opted into a Christian vocabulary —by mythologizing the Holocaust experience.

The theological uses to which the Holocaust has been put by an assimilated American Jewish community are so diverse that the Holocaust has begun to replace the Bible as the new text that we must interpret. There is the danger that the "glamour" of the Holocaust will eclipse traditional religious practice in the eyes of

American Jewry—that, in effect, the Holocaust will swallow up Judaism. In the vacuum where God used to be, we are putting the Holocaust.

I first began to notice the usurpation of the traditional Passover service by Holocaust worship at a large communal Seder in Houston, around 1982. Though rewritings of the Haggadah were nothing new to me (in the late sixties, the Vietcong were compared to the Jews in Egypt trying to throw off their oppressors), the introduction of references to the Holocaust in every second or third prayer seemed to have a different function. For many of the people at that Seder in Texas, the Holocaust *was* the heart of their faith; it was what touched them most deeply about being Jewish. The religion itself—the prayers, the commentaries, the rituals, the centuries of accumulated wisdom and tradition—had shriveled to a sort of marginally necessary preamble for this negative miracle. The table conversation turned to accounts of pilgrimages to Buchenwald and Bergen-Belsen and Auschwitz, package tours organized by the United Jewish Appeal. The ancient Jewish religion was all but forgotten beside the lure of the concentration camp universe.

The importance of the Holocaust for such assimilated Jews must be considered within the broader framework of the erosion of Jewish group memory in the modern period. By group or "collective" memory, I mean simply all the customs, rituals, ceremonies, folkways, *Yiddishkeit,* cuisine, historical events, etc., that used to be the common inheritance of every Jew. The desperation to hold on to the Holocaust is informed by this larger decay. Underneath these anxious injunctions never to forget, what I hear is: "We must never forget the Holocaust because we're rapidly forgetting everything else, so let's hold on at least to this piece."

At first glance it seemed to me a paradox that Jews, ostensibly "the historically minded people" par excellence, should be so resistant to placing the Holocaust in a comparative historical context. But then I came across an illuminating little book by Yosef Yerushalmi, *Zakhor: Jewish History and Jewish Memory,* which argues that antihistorical currents are nothing new within Jewry. The oft-repeated injunction to "remember" is not the same as urging a historical perspective: "Not only is Israel under no obligation whatever to remember the entire past, but its principle of selection is unique unto itself. It is above all God's acts of intervention in history, and man's responses to them, be they positive or negative, that must be recalled."

Yerushalmi points out that for nearly fifteen centuries after the death of Josephus, during the Talmudic period so fertile for commentary about the patterns and meaning of the Bible, there were no Jewish historians. The rabbis felt it unnecessary and perhaps even impious to keep contemporary historical records (except for sketchy rabbinic genealogies), precisely because the Bible was already "sacred history." A brief flurry of Jewish history writing occurred in the sixteenth century, partly touched off by the need to understand the catastrophic expulsion from Spain and Portugal; but these chronicles were not so scientific as Christian histories of the same era; they had elements of messianism and followed a somewhat apocalyptic approach, examining the past for signs and prophecies of an approaching redemption. Even this limited historical activity was submerged, at the end of the sixteenth century, by the greater appeal of Lurianic Kabbalah, which offered Jews "a unique interpretation of history that lay beyond history . . . an awesome metahistorical myth of a pronounced gnostic character. That myth declared that all evil, including the historical evil that is Jewish exile, had its roots before history began, before the Garden of Eden was planted, before our world existed, in a primal tragic flaw that occurred at the very creation of the cosmos itself" (Yerushalmi).

In the modern era, of course, a plethora of Jewish histories and historians came into being, but the new objective methods of analysis have been on a collision course with providential history. "To the degree that this historiography is indeed 'modern' and deserves to be taken seriously," notes Yerushalmi, "it must at least functionally repudiate" two cardinal assumptions of traditional Judaism: "the belief that divine providence is not only an ultimate but an active causal factor in Jewish history, and the related belief in the uniqueness of Jewish history itself."

Forgive this digression; it actually has a point. Our response to the Holocaust must be seen within this broader framework of the ancient Jewish ambivalence toward a historical outlook, which threatens the religious one. The hostility toward anything that questions the uniqueness of the Holocaust can now be seen as part of a deeper tendency to view all of Jewish history as "unique," to read that history selectively, and to use it only insofar as it promotes a redemptive script. Thus, the Holocaust's "mystery" must be asserted over and over, in the same way as was the "mystery" of Jewish survival through the ages, in order to yield the single explanation that God "wants" the Jewish people to live and is protecting them. Being a secular, fallen Jew with a taste for rationalism and history, I cannot help but regard such providential interpretations as superstition. Against them I would place the cool, cautionary wisdom of Spinoza about his own people: "as for their continuance so long after dispersion and the loss of empire, there is nothing marvelous in it."

Sometimes I see the Jewish preoccupation with the Holocaust, to the exclusion of all other human disasters, as uncharitable, self-absorbed, self-righteous, and—pushy. On the other hand, it makes no sense to counsel putting it aside for a while. How can we expect to get over so enormous a tragedy in only forty or fifty years? It takes time, centuries. It took over a thousand years for the Jews as a people to get over the destruction of Jerusalem by Titus, and we may still not have recovered from that. My problem is not that the grief is taking too long but that the orchestration of that grief in the public realm sometimes seems coercive and misguided.

Jewish history is filled with disasters, from which some redemptive meaning has ultimately been extracted. The Holocaust is proving to be a large bone to swallow; it does not turn "redeemable" so easily, and when we try to hurry up that process with mechanical prescriptions and ersatz rituals, compelling governments and churches to pay verbal tribute to our losses in narrowly defined terms, and browbeating our young people to feel more anguishingly the memory of our dead, something false, packaged, sentimentally aggressive begins to enter the picture. Perhaps the problem is that for many alienated, secularized Jews who experience themselves as inauthentic in a thousand other ways, the Holocaust has become the last proof of their own authenticity. If so, they should realize that even this proof is perishable stuff; the farther one gets from personal experience, the harder it is to take the spilled blood of history into one's veins.

An End to Innocence

BARBARA ROGAN

Through a mouthful of cornflakes my six-year-old son asks, "Mommy, who was Hitler?"

I pick up my cup and toss down some coffee, though it's scalding hot. I fuss with the baby. I say, "Don't talk with your mouth full, dear," and point out a squirrel walking a high-wire tightrope outside the kitchen window.

My son eyes me strangely. My face feels warm. "Mommy," he says patiently, "who was Hitler?"

"A bad man," I say rapidly, "a very bad man who killed a lot of Jews and other people. He's dead now."

"Oh," he says and goes back to his cornflakes. Afterward I squander a whole day's work, distracted by this inexplicable fit of panic. It's not my style. My idealized vision of my parental self (honored, albeit, more in the breach than in the observance) is the unflappable earth mother whom nothing can dismay. I believe that if a child is old enough to ask a question, he's old enough to get an answer. I watch the news with my son and we discuss whatever interests him; our conversations on such topics as Middle East politics, child abuse, homelessness, AIDS, and sex have never raised a blush on either of our faces. Why, then, does the mere mention of Hitler reduce me to stammering evasions?

I don't know. The closest I come to an answer is no answer at all, but only a feeling: a belief that his innocence, which I am devoted to preserving, cannot coexist with a knowledge of the Holocaust.

But why not? We warn our children against strangers, we arm them against molesters, and in most cases, we do so without rupturing the fragile hymen of childhood, that indefinable quality called innocence. Whence, then, my certainty that innocence cannot stand before knowledge of an event that preceded, not only my son's birth, but my own?

The sixties were my formative decade and I'm proud to say I lived them to the hilt; but I do truly hope that my children never do unto me as I did unto my parents. I was self-righteous and contemptuous; I opposed them on every front: we fought about friends, values, religion, drugs, and, most of all, politics. I accused them of dividing the world into two arbitrary categories, Jews and others, but saw no problem in my own division by generation. Anti-Semitism was a bogeyman invented by our elders to scare Jewish kiddies into staying close to home.

I wasn't a Zionist and didn't consider myself much of a Jew. I went unwillingly to Hebrew school, learned nothing, shunned the Zionist youth groups. It seemed to me improbable that I should have chanced to be born into the one true religion, and I undertook to learn about others. I visited Buddhist temples, Quaker meetinghouses, churches, and cathedrals. At Christmas I went caroling with my friends. Nevertheless, I'd been an uneasy atheist since the age of five, when my best friend asked me if I believed in God and I said no, then ran home to hide under my bed.

I learned about the Holocaust in increments; I can't remember when the process began, but there were milestones along the way. I read *The Diary of Anne Frank,* wept, and walked around like a tragic heroine for several weeks. I remember watching the Eichmann trial on television, but little of what I saw stayed with me. I knew in a factual sort of way that 6 million Jews died and that all my grandparents' relatives who stayed behind in Europe were killed. But I was far more involved in what was happening in my own world.

The struggle of the blacks in America and the movement against the war in Vietnam mattered far more than atrocities committed in another time, another world. In high school I volunteered as a tutor for disadvantaged—i.e., black—students in a neighboring school; I was an editor on the school paper and a minor-league activist in the antiwar movement. When I was sixteen I was suspended from school, ostensibly for cutting a class but actually for my political activities. The same year, two men in gray suits canvassed my neighborhood, claiming that I had applied for a job that required a security clearance and asking personal questions about me. In fact I had applied for no such job, and we never found out who the men were.

I was no one special, no hotshot organizer or movement child-star. I just happened to be at a passionate age during an era of passionate politics. My attention was fully focused on America. Of my Jewish friends, most, like me, were second-generation Americans. But we had neither our parents' sense of tentative acceptance nor our grandparents' gratitude; and if there was a Jewish factor to my emotional identification with the victims of American racism, I didn't acknowledge it.

Religion is irrelevant, my friends and I agreed. So is race. People should define themselves, instead of gutlessly allowing society to do it for them. The biggest fight, or series of fights, I had with my mother was over my high school boyfriend, who wasn't Jewish. Actually he was half-Jewish, but not the right half; he was raised a Catholic. I screamed at her: "What difference does it make? Neither of us believes anything."

"It's not about belief," my mother replied. "It's who you are." But in those days I never listened to anything she said.

When persuasion failed, my parents wisely tried bribery; as a high school graduation present, they offered me a trip abroad.

"London!" I cried. "Paris!" In Paris students were leading the revolution, tearing up the streets, and using cobblestones to fight the *flics*. I yearned to be there, to witness with my own eyes.

"Israel," they said firmly, "and with a group."

"Israel!" I wailed. "Why not Miami, while you're at it!"

For, despite Israel's stunning military victory in the 1967 Six-Day War, I pictured the Jewish state as a cross between Long Island and the Eden Roc: a country of old men in lime-colored trousers, snobbish girls, and boys with fat bottoms and spotty complexions. (I don't know what my parents imagined—a land full of distant relatives, perhaps, who would see that no harm came to their impetuous child.)

In the end they prevailed; it was, after all, their money. I agreed ungraciously to go to Israel. It was better than staying home, if only marginally.

We landed at dusk and drove directly from Lod airport to Jerusalem. At dawn I stood on the roof of our small hotel, watching the sun rise over the most beautiful city on earth. And the most foreign.

I was seventeen years old. I'd been in love before, but never with a country. It's a disease something like malaria but more virulent. Twenty years later, I still suffer recurrent bouts.

As in most love affairs, the initial attraction was physical. The astonishing crystal light, the mind-altering heat, the countryside slow-baked a golden brown, the groves of gnarled olive trees. Clarity, not only of sight but of all the senses: the deep quiet of the ancient terraced hills of Jerusalem and the Galilee, the braying of donkeys and the polylingual babble of the Old City, the smells of the souk—pungent Arab tobacco mixed with hashish, fresh pita, meat roasting on spits, mountains of fruit from Jericho, the sweetest in the world. Underfoot, stones trodden smooth by centuries of pilgrims and vendors. The streets of the Old City are too narrow for cars; people and donkeys throng the souk.

Jerusalem is a crossroad in space and time. The city is built of stone and the stones are old beyond reckoning, natural conductors of time. Late one night I wandered alone through the Old City and saw nothing I would not have seen a thousand years before. I grew disoriented; I knew where I was, but not when. Everything was strange, yet nothing was entirely unfamiliar. It came to me for the first time that I was a direct descendant of people who had lived in this land, in these very streets, centuries upon centuries ago. Foreign though it was, it didn't feel like a first visit; it felt as if I had come back.

Before we left Jerusalem we visited Yad Vashem, the Holocaust memorial.

All tourists are obnoxious but none more so than American teenagers. We drove to Yad Vashem in a bus, screeching, laughing, hanging out of windows to flirt with passing truckloads of soldiers. We filed into the building, assuming, with more or less success, a solemnity we did not feel.

A director met us in the great hall whose floor is taken up by a giant map of Europe. From walkways above the floor we gazed down at the map, which glittered with innumerable points of light. The lights, the director said, stood for Jewish communities wiped out by the Nazis. Each light might represent 100, 1,000, 10,000 souls. There were so many glittering points that the floor twinkled like the dome of a planetarium. I thought of God's promise to Abraham that his descendants shall be like unto the stars in the sky, the grains of sand on the shore. I wondered if this was what He meant.

We moved into the main part of the memorial, a series of rooms that traces the course of the Holocaust in time and space as it ripped through Europe like a malevolent tornado. Our guides left us there, so that each could go through alone, at his own pace. First we saw documents and photographs of the anti-Semitic propaganda that primed the German people for the Final Solution. I had never before encountered this kind of material and I took it personally. Every vicious caricature, every slander seemed aimed at me. My face burned, and I was grateful for the dim lighting.

Next came the photographs of the camps.

Since that time I have seen many such pictures, and I would like to say that the impact never diminishes; but the truth is that nothing ever hit me as hard as that first glimpse into the Holocaust. It opened my eyes to the depth of my ignorance, not only about the event itself, but also about human nature. Not immediately—it took time to sink in, time till I understood what had happened—but eventually, that visit changed the way I thought about the world and about myself. It reset the parameters of human behavior and permanently altered, in several ways, my feelings about being a Jew.

I was seventeen, on the outer cusp of childhood. Before I walked into Yad Vashem, I thought the world had come into being to produce me. By the time I walked out, I knew that my existence hinged on the merest happenstance.

That's true of everyone, of course. We are all pieces of a chain linked by billions of tiny accidents. But the coincidence of this rude awakening with my first visceral introduction to the Holocaust bound the two forever in my mind.

There was another change. The idea of chosenness had always worried me; it assumed a kind of elite status for the Jews that offended my egalitarian beliefs and that implied a preordained destiny incompatible with my ideas of self-determination. After Yad Vashem, the concept changed colors. The description became empirical: the Jews *were* chosen, but not for glory and not by God.

We had a great deal of freedom that summer of 1968, one year after Israel's stunning, swift defeat of four Arab armies in the Six-Day War. I hitchhiked all around the country on my own and met many Israelis. All the men and most of the women were soldiers, either active or reserve. Unlike American soldiers, whom I viewed at the time as bloodthirsty executors of an evil war, the Israelis' cause was self-preservation and their valor unquestionable. It's not entirely irrelevant that the Israeli men were hard-bodied, deeply tanned, amazingly good-looking, self-assured, and sexy—a great contrast to the American boys I'd known. I fell in love at least three times that summer.

The land itself seemed alive and sensual, its fields abundantly fertile and its deserts full of sweet oases. I wondered that a people who had gone through the horror of the Holocaust could create such a strong and vital state.

My mother says we come from good Jewish peasant stock. Her mother, Pauline, was born in Poland in 1896. At the age of sixteen she ran away from home and traveled alone through Europe to France, where she took a boat to America. She spoke no English and knew no one in America, save an aunt in Wilkes-Barre, Pennsylvania. It took her years, but she saved the money for her ticket by taking in sewing. She knew when she left that she might never see her parents again, and in fact she did not. But she had to go, because in Poland there was no hope. You were born poor and you died poor. America, she believed then and still does, was the land of hope and opportunity, where anything was possible.

My grandfather Morris was Hungarian, the middle child and only son of a Jewish merchant. Unlike Pauline, who fled the poverty of the shtetl, Morris was drawn to America by the promise of freedom and adventure. When Pauline first met him, he was an itinerant peddler; he owned a horse and wagonful of sundries that he bought and sold as he plied his route between Pennsylvania and New York. Later, after marriage and a handful of babies, he gave in to Pauline's practical urging, sold his stock and wagon, and took steady work as a milkman. Later still, he apprenticed himself to a furrier and learned the trade. After a couple of years, he joined the furriers' union and became a fervent socialist. Pauline didn't know from socialism; she knew from bread on the table and a decent place to live. Security, for Pauline, was her own house, and happiness was wall-to-wall carpeting, the lamp on the polished end table, the car in the garage. But she was tolerant of her husband's *meshugas* and he of hers.

There is a family story that goes like this: Once, early on in their marriage, Morris boarded a boat to Europe in the company of a young woman, a singer or dancer. Just before the ship set sail, Pauline dashed aboard with one baby in her arms and another clinging to her skirt. She found Morris, grasped him by the ear, and marched him off the boat.

The story is apocryphal, denied by those who know best; but it persists in the family and the reason it persists is that even if it never happened, it says something true about Morris. Similarly, in a manner hard to define, the marriage of Pauline and Morris seems to me to say something true about the Jewish people.

The Nazis didn't invent anti-Semitism; they just brought it into the industrial age. Centuries of persecution, rejection, and alienation must of necessity leave their mark; and the Jews have evolved several main channels of response to this "chosenness."

It seems to me that two of these channels met in the marriage of my grandparents. For my grandmother, assimilation was the goal and materialism the key to success on the terms of her adopted country. Morris's path was to embrace his alienation, to imbue it with meaning by clothing it in idealism—socialism, in his case, religion in others. That so many early socialists were Jews suggests that socialism represented a secular counterpart to religious orthodoxy, perhaps a preemptive distancing of an un-welcoming society.

When, at the age of twenty-two, I announced my intention to move permanently to Israel, my parents took it like troopers; but my grandmother Pauline would not be reconciled. She said, "It's the most *meshuga* thing I ever heard, a young girl should quit a good job it took a year to find and leave her family to go live in the wilderness."

"It's not a wilderness," I said. "I'm not so young. And it's my life."

"And you think you find a better life in Israel, with all the time wars and Arabs and no money, they gotta come schnorr in America? For that you leave your home, your family?"

"You left your family when you were younger than me."

"That's different. We had nothing in Poland, we never would have. Here you got everything. For what did I break my mother's heart and run off and never see her again—so you could throw it all away? *Oy*," she cried. "You don't know what you got here. You don't know what America is."

"I was born here," I said.

"That's why you don't know!"

I couldn't, at the time, understand why she wished to deny me the adventure she'd claimed for herself; but now I understand more. To Pauline, America was and would always be the Promised Land: a land where Jews were un-Chosen, free to live normal lives, to prosper or fail by their own efforts, to worship or not as they saw fit.

Then I think of my mother-in-law, who was born in Yugo-slavia and spent her adolescence living in the forests around Belgrade with a group of partisans. When the war ended and the Nazis were expelled, Ava came out of hiding and tried to resume her life. Her father and sister were dead, but her mother had survived. They took an apartment together in Belgrade and Ava started studies at the Academy of Art. She was a good socialist and a talented student; within a few years she had established a promising career as a movie set designer. Then, in 1949, she threw it all up to move to Israel.

"I was tired of being a Jew," she said. "In Yugoslavia they never let me forget it. Israel was the one place I could go to escape."

I've come to believe that this is a condition of Jewishness— the desire to escape being what we are, escape being Chosen, escape being other. Pauline sought it in America, Ava in Israel.

I carefully explained to all who asked and some who didn't that my decision to live in Israel had nothing to do with being a Jew. It wasn't Zionism or religion, and it wasn't a man but the land itself I coveted.

The hot and arid climate suited me unexpectedly, and I felt that somehow I knew how to live in such conditions. Also, once I reached a certain level of proficiency, I felt remarkably at home in the language. Hebrew is colorful and direct, much like the people who speak it; it was liberating and instructive to live in a language that was not my own. Altogether I felt more at ease in Israel than I ever had in the United States. But I hardly ever expressed these feelings, for fear they would be taken as some sort of atavistic claim to the land.

The glory of living in Israel is partaking in a life that is overtly political. Unlike Americans, virtually every Israeli knows precisely where he or she stands on every issue and will at the drop of a hat express that view. I've heard this phenomenon attributed to the quarrelsome nature of the people, and there's something to be said for that interpretation, but I suspect the answer lies more in the nexus of Israel's small size, perilous economy, and political situation.

It's hard for Americans who haven't lived abroad to appreciate how different a small country is. The United States is such a huge country, made up of separate spheres that never intersect. Momentous decisions are made at the center, and by the time they reach the periphery, they're barely perceptible ripples. Interest rates go up or down a point, the stock market quivers, the numbers of the homeless subtly increase. But the same decisions made in a small country—Israel, for example—create shock waves that rock the lives of every citizen.

Twice in my life I have lived in countries that were at war, and both times, for different reasons, I have opposed these wars: but with what a variance in personal investment.

The war in Vietnam dragged on for years before the level of opposition rose high enough to stop it. During these years, tens of thousands of Americans, most of them my age, were killed. I knew none of them. I knew no one who'd been wounded, no one who'd even served. The war was being fought in our name, and that enraged us—but it wasn't *our* war.

When the war in Lebanon broke out, I was seven months pregnant with my first child. Overnight, half the men I knew and worked with in Tel Aviv had disappeared, and by the next day the other half was gone. My colleagues, my obstetrician, and the contractor who had just finished demolishing the interior of our apartment were gone. I stood on the balcony of a borrowed apartment with our baby kicking in my belly and waved good-bye to my husband, who was going we didn't know where to fight a war we didn't believe was necessary. The connection between what our leaders in Jerusalem decided and our own lives was exceedingly clear. If Israelis are opinionated, it's because they have to pay the price.

For the past twenty years the main issue has been the disposition of Gaza and the West Bank, called Judea and Samaria by those who would stake a biblical claim. Politics permeates religion and vice versa throughout the Middle East. Bible-based Zionism is politically if not ideologically incompatible with the secular, Holocaust-based variety. I, of course, subscribed to the latter. Biblical claims not only depend on a level of belief I don't possess, they also tend to backfire, bestowing equal validity on the claims of other religions.

Nor did I ever buy the claim of many Zionists that Jews are *obliged* to "come up to the Land." Why should they? Why live where everything is ten times more difficult than it needs to be? I could have written a novel in the time I spent getting a telephone installed. Why would anyone who could avoid it choose to live in Israel—unless something, some inner or immaterial thing, compelled them?

As to why I chose for over twelve years to live there—for reasons I resolutely refused to examine, it seemed necessary. Having through what I insisted was a fluke discovered the one place on earth where I felt at home, how could I leave it?

My Zionist ideology was primitive, based solely on the Holocaust and the stunning indifference of the rest of the world to the fate of the Jews. Having barely escaped total genocide, the Jews had an absolute, self-evident right to take their fate into their own hands by establishing a state. This single-pronged Zionism forged in Yad Vashem was reinforced by meetings over a period of years with dozens of survivors of the Holocaust. My work drew them to me.

Eighteen months after I moved to Israel, I opened a literary agency. I sold translation rights to Israeli publishers and helped Israeli writers get their books published abroad. Since it was, at the time, the only agency of its kind, I was deluged with submissions from Israeli writers. Many came from Holocaust survivors.

Most had no idea how to go about writing a book. Usually they wrote in a language that was not their own. The great majority of the manuscripts were eminently unpublishable and would never be read in their entirety by anyone outside the author's family.

Agents generally don't continue reading a manuscript once they've determined that it's not for them—there are too many manuscripts and not enough time. But I felt obliged to finish every Holocaust memoir that crossed my desk and to meet with the authors, even when I thought the book was hopeless. One couldn't in decency say to these people, "I read the first thirty pages and I'm afraid . . ."

Thus it happened that I read dozens of Holocaust memoirs over the course of twelve years as an agent, in addition to the Holocaust books that flowed into the agency from abroad—since every publisher who issued one felt sure it had an easy market in Israel. The stories were matter-of-fact accounts of deeds so cruel and suffering so great that had they been fiction they would have been called surrealistic. A few of the manuscripts particularly stand out in my memory.

One was by a man who survived the camps by working as a *Sonderkommando,* a member of the special *kapos* unit that did the horrible job of transporting and burning the bodies of the dead. The job they did was the worst in the camp, and though the Nazis rewarded these *kapos* with extra food and other privileges, the other prisoners despised them. I remember the wrenching account of the author's finding his parents among the dead. But what fixed the book forever in my mind were not this man's experiences in the camp but the aftermath: his attempt to deal with overwhelming, abiding guilt in order to go on living.

After reading the manuscript I met the author. Knowing how other survivors felt about the *Sonderkommandos* and having just read his own description of the work, I felt some unease about the meeting, but I couldn't refuse it. He entered my office and sat in the chair opposite my desk, a solid, burly, slow-speaking man, some forty years my senior. He had unusually large hands, which he kept splayed on his knees.

He said he knew the other prisoners had hated him and the other *Sonderkommandos* and he didn't blame them. For years he'd felt stigmatized, and he used to deny what he'd done in the camps, but he couldn't do that anymore. He needed to tell the truth, not as an act of penance or even self-examination, because I could see as he sat there so quiet and contained that he had come to terms with what he had done, but because the truth needed to be told.

"The thing is," he said, "no one has ever written about what it was like for us, and time is running out. I know it's not what you'd call a literary book," he said. "I know my English is not so good and maybe there are some spelling mistakes. But someone had to write it."

And someone ought to have published it, but as far as I know, no one has.

I remember, too, a woman who survived the Holocaust as a young girl, immigrated to Israel, and became a painter of note. She wrote her story in a series of short, stylized vignettes, illustrated with her own watercolors. Together the stories and paint-ings conveyed a vivid, moving vision of a child caught up in the Holocaust.

I tried very hard to place that book. I offered it to every publisher I knew and some I didn't. Everyone admired the work and was sure someone else would publish it. Editors pronounced themselves personally moved but professionally inhibited. Ho-locaust books didn't sell, they said regretfully, unless the author was famous or the book written with the brilliant luminosity of a Primo Levi. But none of my survivor clients was a professional writer; they were just people with one single, essential story to tell and not much time left to tell it.

From years in the industry, I understand the forces that act on editors, whose jobs ultimately depend on their bottom line. Some Holocaust books are published, though only a small frac-tion of those written, and most publishers of any size can point to one or two on their backlist. How many can we do? they ask, and justifiably so. But I wonder: How many can we afford to lose?

The State of Israel embodies the contradictions that en-livened my grandparents' long marriage. In one breath Israel declares its mission to serve as a beacon to the world, just as many young Jewish Americans like my grandfather aspired to lead America toward the enlightenment of socialism. In the next, Israel claims to be "a nation like all other nations," entitled, even obliged, to pursue its own best interest. Like my grandmother in America, the state founded by her own generation set its heart on assimilation into the body of nations. The attitudes of the founders have carried over; thus Israelis today howl with indig-nation at what they perceive as a double standard in their treat-ment by the world press. Once again, they say, and despite all that has passed, the Jews are set apart.

A lot of people feel that, because of its history and genesis, Israel ought to be more sensitive than other nations to the rights of its minorities. I think they're right about the primacy of the Holocaust to Israel's ethos, but mistaken about its effects.

Survivors, like all people, react variously to what befalls them. Some came out of the camps with an abhorrence of racism and a heightened empathy with its victims; in retrospect it's easy to see that dynamic in the identification of American Jews with the civil rights movement. Other survivors emerged with an absolute determination to do whatever was necessary to ensure that never again would the Jews suffer a holocaust. Such disparate premises may lead to political conclusions that are diametrically opposed. All that unites them is the conviction that each has arrived at his conclusions based on his experience of the Holocaust.

No one can judge them. They have a right to whatever conclusions they've drawn. When I meet someone who survived the camps, I am filled with awe because I know something of what they endured. But I do not make the mistake of believing that suffering automatically confers wisdom.

If it did, all survivors would agree on every important issue, but this is manifestly not so. There is no unanimity. One finds Holocaust survivors scattered throughout the political spectrum and on both sides of the Palestinian issue. The survival experience is no predictor of the survivor's politics.

Nor is it a predictor of his or her level of religiosity, which always seemed strange to me. I could well understand how some Jews went into the camps believers and came out skeptics, but how the opposite occurred was a mystery. Less of one now that I've been in enough foxholes to discover for myself the truth of the old adage; but prayers of desperation and sustained faith are two different things and I still wonder how believers reconcile God's omnipotent goodness with his passivity in the face of the Final Solution. It is such a barrier to my belief that I think those who surmount it must have greater faith than Jews who lived and died before the Holocaust.

The survivors' compulsion to bear witness aroused in me a compulsion to receive it; I felt that if I read their stories, then, even if they went unpublished, they would not have gone entirely untold. I didn't know that these stories would stay with me, that they would eventually influence my own work. They were not, after all, *my* stories.

They say that writers need good memories and I believe I have one, but it's almost all unconscious. Things penetrate, disappear, and years later come out in the writing. Just bits and pieces, but authentic bits and pieces.

My first novel, *Changing States,* was about the daughter of two Holocaust survivors who move from the United States to Israel. When the girl falls in love with an Arab, her mother intervenes, and the consequences are tragic. The book attracted rather extreme reviews; some people liked it a lot and others not at all, with the difference seeming to hinge on where they stood on the issue of Israeli racism. But common to almost every reviewer, including real children of survivors, was the assumption that I myself was the daughter of a survivor. The same assumption cropped up in letters from readers. In fact, however, thanks to the prescience of my grandparents, my immediate family (though not theirs) was beyond Hitler's reach.

The whole of my last novel, *Cafe Nevo,* coalesced around the central character, Emmanuel Yehoshua Sternholz, the seventy-two-year-old waiter in Cafe Nevo who survived the Holocaust but lost his wife and son. Another main character was orphaned by the Nazis, and still another was a daughter of survivors. Once, after I spoke at a Jewish book fair in Buffalo, an elderly woman came up and waited patiently till I was free. Then she took my hand and pressed it, and she said, "I am a survivor. Thank you, God bless you for not forgetting."

I was deeply embarrassed. Why should she thank me? I had done nothing beyond the requirements of my job: I had written a novel that reflected as closely as possible the world as I know it: that is, a world permanently marked by the Holocaust.

It was never my intention to write about the Holocaust, but somehow it came into my novels and once inside grew like a weed, fertilized, I believe, by that deep reservoir of vicarious experience. It puzzled me that this should happen when my own connection to the Holocaust was so remote, and for a while I attributed it to the fact that my books were set in Israel. The Holocaust is a potent presence in Israel; state policies are influenced and sometimes determined by its leaders' memories of the period and by the many survivors and their descendants who live there. Nor are the spirits of the dead absent from the councils of Israel. Six million voices, even when dead, raise a clamor, and it doesn't take a writer's ear to hear them.

But now I live in America, where the dead do not speak (at least not to me), and I'm writing a novel about this country in which I am a native-born stranger; and yet, as if I were trapped in a carnival fun house, where every exit turns out to be a mirror, I keep bumping into the Holocaust.

My books guide, they are not guided by, my understanding. They are wiser than I am; they tap into memories and thoughts not otherwise accessible to me. Through them I have come to what understanding I have of the Holocaust.

The images of men and women warehoused like spare parts; worked, starved, beaten to death, turned into soap and lamp-shades; children torn limb from limb; patients tortured to death by doctors; mothers forced to choose which child shall live and which die; piles of stripped corpses awaiting disposal—these images, once seen, cannot be unseen. And the knowledge that this thing was done diligently and methodically by men and women like ourselves, not monsters, demons, or beasts, but "civ-ilized" human beings like ourselves, cannot but alter forever one's notion of what man and civilization are.

There is also the other side. I once read a book about a small village whose residents belonged to a Protestant sect long per-secuted in France. Led by their pastor, a charismatic figure of tremendous moral force and clarity, the entire village trans-formed itself into a clandestine staging facility for Jews fleeing the Nazis. To rescue strangers, they knowingly and repeatedly risked not only their own lives but also the lives of their children. This story and others like it exemplify a level of altruism so heroic it almost balances the moral decadence of the Nazis.

In their wisdom, the architects of Yad Vashem created a tranquil, tree-lined boulevard through which visitors to the me-morial must pass as they leave the grounds. Each tree is planted in memory of a Righteous Gentile who risked and often lost his or her life to save Jews from the Holocaust. That walk reminds those who emerge in despair from Yad Vashem that the Holo-caust enlarged our understanding of the human capacity, not only for evil, but for goodness as well.

We start off learning about the Holocaust as if it were some-thing outside us and end up acquiring self-knowledge. I can imagine myself writing a book that never mentions the Holocaust, but I can't imagine writing anything that is not informed by it. Like the expulsion from Eden, it marks a turning point in human history: an end to innocence, an awakening.

My son is prone to nightmares. When ghosts and monsters menace him in his sleep, he cries out for Mommy or Daddy to save him. We sit beside him, stroke his head, and tell him, "There are no ghosts, no monsters; it was only a dream." We don't lie, but we don't tell the whole truth: that there are worse things than ghosts and monsters in the world. He'll find out soon enough.

Our Houses?
Our Holy Places?

MARK MIRSKY

The knowledge of the Holocaust in me lies as far as I can remember at the age of four, just past my first memories, where its roots are twisted together with World War Two, the pear trees suddenly barren in the backyard, a childhood neighborhood.

We lived in Boston's Dorchester, Roxbury, Mattapan, wood and asphalt-shingled streets into which sixty thousand Jews clung to each other's necks. Our house, however, lay a backyard away from the railroad. Beyond the stone and board fences were collapsing three-deckers of poor Irish and Italians, facing the trains, the district's saddest homes—raveled into the cloth of the Jews. Across three wards our wanderer's tent of black sacking stretched. The smell of chicken fat saved in octagonal glasses, where memorial candle wax had jelled, ascended in hallway after hallway.

On the way down to my family's cellar in the pleasant old house (my father, counting pennies in a fledgling law practice, had redistricted two floors and an attic into three apartments), descending to a furnace still fed by coal, there were oversized posters of aviators in chocolate leather jackets beside brown bomblers. These romantic heroes of the savings bond drives were pasted over the bumpy plaster cellar walls. Plucked onto the cover of a record album upstairs, Hitler, Mussolini, Hirohito dangled frantically from a string as Irving Berlin tunes boomed from the phonograph. "This is the Army, Mr. Jones/ No private rooms or telephones. . . ." Under the brass bands, the good humor of my father in white puttees and khakis getting ready to report for his weekends in the Massachusetts State Guard, I was told (was it my mother in an aside?) this was no ordinary war for us. If the Germans won, I, my little sister, cousins, playmates, would be killed.

"Why?"

"We are Jews," she answered.

When the war was over, sitting on the curb of Warner Street, a playmate whispered, Hitler is alive, living in the attic of an abandoned house at the corner of Kerwin and Talbot avenues, two streets across, one down. Through the war, I felt the looming imbalance. It was, like my grandfather's death when I was four and a half, one of those strokes that set the whole adult world tipping, to come down on my head: like the news of the atomic bomb, which drew lines through my father's and mother's faces as they stared into the fire at our rented cottage at Nantasket beach. Headlines of mushrooming type, a universe poisoned, one in which the adults were helpless, and whispered the opposite of reassurance. In a few days I, my playmates did not forget but, breathing it in, got used to the horror, like the children in the huge steel cylinders, with faces as pale as hospital sheets who were displayed in the iron lungs on the Boston Common. It was part of the fear, futility. It contradicted the homilies of a just world, and like many Jewish children of the forties, I grew up sensing that my parents wanted me to understand what lay beyond conventional assurances.

For a little boy who learned to read and write those first years after the war, in the Jewish streets of Boston, classes in second grade were still divided into Marines (best readers), Army (good readers), Navy (fair readers). The absence of the Holocaust, its discussion in the house, in retrospect, is eerie. I go with the question to my father's youngest sister. Dad and his two sisters had been born and grew up in Eastern Europe. It was their childhood streets, playmates, cousins who were destroyed. My grandfather lost two of his three sisters in the Holocaust. Grandpa had been very close to both and through the twenties and the thirties begged them to emigrate. My father would talk, when I was three, four, about Pinsk, but it was a faraway fairy tale, a place of deep forests, wolves, angry, comic grandparents, and charging Cossacks. In my father's top drawer, mingled with the copper cigarette lighter in the shape of a fat rifle shell casing, was a black leather purse of silver and copper coins with the insignia of the czar, the German kaiser, which smelled of something very old. The Pinsk that had just been destroyed was never spoken of.

My aunt confirms this: "We tried not to think about what happened."

A secret river, the knowledge, ran underneath the synagogue, Hebrew school, holidays. As a boy of nine, ten, at the South End Music School, waiting for a class to begin, I took down a book of photographs from the library shelf. There was a picture of a Russian family frozen in the snow outside Minsk, not skeletons, but in warm fur coats—the boy's face my face, his sister's like my sister's, the father and mother uncannily similar —the cold taste not only of my own death, but my family's. Was I twelve, thirteen, when I discovered on my father's bookshelves *The Root and the Bough*?[1] There the story of the murders began to unfold from the mouths of survivors, in detail. The sentences breathed sickness. I lost appetite, will, breath, as if to survive was a betrayal in me, my family in our quiet street in Mattapan. The descriptions by the survivors set fire to the chicken fat, the soaked wood of the stairs in Dorchester, and the furnace in the basement became a fearful thing. Again and again, I have heard, read, the accounts, and that first time takes hold of my bones.

It was almost sweet, the fever that ran through my body, shame that waxed possessive, the overpowering of horror. I couldn't eat, think. It wore off in a few days that shame, its sugar, had to ferment into a harsh intoxicant. Now I understand the laughter of my demented Hebrew teacher, her curses when asked about Roosevelt, her story about a boat full of Jews fleeing in a leaky wooden ship floating between indifferent continents. I can't shake the story from my fiction or the memories of those pale survivors of the Holocaust who began to appear in the streets of Jewish Dorchester, something bleached out of their skin that no suntan could restore—speaking to my father in rapid Yiddish, the language itself seeming to bear the burden of what had been done.

The information was suppressed, deliberately—along with much of what was Jewish in my upbringing. I had to compete at the Boston Public Latin School, Harvard College. The Holocaust was packed into a sad little suitcase, next to the record of my bar mitzvah haftorah reading, the boy's *tallith* my grandfather gave, old picture albums, and put somewhere among the boxes in the basement.

At Harvard I was faced with Rabbi Ben Zion Gold, who appeared in my sophomore year as director of Hillel. I had an aversion to Jewish organizations, due in part to my father's contempt. Ben Gold was a European, very different from the rabbis I knew from American synagogues, and he sought out students active in the theater and literary circles of Harvard College. One was quickly mesmerized by Ben Gold's considerable knowledge, rabbinic, Yiddish, Polish literature, modern biblical studies. I understood that he had been incarcerated in the death camps. It was a subject, however, he would not talk about. He had funny stories about the postwar period in Europe, a world of black marketeering, lost women, the wandering of refugees over borders, but when we came to the Holocaust, his own experience of it, he stopped. It was simply too painful, he told me, to discuss.

One felt it, however, in Ben Gold's response and in his zeal to awaken students to the culture of Eastern European Jews. The sadness, the poetry, awoke childhood memories, sent me back to my father, and his boyhood, stories I dimly remembered. My father used to drop in at my rooms in Kirkland House, when there was an afternoon lull in his law practice. To my questions, now, Dad obligingly unbuttoned his jacket and tie, sat back to recall in detail his first memories of the house in Pinsk on Lahitianagasse, his grandfather, Yossel the Wild One, his great-grandfather, Baruch, and Sulya, Baruch's wife, the matriarch of the Lieberman house, my grandmother, Devorah's house, in which my father and his two sisters grew up. There were many mysteries in the pages of crumbling manila that I still retain from those typed interviews, but one was especially striking. It would deepen when I sat down with my father at the end of his life, as he rocked between heart attacks, to preserve his memory of Eastern Europe—the murder of his uncle, Menachem.

My father, his sisters, their father, were safe in America during the Holocaust. In 1919, however, when my father was twelve, his uncle was seized by Polish soldiers in front of his eyes. My father got a kick in the rear and a rifle butt to the head when he tried to hold on to his uncle's coat. The young married man, Uncle Menachem, was marched to the wall of the Orthodox Monastery together with thirty-six other men, Zionists, and town leaders. Torn from a meeting at which they were distributing Passover baskets to a starving city—they were summarily shot. My father had never told me the story as a boy.

It was a small massacre but my father's voice was tense, low, as he spoke, his habitual good humor, irony, falling away as he lived through a violence again that shamed him because he was helpless before it. My father, his grandparents, mother, sisters huddled behind closed blinds, only guessing at what had happened as the shots rang out. Later the Polish military forbade the relatives to visit the graves, to mourn openly.

The massacre has been forgotten by the world in the wake of the Holocaust. "It seems like nothing in comparison," one of its eyewitnesses told me, wryly; yet in the telling the old man, a doctor, starts to cry, gasp. At the time, the massacre interrupted the Versailles conferences and awoke a storm of protest across Europe and America. Two victims, discovered alive during the burial the next morning, were shot in the cemetery. Women apprehended at the same time were raped in the police cells. My father remembered American ambassador Hans Morgenthau, who was dispatched to Poland by Woodrow Wilson, speaking in Pinsk's synagogue.

As I began to research the background of my father's and grandfather's city, cousins in Israel sent me the *Yizkor,* or memorial books, of Pinsk, some thousands of pages of material about the city's history from the sixteenth century to the twentieth. I brought them to Ben Gold, since they were in a difficult Hebrew, to find out what in them would bear on my project.

The rabbi asked to take them home overnight to look the three volumes over. In the morning, when I came to his study, he rose from the desk, somber. "You have a duty. You have to bring these books into English. They show what was lost in the Holocaust. Not just a generation. What was lost was five hundred years of Jewish life."

It was so: The Pinsk *Yizkor* books, as I began to edit them and arrange for their translation, were an education. My father died. His detailed memories could no longer serve as a reference for me, but in the books and in the surviving Pinskers whom I interviewed, I learned more and more about my father's and grandfather's city. Pinsk. I also saw the Holocaust, not from the perspective of America, but from that of Eastern Europe. All the marks of German callousness were present from 1915 through 1919: the reduction of a city to starvation through forced labor and confiscations, rations below the level necessary to sustain life —so that a third of Pinsk starved to death each year during a German occupation that seemed at first benign.

Equally grim were the years between the First World War and the Second, in which the Jews of Pinsk were ground into poverty through a host of discriminatory economic and political measures, legislated by the Polish government. The march of horrors—as the band struck up with the entry of the Germans into Pinsk—really began much earlier. Only now it was almost too horrible to bear—so awful one almost had to laugh to keep sane, as in the pages of Nahum Boneh's monograph on the exterminations in Pinsk:

> One day in July, Ebner [the German deputy commissioner] arrived at the "Judenrat" Office [in Pinsk] accompanied by the district medical officer Bilevski. The ghetto was stunned; what next? They did not have long to wait. Ebner asked for a list of the mentally disturbed and of the incurably ill. "We want to take them all to the hospital at Brest Litovsk." The "Judenrat" tried to shirk the issue, saying they didn't know whom he meant.
> "The list has already been prepared by Dr. Bilevski," said Ebner, "and if you don't cooperate, we shall fetch the sick ourselves —but, as a punishment, together with their families." Faced with this dilemma, the "Judenrat," together with the Jewish doctors and policemen, compiled the list of about 40 victims. Two days later, a number of German cars arrived at the ghetto gates for their prey.

The poor sick people and their families knew what was in store for them and they tried to resist the Jewish policemen who had come to take them to the cars.

"It was a heart-rending sight to see the sick being dragged towards the gates by Jewish hands. As far as I can remember, this was the only case in Pinsk when Jews were compelled to deliver their own people into German hands." Two cars, full of Jews, drove off in the direction of Brest. A few hours later they were seen returning empty and very soon the truth became known. The sick had been shot near the village of Kozlakowicz. To calm the agitation that swept through the ghetto after this operation, Ebner and Dr. Bilevski came back . . . and promised that no more sick people would be taken away. "The woman psychiatrist, Dr. Yooz, a refugee from Warsaw and member of the well-known Davidson family, who had been tending these sick with great devotion, committed suicide the very next day. A few days later a madman nicknamed 'Nahumke Tepele Schmaltz' reappeared. 'How did you save yourself?' people asked.

" 'I ran away—how could a town exist without its madman?' "[2]

I went to Israel to meet Pinskers who remembered the massacre of 1919, and the greater, overwhelming massacre to come was always present in their memories. In a remarkable book by Fanny Solomian-Loc, who fled into the forest to fight with the partisans from Pinsk, there is a passage that explained to me, better than any rhetoric, why so few escaped. Such inhumanity was paralyzing—it meant in many cases abandoning parents to certain death. The young people knew that the Nazis had prepared the lime pits into which they were to be machine-gunned and buried. They walked about in apathy, horror. "I frequently spoke with the young people, those whom I had taught in the 'Tarbut' school from 1939 to 1941," Fanny wrote. "I hinted, even appealed to them indirectly, to go into the forests, but I always received the same meaningless, noncommittal answer, something like 'But why should we separate from our families? What happens to them will happen to us too.' " The author will fall victim to this, too: boiling water for two syringes of morphine, one to put her father, ailing, and the other herself out of their misery before the Germans can murder them. "I had to fight," she cried. "The water boiled and boiled, and I kept adding more all the time, turning often to look at my father's gray head.

Then suddenly it seemed to me a way out had revealed itself. As if awakening from a nightmare, I put away the sterilizer, dried the syringe and laid it aside. I did not have the strength to go through with it. This troubles my conscience to this day."[3] Again and again Fanny leaves the house to flee into the forest; again and again she returns to her father, hoping somehow to bring him along. Finally the last possible moment comes. "It was almost five o'clock. The night was over. Outside it was slowly turning gray. I felt that every additional minute made my escape from the ghetto more difficult. I looked at my father and fell on his neck. I seemed to sense that I would never see him again. I pulled him to me as if trying to take him along, but he disengaged himself gently and said in a soft voice, 'Go alone. Perhaps you will succeed in taking revenge for me and all the others.' "[4]

The *Yizkor* books are wet with the blood of the slain. I have seen it—in a living room in Montreal, my father's cousin, May Dines, picks up the *Yizkor* book of Yanover, a small town outside Pinsk, and starts to read, and remembers and begins to scream, telling the story of how her sister, her neighbor, fled into a mill to escape the German soldiers. It was set on fire. They ran into the street. The Germans following them grabbed her, tore her hair from her head, dragged the bodies with jeeps through the streets. Her tears pour over the pages. The memory is too awful; we turn off the tape recorder, the video, ashamed, knowing it is time to look away. The survivors came back to tell the story, and now it is part of the family's life, their memories, ours. It has happened to us.

In the absence of religious belief, the sense of shock, terror, has brought many Jews closer to Judaism, its languages, Yiddish, Hebrew, its customs, its East European history. For me an identity based on pathos is not sufficient, and I have tried to live as a religious Jew, committed to as much observance of the law as I can muster, and if not observance, study, understanding, since that is the tradition as my grandfather and my father practiced it.

Still, the hold of the pathos is very strong. It led me, I don't doubt, to trace my father's and grandfather's lives back to their small city, Pinsk. The sadness of Jewish life, crossed with laughter, an angry, often personal laughter, is what has informed me as a writer of fiction, a riddler. Here is the enormity of the Holocaust, there the diminutive scale of the individual Jew. It seems impossible to repress consciousness of the slaughter, but as in most American writers who are committed as Jews, the ghost of it is there at every margin.

Almost the first prose I wrote in a voice of my own—although the story, written when I was a student, is callow and adolescent—touched this. The line popped into my head as I left Hillel House one day, "So it was Epstein, the butcher's boy, who had painted the swastika on the wall of the Beth El Hebrew School. Oy." The desire to shock, to ridicule, to be loose of Judaism, its limitations, its restrictions, its bourgeois cant, came up against what had happened in Europe. Not to identify as a Jew at Harvard College was to separate oneself from a community which had gone through a disaster equal to the destruction of the Temple. I separated myself from most of my fellow Jewish students at Harvard with ease—in retrospect I am a bit ashamed, even as I wanted to experience new worlds. European Judaism, however, could not be evaded. One went to Professor Samuel Beer's showing of *Triumph of the Will,* Leni Riefenstahl's Nazi propaganda movie, in his Government course and was left shaking with anger.

The loss of the great European community of Jews became a metaphor for all mourning, in the wake of my mother's and father's deaths. Strangely, turning to the *Yizkor,* Remembrance prayers in the synagogue, that is exactly their structure: first to mourn one's father, mother, relatives, then to mourn for the martyrs of Israel, who died as Jews, only because they were Jews.

One year, traveling in Europe, I was staying with Max and Marianne Frisch. It was the time of the Jewish New Year, Rosh Hashanah, and it became an imperative to go to services. One of the reasons I had come to Zurich was Marianne's promise to arrange a dinner with Gershom Scholem, the scholar of Jewish mysticism, who was in the city. The Frisches called Scholem and directions to the Orthodox synagogue were given to me over the phone. ". . . I want to hear the ram's horn, shofar, the duty of every Jew," begins my diary.

"So, following the instructions . . . Friday night, I thread my way down unfamiliar streets to the Orthodox temple.

"But I don't have a hat. All of Max's collection consists of berets. . . . So I reach the gate nervously, hoping they have a box of spare skullcaps by the door of the sanctuary. Just as I arrive, two old men get out of a taxi. I ask them if they know where I can find a yarmulke. They laugh. It's their first time here too. Am I American? they ask. They pull out their American passports, wave them at me. See, they have lived in America too!

"We go into the building to try to find its prayer hall, scare up a yarmulke for me. Speaking fluent Yiddish, they waylay some of the Hebrew teachers in the hallway. The synagogue has no spare skullcaps, it turns out, but clustering around the teachers are a few students, and one loans me his yarmulke. The prayer hall is in the back of the building. We tramp around, services not yet begun. The two old men ask me questions, where have I been in Europe?

"When I mention Bergen-Belsen, they sigh. 'I hear it's very pretty there,' one says.

" 'Yes,' I answer. 'Like a country club.'

"We all laugh, a bitter, quiet laugh. 'I lost my daughter there,' one of the men adds. And they both tell me the names of the concentration camps they were in during the war. We are joined by a third elder, an Italian who fled from Venice to New York during the war. They all beam at me—an American. America has been good to them.

"After the service, they ask me where I am going. 'To friends,' I reply. I feel so strange leaving the bosom of the synagogue, to rejoin the world of literature, a night of conversation about books, easygoing laughter.

"Marianne Frisch has put herself out for me, making fish for supper so I can stay kosher for the holiday. She is curious about the synagogue. I try to describe my sense of it, a very sober group of men, most with beards, and even the clean-shaven ones have the smell of strict adherence to the traditional law. The three old men who cluster with me at the back of the synagogue are from another, more tolerant, amused Judaism.

"I invite Marianne to come the next day. I haven't heard the ram's horn yet. She goes up into the women's section, while I creep into the back of the synagogue again. In the sacrosanct atmosphere, though I am wearing a black corduroy cap of Marianne's, I feel the need of a skullcap again, and as I go in the door I ask a dignified, bearded young man. He goes to a locker and loans me one of his. I join the old men again. Now the whole synagogue is swathed in white for the New Year over which the black-striped prayer shawls are thrown. Afterward, Marianne will wax enthusiastically over the poetry of that assembly, a sea of bobbing black and white bodies, although she complains that the singing is a cacophony. True enough—the Zurich synagogue does not have a very sweet melody, its music a bit dry, harsh.

"On my way out, the man whom I have borrowed the skullcap from invites me to eat with his family. I find myself moved, shaken. This is a very old Jewishness—the traditional invitation to the stranger that I have heard about, read about, still alive. I want to go, but Marianne is waiting for me . . . and there will be explanations to make to a sober religious family—where am I staying? how did I get there?—which will not jibe with an Orthodox world.

"The old men from the previous night come along as I reach the sidewalk. They ask me to join them for a cup of coffee. I have to decline, I explain, because I am with a friend and we are going off together. I introduce them to Marianne. They are instantly curious about her—where are you from? The conversation begins in English, but when she replies 'Dusseldorf,' they smile shyly and begin to speak German. How strange—to stand on the sidewalk on Rosh Hashanah listening to Marianne and the two old men speaking in the language of their childhood together.

"Afterward, as Marianne and I walk off, she speaks of it too, wonders if they have not come to Zurich to observe the holiday because it is too painful to celebrate it in Germany, where they have returned to live. . . ." I pause in the writing of the diary, trying to find words for the pathos of the voices on the sidewalk outside the Zurich synagogue. "Speaking the language of infancy together, the enormity of a whole people with whom one shares the bond of linguistic roots, to have been torn out of a nation and destroyed. A Spanish-American critic spoke to me of his horror, watching a filmstrip of the Rumanian Jews being taken away by the Germans to the death camps, at hearing them cry in Spanish, the language they had preserved four hundred years in Central Europe, 'Madre, Madre,' not only Jews but 'Spaniards' being taken to the slaughterhouse. Slowly the realization of what the Germans have done to their lost selves, to the speakers of their language, their infancy."

At Dachau some seven months later, my girlfriend will burst into tears, unable to go through another room of pictures, although an insane electricity takes hold of me as I stare at the back gate's slogan in wrought iron, *"Arbeit Macht Frei,"* see the meat hooks, memorize the jolly sign that invites the tourist at the front entrance to visit, as well, "Historic Dachau Castle!" And as we leave, the heavy women in the field, pulling turnips, potatoes, of an age to have pulled them as the trucks and trains carrying Jews went into the camp.

What did they see? I want to ask it of every German, European. And so I have to ask Inger's, my girlfriend's, grandfather, what he saw. I write, "The answer is not as heroic as Inger hoped it would be. It is only honest and its honesty is frightening in the bright sun of the living room, then the patio outside, where the Norwegian flag is run up on the pole in honor of my visit. We overlook the town, Alesund's, wharves.

"Yes," the old man, a sailor in World War Two, remembers the Jews from the town across the fjord, Molde, being taken away. Below us are the blue harbor waters, sparkling above the wooden boards of his old house. The boat anchored there by the dock and the scene is as clear as a tintype, the ten, twelve Jewish adult males of Molde, dressed carefully in black suits, white shirts, ties, sober, respectable businessmen. They were deferentially treated by the Germans, being taken quietly to their death. Below in the hold were Russian and Polish peasants, chained, half naked, thrown food and water like dogs.

"A few months later, the children and wives of the men, the Jews, are collected and shipped after the heads of the families.

This has gone on, been watched, under her grandfather's window."

I remember this.

The Holocaust has become political and religious myth—and in that sense it is going to survive its survivors. As a Jew drawn to observance, the "way" of the law, the slaughter stands as a frightening fact in my path. Its dimensions and its very personal threat provoke both awe and anger—belief and defiance. On the one hand it is shameful to believe in a Holy One who could permit such a destruction. On the other, its very scope mocks the scale of human arrogance and makes me desire to hear, if not the voice, then the echo of the Unknown. Sitting one evening at supper with friends, one of them a prominent literary psychiatrist who would subsequently write on the Holocaust, I began to repeat a gloss of Rabbi Joseph Soloveitchik's. I was hooted down—and I realized the resistance of the professional American world of Jewish assimilation, doctors, lawyers, social workers, all wedded to secular structures of explanation, when faced with theology and metaphysics. The notion of an Unknown, capable of emotions, and the crisis of the Holocaust created rage around the restaurant table.

Still, these were not survivors who got angry with me but intellectuals, in most ways distant from the Jewish community who were expressing themselves as Jews through the Holocaust. Out of context, the description of an Unknown, turning away, hiding, letting a world run on mechanical laws without compassion, may sound almost childish. In the context of men and women who cling to a closeness with a mysterious and personal numen, a principle of order who can speak uniquely, and individually, the idea of the withdrawal of God is frightening. So Rabbi Soloveitchik's words: "In Deut. 31:17, the Torah describes the ultimate punishment of *Hester Panim* [Hiding of the face].

> Then My anger will flare up against them in that day and I will abandon them and *hide My face from them,* and they shall be devoured and many evils and distress shall befall them; so that they will say in that day, "Are not these evils come upon us, because our God is not in our midst?"

"*Hester Panim* involves a temporary abandonment of the world, a suspension of His active surveillance, as Rashi clearly explains, 'as though I do not see their distress. . . .' "[5] Rabbi Soloveitchik's essay is about the creation of the world from nothing—God as Creator, rather than merely fashioner of preexistent material (as in the Aristotelian universe). The world is first brought into existence *tohu vavohu*, chaos and confusion, then refined by fashioning, or *yetzirah*. Ordinary punishment has to do with God's involvement in the world, as it was fashioned, *yetzirah*, punishment according to law according to the Rav. "The Holocaust in contrast was *Hester Panim*. We cannot explain the Holocaust but we can, at least, classify it theologically, characterize it, even if we have no answer to the question, 'why?' The unbounded horrors represented the *tohu vavohu* anarchy of the pre-*yetzirah* state. This is how the world appears when God's moderating surveillance is suspended. . . . [6] He turns His back, so to speak, on events and leaves matters to chance. Under such circumstances, the usual vulnerability of the Jew invites the threat of total extermination. This is strikingly conveyed by the words *vehayah le'ekhol*, 'they shall be devoured.' What ensues is not circumscribed by considerations of measure for measure, and the magnitude and severity can be devastating. Without God's governing control, events may simply go beserk."[7]

I was to witness the Rav during *Tishah-b'Ab*, the midsummer fast that marks the destruction of the First and Second Temples, wrestling again with the subject. The Rav's *shiir* (lecture) lasted through the morning. It moved between singing of the *kinnot*, or traditional laments, and meditation. Lines from succeeding years echo in my head as well, but as variorum on the drama of that summer morning in 1981. In front of his students, young men, silver-haired elders, women, all fasting in memory of a faraway day in Jerusalem, Rabbi Soloveitchik began to try to make sense of what the destruction of the Temple meant today. It was not to a distant, removed Unknown that he spoke, but to a close one, the *Kodosh Boruch Hoo*, the Holy One, Blessed be He. The three hours of stream-of-consciousness were dependent on an understanding of associations between biblical and Midrashic texts, in which *kinnot* of the seventh-century poet Eleazar Kalir blended with the Rav's commentary. Yet even I, an unprepared student, was arrested by the anger that kept breaking through.

"Why does the prophet [Jeremiah]," asked the Rav, "emphasize the phrase—*Tsciyah Moyess?* [It] means refuse, dirt [Lamentations 3:45. 'Dirt and refuse you have made us in the midst of the nations']. What is horrible in the *gollus* [Exile] experience is the fact that the *ahmim* [peoples] . . . we expected those people, who will respect us, who will honor us, those people *look* upon us as *Tsciyah Moyess,* as refuse and as subhumans." The shame, the horror of that degradation, is an assault on the Divine Name, for it degrades what is spiritual in man.

The Book of Lamentations (in Hebrew, *Aychah,* How?, from its first word, "How does the City sit solitary?") is disputing what God has done—according to the Rav. This "How?" implies "How did this happen?" The effrontery of questioning the Holy One—this became part of the Rav's discourse. "This *aychah* is an expression, a very strange expression which *Yermiyohoo* [Jeremiah] shouldn't have used, but he *did* use it, because *Ha Kodosh Boruch Hoo* told him to use it, namely, *Aychah*—how is it possible?—means 'I don't understand it.' He has no right, *Yermiyohoo* had no right to say, 'I don't understand.' "

Answering the prophet who has the nerve to question—to ask, " 'How' did we become 'dirt and refuse'?"—the Rav thundered in the voice of God, "What do you mean you don't understand? Why should you understand?

"But this was one of the privileges, the privileges that was given to *Yermiyohoo* . . . in *Megillas Aychah* [the scroll of Lamentations], to address *Ha Kodosh Boruch Hoo* and ask him questions, something we mustn't do in regard to our private lives . . . we don't ask the *Kodosh Boruch Hoo* questions, like Rabbi Akiba [who] didn't ask questions [but was] anxious to fulfill the mitzvah of *kiddush ha shem* [martyrdom]—this is the way you approach the *Kodosh Boruch Hoo* in times of disaster. . . . Again the words which were formulated by the *Kodosh Boruch Hoo* for *Yermiyohoo.*"

The martyrdom of Rabbi Akiba and the other rabbis who after the destruction of the Second Temple accepted Roman torture, the skin raked off their bones, cannot compare to the Holocaust—the martyrdom of the rabbis, according to the Rav, was still a phenomenon of a world of punishment by Divine law, however cruel. The Holocaust signaled a world of no God. As the hours wore on, the fate of the Jewish houses of Eastern Europe towered over the destruction of the Holy One's House in Jerusalem thousands of years before. The Rav began to speak almost sarcastically, in the language of Lord Byron. "When *Ha Kodosh Boruch Hoo* comes to *Yerushalayim* [Jerusalem] He simply has no house to dwell in. He has no house to dwell in. It's His *House* that the Romans have burned. Not *our* house, we don't care. We can get along without, without the *Bays Ha-Mikdash* [the Holy Temple]. . . ."

In that circle of the pious, fasting in Brookline, Massachusetts, over the destruction of a far-off Temple, the Rav insisted, let the Holy One mourn His Temple—let us, contemporary Jews, think today about what we lost, our house, houses, our holy places! "Basically we read very much, a lot about the Holocaust. Over six million. It's very hard to pronounce it—six million. How many houses were destroyed. Each Jew did not live on the sidewalk, not in the woods. Each Jew had a house, a home. A rich house, or a plain house, a poor home, but he had a home. Each home was a *Bays Ha-Mikdash*. Why only the *bayt midrashiim* [study houses]? Each home throughout Lithuania, and Poland, and White Russia, was a *Bays Ha-Mikdash*. Each home had its own traditions. . . . If only a *Bays Ha-Midrash* [House of Study] was burned, I wouldn't care so much about it. . . . But they destroyed the true *Bays Ha-Mikdash,* which actually is responsible for the survival of the people, the private home of the children.

"I begin just to see images. And one image I see. He was a carpenter. Eliyah Ha-shtoller [the carpenter], a carpenter, a short fellow, and he also rented out a room to my *melamud* [teacher], in order to make a living. A plain Jew, a plain carpenter, not too much of a *charif* [shrewd person], *ponkt* [sharp]—a Jew. But I mean, the way he used to work as a carpenter and say *tillim* [psalms], he learned *tillim* by heart. And actually he somehow found a system, a parallel system, certain *psukiim* [verses], for instance, [Hebrew] when the table was completed. Or another *possuk* [verse] when he started to do his work. He was a plain Jew. Is this not a *Bays Ha-Mikdash*? Who lives now in those homes, those houses? Many of them, most of them are destroyed. Many of them."

The Rav's voice broke, in tears. "Who lives—*Aysov* [Esau—traditional name for the oppressor of the Jew]. Those people who killed them. They live in their homes. *Tishah-b'Ab* is the *zman* [time], the day of *Avayliss* [mourning], and the day on which we should tell the story of *Chorban* [sacrifice], which begins of course with *Aysov* . . . the story of *Chorban* which is the main experience in our life—in the last two thousand years, nineteen hundred years. It is not a question of houses, of the *Kodosh Kodosh* [Holy of Holies, the inner sanctum of the Temple]; the question is of the *Bays Ha-Mikdash,* which every Jewish home *was.* What about this *Bays Ha-Mikdash?* It's irreplaceable. This is irreplaceable. A *Bays Ha-Mikdash Yerushalayim* is replaceable. . . . It is theoretically, historically, *possible* to replace. But can you replace the house of Eli der Shtoller? And draw a figure of him? You can't replace it, you can't replace his home. His home was a *Bays Ha-Mikdash.* He used to be present when we davened [prayed] for the *ma-ariv* [evening service]. He was a strange person. My father used to say that he belongs to the *Lamed Vovnicks* story [thirty-six righteous men who sustain the world]. All right, you can take the statement for [truth] or not, but he was certainly a rare type. And this was not only he, thousands and thousands of Jews. . . ."

"A home was a tradition!" cried the Rav. It was a part of the Law, the Law not in the scrolls but the equally holy law passed down by mouth to mouth, the oral Law, Torah. "Torah *shebalpeh* was not just of one individual you know, [but] a family, a household, a home. This has been destroyed." The Rav in his firm, high voice began to sing the lament in Hebrew.[8]

> My temple which you did establish
> for my fathers of old, [who]
> in a tremor asked: "Who is it [that will destroy it?][9]
> Why has it been cut off forever by its adversaries,
> Whilst thou hast become like a solitary bird on a roof,
> lamenting bitterly, "What has my beloved to do here?"

"Who are these fathers of old?" asked the Rav. "Abraham, Isaac, Jacob—the Judges?" Oh no—"Why only Abraham? Why only Abraham as a 'Father of old'? Abraham was mighty, great, no doubt. But many people, his descendants who were not as great as he, they had the same faith. Their homes are also houses of study." And again the Rav's voice rose in the words of the lament, speaking not of the faraway Temple, but the houses of Eastern Europe. "Why did you destroy it forever? For there is no way out of it. Unless the *Kodosh Boruch Hoo*. . . . And now it is not only the *Bays Ha-Mikdash* to which the Jew is not admitted —but the *Kodosh Boruch Hoo* himself. . . .

"I read an account by one who—he didn't live through the Holocaust because he was deported to Russia. And that saved him from being executed by the Germans, exterminated by the Germans. So he had a mother, before the war, before Germany occupied Vilna, he had a mother, the mother was a *nahlich yiddeneh* [an uplifted Jewish woman], as all Jewish mothers were so many years ago. And so the mother . . . used to come on Yom Kippur to shul of course, daven, but when it got to *Maftir Yoneh* [the book of Jonah], she was tired already, the mother, and so she had a a job. She used to leave the shul—I would say for half an hour, and feed the cat at the home. She had a cat. On Yom Kippur who paid attention to the cat? On Yom Kippur? So she used to remember that. . . . *Maftir Yoneh*, the end of Yom Kippur is [in sight]—you examine the *mahzor* [prayer book], there are so many prayers to say, but you've said them already, and there's *Maftir Yoneh, Nillah* [final service of the day], and that's all, you'll be able to go home and eat and to make the sukkah.[10] That's what the Jew thinks at *Maftir Yoneh*, it's very nice; but she, she used to think of the cat. So she used to go. The cat used to wait for her . . . after she got through feeding the cat, she came back to shul.

"He spent the Yom Kippur after the liberation of the territories from German rule, so, he came to spend Yom Kippur, in Vilna, in the Vilna shul. Whether this is true or not, I can't guarantee, but anyway, it could have happened. *The only one who met him was the cat.* The only one who met him was the cat. She came—he felt, he told me, as if the cat was waiting for him to feed her. 'The way my mother used to.' She was killed. . . ." The Rav's voice whipped at his audience, which was sighing. "Do you think—it's a nice story?—yeah.

"But it's more than a story—that's all—the mother, a *nahlich yiddeneh,* a second Sarah. All right—it's very hard to replace that." The Rav's voice, harshly guttural, cried out in Hebrew. Instead of the lone bird, hovering over the roof of the ruined Temple in Jerusalem, the cat of Vilna shrieked and cried aloud " '*Mahr tzorayach, Meh leeydeeydeey fo-h*' What did he say, '*Ktzee-poor bodaid ahl gohg,*' A cat on the roof. '*Mar tzorayach*' [a bitter shriek]. The cat also probably emitted certain sounds—ahh, ahhh, ahh—she is hungry—but there was no one to feed her. '*Mahr tzorayach*' Bitter, hopeless, *Meh leeydeeydeey fo-h*—[what does my beloved here?] who are you? Who are you?' And people told me, many told me that the sense of emptiness, of vacuity, which actually accompanied those survivors when they visited the towns and cities of old, where they were raised, was unbearable. A cat, whoever knew what the Vilna *schulaysh* [synagogues] meant on Yom Kippur, and then—and suddenly there is one cat. And that's all. . . . You can't restore it.

"So this is not just a question about a cat but about every Jewish home."

Aychah—how?—how can those individuals, those homes, be replaced? How? The Ninth of Ab is not a distant historical event but a contemporary one, its book, *How?*, in which the third and most terrible destruction of the home of Judaism has taken place.

I go groping, back to religion, back to my father's, grandfather's, great-grandfather's world, in all its complexity, for it was not always religious—it was often skeptical; back to Yiddish, not necessarily to speak it, but to hear its echoes. Working on a short sketch of YIVO, the Yiddish Scientific Institute, which has been one of the centers of Holocaust research, study —and study in Lithuanian Torah, my grandfather's teaching, is a form of religious practice—I came across an address given by Israeli Yiddishist Dan Miron to a YIVO gathering. He is quoting Max Weinreich, a sober scholar, one of the founders of YIVO, the man responsible for its survival in America, after the destruction of Vilna. Weinreich is saying good-bye to Miron, his student. It is the end of Weinreich's life and he speaks with a strange secular faith: "If American Jews still dream as a group, Yiddish is the language they speak in their dream. . . . For their personality to be whole they—at least some of them—will have to go back to Yiddish one day. . . . They will come back to look for the hidden parts of their national personality. Once they realize that their Jewishness, lived on an abstract level, is moribund, and that the mere presence of the Jewish state cannot by itself revive it, they will have to come back. And there we shall be, waiting for them down in the Yiddish cellar with a strong torchlight in our hand. Someone will have to spell for them the contents of their dream, to elucidate the vision they saw with bleary eyes, and we, because we made Yiddish *vissenshaft* the thing we live and die for, will be able to throw light and heal."

It is not only Yiddish that lies waiting in the cellar of Jewish dreams, or Hebrew, or the secular, or the religious worlds of Europe—it is the fear of a final and absolute extinction of a people, a tradition. A Jew who wishes to inherit from the European *Yiddishkayt* is incomplete without going down into these shadows—though whether he, she, can be healed is more a hope than a certainty. The Jews cannot assimilate, for that means forgetting. One of Bernard Malamud's most powerful stories is about just that—"Lady of the Lake," in which the magical woman of dreams becomes the experience of the Holocaust, manifest in a woman, like the women half divine of the Provençal poets, of Dante, a union with the Holy One. To deny the Holocaust, not to identify with it, is to lose the best hope of oneself, a secret partner, an experience of the other world, in this world. The sensation of its pathos is a terrible yet overwhelming one—love and death.

Those preoccupied with the Holocaust, who talk, walk, with the men and women who were in the flames or lived at the edge of the fire, have also been called to witness what we heard, though it was only echoes—though speaking with survivors we saw only images. What did it mean? The survivors cannot tell us. As the great sleep of horror in which they were silent has begun to lift, however, they speak and ask us to begin by remembering, to make part of our dreams what they suffered.

In front of these mariners of a shattered Jewish Europe, I became an anxious wedding guest. Only a few weeks ago, out for a Thanksgiving weekend with friends on an island, the host's parents, who came as refugees from Germany in the thirties, attract my attention—to the exclusion of children, gossip, a stroll along the beach. The details of the flight from Berlin are narrated by a balding gentleman in his eighties who came as a young man. He described his "incredible luck" in getting a visa to America through a cousin in Brussels who was a tailor to the American consul. He tells me how *his* father had put aside money to match the tips of his delivery boy, depositing both sums in a bank. When the Nazi laws made it impossible for Jews to employ gentiles, the father turned the bankbook over to the boy. Later the boy would reappear as an S.S. man, during the smashing of Jewish windows, and save the shop. Again, the night before the father and mother were to be arrested, a phone call warned them and they were able to get away, first to Paris, then Marseilles, then the Caribbean, finally America, to join the son who is telling me this, ending the story with the ironic tag, " 'If only all Jews were like you!' they said. They [the Germans] all had one Jewish friend." I sit, memorizing it, remembering another night of this hypnotic narration—from a couple who had met when both were prisoners in a Berlin jail, 1944. She jumped off a train taking her from Hungary to the death camps. He was a half-Jewish German who had defied his family's wishes and insisted on a bar mitzvah in the middle of the thirties. Then with the beginning of the war, he ran from the door of one gentile relative to the other relative, demanding that they hide him, leaping from the backs of trucks that took him away several times, to return to Berlin. Boy and girl had fallen in love, while the Reich burned, prison walls bombed out around them, Russian tanks rumbling to their liberation. The Hungarian girl, German boy, had refused to accept, and against all odds, they had survived. They laughed, telling the story, yet they could not stop telling it, once it started. Afterward they drove me, my wife, home to Manhattan, from the supper in Queens. We were all numb—did they survive? And our host, who marched with bare feet in the snow, ahead of the German armies, to draw the artillery fire? He had begun the evening telling stories of men freezing to death, as they went out to urinate, the cold so intense the stream froze as they stood there. How did he, they, survive—even as they turned around in the expensive car and talked to us—hard to believe.

A Jewish writer is responsible to a nation of ghosts, their

stories; must record, decipher, dream nightmares, write for the clap of the pale hands, listening in the night. Who survived? What survived? What did it mean? How did it happen?

NOTES

1. Leo W. Schwarz, *The Root and the Bough* (New York: Rinehart, 1949).

2. Nahum Boneh Mular, "The Holocaust and the Revolt," in *Pinsk, Historical Volume, Number Two,* edited by Dr. Wolf Zeev Rabinowitsch (Tel Aviv, 1977), p. 116.

3. Fanny Solomian-Loc, *Woman Facing the Gallows,* privately published, based on a translation of *Na'ara Mool Gardom* (Tel Aviv: Moreshet and Sifriat Po'alim), p. 89.

4. Ibid., p. 96.

5. Rabbi Joseph Soloveitchik, "The World Is Not Forsaken," from *Reflections of the Rav,* edited by Abraham R. Besdin (Jerusalem: Alpha Press, 1979), p. 35.

6. Ibid., p. 37.

7. Ibid., p. 36.

8. The *kinnot* can be found in *Tisha'Bab Tephilot and Kinot,* translated and annotated by Abraham Rosenfeld (New York: The Judaica Press, 1986), p. 104, lines 4–6. (The variant reading, *kedem,* is found in the footnote.)

Ohohleey ahsher komamtoh
laysohnay kedem
Bcherduht mee ayfoh
Lomoh lohnehtzach tzoomuht byahd tzorim,
Vehneehyahsoh ktzeepoor bodaid ahl gohg
Mahr tzorayach, Meh leeydeeydeey fo-h.

9. Isaac, one of the three patriarchs or "fathers of old" trembled violently and asked, "Who is it?" (Genesis 27:33) when Esau entered his tent. Esau was identified by the rabbis with Rome, which destroyed the Second Temple.

10. It is traditional to begin building the unroofed booth or sukkah for the Feast of Booths immediately after Yom Kippur.

III

Absence

SUSANNE SCHLÖTELBURG

The great psychological fact of our time
which we all observe with baffled wonder
and shame is that there is no possible way
of responding to Bergen and Buchenwald.

—Lionel Trilling

"Denn das Vergessenwollen verlängert das Exil,
und das Geheimnis der Erlösung heißt Erinnerung."
—Jewish proverb, quoted by Richard von Weizsäcker on May
8, 1985

For Shoshana

In 1977 I stood in Auschwitz. I looked at the
mountains of suitcases, heaps of glasses, sacks of human hair
without comprehension. I walked past these relics of horror in a
daze, wide awake to the sensation of an immense ugliness, but
senseless to the meaning of these objects. My mind was vacant.

They were just objects, revolting and hideous like the installations by a certain modern German sculptor. But there was a pit somewhere waiting for me, the pit of comprehension. I turned away from the exhibits and walked toward the exit of the building. Not far from the door I was overcome by an intense nausea which sent me running into the open. I threw up. The pit had opened. I was in it. It had opened by an act of the imagination. My mind had connected the objects just seen and now remembered with other memories: images of the owners of these objects in the process of being deprived of their humanity. The suitcase with the inscription "Wien" belonged to the gray-bearded gentleman who had to get down on his knees and scrub the pavement with a toothbrush, much to the amusement of the bystanders; some of the dark hair—*"dein aschenes Haar Sulamith"*—belonged to a pregnant woman sent into the gas chamber by a movement of Mengele's hand. Films, photographs, documentaries, histories connected themselves to the exhibits and hurled me into the pit. The nausea had arisen in the falling. I sat down on the grass under the Polish summer sky trying to think, trying to establish some order (of all things) in the pandemonium inside, trying to think what my reaction *should* be. I began to cry, and as soon as I noticed it, I cried harder—out of self-disgust. To just sit there and cry was the easiest of all solutions. It established a personal relation between myself and the Holocaust. It privatized a horror whose historic dimensions and philosophic implications I was not able to fathom. It neatly enveloped the unfathomable in tears (always unimpeachable) and thus reduced it to the proportions of my private world, where I could deal with it. I could feel sorry (for whom?). Crying made the Holocaust personal. And this seemed to me a most inadequate, suspect, and perhaps even despicable response.

The bewilderment and agony of that day came back to me when I was asked to contribute an essay to a collection of personal reflections on the Holocaust. It seemed as if, for all who had not been immediately involved as victims or as murderers, the Holocaust defied the personal. For me as a witness *post factum* the "Holocaust" and the "personal" were a contradiction in terms. The one was not contained in the other. The Holocaust was not part of my life. An essay of personal reflections on the

Holocaust seemed to demand the psychologically impossible. How could anyone bring into his or her personal realm that which at every moment, in every deed and detail, had enacted the destruction of the personal? And if one could bring oneself to sit down and think about what the Holocaust meant to oneself or to others, did this endeavor not involve an element of reduction? But one had to remember. *"Denn das Vergessenwollen verlängert das Exil, und das Geheimnis der Erlösung heißt Erinnerung"* (For the wish to forget prolongs exile, and the secret of redemption is memory). But was personal reflection the basis for that memory? The slaughters of the First Crusade in 1096 are still remembered. The inclusion into the *machsor* (holiday liturgy) of prayers and poems written in Mainz after the bloodshed suggests that the basis for remembrance is a certainty of continuity which does not rest on the personal.

This certainty was present among the Jewish people even in times of despair, and it induced the chronicler Shelomoh bar Shimshon of Mainz to use the events on Mount Moriah as a foil for what happened in Mainz during the Crusades.

> Who has heard or seen such a thing? Ask and see: Has there ever been an *akedah* like this in all the generations since Adam? Did eleven hundred *akedot* take place on a single day, all of them comparable to the binding of Isaac son of Abraham? Yet for the one bound on Mount Moriah the world shook, as it is stated: "Behold the angels cried out and the skies darkened." What did they do now, why did the skies not darken and the stars not dim . . . when on one day . . . there were killed eleven hundred pure souls, including babes and infants . . . ? Wilth Thou remain silent for these, O Lord! [1]

Those who are not bound by *akedah* or *brith* do not remember the slaughters of 1096. In a few decades they might not remember those between 1939 and 1945, unless they read history books. Personal pain seems ephemeral. This is bitter. It would seem that to ensure remembrance the Holocaust would have to be made transpersonal rather than personal. Much of memory will be based on the works of the chroniclers and *paytanim* of the Holocaust who wrote and write in the tradition of Shelomoh bar Shimshon: among them Nelly Sachs, Paul Celan, Uri Zvi Greenberg, and Primo Levi.

As a chronicler of lesser capability who remembers by personal reflection, I needed a theme which reconciled the contradiction of form (personal) and content (Holocaust) and established continuity. The experience of Absence and the memory of Loss constitute community through time. For Diaspora Jewry, memory of Loss seems to be as binding as the Covenant itself. In the experience of Loss, the personal and the communal, the need for comprehension and for remembrance come together. From my point of view, that of a noncontemporary witness, relating the Holocaust to my life meant to make personal what I had not experienced. This is not absurd, because the Holocaust is omnipresent in the modern Germany where I grew up. It is an omnipresence which cannot be personalized because it is the omnipresence of a negative—Absence. I hesitate to qualify this Absence for the sake of clarity by saying, for instance, "the Absence of Jews," because any attempt to define this Absence by juxtaposing concrete terms begins already to alleviate the *horror vacui*.

Absence is a decisive element in postwar German history. The first decades after the collapse on May 8, 1945, saw a frantic filling of the vacuum left by the mythic *Stunde Null* (Zero Hour) with houses, goods, and culture. But in recent years the ghastly recognition has become unavoidable that in some sense Germany is still empty, the vacuum still there. An earnest search has begun. Survivors, Israelis, American Jews are being imported and asked for help in conference after conference. Synagogues are being restored (and made museums), *Gedenkstätten errichtet* (a German idiom by now) at which official wreaths are being deposited; documentation centers are being founded and visited by schoolchildren. But all this activity around the national pit can neither sound it nor fill it until the courage has been found to face the Absence in today's Germany and to integrate it into the nation's sense of self. It is not enough to constantly think about what caused the loss of an eye. It is equally important to learn to live with the hole in one's face. Germany is finding out that a glass eye and paint are not fooling anyone other than itself.

That the integration of Absence into the nation's self-understanding might still take a while was made clear by the speech which the president of the West German Parliament, Philipp

Jenninger, delivered on the fiftieth anniversary of the so-called Reichskristallnacht. He dove into German history trying to reconstruct the nation's sense of itself in 1938 and what had formed it. He became so absorbed in the task that he forgot what was actually expected of him: to acknowledge, representatively for all Germans, his consciousness of the Holocaust today, to recognize Absence, or that all was not well. The German historian Sebastian Haffner commented bitterly: "He has no sense of the occasion. When a man was murdered, you cannot speak at his grave of the interesting personality of the murderer." But Jenninger also avoided the ambiguous tears of the murderer's relatives. He is an honest man.

Jenninger resigned. His speech was reprinted in a major German weekly, analyzed, and extensively commented on by a number of intellectuals to compensate for what he did not say. The same paper printed his picture at the lectern with the speaker's space a white blank. It was a deeply satisfying consolation that onto the blank space left by Jenninger the nation could project its one representative moral hero, Richard von Weizsäcker, delivering on the same spot three and a half years earlier as president of the Federal Republic of Germany his by now famous speech on the fortieth anniversary of the German capitulation. Paradoxically this speech became almost an occasion for joy because it seemed to relieve the nation of a great burden: there was hope that the impossible could be achieved, that the past could be integrated into the present, that knowledge about the Holocaust and the permanent consciousness of its reality could inform Germany's sense of self without completely crushing and eliminating it. How does one *live* in the presence of an all-devouring Negative? Richard von Weizsäcker showed that it could be done.

How does one live in, grow up in Absence? What does it need to become "aware"? These were questions that this essay asked me to confront, and my task seemed to be to describe in what way the life of a German born in the Black Forest in 1959 was touched by the Holocaust. The answer was simple: in every way. Its reality, its all-pervasive presence, that is, Absence, was the single most important force that shaped my mind. But to describe the formative power of a Negative is difficult. In addition to that, with images of the *Shoah* constantly before my eyes,

I find it preposterous to talk about myself. I was "sheltered." Therefore I speak with reluctance and the sense of being a usurper.

I should begin by saying that my presence here is due (in complicated ways) to a letter I received from a writer in June 1987 in reply to my request for an interview later in the year, when I would be in the United States for studies. The letter cut me to the quick. But mine, too, had hit on a sensitive spot: "[A] letter from Germany inflames me, ignites furies that are never dormant, and arouses in me huge storms—contradictory storms, since it is elating and exciting to learn of your interest, and yet the German context drives me to rage and an agony of boiling irony. Germans singing Hebrew songs in a Judenrein land! Jews who can still live—sleep and walk and buy groceries and go to school and all the 'normal' rest of it—on that blood-and-ash-saturated soil!"

"Blood-and-ash-saturated soil"—the phrase made me sick. It did not concur with my image of Germany. Everything was neat and tidy where I had grown up. *Oh Deutschland, bleiche Mutter/ Wie sitzest Du besudelt/ Unter den Völkern/ Unter den Befleckten/ Fällst Du auf.*" But Bertolt Brecht's pale, stained Mother had gotten up and was cleansing herself, wasn't she? And I was part of this cleansing process, wasn't I? I had been given a full-time job in the English Department at the University of Mannheim (when such jobs were rare) to teach American Jewish history and literature. While other professors had difficulties filling their courses with students, mine were overcrowded, and not because I was making things easy. In the first session of my seminar on American Jewish history, 1654–1880, I asked my thirty students what they knew about Jews. Embarrassed silence. Finally, when it was clear that I was not going to liberate them from their embarrassment, a student, who later turned out to be a great cynic, said that in Spain in the Middle Ages Jews were believed to have long tails. He said it with a straight face, and it was obvious that he was not going to qualify his remark. With him I would never be sure how much was naiveté and how much was cunning. I spent most of the semester (spring 1986) on an introduction to Judaism. All the students stayed, even the cynic, although very few needed the course for credit.

During the following semester I dealt more particularly with the history of Jews in America up to the present, and I smuggled in long excerpts from Claude Lanzmann's *Shoah*. During the last semester of my appointment I taught a seminar on Jewish women writers and assigned among other texts four stories by Cynthia Ozick. "The Suitcase," from her first collection *The Pagan Rabbi* (1971), triggered a heated discussion. Some students were offended by the Jewish woman saying about the German artist (who happens to be her lover): " 'Shredded swastikas, that's what,' Genevieve announced. 'Every single damn thing he does. All that terrible pre*ci*sion. Every last one a pot of shredded swastikas, you see that?' " Wasn't Genevieve summing up the author's own prejudice? Some of the students did not feel treated fairly by Ozick, whom they supposed to be like Genevieve of "the sort who, twenty years after Hitler's war, would not buy a Volkswagen. She was full of detestable moral gestures, against what?"[2] Exactly. They were twenty years old; they had not shed blood, had they?

But Ozick's novella "Rosa,"* the story of a woman half crazed by the losses inflicted on her by "Hitler's war" and the *Shoah,* shut up the hardliners ("Prejudice, prejudice!"). They were touched by the pain in this woman who smashes up her little store in New York to move to yet another exile. Rosa's pain made them aware of the fact that for the victims the *Shoah* is still a reality; it is not the past, it is the present. It is a maddening sense of loss, loss of home, language, kin, of every element creating "belonging" and thus making for "sense" in a person's life. My students had immense sympathy for Rosa's suffering but no grasp of the dimension of her loss. They were glad when they found out that Rosa could be criticized for making an idol of her murdered daughter Magda. They had not experienced loss beyond the ordinary incidents of everyday life; and yet they were living in the midst of Absence. But that was precisely the problem.

They were not aware of Loss; their lives were filled with the goodies of the German *Wirtschaftswunder*. The Economic Mira-

---

* "Rosa" was first published in *The New Yorker,* March 21, 1983, pp. 38–71; it was reprinted in Cynthia Ozick's *The Shawl* (New York: Alfred A. Knopf, 1989).

cle had produced the most astonishing lifelike glass eye for the hole torn by the past. The hole had disappeared. The continuity between past and present, between Destruction and Miracle, was not visible in modern Germany except in a few places, in Berlin and Munich, for instance. My students were hardly aware of such a continuity. They had never seen anyone with a blue tattoo number, nor did they know anyone who was still waking up night after night shrieking in terror. Of course, they *knew* about the Holocaust from history courses, books, films, and so forth. But they were unable to connect this knowledge with their lives because the link between Germany's past and their present had been obscured by their parents' creation of a New Germany. Loss, the most powerful constituent of memory, had seemingly disappeared. Unaware of their visual impairment, my students could neither see nor imagine that they lived in a vacuum. What there was, was just all there *was*. They knew no Jews and nothing about their belief and culture. There was much talk about Jews, and their grandparents (and perhaps parents) were charged with their murder. So they became interested. But there was no pain about the absence of Jews; of course my students did not miss them; the vacuum was what had formed their sense of normality.

How does one make Absence visible? How does one explain that the normal is not the normal but the exceptional, that the present culture is the result of an enormous destruction, and that everything that is there suggests what is not there? My task, then, was to transform my students' "literary pain," which Cynthia Ozick suspected to be never "anything more than ephemeral or skin-deep," into real pain, into a sense of Absence. My strategy was simple: to make Absence visible by contrast. By teaching Judaism, Jewish history, and Jewish culture in the university, and by bringing (as a journalist) its continuity elsewhere (in the U.S., in Israel) to the attention of a German audience, I hoped to make visible its absence from our present culture and thus to show that we were *not* back to "normal."

Why this emphasis on Absence? Because the Germans (and myself possibly among them) had begun to fill up this vacuum, too. In 1980 an Academy for Jewish Studies *(Hochschule für Jüdische Studien)* was established in Heidelberg loosely affiliated with the university, somewhat like the *Hochschule für die Wissen-*

schaft des Judentums in Berlin closed by the Nazis on June 30, 1942. The academy was crowded by non-Jewish students and auditors, some of whom eventually converted. I remember two students in my *Ivrit* class, who both converted and not long afterward got married to each other. The members of the faculty, all of them either native speakers of German or Yiddish (except for the *Ivrit* teacher who was a *sabra*), were polite, tried to be professional in a situation that must have struck them as completely crazy. What were all these Germans, Protestants and Catholics, *doing* here? When I looked at the pained face of our professor of medieval Jewish history, whose *mameloshen* was Yiddish and who taught in German with difficulty, I wondered what *he* was doing *here*? Perhaps the answer was contained in his name. It was that of the city without the first letter H. I left the *Hochschule*, after three semesters to pursue my studies in American literature at Brandeis University. The futility of the state-sponsored enterprise *Hochschule*, the forcedness of its social atmosphere in its diminutive library or its small kosher cafeteria, the tyranny of the two-hundred-percenters (non-Jews who *knew* everything *about* Judaism), my sense of (self-)disgust became clear to me only in the freedom I experienced at Brandeis.

This experience brought into sharp relief the causes for my unhappiness in Germany: isolation, the museum-like character of my interests and concerns, a sense of claustrophobia in the extreme homogeneity of German culture. But freedom at Brandeis did not mean liberation from German bondage. I had never been more intensely aware of the inescapability of being born German and settled with that country's historic burden than during this year at Brandeis. Whoever talked to me and detected my accent needed to know who I was in order to feel safe: What did your parents do during the war? I began to understand that for those who might have become its victims the reality of the Holocaust extended into the present. For those bound by *akedah* and *brith*, there had been no Zero Hour from which to start anew. My own sense of continuity between past and present had been obscured by the myth of the *Stunde Null*. One day I relived the *Stunde Null*. The Anti-Defamation League had arranged a small exhibition in the main lobby of the Brandeis library on the occasion of the fiftieth anniversary of Hitler's rise to power in

1933. I was busy and always rushed past until one day something familiar caught my eye. I went back to look again at the blown-up photograph. It took me a few moments to locate the familiarity. But then in a flash past and present were linked. The photograph showed the usual postcard view of Heidelberg with the castle halfway up the mountain and a few streets with baroque houses below, just as I had last seen it in reality, except that all the houses were decorated with enormous swastika flags. In the Zero Hour they were taken down. That was it.

When I returned to Heidelberg six months later, I looked at the city with this picture in mind. The double vision linked past and present. I did not go back to the *Hochschule* because I could not endure the flag-waving students there. I finished my exams and in January 1986 began teaching in the English Department at the University of Mannheim as a specialist of American Jewish culture. In spring 1987 I happened to see a poster announcing the group Aschira with a program of "Contemporary Jewish Songs from Israel." The concert was to be held in the *Aula* (assembly hall) of the University of Heidelberg. I decided to go, because I liked Israeli music and had not heard much since I had left Brandeis four years before. The hall, a fancy, stiff wooden affair in a baroque building, was packed. I studied the program and was in for the first surprise. Instead of the expected Israeli music I found traditional Jewish songs from the liturgy as well as from Hebrew and Yiddish folklore. Everything was there, from *Ma tovu* to *Hine ma tov* to *oifn pripetshik*, relentlessly concocted into a charming Jewish potpourri. The program informed me further that Aschira was a group consisting mainly of Protestant theology students who, with the "pre*cis*ion" of German scholars, had added copious illuminating notes to various items on the program. But where were the *partisaner lider, Sog nisht keinmol, S'ligt ergetz fartayet,* or *Shtil, di nakht is oisgeshternt?* While I was deciding whether or not I should stay, the group came in and commenced. After two or three songs they asked the audience to sing along and in order to facilitate this, they unfurled huge scrolls of paper on which the text of the next song was written in Hebrew script and in transliteration. But this seemed hardly necessary. The audience, about two hundred people between the ages of twenty and thirty-five, was all aglow singing along with *Inbrunst*. I looked around. Except for the woman on my left (who was Israeli), there were no Jewish faces in the crowd. Of course not, it was Friday night. A mock Shabbat celebration complete with *Ma tovu* and scrolls in Hebrew script. I couldn't endure it and left during the intermission.

The letter I received a few weeks later was very clear on that issue: "The story you tell me (if I've understood it correctly) of a hall full of Germans singing Jewish songs, and no Jews present, fills me with a horror so dense that it is beyond thinking of. Nostalgia for ghosts, nostalgia for smoke and ash!" That was one interpretation. Was the eagerness of my students to learn about the people and the culture their relatives had destroyed "nostalgia for ghosts, nostalgia for smoke and ash"? Or was there something else, just as there had been "something else" in this "hall full of Germans"? Was I helping to fill the vacuum instead of making it visible? "Germany," the letter continued, "is a Jewish vacuum, and the means of my 'memorial' to the dead is to avoid filling that vacuum with Jewish tokenism." In a sense I was forcing Jewish authors to acquiesce in just that by assigning their stories. "Do I know how I feel about that?" the letter went on. "Not exactly. I am wary of being a token collaborator in a job Germany must do on its own: it's a job of moral reclamation, generation by generation. I am not certain it's the place of Jews to rush, in less than half a century, from being Germany's victims to being Germany's teachers. [Moral reclamation] isn't something that can be imposed from without. It has to be a spontaneous, voluntary, uncoerced (except by conscience) movement [like the singing? like the seminar attendance?], or it's nothing at all: or it's only the meaningless self-exculpating stuff of official conferences and official pronouncements. So I'm not certain whether Jews, whether as teachers or even as writers being read, ought to be participants in what should properly be an internal German national task. The word 'collaborator' may well apply. Is a Jew living in Germany today—by virtue of lending his presence as a sign of the ostensible return of 'normality'—a kind of collaborator? Is a Jew living in Germany today helping to build a German Potemkin Village, a cover-up for the guilty recent past? Today, it seems to me, the definition of a collaborator would be one who assists in the exculpation of the past by insisting on the innocence of the present: as if the children of the present had been born on Mars, and not in their grandparents' and parents' Germany! I am afraid these are my unblinkingly harsh views. . . . You may not welcome them. . . . But the subject of the Six Million and the memorial owed them is the one subject in the world, I think, that requires truth-telling over good manners. The least courteous text ever written may well be: 'Your brother's blood cries out from the ground.' If that text reminds us of anything, it is where we set our daily feet."

This letter (not sure if it was addressing a Jew or a German) not only cast strong doubt on my strategy of making Absence visible by contrast, which relied somewhat on the cooperation of survivors or American Jews. I even went a step further and put a moral question mark on Jews who stepped on German soil. But how could the "job of moral reclamation" be done in a vacuum? About the older generation, people in their sixties and beyond, I had no illusion. I wasn't even sure if most of them felt any need at all for "moral reclamation." This doubt had bizarre consequences. It made their presence unendurable for me. Riding a streetcar or a train, waiting in a bank or a fine neighborhood bakery (which on Saturday mornings was crowded with a horde of particularly undisciplined Germans, Germans who in their jobs were not used to waiting but to be waited on), I was plagued by the double vision: I imagined the same scene, the same people forty or fifty years earlier, and was overcome with deep revulsion. What did they all do in the thirties and forties? Maybe the man sitting next to me served on the Eastern Front? One day in a neighborhood butcher's shop which sold the best sauerkraut in Heidelberg (I am a vegetarian), the queuing women talked about dogs. The owner of a German shepherd said with deep conviction: "People who understand and love dogs, also love human beings." *Sancta simplicitas!* How often can one run away? When on a Sunday morning in New York I saw a man with a kippa walk his German shepherd, the picture pained me like the sight of something monstrous. But if I had given up on the old people, there were still the young. And here it seemed to me that the letter's politics (though not its moral stance) were erroneous. The perpetuation of Absence would prevent moral reclamation. Of course, some of my students might well think of themselves as having been born on Mars. So what if one set out to show them that they were not? If one insisted not "on the innocence of the present" but on its connectedness with the past, to evoke not guilt feelings (that did not strike me as adequate) but pain? In regard to myself, however, the question was academic, since in another two months I would leave Germany to finish my dissertation in Cambridge, Massachusetts (where I am still). Had I been a collaborator or even a usurper? Had I stepped into the place left empty by Anne Frank, to whose house I had made a passionate pilgrimage at fifteen? Had I been filling a vacuum which my correspondent considered a " 'memorial' to the dead"? I did not think so. Our moral needs were equally valid, but the resultant actions put us in opposition to one another. Her decision to perpetuate Absence was based on distance; for me, lack of distance had eliminated choice. And the way in which I became a usurper (or perhaps a moral reclaimer) was quite accidental.

I was born to absence, to a Swiss-born but Catholic mother and an absent father. This father, in turn, had been born out of wedlock to a woman of uncertain religion and very humble social status and an absent father, a Jewish merchant from Hamburg. Whatever his parents' social situation was exactly, it seemed to have been impossible to keep the child (born in 1931). In early childhood my father was given to a childless, financially secure though not affluent Protestant couple. They adopted him and raised him in a cult of gratitude ("If it wasn't for us, you would be dead!"). Religious education of any kind was out of the question, but attendance at the local Gymnasium (secondary school, which one attends between the ages of ten and eighteen) was all right because the adoptive parents counted among the "respectable" people in the small town in rural northern Germany. During the reign of the National Socialists, "respectability" included the profession of the dominant ideology. The adoptive parents were believers in the Führer's secular redemption. But like all believers they were haunted by the sense that their sinfulness obstructed the course of salvation. Their sin, committed in secret like any sin, consisted in the adoption of this angelic-looking devil's child, which the woman, who had been left paralyzed from the waist down by polio and thus could not have any children, wanted so much. She, rather than her husband, lost control over her inner torment and transformed her sense of guilt into tyranny of the child. My father did not talk very often about his youth. But the social environment of his youth comes to life in his last novel, *Der Mörder und die Heiligen* (The Murderer and the Saints), published in 1979. It tells the story of a not so *comme il faut* reverend who, as an act of penitence, brings the Gospel to an anarchic town in the Wild West. It is hardly possible to mistake the cruelty in this deepest province of mankind—the everyday banality of evil, the debasing hypocrisy of the town's petite bourgeoisie—for a portrait of mid-nineteenth-century America. This town in the Wild West is the Nordic hamlet Nordenham in the late thirties and early forties. It took my father forty years to find a language to describe his childhood —that of blackest humor.

The child, Horst as he was called, was smart but overly sensitive, blond and blue-eyed, had tiny ears and a shy grin. In photographs of the period, which, in compliance with the demands of German racial theory, depicted Jewish children with one ear clearly visible, no "hateful, offstanding ears"[3] would have shown. The child was obedient, perhaps even meek. But eventually the relentlessly enforced gratitude deformed him into rebelliousness. Shortly before graduation from Gymnasium (at about age seventeen or eighteen) he ran away and drifted through Germany supporting himself with odd jobs (such as mining). By the middle of the 1950s he arrived in the south, in Konstanz, a medium-sized town on the Swiss border. By now he had discovered that he could make a living by being original and was working rather successfully as a writer of ads (he would later become a writer of short stories, radio plays, novels, and, above all, letters). For some reason he came to the home of my mother's father fairly regularly on Sundays to play chess. Games of any sort, but chess in particular, fascinated him. At the chessboard he could imagine himself in complete control over the world, which showed to him the familiar structure of Me against the Other. Here one had a chance to beat the enemy by being smarter. Reality was different.

My mother, daughter of a gifted woman whose artistic talents had been frustrated in her marriage, discerned a similar suffering in the thin, good-looking young man who was bent over the chessboard, trying to devise an ingenious move that would checkmate his opponent. His otherness appealed to her, his irreverence for conventions, his self-consciousness, which was the result of a deep-rooted cultural split between what he called his "Jewish self" and his "German outfit," fashioned during his torturous northern German childhood and adolescence. My mother thought of herself as a dislocated Swiss. Both had a similar desire for order and stability, and my mother radiated the strength to achieve it. They were married in 1957. But the burden which the maintenance of familial stability and comfort (home, clothes, food) imposed on my father was too much for him. He began to lose ground and took flight into a world of imaginary control. A vicious circle began, or, rather, a downward spiral that hit bottom in 1960, while my mother was pregnant with her second child. Bourgeois bliss exploded and sent my mother reeling to northern Germany, where she gave birth to my brother. She spent the worst year of her life at age twenty-six in the house of her husband's adoptive parents. Although a kind and generous woman, she would never be able to speak of them (which she hardly ever did) without bitterness and pain. (When at age ten I received in the mail my one and only gift from Nordenham, an eighteen-karat gold cross to be worn as a pendant, the sight elicited from my mother, a believing Catholic, a bitter laugh. When a few years later the wearing of a cross around the neck was the *dernier cri* among my schoolmates, as Arafat kerchiefs would be thereafter, I gave the cross away.) The moment came when Mother could not endure it any longer in Nordenham. She put her infant in a home, sent me to her parents, and headed back south. Early in 1963 she had secured the basic elements of a new home: a tiny apartment and a job with the German railways (of all possible employees). She took me back. And then the great day came. We traveled north to fetch my brother. It is my earliest memory, and it is clear and distinct, how the door opened and a nun brought into the waiting room a skinny creature, supposedly two and a half years old, with long wheat-blond hair and large brown eyes in a pale, skull-like face. He could not yet speak.

The 1960s were a tough time. My mother put herself

through night school and worked (those were the days when one worked six days a week and every two weeks on Sunday morning). My brother and I walked about a mile to kindergarten and later two miles to school every morning. I had a better time growing up than my shy brother, because our lower-middle-class-to-proletarian neighborhood not only permitted but encouraged loud and roaring play in trees, the lumberyard, freight cars, and trucks. We kids were accepted by the neighborhood kids, but my mother, a nondivorced woman with two kids and no husband in the 1960s, was avoided by their parents and of course by her former peers. She did nothing to break her neighborhood isolation because she felt she did not belong there. She was on her way out. She was going to make it. She would regain her social status. The poverty was hard, but my mother suffered more from the loss of social status and of the intellectual and cultural pleasures in which she had indulged at home. We kids had an acute sense of Mother's fall and of our social ostracism. This ostracism was not merely a class issue. Somehow there was another embarrassing element involved of which we children were conscious from early childhood through adolescence. We could not help but be aware of it, as two examples will show.

My mother had a cousin on her father's side who happened to live in our city. He was a baker and a very kind man. He had scant feathery hair, pink baby features, and watery blue eyes. When my brother and I were about five and six years old, he had come to visit us two or three times on Saturday afternoons. Each time he brought two large bags full of the most delicious rolls and white bread. The fragrance of the fresh bread which soon filled our small apartment was a feast in itself, and the flour with which in southern German fashion bread and rolls were dusted seemed to taste different from the stale flour we bought at the local store. I don't remember the cousin very distinctly because in my memory his kindness and the gift of bread have fused. It turned out that this cousin was married and had two daughters, one still an infant, the other about three years old, and that we had been invited to pay a visit. For us this meant a long journey by streetcar and bus to a distant suburb on one of Mother's precious Sundays. We were welcomed into a one-family house and ushered into the living room. We children were amazed at the whiteness of the upholstery and did not understand why Mother's features suddenly froze and the cousin turned to her with an expression of grief and shame. Mother told us later that the cousin's wife had insisted on covering the upholstery with bedsheets so that the *three* of us should not soil them. We never went back.

Five years later, in secondary school, my best friend was a plain but extremely bright girl, the class genius. Her intelligence, combined with a disarming honesty and a complete lack of social graces, made her another outsider, so we naturally joined forces. Her parents had fled Silesia, an eastern German province (now belonging to Poland), to escape the Russian occupation. They had arrived in Mannheim with not much more than a few suitcases but a good education. Both had finished their studies and had become pharmacists. They began to rebuild their lives, opened a pharmacy, and after a while even managed to buy the apartment house in which the pharmacy was located and in which they, too, lived. During my first years in Gymnasium (between ages ten to thirteen), I frequently went home with my friend after school which ended at ten of one P.M. Nobody (except a few cooking utensils with which to produce my eternal omelettes) expected me for lunch, whereas my friend had to be home at one o'clock sharp. This was when the pharmacy closed for lunch and the *Mittagessen,* the most substantial meal of the day, was served. In their household this was literally true: the meal was shopped for, prepared, served, cleaned up by a cook. If my friend did not show up on time, she would be scolded, which she detested; so we hurried. On entering the apartment, which always seemed to smell of a particularly nauseating disinfectant, I usually became tense because I would have to greet my friend's parents. But at one o'clock sharp I would be released. The family —mother, father, two children, aunt, and grandmother—would sit down to their meal while I disappeared into my friend's room (childhood dream: A Room of One's Own), looked around for a leftover piece of chocolate on my friend's desk, and started my homework. In the adjacent room I could hear silverware scraping china. It distracted me from doing math. Sometimes, though rarely, the cook would come in and bring me a plate of food. Then I would sit on my friend's bed and eat while balancing the plate on my knees. The desk was cluttered with papers which I did not dare disturb. I was always a little embarrassed when the cook handed me the plate. But the most painful moment would be (if I hadn't eaten fast enough) at one forty-five sharp, when my friend would come back to her room and see me hunched over a plate, gobbling food. Then tears would come to my eyes from shame. (Only later was I ashamed for her.)

As children my brother and I developed a strategy of defiance. But it did not always work. When we were not with the kids in our street, knowledge of our social ostracism informed our behavior. Three things were self-understood: (1) that the family had absolute precedence, (2) that we would restore our mother's "honor" and regain what she had lost, and (3) that as far as WE were concerned THEY could all go to hell. Our vulnerability is obvious in the contradiction. We never asked, as far as I can recall, about our father because in his absence and its reasons we sensed the very source of pain. I discovered his history one day when I was poking around my mother's files. The discovery shocked me, but I began to understand what was expected of me. Our parents' absence allowed us to grow up in singular freedom—freedom of mind and behavior. This together with my "ambition" created problems when I entered Gymnasium, in 1969.

That my brother and I would attend Gymnasium was a matter of course. For us it was the decisive step out of the neighborhood into an alien world, not culturally alien (because books were the one thing in which we could indulge freely, except for the restraints imposed by the public library) but socially alien. It was clear to us that this was our opportunity to kill two birds with one stone: *Mutter Ehre zu machen* (a German idiom for the Americanism "to make good") and to defeat THEM—the Philistine kids who had all these wonderful things created by their Philistine parents out of the ruins of Germany—by being somebody. These new kids talked about Mister Spock and Captain Kirk, about Buster Keaton and Mister Cartwright. I had no idea who these characters were, but I was pretty sure they had nothing to do with books. So I wouldn't have to know about them in the world in which I was going to make it (though I wasn't exactly sure what "it" stood for). My heroes at the time (age ten) were David (against Goliath), the Spartans, and Ulysses. In school I demanded to be taught, to be paid attention to, to be singled out for special tasks in which I could excel. I was a pain in the neck, but I found a few generous teachers. All was fine until, in 1973 or 1974, the slogans of the student revolt found their way into my school. "Democracy" was all the rage; the elite had to be leveled with the mass. My grades in German, history, and geography dropped from their constant high to somewhere in the middle of the scale. The middle-aged teacher of these subjects was newly assigned to the class. She had a weakness for Japanese and Chinese culture which did not stop at an appreciation for their art. She was not a communist, but the idea of toppling the elite and of creating uniformity by forcing all elements to adhere to a strict code apparently dictated by the masses appealed to her. I would have to conform. At that time this did not trigger historic recognition. I was fighting back, which made school a little bit more interesting until I graduated, in 1978.

On the whole, school was not enough. What it had to offer I gobbled up and cast around for more. I read mountains of books, but they did not do anything for me. I was fairly directionless and lonesome. And for all my knowledge my mind was vacant. One day in 1973 all students of my grade were asked to attend a lecture instead of religious education. The lecture was to be an introduction to Judaism. The Protestant pastor had asked his Jewish colleague to come and talk about his religion and his way of life. What would he look like? I knew Jews from books and I knew that my mother met some in a monthly discussion group on Israel (in 1980 an affluent German of this group anonymously gave me half of the costs for a trip to Israel), but that there were Jews living like everybody else in our city was news to me. The door opened and in walked an extremely handsome, Mediterranean-looking young Frenchman who could have talked about anything at this girls' school and won our hearts. At the end of his lecture he offered Hebrew instruction to anyone who would like to come to the Jewish community. The next Monday ten of us went to the synagogue hidden in a noble part of the city. Half a year later I had the instructor all to myself.

He was the community's *hazzan,* a deeply believing Orthodox man who had recently come to Germany from the large community of Metz in France on a double mission: first, to provide spiritual guidance to Jews in Germany and, if possible, to build up a functioning community, and second, to participate in a Christian-Jewish dialogue. After a year he asked me why I was still coming. I told him that my father, whom I saw occasionally in Munich, talked about his "Jewish self" and that I wanted to know what that was. Besides, I didn't have anywhere else to go. I liked the world I began to discover. From now on we worked seriously first on biblical Hebrew and Torah, later on Mishnah and Gemara. He was not a great linguist or a great Talmudist (as I found out later when I knew more and studied with "scholars"), but he was a man with a deep sense of what it meant to be a Jew. We worked for two hours every week for the next seven years until he quit his job in Germany to return to France. "In Germany you will always remain a *ger*" were the words with which he announced his decision to give up. The problem was not the Germans but the Jews in his community. They resented his active participation in the Christian-Jewish dialogue. The community comprised about four hundred members; most of them were returnees, a few had immigrated from Eastern Bloc countries. The level of Jewish knowledge, particularly among the returnees, was very low. Their Jewishness consisted of a sense of having been victimized by Germany. This definition of Jewishness was reinforced by the enormous gratitude shown them by Germans and Germany for having come back. As victims of the Nazis Jews now enjoyed the highest esteem, a certain exclusiveness and moral impeccability. But they did not have much to offer in a Christian-Jewish dialogue. Their sense of themselves as Jews was not religious, as was the *hazzan*'s, but resulted from recent German history and as such was extremely vulnerable. The dialogue in which the *hazzan* engaged with his colleagues and interested laymen posed a threat to the community's exclusiveness and thus to their fragile sense of self. There was constant tension between the community's spiritual and its worldly leadership. The scarcity of children and adolescents added to the general despair. By the time the *hazzan* left, I had learned to think the way he thought and felt comfortable with it. I had found out what it was to have a "Jewish self" and had made good my father's absence. The *hazzan*'s rigorous train-ing had filled a vacuum and created a home, not in a place but in a way of thinking about the world.

In the late seventies a friend told me of a survivor of Buchen-wald who gave Yiddish lessons in Heidelberg. Over thirty years after his "liberation," the terror was still visible in his face. The university paid him to teach "courses"—an alien notion to him. We read Peretz as soon as he found out that I could read the *oisjess*. Why waste time? Once in a while he looked at me and shook his head sadly. I was too embarrassed to ask what was wrong. He was the one teacher by whose humaneness I was awed. Recently I learned the answer to my unasked question, but I don't know what it means in regard to the question of Absence. After an evening in the company of a few New Yorkers, in temporary Californian exile, the writer of the letter I had received in Germany reached out, touched lightly my blond hair, turned to the others, and said: "Do you know that under the shiksa hair there is . . ." " . . . a Yiddish *kepele*?" I completed for her. She smiled in agreement. Collaborated with, usurped, re-claimed—the history of my coming to terms with Absence. It has caused another loss. I was taught to see the Absence in Germany and I found it unendurable.

NOTES

1. Quoted in Yosef Hayim Yerushalmi, *Zakhor: Jewish History and Jewish Memory* (Seattle: University of Washington Press, 1982), p. 38.

2. Cynthia Ozick, "The Suitcase," in *The Pagan Rabbi* (New York: Alfred A. Knopf, 1971), p. 109.

3. These are Ludwig Lewisohn's words about the ears of his gentile tormentor in a Charleston, South Carolina, school; see Ludwig Lewisohn, *Up Stream: An American Chronicle* (New York: Boni and Liveright, 1922), p. 65.

Threads

MAX APPLE

INTRODUCTION

When I was a child, I had to struggle to leave our yard. Around the house a five-foot hedge blocked my view of the neighborhood. My parents and grandparents thought it was fine for me to stay within the hedge. We had a shady arbor where concord grapes grew over their supports to rest against the house. There were fluffy white flowers that my grandma called snowballs. I could blow them apart with my breath. In the sunniest place in the yard, surrounded by their own little fence, we grew currants and gooseberries, fruits that I never saw anywhere else. I was a college freshman reading a Chekhov story called "Gooseberries" before I realized that my grandma planted her gooseberries in Michigan for the same reason Chekhov's character planted them in Russia: she wanted to feel rich.

As far as I was concerned, she succeeded too well. I felt guilty for having a yard in bloom while our neighbors harvested broken glass and bottlecaps.

"Schleppers," my grandma said. "Stay away from them."

"I don't care," I argued. "I want to go out to play."

The schleppers were having fun. They were throwing balls against their crumbling cement porch steps; they were riding bikes and pulling girls' hair and sometimes laying their hands on firecrackers, while I was in the yard waiting for the gooseberries to turn pink.

When nobody was watching I began to sneak out to play. I saw the dollar bills that some of the neighborhood boys got when they went trick-or-treating at the Alamo bar. I crawled into a secret clubhouse beneath a porch to watch a boy named Kenny take off his crepe-soled shoe slowly, like a stripper, to show off his sixth toe. The boys told me about their family life, about drinking and child beating as routine as meals and bed-time.

The more I mingled in the neighborhood, the more lurid my stories became. When I repeated them to my grandma, she put cold compresses on her head and begged me to stay home. She thought even school was too much exposure to the schleppers.

My grampa said I would grow up to be a criminal, and this prophecy became part of his arsenal of facts, all of which proved the superiority of Lithuania to America.

They didn't have to worry. I knew when I was five or six that I was not like the neighborhood boys and was delighted to be different. I didn't envy whippings and seven o'clock bedtimes, but I was jealous of one thing. The schleppers all had cousins.

It seemed as if they had as many cousins as we had mitzvahs. They had cousins who came over to play, cousins who gave them see-through marbles and compasses, cousins who took them to the zoo and ball games—and I had two first cousins. They lived in Ohio and I saw them about every six years and even then only at weddings or bar mitzvahs. The only cousins who played with me were Jack and Max, furniture buyer brothers from Pough-keepsie. They came to visit us twice a year because there was a furniture exhibition in Grand Rapids. I loved them both, the boisterous Jack who could eat *latkes* by the dozen and his quiet thoughtful brother, Max, who smoked Regent cigarettes and gave me the maroon boxes.

To Max I wrote my first letters, block-printing, telling him I was fine and hoped he was and would come to visit us soon. I was glad that we had the same first name and I liked writing out that hard word, Poughkeepsie. He always wrote back on a type-writer that used blue ink.

During one of his visits I introduced him around the neighborhood. Later the boys told me they didn't believe he was my cousin.

"He's your uncle," they said. I insisted he was my cousin, even got into a fistfight to prove it.

I was right, but so were they. Boys who had more cousins than we had gooseberries didn't know how I envied them their horde and what a treasure that fifty-year-old man was to me. After the fight to prove that I had cousins, surrounded by boys who stole hubcaps and would grow into reform school, I began to realize that what we called "Hitler" at our house had robbed me of cousins. Years before I had any historical or emotional understanding of the Holocaust, I was lonely.

The loneliness *has* stayed. I never knew my aunts. One of them was a music teacher. I imagine her trying to sing with my sisters and me at a Seder. The only tune we can approximate is *"Chad God Yow."* I can see her laughing and teaching us to sing like her children, the cousins who would have come from Poland to visit us. I imagine the trips I would have taken to Serai, the village my grandma described so well that I knew it better than Grand Rapids. These are daydreams that my cousin-rich friends would not understand. My entire generation of American Jews is in a way like an only child. We who were born just as the Final Solution began have cousin-loneliness in our bones. There is no word to describe it, but even in our satisfaction we know that we're missing what so many others take for granted.

The Holocaust disrupted time. Family histories only a generation past are lost, as distant and mysterious, as full of lacunae as if hundreds of years separated us from them.

For my vanished cousins there is at least a label. To say they perished in the Holocaust is no comfort but it is a finality. For an uncle not directly connected to the Holocaust I have far less certainty. He left Poland before the war, wrote to his two American brothers from Argentina, and then disappeared for thirty years. Only weeks before my father died we received a letter from him, and I became his correspondent until his own death a few years later.

I learned little about his life from his letters. Only once did he give me a clue. In cryptic Yiddish he wrote that since the moment his sisters were murdered by the Nazis he had not been himself. This was all he said about the thirty silent years. He died without any further explanation.

I felt little grief for this uncle I did not know and who told me so little about himself. Still, ten years after his death I was a tourist in Argentina and tried to find people who had known him.

I located the elderly woman who had translated my letters to him, but hardly knew him. She let him use her address because she could read English and was happy to help a lonely man. His boss was dead, his boss's son also knew nothing about this obscure loading-dock worker. I heard only clichés: a nice man, a quiet man, he minded his own business. . . .

I walked through the streets of the Buenos Aires garment district where he had lived; then, anxious for any solid piece of information, I went to the Jewish Federation Building to look for a record of his burial. In the basement, surrounded by posters advertising Israeli tourism, I searched through the names of the Buenos Aires dead.

I didn't find him among the dead either. I read alphabetically a to z, so maybe I passed him without knowing what name he had selected for himself. I would have settled for a *yahrzeit* date, at least something specific about his death, but there too I failed.

And that's all I can tell you. Cousin and uncle hungry, I wrote a story, "Threads." About the mass statistics of loss, I can add nothing; about my father's little brother living and dying among strangers, I can wonder and imagine.

1

In a Buenos Aires warehouse, only a few blocks from the landing where travelers awaited the ferry to Punta del Este, Ira Silvers of Baltimore examined a replica of the interior of his Charles Avenue apartment. It was not an exact copy, but close, down to a version of his fuzzy green sofa.

In Baltimore, Ira would be on that sofa, one foot over the

worn back. Here it was occupied by the actor Emile Delgado, who sipped sweetened coffee as he went over his lines.

Ira did not understand the Spanish script, but as he roamed the set, every once in a while he heard his untranslated name. He heard it as one word: Irasilvers. In the midst of all the Spanish it sounded as patriotic as "The Star-Spangled Banner."

Even though the strike began at noon, the actors thought it would be over in a few hours. Those already in costume kept their antennae and aluminum foil vests in place. The camera crew and the technicians, already on strike, didn't leave. They were out front, in the trailer of a semi truck playing blackjack while they waited for permission to return to work.

Silvers, on his second day in Argentina, didn't mind the strike. He enjoyed the breeze as he looked across the wide Rio de la Plata, toward Montevideo.

Only ten days ago, he had been lying on his original couch watching the Orioles in the midst of a record losing streak when Feldman called, offering him two hundred dollars a day to stand by in case they needed new material during the shooting of *Filth*.

Ira didn't even know the film was going to be made. A year ago Feldman had run across Ira's story and had paid Silvers a flat fee, ten thousand dollars, for a ninety-seven-page film script. Feldman himself translated it into Spanish.

"I'm not Warner Brothers or Twentieth Century-Fox," Feldman told the surprised writer. "I make movies on less than their catering budgets, but below the equator, people think Victor Feldman is Cecil B. DeMille."

Silvers wrote the screenplay in a week, pocketed the fee, and considered himself the luckiest man on earth. When the producer called a year later, during the seventh inning of a 4–0 loss to the Tigers, Ira was too stunned to answer.

Feldman mistook surprise for greed.

"Two hundred dollars a day is all I pay the stars," the producer reminded him, "and we can do this without you. You're like an insurance policy. In case something doesn't work you write out a new scene or two and I put it into Spanish on the spot. We don't even have to type out scripts. Exact words don't make any difference."

Silvers accepted, and here he was, in midafternoon of shooting day. The cast was edgy after four hours of waiting, when Feldman entered the warehouse and called everyone together.

"Under the military government," the producer said, "I made twelve films. I put Argentina on the movie map. Now they torture me with taxes, and permits, and every couple of months, a strike. Well, they've jacked Victor Feldman around once too often."

Emile Delgado, who now held his antennae in his hands, asked when the shooting would begin.

"When somebody who knows how to run things takes over this country. Believe me, I told the minister of commerce a year ago that Feldman Productions did not have to stay in Buenos Aires. I reminded him that there is Santiago de Chile."

As the actors dispersed, Feldman called the writer aside.

"Check with the hotel every day," he told Ira. "I'll leave you a message. In the meantime, enjoy it. You're on a paid vacation. See if you can write a script for a quick coup to bring the generals back."

2

The writer had other business. In his briefcase next to the annotated screenplay were the letters regarding his Uncle Carlos. Two years late, the nephew arrived in Buenos Aires. Carlos had died in 1986. The year of his death was the only thing Ira knew about his uncle. Ira's late father, Howard, told his son about the brother he had never seen; the boy who had been born in Poland after Howard had left. The boy who somehow escaped the Holocaust and turned up in Buenos Aires wrote Howard a letter in 1947; then he neither answered any letters from his brother nor contacted the Silvers family in any other way, until a brief letter arrived in 1985, four months after Howard Silvers' death.

Ira, the male heir, answered at once. And to nobody's surprise, the junior Silvers also received no response until the note in February 1987, from a Señor Cardozo, informing Ira that his uncle had died in 1986.

Ira felt no grief when he read the news. How could he mourn an abstraction, an uncle who was less real to him than other family exotica, the tablecloth from Shanghai or the tea service from Budapest, historical items that came out on special occasions? Carlos stayed hidden. A name, a South American. "Maybe a gangster," Ira's mother guessed.

If Howard Silvers had an opinion about the fate of his unknown brother, he never told it to his son. When it came to immigrant tales Howard preferred his own, and Ira didn't blame him.

The Howard Silvers saga had no Nazi terror or Jewish blood. The adventure of a happy-go-lucky boy who takes on the world, to Ira, was like Robin Hood, only this one starred Howard Silvers. Ira could still hear it in his father's intonation.

"I was born with a smell for the big world," Howard Silvers would say. "I had an American soul, but in my village there were only two things: study and pray. Study, study, study, then pray, pray, pray. It was making me crazy. When I was thirteen and they said I was a man, I made up my mind to act like one. The next time one of those black-bearded teachers hit me I told myself that would be it, and it was. I ran away. But don't think I was thirteen the way American boys are thirteen. I *was* a man. I passed for seventeen and got a job on a merchant ship. I shoveled coal across the Atlantic. I had muscles like this."

"It's true," Harriet Silvers would interrupt. "Your father was as strong as a horse."

Ira's mother, Harriet, a third-generation native of Savannah, Georgia, raised her son as heir to the Old South rather than the Old World.

"By the time I met him," Harriet would say, "your father had no accent and was already an accountant. I didn't believe it when he told me he had run away from Poland in 1929. He was a self-made man. I fell in love."

While Howard Silvers established himself in Richmond, Virginia, Carlos of Buenos Aires sank into obscurity, became a name.

To Ira, growing up in Richmond, Buenos Aires meant Uncle Carlos the way Texas meant oil or Africa meant lions.

Then, in the mid-1950s, after eight years of unanswered letters, Howard Silvers gave up contacting Carlos.

"If he wants a brother, he knows where to find one," the accountant said, and that was it, until 1986.

Ira, looking for clues to his lost uncle, had only one. The letter announcing Carlos's death was signed by Señor Elisha Cardozo, and it carried a return address.

Silvers telephoned, then took the number eleven bus as directed in his pocket guide to Buenos Aires. The pocket guide also informed Ira that he was heading toward the Buenos Aires garment center, "similar to New York's Seventh Avenue," the pamphlet said, but when Silvers got off the bus and walked away from the Avenida Corrientes, the expensive luggage and shoe stores disappeared and he saw twisted streets full of shops featuring yard goods, fabrics, notions, liners, crowded nineteenth-century facades that reminded him of the Lower East Side.

He found the address, No. 97 on Calle Larrea, a wooden gate between a store of curtain hooks and an emporium of mothballs and Velcro.

Until the woman came to the gate to admit him, Silvers did not know there was a Señora Cardozo.

The elderly lady led him to her apartment through a small courtyard half in bloom. Next to a banana palm, Silvers saw the open shower and what he guessed was the shared toilet. At the rear of the courtyard Señora Cardozo welcomed him to her three tiny rooms.

"It is I," she said, "who wrote you the letter. I speak the king's English."

Already awaiting the American on her mahogony dining room table were tea, date cookies, and, ubiquitous in Buenos Aires, a plate of sliced beef.

Señora Cardozo welcomed Ira as a guest, but Silvers, too curious to be polite, asked what she knew about his uncle even before he sipped his tea.

Señora Cardozo unfortunately had scant information.

"Maybe I saw him in the synagogue," she said, "maybe not. My husband, he will tell you."

Señor Cardozo, she said, was expected at any moment.

While they waited, Señora Cardozo wanted to show the American a few things. From a bookcase she pulled down her albums. Expecting grandchildren, Silvers was surprised to see women in evening gowns. He thought Señora Cardozo was showing him a photo album of an old Miss Buenos Aires pageant.

"All mine," the señora said.

"Daughters?"

"No"—she laughed—"the gowns. My life's work. Since I was eight years old my mother taught me dressmaking, in England, before I came here."

She held up her right hand, then, as if an afterthought, her left.

"Who knows how many dresses these fingers have made?"

Señora Cardozo began to narrate her way through the smiling women in prom gowns.

Silvers looked at his watch.

"This one you will know," she said.

Silvers shook his head.

"Gisela Glandt."

She skipped a few laminated pages and pointed to a woman holding a microphone desperately as if it were a life raft.

"Her you will know from the radio all over the world."

"I'm not up on radio," Silvers said.

He had had his fill of beehive hairdos, plump smiles, and 1950s gowns. He didn't want to be rude, but he closed the album and moved it from his lap to the table.

"Some of the girls," Señora Cardozo said, "are not girls anymore. Some have already left this life. But the dresses they passed on to their daughters. My work lasts."

To distract her from opening the second album, Silvers told her about his own work.

Señora Cardozo immediately offered her services to the film industry.

Silvers told her that the film he was working on was science fiction.

"They don't need gowns," he said. "The characters aren't human."

"Still," the dressmaker said, "there must be females and formal occasions."

She opened the second album, looking for Helena Ferranto, an actress. Silvers decided he had seen enough.

"I have to get back to the set," he said. "I'll call your husband tonight."

He was already planning to meet her husband in a café.

"No, no, no," Señora Cardozo said. She blocked the doorway with her bony self.

"Señor Cardozo will not forgive me if he doesn't see you."

When Silvers had moved back to his seat, the señora, moving as quickly as a child, went to the bedroom. Silvers heard her excited voice on the telephone. When she opened the door he spotted, above the unmade bed, a crucifix.

"Cardozo will be here faster than a pig can eat," she said, proud of her colloquialism.

Silvers wondered about the crucifix but decided it was none of his business.

An hour later, after he had finished the platter of meat and all the cookies and had looked through the second album, Silvers told the señora that he absolutely could wait no longer.

"I'm late. People are waiting."

She blocked the door again, but this time Silvers was prepared if necessary to move her aside.

"Five more minutes," she pleaded. "It will be worth it, you'll see."

The door opened, and above the old woman's head Silvers looked into the eyes of a movie star.

"Nora Cortez," she called herself, "an actress."

Silvers could not look away. With twilight and the dingy courtyard as backdrop, Nora modeled a gown that only Señora Cardozo could have made. The red material dipped into the young woman's chest, made a sliver of her waist, then blossomed into a garden of flowers that wilted at her ankles.

Nora, perhaps a model as well as an actress, did not mind being looked at. Without posing or becoming embarrassed, she accepted Silvers' stare and seemed equally intent on looking at him.

Señora Cardozo stood between them. When she was sure of the writer's interest, she taunted him.

"Mr. Silvers is late," she told Nora. "He has to leave."

Silvers no longer noticed her. The three of them stood in the doorway for a few seconds, then the old lady, satisfied, went into the kitchen.

3

Silvers walked with Nora through the crowded streets of the garment district. Workers, on their way home, stepped aside for the beautiful woman in the hooped skirt. Nora was embarrassed.

"Señora Cardozo insisted that I wear this," she said. "Please forgive me. I did not want to disappoint her."

"If I knew where to rent a tuxedo around here," Ira said, "I would do it, and we could go to the opera or something."

"I've never been to an opera," Nora said.

"Neither have I," Silvers told the truth. "I was just trying to sound impressive."

When Silvers invited her to dinner, Nora gave him the address of a restaurant and went home to change. He offered to take her home by cab, but Nora insisted on going home alone and on foot.

Silvers watched her disappear among the bookstalls on Avenida de Corrientes. When she turned the corner, he had a terrible premonition that he would never see her again. He waited for a minute, trying to act rational; then he attempted to follow her, but when he came to the crosswalk there were only pedestrians on the sidewalk, no Cinderellas, no dark-eyed Spanish beauties who just stepped out of eighteenth-century paintings.

At the Parilla Restaurant, which he quickly located, Silvers drank a salty beer as he awaited Nora. He tried to remain calm. In the men's room he washed his face and ran wet fingers through his curly hair. He wanted to look good for her even though he had resigned himself to believing she would not come to the restaurant.

If this happened, he would return to the Cardozo apartment and find Nora on one of the album pages. On the back he would read her biographical facts, her statistics, or if not, the old dressmaker would give Silvers her phone number.

Then, on time, actually ten minutes early, Nora appeared. Though she now wore blue jeans and a man-tailored shirt, she still looked to Silvers as if she could perch on a museum wall.

She laughed when he told her how worried he had been.

"Señora Cardozo told me you could help me find a film role. She convinced me that I had to appear in costume. I was so ashamed. I felt like—what you call her—Scarlett O'Hara."

"You could be a movie star," Silvers said. He could hardly believe such a cliché could come from him. It was a phrase his mother used. "I mean, you certainly have what it takes."

"What it takes," Nora said, "is an opportunity, no?"

Silvers knew what she wanted and felt his insignificance in Feldman's project. Briefly he imagined going to the producer with new scenes, a new character, Nora, the Queen of Baltimore, riding along the waterfront on a barge like Cleopatra entering Rome.

"I wish I could help," he said, "but it's already cast. Anyway, you would not want to be in this film." He was embarrassed as he told her the plot.

"It's about microscopic creatures from another planet who land at the Baltimore County Sewage plant. To them human waste is paradise. It's the ultimate power source, what nuclear fusion would be to us. They use one day's worth of Baltimore sewage to take over the world. The producer thinks it's so disgusting that it will become a cult classic."

Silvers was smiling an embarrassed smile, but the actress looked intent, as if he had narrated to her the plot of *The Brothers Karamazov*.

"I have heard of Feldman," she said. "He makes many films."

"Don't judge me by him," Ira said. "I hardly know the man."

"But you work for him."

"Yes, maybe for a few weeks."

Silvers wanted to move the conversation away from business.

"Let's make a deal: you won't connect me with Feldman and I won't connect you with Señora Cardozo."

"Without the señora," Nora said, "we would not know each other."

Silvers raised his glass. "To Señora Cardozo, in gratitude."

They drank several more toasts to the señora, and one sweet one to their new friendship, but once the food arrived, the evening took an awkward turn. Silvers, unaccustomed even in the States to dripping barbecue sauce, needed a dozen napkins to dab at his lips. He was embarrassed and felt that he seemed coarse to this Argentinian beauty who could hold a sticky rib with her fingertips and gnaw at it the way a cat might, hardly disturbing the flesh, making it melt toward a blackened bone.

He was so busy with chewing and wiping his lips that he felt unable to charm or even interest her. He needed to count on the lure of his connection to the movies. For their next date he was already planning a café setting. They would order small, clean pastries and white wine.

He did learn that Nora was twenty-two and had been taking acting classes. By day she worked as a typist in an insurance office. Recently she had given up the classes because they were too expensive. She was looking for a second job in the evenings.

"The inflation," she said, "it makes people crazy. You think there is never enough of anything, and it's true."

She also wanted to improve her English.

After dinner, Nora arose, shook Silvers' hand, and said good-bye.

"Wait," he said. "I'll take you home. I would love to help you with your English."

Silvers had been imagining a few drinks, maybe even, depending on the situation and of course, her attitude, an invitation to the Hotel Grand Plaza. She was already out the door before Silvers, leaving a wad of cash on the table, rushed from the restaurant to catch her. She gave him her phone number but refused his plea to walk her home. Still, as she handed him the slip of paper with her number, Nora kissed his cheekbone before she disappeared among the early evening shoppers.

4

Nobody answered at the phone number she gave him. Silvers tried all day, until midnight. After that hour, he thought, it's not my business. The day after that when she didn't answer, he couldn't stand it and returned to the Cardozo apartment.

This time the gentleman himself awaited Silvers. He was a dapper man, in his seventies, with a trim white mustache and a silk cravat such as Silvers had seen worn only by characters in films.

Señor Cardozo bowed at the waist to his guest. It only took a few minutes for Silvers to realize that his host modeled himself on Douglas Fairbanks, Jr.

Though still curious of course about his uncle, Silvers wanted information about the living, about Nora.

The dapper gentleman ignored Silvers' straightforward request for Nora's work number. He looked at the ceiling of his squalid apartment, held his hand to his heart, and seemed to be fighting off painful memory.

"I hardly knew the man," Cardozo said. "He came to the synagogue on high holy days only. I'm not much better. You know how it is, one forgets the old days."

Recalling the crucifix in the Cardozo bedroom, Ira suspected just how much forgetting there had been.

"I regret," Cardozo said, "that I don't even know his last name. I only knew him as Carlos."

With shame, Silvers admitted he was not certain.

"Our name is Silvers. In Poland it was Slavititsky. I don't know what name Carlos went by here. I addressed the letter that your wife answered to Carlos Silvers, care of this address. It was the address he used."

"Of course," Carlos said. "So that my wife could read him the English. I do know that he was a modest man. He prayed in a corner of the synagogue. I believe he worked on a loading dock. He was a strong man. Arms like this."

Suddenly, in this detail, Silvers for the first time recognized his uncle. Carlos became a man, like Howard the sailor, or Howard the father who had entertained his little son by making his huge biceps jump. Ira himself had none of the Silvers' arm strength. Tall and thin as a Virginia elm, he resembled the delicate Georgians, his mother's relatives.

"How did your wife happen to write the letter in English to me?" Ira asked.

"Carlos brought your English letter to us to translate. He was very sad to learn that his brother was dead. I offered to write for him, but he said not now. He left your letter here, so naturally when we heard he was dead, she wrote to you."

Finally the aged fop turned his mournful look to use. "You

could give a donation to the synagogue in his memory," he said. "It would be very helpful."

"I'm not a rich man," Silvers said. "This movie job is a rare experience for me."

Silvers asked again about Nora Cortez.

"Yes, yes, Nora," Cardozo said, "a true beauty."

Before he said anything else about Nora, Cardozo extracted a promise from Ira to visit the synagogue on Friday night.

"There's no rabbi, no cantor," he said, "just a group of old men. We used to be a burial society. Now it's more like a religious club. You'll visit, you'll sip a little wine, then you'll decide about a donation."

For the third time the writer asked for Nora's number at the insurance office. The old man gave him the same phone number he already had.

"That's all there is," Cardozo swore. "Even my wife has no other number."

The señora, of course, was not at home.

"Fitting a gown for a circus performer," Cardozo said, although Ira was certain he heard her whispering to her husband when Cardozo went into the bedroom for the phone number.

5

Though he knew it was hopeless, Silvers looked for Nora on the streets. He spent two whole days at outdoor cafés on the Ricoletto. He sipped coffee after coffee and went, on the half hour, to use the men's room and the telephone. Waiters began to recognize him. Nora did not answer.

At a bookstall he bought an English grammar, a gift for Nora, so she would know how genuinely he wanted to help her with her English.

Surrounded by verbs, Silvers' lonely imagination raced. He would invite her to America, help her find a typing job in Baltimore. He would do this out of disinterested friendship, asking nothing in return.

Still Silvers, breathing in the cigarette smoke of the Buenos Aires literati as he read his English grammar in a café beside the carved tomb of Eva Perón, dreamed a man's dreams. Wearing the red dress, Nora came to his apartment on Charles Street. She carried a tiny suitcase like a stewardess. At first she was shy. Then she kissed his cheek and whispered in his ear. And soon his bony American knee pressed against the roses of her red gown.

At the surrounding tables couples whispered, talked with their hands, blew dark smoke to heaven. Silvers could stand it no longer.

Breaking into a jog as he left the street of cafés, he ran toward the Jewish Federation Building. If he could not find the living, he would divert himself among the dead.

6

This was no easy job. The officials of the new three-story building a few blocks from the Cardozos' apartment were not sympathetic. He was seeking an uncle, dead for two years, whose last name he did not know. For that matter even Carlos might have been a nom de plume. All Silvers really had was the date of death, and that was accurate only within months, in the summer of 1986. In spring the Cardozos had seen Carlos, but by the high holy days he was no more.

Finally, after being shunted from office to office, Silvers sat alone in the basement of the Organización de Judios de Buenos Aires reading alphabetically the 1986 list of Jewish dead.

Under Silvers he found four entries, even one about the right age: Emanuel, but this departed Silvers had been born in Buenos Aires and had left a half-column list of survivors, hardly the thick-muscled Polish-born dockworker that Cardozo described as his uncle.

Under Slavititsky he found no listing. There were no other reasonable possibilities, but because Ira had nothing better to do, he read through the entire list of 1986 Jewish dead. None could have been his uncle Carlos.

When he returned the volumes that looked like the ledger books in his father's office in the precomputer days, the clerk told him there was only one other possibility.

"If your uncle had nobody, he might have been buried by the gentiles at the public cemetery."

"Would they bury a Jew there?"

"This is a big city," the clerk said. "If there's a corpse and nobody claims it, the authorities bury it. Jew, gentile, whatever."

"But would there be a record?"

"Of course," the clerk said. "This is not a primitive country."

"I'm surprised," Silvers said, "that the Jewish community has no record of a man who lived in Buenos Aires for at least forty years."

"The Jewish community," the clerk reminded the American, "relies on names. We are not magicians."

7

On Friday morning, Silvers, still in bed, heard from Feldman. The producer, calling from Santiago de Chile, had canceled the production. Instead of Silvers' script, he was going to remain in Chile to shoot a vampire movie.

"I'm sorry," Feldman said. "Still, you got a week below the equator out of this, and you learned something. Never trust the unions. They're all Communists."

The producer had managed to get Silvers a seat to Miami on Sunday even though the Argentinian airline was on strike.

"You're going on AeroPeru. Let's keep in touch."

The end of his film-writing career was no disappointment. Silvers even felt relief that he would not have to see Feldman again, but how could he leave without seeing Nora?

On Friday evening, as he promised, Silvers went to services in the company of Señor Cardozo. The gentleman appeared even more dapper in his linen suit plus cravat. Silvers, a reform Jew who went to temple on the high holidays when he remembered, had no idea what to expect from Cardozo's congregation.

He suspected there would be old men passing around Torahs wrapped in dark velveteen. He would not have been surprised by incense or stirring harangues in Hebrew or Yiddish, languages obsolete and meaningless to him.

No matter what, in advance Silvers had made a policy decision. He would make a donation in his uncle's memory but only fifty dollars, not a penny more. To a live uncle he would have been generous, but for the nameless dead he set a fifty-dollar limit. Like his father before him, for cash Silvers wanted results.

To the Cardozos he owed nothing at all, especially since neither the aged señor nor his wife gave him any information about Nora.

Silvers, without any options left, played his last card.

"It's too bad about Nora," he told Señor Cardozo. "I've tried to phone her. There is a part, but if she doesn't reach me by tomorrow it will be too late. A shame. I did everything I could. I'll be in my hotel right after services."

In the synagogue, actually a room in an old house with a dining room table and some folding chairs, Silvers prayed for a message from Nora. He knew it was crazy, but he said his prayer like a mantra: "Call me, call me, call me." When he stopped chanting to himself he wondered what he would do if she called. What if she even fulfilled his fantasies and slept with him? So what? He would be back in Baltimore and she would remain in Buenos Aires, typing to fight off inflation. His romance, like his film script, was a stillbirth. No *Filth*, no love, not even information on his uncle. His week in Buenos Aires amounted to three strikes, even worse. He now dreaded going back to his solitary life in Baltimore, feared that his old defenses against solitude would no longer help. In this makeshift synagogue among less than ten old men, Silvers, without moving his lips, repeated Nora's name in rhythm to the Spanish songs around him.

"It's a friendship society, even more than a synagogue," Cardozo told him.

"Did my uncle come often?"

"No," Cardozo said, "just on the holidays. He had his own book."

A new fact. Late in the game, Silvers discovered that Carlos owned a Hebrew book.

"Would the book be here?"

Cardozo shook his head.

After the service one of the congregants shook Silvers' hand, spoke in English, and gave him a gift, a small red Gideon Bible. Silvers was no stranger to the book. Such Bibles were regularly given to children in Virginia, but by Christian missionaries, not by Jews.

Silvers dropped the book into the pocket of his blazer, as useful to him as a ticket stub.

Cardozo watched the transaction and looked embarrassed.

"What kind of synagogue is this?" Silvers asked his host as they walked out together. "That man gave me a Christian Bible."

"It is all one God," Cardozo said. "The Christians come, you tell them fine. Jesus was a good man. Things stay peaceful."

"You've got a cross in your house," Silvers blurted out. "What kind of a Jew are you?"

Silvers' passion surprised him. He pulled the Gideon Bible out of his pocket and handed it to Cardozo.

"I don't believe my uncle was part of your congregation," Silvers said.

"On high holidays," Cardozo said, "it's all Jews. Then we pray in the old ways. The rest of the year, who cares? You go out for a little company."

In the sweaty palm of his right hand Silvers clutched a fifty-dollar bill.

"I'll give you a donation," Silvers said, "but only if I can see Nora. No lies, no excuses."

The elegant gentleman pulled a watch out of the pocket of his trousers, snapped it open.

"I know my wife," he said. "Nora has already called you."

Silvers gave him the fifty, then ran as fast as he could through the crowded streets toward the Avenida de Corrientes, where the cabs on Friday night were plentiful.

8

When he got to the hotel Nora sat on a flowered couch in the lobby waiting. She was wearing a gray jersey dress. Her eyes were swollen.

Silvers, a madman, ran to her.

"I've called you every half hour for days," he yelled.

People in the lobby looked at him. Silvers didn't care. Nora stood. Silvers pressed her against him.

"I love you," he said.

"I know," she said. "I heard the phone ring."

In his arms she sobbed and let him kiss her. He led her toward the elevators.

9

In his room Silvers, a starving man, kissed her ears, her cheeks, her eyes. Her tears wet the back of his neck.

"I lied," he said. "There's no part, no film. I just had to see you. I've been losing my mind."

Nora did not resist him. He buried his face in her neck. He kissed the soft tops of her breasts, drew her waist to him as a lover.

"No," Nora said, "we cannot. There are things you do not understand."

She moved away from Silvers, straightened her dress.

"I wanted to tell you right away but I could not."

She closed her eyes, then said it. "I can avoid it no longer. I am your uncle's daughter."

10

That night Silvers learned some of the facts.

"My mother is a Christian," Nora said. "My father lived like us. Only once a year he went among the Jews. We knew he had a brother in America, but he made us promise never to tell."

With Nora's help Silvers located his uncle. Nora led, and Silvers carried the flashlight. As he stood beside Carlos, a tiny hump beneath a cross, Silvers grieved for his father's baby brother. Tears of love and sorrow fell from his eyes, and from his cousin's.

"Now I've told," Nora said. "Forgive me, Father."

She encircled Ira in her strong Silvers' arms. His lips on Nora's wet cheeks, his heart as confused as it was aroused, Ira mourned his uncle and foresaw himself surrounded by family.

Notes Toward a Holocaust Fiction

NORMA ROSEN

1. THE BOY IN THE PHOTOGRAPH:

Later in these pages there will be a story, a fiction based on truth (though with altered characters and point of view), an almost-memoir about the way something happened: a trip to Vienna with my husband, who was born there. With or without these fictional changes, the story asks the one question I believe worth asking: How, after the Holocaust, can we live now?

Why do I want to write a fictionalized account instead of a memoir? Perhaps to give distance; maybe to give some hope. Also to be truer: left alone, reality can't be trusted to convey itself.

I can't dictate to others, but for myself, I never want to invent Holocaust scenes. In fact I have a horror of it, as of something that might add to the sum of pain. And this despite my knowing that in Holocaust fiction there can be no invention of event. Whatever can be imagined has happened. The Holocaust transformed to reality what should have occurred only in nightmares.

I do not want to invent Holocaust scenes. Maybe that is why, now, I want to write real Holocaust scenes as fiction.

Maybe this, maybe that. The truth is I don't know why.

Somewhere in a Bellow novel a character tries to get another character to shape up: "Your father had rich blood in his veins, he sold apples." Our fathers and mothers had rich blood in their veins and it was spilled and spilled. Whether or not we're crazy with the weight and grief of it, we are astonishingly sane. Only sanity remembers. Sanity makes a home for the dead.

This raises a terrifying question: How are we to create anew, how go forward into life at all, if we are so weighted with memory?

There is no beginning and no end to thinking about the Holocaust. We spend our lives reading witness books, looking at films of testimony, and we know nothing. Behind every degradation, every terror published or recounted, horrors we cannot know lie buried with those who could not survive. The worst of sadistic fantasy? Decency once warned us to push it down. Allow it free rein now. What is your most bestial imagining? No, more than that. Worse. Given power by actuality. Caring for a child, reading Wordsworth with students, comforting a sick friend, we are all caught forever, at the bottom of the mind's mud, in mockery of love. These things have been. And quite, quite recently, polluting the human psyche forever.

My story asks the question: How can we live now?

Not long ago the poet Czeslaw Milosz published a letter in *The New York Review of Books* defending himself against a *favorable* review of his work. What upset him was that he had been characterized as a witness, "which for him [the reviewer] is perhaps a praise, but for me is not." Milosz went on: "An insane course of history tore out of me during the war anti-Nazi poems of anger and solidarity with the victims. And yet we should distinguish between our duty to preserve memory and our natural desire to move forward with our affairs of the living. People should not freeze, magnetized by the sight of evil perpetrated in our lifetime." The poet then goes on to speak of "the dynamics at the very core of any art: ". . . a poet repeatedly says farewell to his old selves and makes himself ready for renewals."

Compare this with another statement. It is from Primo Levi's

The Drowned and the Saved. "Anyone who has been tortured remains tortured."

Milosz's wisdom is akin to nature's wisdom: death and renewal. We say easily enough that the Holocaust is the central occurrence of the twentieth century, but we act sometimes as if we don't believe it. We slide out from under its weight now and then or we can't live as artists or as human beings, either. If we allow the full weight, what then? A literature of apocalypse—dark, satanic, black with wretchedness and grieving. If we wish to go on writing about lovers and children and trust and hope and families and springtime, we suppress knowledge of the Holocaust, relieved to be, now and then, inauthentic beings who hide from ourselves what we know. *Henderson the Rain King* is Saul Bellow's vacation from the Holocaust. Creating a gentile Henderson (or at least proclaiming him so) with no duty to preserve memory was one means of sending a character out into the world in free search of adventure. Jewish writers take such working vacations, creating an "as if" world. As if it never happened.

I have written my share of "as if" pieces. I have also published essays with such titles as "The Holocaust and the Jewish-American Novelist," "A Second Life of Holocaust Imagery," as well as a whole series of short stories that spring from a different "as if"—as if we were never free to stop thinking of the Holocaust. In my novel, *Touching Evil,* American non-Jews respond to their first knowledge of the Holocaust by asking themselves, "How can we live now?" Non-Jews, says that book, suffer from Holocaust-knowledge, too. This is what human beings could do, and did. It was the peculiar genius of the Jew to fetch it forth, but the malaise, the malediction of that knowledge has entered the psyche of Jew and non-Jew alike.

I wanted to call my novel *Heart's Witness,* or *Witness Through Imagination.* My "as if" world is as if no one can escape the knowledge. One character encounters it as an undergraduate in the forties. A teacher, in despair at his own discovery, makes a sexual conquest of her: seduction through concentration camp pictures, initiation into the facts of grown-up life. For her, thereafter, the symbolic figure is the woman who claws her way up from the bottom of a pile of corpses, barely buried, the earth spouting blood at that spot. A woman of the next generation, pregnant and watching the Eichmann trial televised in the early sixties, with its testimony of surviving victims, is overcome by terror, the child in her womb menaced by what has been loosed in the world. For her the symbolic figure is the pregnant woman in the death camp, laboring on lice-infested straw, giving birth at the booted feet of a guard who watches "to see how life begins," after which he flings the newborn into the crematory fires.

I too was pregnant in 1961, watching the Eichmann trial every day through the promising spring and the suffocating heat of summer, asking the question: How can we live now?

How we first encountered the Holocaust and how we reencounter it over and over—these are the touchstones of our time. A very old Japanese painter once said, near the end of his life, "I am just learning to draw a straight line." If I live a long life, I, too, will say, "I am just learning to draw a line from myself to the Holocaust."

When I wrote of the devastation in the woman who makes her discovery at the time the camps were opened and photographs were released, I believed it was invention. Later, I read Susan Sontag's *On Photography* and found her description—"a negative epiphany"—of her first sight, at age twelve, of photographs from the camps in 1945:

"Nothing I have seen—in photographs or in real life—ever cut me as sharply, deeply, instantaneously. Indeed, it seems plausible to me to divide my life into two parts, before I saw those photographs . . . and after, though it was several years before I understood fully what they were about. . . . When I looked at those photographs, something broke. Some limit had been reached, and not only that of horror; I felt irrevocably grieved, wounded, but a part of my feelings started to tighten; something went dead; something is still crying."

When I started I didn't know about that. Between 1961 and 1962, when I was reading and taking notes in preparation for writing the book completed in 1967, little in the way of the subject's present astonishing bibliographical richness had surfaced. But I was not doing research. I was stumbling upon books —memoirs, diaries, factual accounts like dirges—*The Black Book of Poland*—and recoiling, then making myself go back and read on. Those texts, and the televised recollections of witnesses at the Eichmann trial (supplemented daily in the *Herald Tribune* far more fully, I seem to recall, than in *The New York Times*), were enough to start the landslide of images that were to become my novel. A sliver of any one of them would have been sufficient.

Most of all I listened to my husband's accounts of his childhood in Vienna before he left on a children's transport a few weeks after Kristallnacht. The Jewish *Kultesgemeinde* managed to save his life, but not the lives of his father and mother or of a large extended family. More than four decades later we went to Vienna, that flower-planted city, and saw it in inverse relation to its perfection now: the shadow that lies beneath, the past within the present. That also is a part of the story that follows.

Ordinary pleasures and, I suppose, in Nadezhda Mandelstam's phrase, "ordinary heartbreak," which we try to encompass in our post-Holocaust era in order to create life out of survival, are in some way forever beyond us. The delicacy of a sweetmeat, a delectable food that completely fills and satisfies, cannot fill and satisfy us because we are already filled with our history. Even if we wish to forget the past, so simple a thing as a fork knocking against a fish bone may remind us.

People in my story dine on trout. The fish known as trout is also "The Trout," the Schubert quintet of melting beauty, *Die Forelle*. What do we think of beautiful German music? Do we think or do our nerves react for us? Concentration camp commandants were often men of "culture" who would finish the day's hideous work and then repair to an evening of beautiful German music. In Auschwitz the S.S. commandant kept a quartet of gifted prisoners playing German music day and night as Jews stumbled to the gas chambers.

I once heard an innovative cantor lead the singing of *Adon Olam,* God of the world, to the "Ode to Joy" theme of the last movement of Beethoven's *Ninth*. No one was entirely happy, but no one thought it right not to be happy, either. "What is it? What do you want from a melody? What is a melody anyway? Besides, it predates all that. And when did Jews have melodies of their own . . . ?" The beautiful can't be enjoyed unless the moral component is evaluated in it, and that makes life a burden, but when was a life unburdened by moral component ever worth living?

And yet—when is memory an act of homage, and when does it hold us hostage? Buildings, monuments, national and personal relations bridge themselves over the past. Repair, repair, says the world. The act of memory is an affront to life, which reseeds each season. Jews affront life, with their eternal remembering: life affronts Jews, with its eternal obliterating.*

On and on it goes, this argument with ourselves. When we commit to our pastimes—when we eat, make love, reproduce, create shapes of language on paper—each stroke of joy casts up a dark echo. That is my story, or rather, it is mine to the degree that it is not mine alone.

When I was about twelve years old, the same age as Susan Sontag when the photographs of Dachau and Bergen-Belsen produced her "negative epiphany," I also saw a photo. My parents were sent a picture from Germany of a boy of about the same number of years as I. He was stocky, with round, smiling cheeks, he wore knickers, and his arms hung awkwardly by his

---

* I have argued with a friend, D., about the images in a film whose story was written by the German writer Peter Handke, in collaboration with the moviemaker Wim Wenders and called in English *Wings of Desire:* concentration camp inmates, S.S. guards (even if they appear only in a movie within the movie), bombed-out German cities in World War Two, and young Germans wandering about in a general air of malaise and confusion. Mystical German angels float in the air, listening impassively to the inner anguish of the populace, and then moving on in what seemed to me an inadvertent parody of the German people themselves who could hear, and not hear, the anguish of Jewish neighbors forty years before.

D. argued that Germans and Austrians are victims of their history and, like all victims of catastrophe, can't allow themselves to remember. He likes it that these two German artists aren't trying to say too much, that they admit impotence and inability to make meaning of their own and their nation's history. It is an anti-meaning film, says D., because, after all that happened, they do not trust meaning, they have limited ambitions, which D. approves in art. He prefers this confession of impotence, this anti-heroic admission of damage.

For me such Holocaust aesthetics don't exist. Concentration camp prisoners in their striped uniforms, bunks from which those haunted eyes peered out, booted S.S. guards—these images strike upon the synapses so violently that they skew the weights and balances of things, they tip and sink other cargo like a capsized *Titanic*. For me Holocaust images cannot be some among many. Writers have the responsibility to avoid resisting meaning with all their strength.

side. His parents, who were distant relatives of my father's, were pleading for us to send an affidavit so the boy could escape Hitler.

My mother grieved that it was not a girl, and said she would gladly have sent for her to share my room. But without an extra bedroom, where could a robust boy like that be accommodated?

The photograph was put away somewhere. The boy no doubt died somewhere else. The rest of us went on in some very different fashion, although it is true that I am married to a man who escaped from Austria at about the age of the boy in the photograph.

2. THE CHEEK OF THE TROUT

"Enjoy the city for me," he kept saying, as if he *counted* on the difference between them. He had lived there and she had not, he was European and she American, he steeped in politics and she in art history, on the lookout for the interesting and beautiful. They were the same age, but on this trip she felt younger than her husband. He kept trying to explain something and then stopping, as if he thought it was hopeless, she could never understand. She almost agreed. His explanations seemed to be falling into some part of her that was missing.

This didn't happen so much when they were going around the official part of the city: he had not lived his boyhood there. But when they walked into the old, outer districts, he would now and then stop in his tracks. She found herself stopping too, and when he stared at a house or a corner of a street on which there was nothing, she also stared, and her heart began to pound.

Once, stopping, he said, "My uncle's store was there, someone must have stepped right in, right away, afterward. Look, it's still going strong, which neighbor could it have been?" And he stood trying to imagine which one, but making no move toward the place.

As they walked away she said—like a fool, but it was out of tenderness for what he had said, and tact, a certain kind of tact that knew he required her not to speak directly or with pity for any of this—that she loved the old-fashioned wood dividers of the front windows. He nodded, he acknowledged what she said, but had no reply to it then. Later, in another place, he said, "Here's a carved door for you!" pleased to have found it for her.

In the formal part of the city things were easier. "Be a tourist," he said. "Look at everything and enjoy it, otherwise it's not fair to yourself."

Sometimes she complained, "You think I don't know anything about life because, compared to this, I've only been happy." It was her happiness grumbling. She accepted her role. The beauty of the city was making her drunk, in spite of what she knew—of course she knew it! And to be there with her husband, who had at his fingertips history and politics and languages and art, too, though he lingered least on that, felt to her like the supremest security.

He relied on her too, of course, to see the beauty of the place where he had been born, leaving him free to be as blind to it as he needed to be on this first return after four decades. Had she expected to see bridges sag? Facades pockmarked by corruption as if they were paintings by the Albrecht twins? As if a place could be punished like the picture of Dorian Gray? She reported to him, as if he were blind: Now there is beauty, wholeness, prosperity, repair. Buildings bore fine stone sculpture, even the ones without special plaques. On rooftops, life-sized stone figures offered books, instruments of music and science, to the populace below. She turned her gaze up to them, drinking in their gifts. Doing her job, she described them, she snapped their pictures with her camera.

When they needed directions, he did the asking, caught for a moment with strangers in the intimacy of mother tongue. His manner with people seemed perfect—his dignity, his self-control. He was stocky, handsome, gray-haired. She would watch him approach each one, guessing at whether they guessed why he was a stranger now, though in command of their dialect. Nothing was betrayed on either side—polite, polite.

When people in the street seemed about the right age she asked, "Can any of these possibly be the same as the ones who were here then?" And to show how much she knew—of course she knew!—"I mean the neighbors who put on their swastika buttons right after Hitler marched in—you told me they did that —as if they'd already worn them hidden under their coats?"

Then, her voice rising in a kind of anxious demand that he acknowledge that she knew: "The ones who attacked your father? Who slapped you in the street one day, a child on your way to school?" Her voice broke on that, ample warning, if she needed it, that this was the wrong tone. She stopped at once.

In silence they stood before the doorway of the house where he had lived; in silence followed his path to school through the tree-shaded alleys of the *Augarten,* a park so clean and neatly planted she might never have believed in its existence; in silence sat on a bench beside the broad road called the *Hauptallee,* where his parents rested in the open air on Sundays and his little-boy self, untouched by sadness then, played with friends. When the bench sent forth too many emanations, he got up and walked rapidly away. She shot after him, catching at his hand. He fumbled with the other across both their chests, not looking, to give the side of her hair a quick caress—he reassuring *her!*

From the beginning they knew the trip would be too painful. From the beginning it was too full of silences between them. She filled them in for herself. She imagined they were not who they were, a couple approaching this pain from their own chronology, one of them having had the worst experience it is possible to have, and now for the first time going back. She invented: We are a young man and young woman, his name is Joshua, hers is—whatever—Joan, it's better to be young here, we're intimate with each other but in a different way, we have empathy for the past, but with veils of distance, we'd each have parents, but it's Joshua's father who's the Holocaust survivor, his pain wouldn't so immediately be ours. She imagined this as much for her husband as herself, wanting him to have some refuge.

She'd read of people, there are case histories about them, who under the assault of pain split off into other personalities. But she was fearful of what she was doing. How could she dare attempt such an alleviating gesture? After a while she developed little ironies about it. "Really? You're not just yanking away a few years? Not just preening yourself on giving comfort where there's none to be given?"

It came anyway—little waves of Joshua and Joan, invention making its own complications.

Joshua telephones his father and Joan hears him too in the echoing booth warning Joshua to keep this, keep that, afraid of more losses.

"Keep your dignity," his father says. "If you accidentally bump into someone, keep your head high. Keep your distance, you're an American, you're looking them over. Right now I'd like to pull you out of there but all right, you're another generation, you can keep separate, it's not the same for you."

Then Joan calls her mother and Joshua has to hear her tell Joan to give everything away. "You're holding back for Joshua's sake, and that's not right. There's not a thing in the world wrong with that city, it's the cleanest and safest of any in Europe, your father and I had a wonderful time when we were there, but you're not giving yourself to it. It's not Joshua, it's his father I blame, someone who can't allow people to give themselves to the present now where they're completely safe and well. . . ."

Joshua is small-boned, with curly brown hair, unbelievably watchful eyes, and now a new reddish mustache, started for their trip. Joan thinks: *their* trip, but it's Joshua's, it's Joshua's father's with Joshua making it for him. The complications of the invention grow. How, for example, did Joan meet Joshua? In an art history lecture at a university, the same as themselves? Yes, Joan made a beeline toward the vacant seat beside Joshua, toward the two expressions in his face, sadness and the wish to be happy. "Oh, I'll see you're happy," Joan is always thinking.

On the second day they went to the Jewish cemetery, they themselves, not Joshua and Joan. They searched for a gravestone arranged for from America. Her husband held a slip of paper with location, row and number, and a lone laborer encountered in the otherwise empty vastness, a Yugoslav worker, helped with hand signs. At last they found the place, swellings in the earth, neglected stones pushed crooked like teeth in an infected gum, but it was not from his parents, they were not buried anywhere, though her husband for this moment wanted to believe his father's ashes were here. Would they be? Would the bureaucrats of Buchenwald where his father died of typhus have ordered the ashes of individuals to be carefully scooped and labeled and sent home because it was still in the early years of killings, or had they shoveled and dumped the bushel-loads and picked names to call them? Did it matter whose ashes these were? Yes, for now, to her husband, it mattered, and mattered that his mother's could never be reclaimed. Where is Antigone in a world of human ashpits?

Late afternoon summer sun spilled over the ground and honeyed the leaves on the trees. In this prodigality of light, who would believe in darkness? She stood apart. Her husband began to speak a prayer before the writing on the stone. Mother and Father, names on a gravestone. When his voice broke into tight, fought-off sobs, she thought, Where are Joshua and Joan? But it was no use, it was themselves standing there. A little door opened in her husband's broad chest and a twelve-year-old tumbled out weeping. She opened her arms to catch him.

Leaving, they lost their way. The gravestones on this path were bigger, they had elaborate gothic lettering, titles. *Vize-burgermeister* and *Obermedizinalrat* and *Kaiserlicher Rat* and *Reichsratsabgeordneter*. "What's this, what's that?" she asked. "Heads of things," he answered. "Medical organizations, city councils." "Why are these so bare?" She meant the names beneath the ornamented ancestors. Then she noticed the dates, 1937 to 1945. There was luck even among the dead.

She could sound out these words herself. *Vergast Belsec, Gestorben in Theresienstadt.* Jews of the world, you know more German than you think. *Verschleppt nach Auschwitz. Umgekommen in Dachau. Ermordet in Belsen.* She copied words into her notebook, but not fast enough, and turned to snapping the camera. Sun glinted on granite, obliterating names, but she went on snapping till she couldn't anymore, and ran down the path, he after her.

Then they were back at the beginning, and entered a low room, cryptlike, filled with filing cabinets. Her husband spoke to a man reading behind a desk who rose, a long cotton coat of rusty black uncreasing itself down to his shoetops.

At first her husband translated for her. "This gentleman is the keeper of records here. He spent the Hitler years in Argentina." Then the man spoke to her in good English. "Enjoy this beautiful city." The man's smile was sweet. Not a melancholy smile, only slow. "It is your first time here, enjoy it."

She flinched a little at that, as usual. "And also go to the mountains," said the record-keeper, the cemetery man, like a sybil, like a good elf, "my mother's favorite place, ah, the wonderful air. In the mountains was always my mother's cure, you should go, enjoy everything."

An encouraging breath expanded inside her. She blurted, God knew why, knowing it was idiocy the moment she spoke, "Is she there now?" The record-keeper's smile slowly faded. He gave her a prolonged look, as if assessing how it might be possible to infuse intelligence into her at last.

On the trolley ride back to the hotel, silent again, she imagined the life of the cemetery man in Argentina. What was it? He had to learn Spanish. All right, that was no problem, she quickly arranged for him to do so. He had to learn to live. How? She pictured the little man in rusty black duster (take that off him, for God's sake, he's not wearing it in Argentina!) blundering with a prayer book under his arm among the gauchos and tango dancers. At first the fantasy diverted her. Then in winding streets it turned grim. Searching out a fellow Jew to speak German with, he encountered instead a fled Nazi prospering there. Mengele, who delighted in medical experiments, would ask if he had a twin, would fancy the special shape of those ironically slanted eyes, those drooping earlobes.

No—no, have him meet Borges, the great Argentinian writer! "You yourself, dear man"—it's Borges speaking so kindly —"even without your old texts and Talmud-study companions, may dream commentaries. You yourself can write *A Guide to the Perplexed* by Maimonides." When the little fantasy was over she still saw the cemetery record-keeper in his long black coat, standing at the low window of his cryptlike room. Her husband stared through the window of the swaying trolley. A recorded voice announced street destinations in guttural German: *"Karl Lueger Strasse. . . ."*

For days after that they quieted themselves in the gilt-and-marble vaults of the Kunsthistorische Museum. Rembrandt, Brueghel, Bosch. . . . They followed a guide through the royal red-brocaded rooms of the Hofburg castle, stepping backward through history to the safe rococo Hapsburg monarchy. Hoopla! The empress installed handrings in her apartment so she could turn somersaults.

Her husband said, "I feel the city's about to explode." But it was in themselves that the explosion came. One evening in a restaurant they encountered a couple from the States eating dinner at an adjacent table, the woman a small, neat body quietly consulting her guidebook, the man enormously fat and talky, his belly a Humpty Dumpty belted barrel. They had been, the man informed them from his table, on a whirlwind tour of highspots in the Slavic countries—Budapest, Prague, Dubrovnik, Warsaw.

"And what did I come for?" the man asked rhetorically, though they hadn't inquired. "I came to see a concentration camp." His little round eyes filled with tears, his voice choked off, he was unable to speak another word.

In their room that night she asked indignantly, "What right has he to cry like that? Why hasn't grief taken off a few pounds, why didn't he first lose weight if he was going to be a public mourner?" Her husband turned on her with a violence like the swing in a weather vane, like the stiff sudden movement of the medieval figures in the Hoher Markt Anker Clock.

"He has a right to his feelings no matter what he looks like!" Aesthetics had perverted her, he said in a fury, the city had done its work and seduced her with its beauty. "It's all you care about!"

"Then stop telling me to enjoy myself," she shouted back. "I'm not a tourist! How could I know you and not think of what went on here? I would think of it even if I didn't know you!"

What was horrible to them was that in this place he had fled as a child, had to be rescued from it before it hacked him to bits, they now hacked at one another. This was happening in their hotel room, itself a work of beauty, stuffed with darkly polished Biedermeier furniture, or at least with good enough imitations of it, its balcony overlooking the stone figures giving counsel to the populace below.

She had backed away from his outburst into the brass lock of the gleaming armoire and had hurt her elbow. He was pacing up and down the room in a rigid line while he circled his hand over his chest, like someone practicing a complicated coordination. She rubbed her arm, he circled with his palm what gripped in his chest. It was as if they were solving the riddle of where to locate pain. That was when they remembered the advice of the cemetery man, and wondered if it could save them.

"This reminds me—yes, the contrasts!—something like a Bosch"—in the mountains it was easier to recover the enthusiasm they both required of her—"or one of the Brueghels we saw, was that Salon Twelve or Thirteen?—never mind!" She would look it up later, but he knew what she meant. "At one side someone's painted a multitude climbing up, at the other side, what? All those people treading the downward path to the boiling lake?"

She had succeeded in making him laugh. He was relaxed now and wryly commenting. "So it's a level of hell after all?"

Enthusiasm always made her exaggerate, but there surely was this duality in the little mountain resort. The two important places were several miles apart. At one end of the village was the entrance to the mountain-climbing trails, at the other, a little beyond the center of the village, were the thermal pools. The place divided itself between the healthy and the sick.

"Everything's in twos!" she announced. "The city and the spa, the monument and the mountain, this generation, that generation. . . ." She let him know what she had been thinking about Joshua and Joan, too. He brushed his lips back and forth on her cheek—"Thanks for the mustache"—so they could both imagine the feel of it, bushy and red.

The dining room of their hotel was vast, but with only five tables set for breakfast. In the morning, among the scattered guests, they heard Italian, German, French. The waitress, a robust young woman, greeted them in a cheery voice: *"Kaffee zweimal?"* After she brought the two coffees and rolls she ran to the window to watch her husband drive the crane that was dismantling the hotel next door.

The proprietress was on crutches. Not, she assured them, from a skiing accident, but only a stupid slip in her bathroom. Dressed in sweater and skirt of matching loden green, she hung genteelly between her props. "The young people nowadays prefer beaches in the south of France. They have forgotten the mountains of their parents." Not her voice, but the striking of her crutches on the flagstones of the lobby, made the bitter sound.

The parents were out in full force. Handsome, hearty couples in their silver-haired age strolled the streets. They wore sweaters beautifully embroidered with edelweiss, knickers of moss-green suede, knee socks of double-woven wool patterned in lozenge. Their shoes were stout-soled brown leather, their alpine staffs armored with medallions: mountain goats and silver jugs and green garlands edging the curved silver shields, emblems of Bad Gastein and Salzburg and Bad-am-See.

One day her husband said, "An attendant gave me some information about this place. There are special baths here that contain a form of radon. The sick ones come for the radon cure."

The absurdity seemed to fit in perfectly—soaring beauty above, deadly emanations from below. Radon treatment was offered in the special baths as well as in the various inhalings and absorptions from the gold mines deep underground. The brochures showed men and women lying on cots in full nakedness, with lifted relaxed knees exposing the shadowed entrance between the thighs, or the winesac of the scrotum and its soft spout.

The proprietress, confronted on her crutches, said forthrightly, "Sure, before this, people came and sat for hours in the baths or baked in the mines, then they went home and got sick! Now they know better. They must consult a doctor here, who will regulate everything."

One afternoon they sat at a table of an open-air restaurant at the foot of the mountain, sipping coffee and breathing in the thin, delicious air. They watched the climbers in their suedes and lodens, as frozen in time as if the hands of the clock had never moved. She saw from her husband's face what was the matter, and didn't need to ask. They were all about the right age.

They decided then to consort with the sick. It was there, among those wanting to be healed in the warm bubbly water, that they began to encounter other Jews. Before they left home, she had bought a tiny gold Shield of David on a chain to wear around her neck. All sorts of Jews swam up to them because of her star, she believed. All of them expressed preference for people of a different part of the world.

A Rumanian couple, widely traveled, said they could stomach all nationalities except Poles: "Terrible, terrible anti-Semites." "Personally we were made to feel comfortable when we visited Poland," said another couple from Europe. There were those who would not "set foot in Germany" and those who made a point of it. No matter which country was mentioned, someone was sure to say, "Others were as bad or worse." "And where we are this minute, Austria, do you want to start on that? We have to show that we are again a part of the universe."

These Jews, some younger, some older, seemed to be struggling to regain a kind of global poise. What attitude should they take toward the world? "This generation," they said, "is not that generation; this decade is not the one of forty years ago."

An Israeli couple swam over. They were leaving soon for Munich. They reported that Germans, Austrians, and Poles had been personally very nice to them when they visited there. "Israel is a small country, you have to travel."

Outside the pool they met a bearded Belgian Jew of about fifty who walked with a hip-hiking limp. He was married to a German woman in her twenties with piercing blue eyes, buck teeth, and a frank manner. The Belgian had a way of not speaking until he had taken one or both of them by the arm and moved a little ways off from where they had been standing: he could only be understood on fresh ground. He spoke in a confidential manner, even his jokes imparted directly into the ear like state secrets. He had one about the countries of Europe where Jews lived before Hitler: "They only killed you there"—he smiled and whispered—"you could live with it."

One day he drew both of them to one side, though not so far that his wife couldn't hear. "She is a better Jew than I am," he said, dipping his head toward his wife. She approached, laughing. "What he means is that when we married, I tried to wake him early so he could attend Saturday services, but always he went back to sleep."

At night in their room they compared notes about the people they met. She wanted to say that the Belgian was too intimate about trivialities, too public about what should be private. But she remembered how they had quarreled over the fat man's tears and kept it to herself.

One day she sat the edge of the pool, waiting for her husband to finish his swim, when a female voice beside her said, "Too much illness and bad legs, how will I stand it here!" She turned to see an attractive young woman in a red bikini, beating up small waves in the water with her feet. "Still, if it helps Heinrich, I will certainly stay."

At that moment her husband emerged from the pool in the company of a man. "There he is," the young woman said, "there's Heinrich!" "And that's my husband." "So we have all become acquainted at the same time." The woman stuck out her hand with a smile. "Elsa. From Germany."

Elsa and Heinrich were both in their early thirties, an attractive couple. Heinrich looked struck by sunlight—even his eyebrows and lashes were blond. But he was melancholy. "I am supposed to be young, but this knee doesn't know it. After one little skiing accident, it refuses to heal properly and becomes arthritic."

"Heinrich is bored," Elsa announced.

"This literary conversation in the pool with your husband," Heinrich said, "is the first interest that has penetrated my life here."

"Heinrich is depressed. And we will have two more weeks of this." Elsa was laughing.

"Shall we meet for dinner tonight?" Heinrich asked in his drawling yet somehow excited English, "if we are not too boring and depressing for you? There is a restaurant called The Trout that serves fresh fish. A rarity in the mountains, yes?"

"What do you think of the young couple?" she called through the bathroom door while her husband showered. After glancing briefly at her, he had agreed to dinner in the most matter-of-fact way. His answer came muffled, but when he emerged, his naked body ruddy from its toweling, he looked directly at her and asked, "Did you feel we shouldn't go?"

In the shower, water drumming on her head, she'd heard an echo of *Heinrich's* father this time, telephoning his son with homilies from Hamburg: "If you meet any Jews, don't hang your head. It's true your grandfather joined the Nazi party for business reasons, and I became an S.S. officer when I was young, but whatever we did you're another generation, you had nothing to do with it, you don't owe an apology. If you meet a Jew, you can be friendly, offer a glass of wine if you can stand to be with them, but on no account are you required to apologize."

Her head was becoming like the thermal pool—there were traces in it of everything. "Oh, no!" she had answered, "of course we should go!"

In the restaurant, still another pool, this time a long narrow one built into the length of the floor, where the dark shapes of the trout twisted slowly back and forth. Everyone made a quip. "Look, they're in their own thermal bath." "Rheumatic trouts, poor things." "Perhaps they need a little radon bath?" She hadn't made her quip yet, so she said, "Now we'll have to choose our victims," and was horrified, but no one seemed to notice.

At the table, Heinrich satirized his own obsession with his cure. In a mock-elderly voice, he gave a little lecture about the healthfulness of eating trout prepared "blue."

"Plain boiled," he said, lifting a finger, "what more can anyone want than that?"

When the waiter came they all humored Heinrich, an agreeable moment, everyone smiling indulgently. Then they sipped wine.

"Heinrich's digestion is unreliable," Elsa said. "His nerves are in a state." Her voice was quick and light. "He works in a publishing house his family owns. Sometimes he writes poetry. It's very good!" Heinrich's melancholy was being visibly broken up, pierced everywhere by bright, deft arrows. "Heinrich and I have been living together in Munich for three years. And"—Elsa never faltered for a minute over this—"Heinrich could not make up his mind to marry. I waited and waited, now there is a child coming."

"So that, of course"—Heinrich's voice, pleasant and open and unembarrassed, broke in—"was the help to deciding."

In the telephone booth of her head a voice said, "It's the right way. You do that too, be more open and that will help." Her husband could sit with this couple and eat a meal and speak of books with them because he thought they were innocent and because they were in the world together, and he was a man who felt responsible to what was in the world, but the rest she must do.

"Sometimes," she said, "my husband and I have trouble looking at Germans or Austrians of a certain age. We think of what they were doing during the Hitler years."

After only the slightest pause, holding their wine midair as if wand-struck, Heinrich and Elsa cried out together, "Yes, yes, that is natural, understandable!" They were dressed in the softest of colors, Heinrich in a pale blue wool sweater and beige slacks, Elsa in a peach knit dress that showed not the least bulge of baby. Her husband was wearing his navy blue jacket with a checked blue shirt open at the throat. The convex metal buttons on his sleeves caught light, and light-formed shapes at the edge of the buttons gave off twisting gleams. She felt his eyes on her.

The dinner arrived. Each fish was covered with a skin that had turned to blue velvet, each was propped, seallike, on the plate, fins like hands supporting the body's upper part, head raised above the curving breast, a mythological creature about to speak: "Consume me and be cured."

For a moment she was afraid she might blurt: "I can't eat this, it's like a character in a children's book!" But she said no such thing. She worked open a snap at the neck of her blouse and waited.

Elsa at once contributed something special to enjoy. "The cheek of the trout is the best part. Not easy to find, though!" Wielding knife and fork precisely, her blond head bent to the task, she folded back a flap of blue velvet in the head of the fish, searched carefully, then put something into her mouth with her fork and looked satisified. Heinrich also lifted a velvet flap on the head of the fish, poked with his fork and knife, and brought something to his mouth. "Aha."

It was hopeless to try for Elsa's prize; she was not adept with fish, but her husband had the European knack. He began to press a bit of trout against the back of his fork in case of bones. Had he found the small delicacy? She had been staring around the table and might have missed it. She felt certain, somehow, that he hadn't even tried. Why should so silly a thing become an emblem of happiness? Her heart flooded with sorrow for her husband, for what had been stolen from him. If he were Joshua, if she were Joan, she would call out to him, "Find it, oh, please, find it!" Her husband lifted his gaze as if she had spoken, smiling as if to encourage her to find it.

What was it like? The nugget of meat in the little spoon-shaped pelvic bone of the roast chicken? The heart of a boiled artichoke, when you finally got to it, dipped in spicy vinaigrette sauce? The eye of a tiny, butter-soft, baby broiled lambchop, her favorite meal that her mother had cooked for her again and again all the while she was growing up? Her mouth filled with remembered tastes of things that were rare and delicious, gone in a minute.

Jew-Killing

GORDON LISH

*. . . all the bodily oppressiveness
that is inflicted
upon the representatives
of interpretation . . .*

—Harold Bloom

This must be some kind of fucking joke, a
book like this one is. Granted, no book is not at least a little
bent, writers being people. Just to begin with, the heart has no
fingers. The impulse that makes its way to the pencil cannot
come to it uncrippled by its commerce with the snare of words.
I know that you do not need me to rehearse for you the inde-
feasible fraudulence of the written enterprise. The physics of it
goes against us—or anyhow the physiology that puts utterance
at a distance from thought is no friend of exactitude, though a
great one of decorum and of theatre. So what is the harm, really
—given that we all of us know what the score really is and are
accordingly skilled at making allowances? Yet a book like this

one is—I tell you, I do not see God forgetting to dream up certain agonies for each and every one of its perpetrators—me, please, at the head of the list.

The hell with it.

Isn't every living Yid one of us not convinced he's got it coming?

Christ, when it comes to reasons, I can think of at least 6 million of them without even thinking.

Here's something.

There was a kid on the block who did not really belong to a house on the block. He belonged not to a house but to a maid on the block, which was a Jewish block—except for the maids on it and also for sometimes their husbands, who were the butlers and the chauffeurs for the Jews on the block.

As to the kid, I used to think Adriance, Adriance, what a beautiful name—Roy Adriance, this is a beautiful name. Anyway, the kid whose name was Adriance used to often come climb the beech tree out in our front yard and then come down from it and stand with me much taller than me in the bed of ground cover my mother kept trying so hard to keep growing under it.

It was a kind of evil to me, climbing this tree, when there was no way for a boy to do it without doing damage to the pachysandra.

What a word that was for me then.
Pachysandra.

I remember this time as a time of your mother and your father trying to make you see that they were trying to keep hard things going.

1941.

This was the thing about the kid whose name was Adriance, aside from the other things—these being that he was no Jew and that he belonged to a maid. I mean, the thing that Adriance just had a mother, not a mother and a father.

Not that Adriance did not try to get us to believe that he had a father.

Just that I do not think that any of us believed it—not even when Adriance stood there in the pachysandra swearing up and down to every single Jewish one of us that he had a father who had gone off to sign up in Canada with the Royal Canadian Air Force to fly for all our sakes against the Germans in the Messerschmitts.

Here is a thing for us to think about.

How come we did not believe it when Adriance said that he had a father but did believe it when Adriance said that if his father could not beat them back with his De Haviland, then the first thing that they were going to do when they got over here was come and get the Jews?

Not him, not Adriance, but us, the boys in the pachysandra with him, the Jews.

The Germans and the Jews.

Where we lived would have taken no time at all for all of their tanks to get to after they had rolled them out of all of their U-boats and all of their bombers and clanked them up onto the beach.

The Germans and the Jews.

This was Long Island in Lawrence and the beach was called Atlantic Beach.

I started having dreams in the nighttime and dreams in the daytime of the U-boats coming up out of the water and of the bombers coming down out of the sky and of torpedoes and cannonballs killing me for being an American and of this being a better thing to happen to me than for the Germans to come and kill me for being a Jew.

Yes, I am being paid for this.
Yes, I am glad I am being paid for this.

No, I did not say that I did not want to be paid for this.

No, I did not say go give instead what you are paying to me to somebody who paid with his bones for this.

A word to the wise.

If it looks as if anyone is possibly ashamed of this, then just chalk it up to strictly looks.

We are writers writing sentences.

We are writers thinking about writing the right sentences.

We want the money. We want the prize.

The Holocaust?

Fine, fine, but now make up your mind whose sentences are the right sentences.

I do not have one useful thought about the Holocaust.

Except that I think it is just more of a holocaust to call it the Holocaust.

You want to hear the closest I think I came to the Holocaust?

I will tell you in two quick stories that have nothing to do with the Holocaust but which I will bend and bend so that they might take on the look that they do have something to do with the Holocaust.

One was when I once went to Silver Point Beach.

The other was when I went with my father to New Lester's.

The first story has in it the first time I ever saw a woman naked.

The second story has in it even less point than that.

You see what we are trading on?

It costs nothing to be a Jew on a page.

My bones are all in place.

This is the crime of free speech; so now you know what free speech is worth.

Actually, it was called Lester's New Extravaganza Barber Shop. New Lester's was just the name I heard my father call it. My father said that that was how you would be able to tell who were the insiders and who weren't. My father said that if somebody said Lester's New Extravaganza Barber Shop instead of New Lester's, then that person was giving it away to everybody who heard him say it that he was not one of the bosses on the inside with the insiders.

First things first—and the Silver Point Beach story will tell you what happened first.

It was the summer when I first got psoriasis.

It was the summer when I was seven.

It was 1941.

I was going to the Peninsula Athletes Day Camp and it was August and they took us on a bus to Silver Point Beach for a day at the beach as a day trip and all of the boys had to go into a locker with another boy to change from their uniforms into their swimming trunks, but I did not have to go into a locker with another boy to share a locker with him because of the fact that I was covered with psoriasis on my backside and my mother and father had asked the camp not to make me have to take off my clothes with any other boys looking because I on account of my psoriasis would be ashamed to have them doing it.

So I was in a locker by myself and no one had seen my backside and I had by now got myself into my swimming trunks, but I did not want to open up the door and go out because I was trying to make up my mind as to whether I could leave on my socks because I also had psoriasis on my ankles, which would be covered up if I kept on my socks, but I knew that the boys would say things to me about my socks on if I came out of the locker and had on my swimming trunks and still had on my socks.

Oh, just look at me, all in a sweat to invent a moral mechanics so that I might somewhere wedge a lever in.

All sweet fucking innocence.

It happened like this.

Sitting there, not being able to make up my mind which would be worse.

Sitting there on the little bench affair.

Maybe looking at what was hanging from the pegs.

The clothes of the people who had already been in there.

When:

I saw it!

I saw that I could see through a hole in the planks.

The back of the locker I was sitting in was also some of the wall of one side of where the ladies went in for their showers and I saw that I could put my eye to the hole and see right into through the planks inside of where the ladies went for showers.

It was light and bright in there because it was wide open to the sky in there.

There was no top built over it.

The sky just came right in over the planks.

So that I could see everything.

Except for the fact that the hole I was looking through cut all of the people off from the knees down and from the neck up so that you could not really see all of them. In other words, I was seeing middles—mainly bathing-suited middles—because mainly the women just kept their bathing suits on all over themselves to rinse themselves off with the shower water as a way to get rid of salt.

Of the sand and the salt.

But one person had hers off.

Was rinsing her middle naked.

A sentence I have been working on.

The price of no jeopardy is severance from Jewishness.

The whole thing of it, of course, was this—that I was looking and seeing that she had a little string hanging down from up inside of her.

There are no Jews writing this.
There are just writers writing this.
For money.
For sentences.

All right, now let me put my back into it some more and bend it a little more—make it a Holocaust story a little more—claiming that for perhaps all of two seconds I had the thought that the Germans had come. Had the thought that while I had been in there afraid to come out, that the Germans had come up out of their U-boats and down out of their bombers and had got the first Jew that they had come across—in her privates.

I mean, I thought it was a bandage.

Okay, maybe not for two seconds—maybe only for fewer seconds than two seconds.

As to the second story, it starts with taking the train with my father in from Lawrence for me to go spend the day with him in New York City to be with him and visit his office with him and then go shopping at De Pinna's with him for me to get some new dress-up things—mainly, I think, leggings.
But never getting to De Pinna's.
I cannot remember the reason for our never getting to De Pinna's.
I just remember going to a Schrafft's for us to get Brown Cows and then going across 38th Street between Broadway and Sixth Avenue for us to go instead to New Lester's.

The idea was for me to get a treat by going to New Lester's to get my first grown-up haircut instead.

I must have been nine or ten or eleven.

I could have said that there was blood on it, you know.
Some blood dropping off the end of it with the dripping bloody water.
But I didn't.

I could have said that there was steam.

But the water they had at Silver Point Beach was only cold water, so there really was not any steam.

Here is something perfectly true.

I was always thinking what if they come and look but cannot tell that I am Jewish.

How's that for my Holocaust story?

So which was worse, thinking that or thinking that Adriance would come and tell them I was just as Jewish?

Worse?

Worst?

This is disgusting.

But at least I did not say steam—steam would have been even more disgusting.

All right, the second story.

Here is the second story.

We are there at New Lester's, remember?

This was the barber shop my father said all of the bosses went to—the bosses of the hat companies and of the dress companies and of the coat companies and so forth.

My father was a boss.

Paul.

This was the barber who my father said he always had Lester set aside for him as my father's special barber.

My father said that whenever he went to get a haircut at New Lester's, Paul was the only barber that my father would let be his barber.

Maybe I was just a little bit less than eleven by then because by then the war was not that far away, I think, from almost being over.

Stop and think.
Will God come and kill us for this?

Not even Germans are going to come and kill us for this.

Oh, this is beautiful, this is gorgeous.
"The felony that we do in the sentences that we write, the felony that we do in that there are any sentences that we write, these are crimes you have no bones to pay for."

Or look at it this way.
You are in a place like that and you smell the smoke of your mother cooking like that and you cannot help it, you are simply famished—so, bingo, your mouth just automatically, you know, waters.

You see what I mean?
It just makes your mouth automatically water to smell the smoke of anyone cooking.

Hey, but does even this, even this, even this entitle you to talk about anything but just what it feels like in your mouth when it is your mouth that is watering?

The quotes were fake.
I just made up the quotes.

I mean, let's face it, it wasn't you cooking.
No one came and cooked the smoke out of you so that one fine day you could sit yourself down and write about the smell of you cooking.

Here is the limit of your authority.
The fucking quality of your fucking sentences.

Paul was small and bald.
My father was small and bald.
But Paul was an even more exorbitant case.

You will not believe it, but in fact my father's special barber had to get up on a one-step stool to give anybody a haircut.

I saw this.

I sat there seeing this.

My father went first, and I sat there seeing the barber get up and then off and then with the toe of his barber-white shoe push his stool to the next station and then get back up on his stool again and go back to cutting my father's little ringlet of hair again from where the barber was now standing on his stool at the next station as he went with his stool around my father's hair.

Anyway, Paul never cut my hair from anywhere.

It was the psoriasis again.

Like it or not, it is not suffering unless you have suffered it.

I am so lonely, so wrong, so unpunished.

You know what I think?

Fuck them.

Fuck the writers writing about this, but fuck them obviously more than probably fuck me.

In other words, Paul.

He sees me see him wave me over and he goes and gets the child's seat.

He says hello, hello, welcome with open arms to Lish Junior, and gets me seated safe and sound on the board that makes the chair a child's chair.

He gets me all set up with the tissue they unwind around your neck and then with the sheet they wrap around your chest and then with the towel they tuck down in and then with everything as pretty as a picture named Lish Junior.

Then Paul says, aah, so let's see.

You know something?

To speak about something is to come to think it only exists for you to speak about it.

Safe and sound up in the child's chair.

I could feel the man feeling around in my hair.
I could feel the man opening up different places to look at me in my hair.

I opened my eyes and saw in the mirror Paul getting down from off of his barber's stool.

We all sit here pretending.

The biggest suffering is the suffering of not making the best sentence.

I could hear it.
Everyone could hear it.
You could hear it wherever you were if you were somewhere in New Lester's.
"I want that mamser fired! Do you hear me? Do you know who I am? Fire him! I want you to fire this man this very instant! Lester, are you paying attention to me? How dare he, how dare he—*catch* it! Just who does he think he is, catch it, catch it? A little putz like that, catch it! And not to cut the son of Philip Lish's hair!"

A writer has no bones.

All there was was a string coming down.
The rest is writing.
(Even that was.)

Here, let me be at least a little useful.
Find out who first called it the Holocaust and then kill this person for not calling it Jew-Killing instead.

One wants the weight of one's Jewishness.
But a living Jew is nothing but a skinny-malink.

You know the question?

Here is the question.

What if when they came, if it was you, if you had, if you had been one of the ones, if you had actually been one of the ones who, when they had come, who came *with* them?

Did I really think that tanks were going to be out there when they made me take the latch off?

I am going to get money for this.

I am going to have a good opinion about the people who are going to have a good opinion about what I did when I did this.

A little more bending.

To wit:

You heard them shrieking in there and shrieking in there—but those were beach showers in there. Well, the water must have been terrifically cold in there, the water must have been absolutely totally lethal.

Here is me suffering—going crazy making the second one look a little more like something that will maybe look a little more generally in keeping.

Look.

If showers in the first instance, then, notice, so not haircutting in the second?

Besides, there is a moral.

The moral.

"Adriance, Adriance, God loved me and made me so you and your Germans wouldn't ever have the stomach to actually touch me!"

More fake quotes.

200
201   Psoriasis.
202   Pachysandra.
203
204   So much for me and the fucking Holocaust.
205   Okay—now where is my money?

The Longest Shadow

GEOFFREY HARTMAN

In memory of Dorothy de Rothschild

I am sitting in a room with a dozen boys. We are glued to a small, crackling radio. On the wall is a map of Europe and Russia. As we hear the latest news we shift colored pins to indicate the progress of German armies that have invaded Russia. To us it does not matter whether the pins move forward or backward. It is just too exciting to follow one battle after another.

I remember receiving two postcards from my grandmother left behind in Frankfurt, after my mother emigrates to America in December 1938 and I go to England in March 1939. She is sixty-five years old, perhaps more. The postcards come from a place called Theresienstadt, and the stamps (I am an avid collector) interest me. A message forwarded by the Red Cross says: I am in good health; everything is fine. The idea forms in me that Theresienstadt is a vacation spot, or where old people go to be cared for.

My passage to England was uneventful. But during the long train ride to the port in Holland, the boys with whom I traveled (all from Frankfurt, evacuated with the help of James de Roth-

425

schild on a Children's Transport) become restless; they fool about with the one family object I was able to take along, a violin. We all play on it, or rather with it; a string breaks. Later, in Waddesdon, we play some more with it; another string breaks. Eventually the case cracks, we can see a label inside. On it there is a signature. It identifies the unrepairable instrument as a Stradivarius.

I cannot say I was happy in England, my place of refuge. I lived there from the age of nine to nearly sixteen. But my unhappiness did not affect, and even stimulated, a thirst for knowledge that coursed through me and covered just about any subject. I devoured books about airplanes, learning each silhouette; books about trees, learning to identify them by shape and leaf; Latin grammars; botany texts; Penguin puzzle books; encyclopedias. I sat near the main road from Waddesdon to Aylesbury noting the make and registration number of cars. I collected stamps, poring over catalogue details characterizing the country of issue and memorizing prices, watermarks, valuable printing errors. Fantasies overcame me of how I would rescue Her Royal Highness, daughter of the King of England, and be awarded a thousand or . . . one hundred thousand pounds. I would then spend hours figuring out which stamps to buy.

My determination to know everything was part and parcel of a wish to communicate that knowledge. Learning was its own reward; nothing, I thought, could be more enjoyable than telling others what I had absorbed. This delight in passing on what had given me pleasure reminded me later of the child in William Blake's *Songs of Innocence,* who goes from church or schoolhouse straight into the fields to catechize the creatures:

> *Little Lamb, who made thee?*
> *Dost thou know who made thee?*

I did well in school; the absence of my mother (my father, divorced when I was an infant, had emigrated to South America), childish rebellion against the family in charge of the Waddesdon home, and ambivalent feelings about many of the Cedar Boys (named after two stately trees marking the large house in which we lived) merely spurred more delight in learning.

Only here and there did the consciousness that I was a Jewish refugee disturb me enough that I recall the very moments. At another level, of course, I was always conscious of it. The Germanic upbringing which continued at the Cedars stressed obligations and also therefore that our food, our clothes, our education were provided by charity. Not that James de Rothschild ever intervened that way. We saw him rarely. He sometimes appeared on Jewish holidays, accompanied by his young and beautiful wife. He would sit very straight, his gaunt face augmented by the aristocratic monocle covering an eye lost in a polo accident; Dorothy de Rothschild always stood beside him and tempered his severity with a smile, as we passed in review. Whether my dislike of dependence, and my intellectual passion to know the world through my own powers, preexisted this experience of indebtedness, I can't tell. Brought up without father and mother, I would let no one else fill the vacuum.

Yet I was always aware of a greater debt: to creation itself. That sounds mystical, and perhaps it was. The joy in simply being alive was so strong that I noted with alarm when some of the delight faded—when a birthday or a vacation or waking early and feeling I was the only awake person in the whole world made the heart glad, but not as before. My social unhappiness had no bearing on a gratitude that "wasted" itself on the Bucks countryside with its ponds, open fields, and lovely old trees. English nature invited the trespasser: We went berrying or hunting or on long, aimless walks, leaping over hedge and stile. Wordsworth opened himself to my understanding as soon as I read him.

I distinctly recall brooding on continuity. What held matter together? Why didn't the table before me disintegrate? (I would later read with perfect understanding the famous question: Why does the world exist rather than not exist?) Who or what kept me alive, and so intensely aware, moment to moment? In school the only subject I failed was geometry. The idea of proving a theorem by extending a triangle did not make sense to me. I needed to know the principle behind the proof; mere extension was too much of a mystery in my own life.

Yet there were incidents which made me conscious of being Jewish and a refugee. One of them also revealed the pressure to assimilate, a pressure that did not come from admonition but from homelessness. The recreation hall in Waddesdon, the only place large enough for socializing in a village of two thousand, was packed full one day with a motley, unwashed crew. We were told that they too were refugees, but from the East, *Ostjuden*. The inhabitants of Waddesdon, who could scarcely distinguish German refugees from German spies, were faced with people whose habits were utterly unlike theirs or ours. These colorful D.P.s were given to talking and gesturing unintelligibly, and . . . to haggling in the shops! I remember disavowing them: *We* (the German refugees) have nothing to do with *them*.

The portion I read on my bar mitzvah happened to describe the attack of the Amalekites on the Israelites as the latter wander through the desert toward the Promised Land. The biblical writer is vengeful and does not mince his words. Amalek is to be destroyed, completely. "Remember the Amalekite. Thou shalt not forget." The good rabbi who traveled from London every week to give us an hour of Hebrew mingled with moral instruction or a schmooze on the virtues of the patriarchs, and who presided over the bar mitzvah of each Cedar Boy, did not fail to draw the lesson that the Nazis were the new Amalek. I was personally charged to remember and offered a Bible inscribed with that dire slogan.

In retrospect, it seems as if some God had wrapped me about and kept me immune from the worst. Though a quasi orphan, I felt at home in the gentle countryside of Buckinghamshire, my life somehow part of its life, and sheltered by an active sense of belonging. This curious trust in life rather than people may have been there much earlier. A separation from home that could have been traumatic at age nine was not. In Germany I was occasionally beaten up by Nazi youngsters, but that was merely part of life: I would have been beaten up anyway, by some group of kids. Only once did I return home crying, not only roughed up but pushed deliberately into dogshit. Where was God? I bitterly asked.

Nazi parades were thrilling; physical hunger was moderate. Because I didn't look Jewish, and was adorned with likable flappy ears, my mother would send me out to see whether a warmhearted grocer might be induced to sell me an egg. Every Saturday I came back with something. Perhaps the tendency then to protect children from adult knowledge made me understand very little of what was happening to relatives: Kristallnacht exists in my mind as a vague rumor of uncles who left home for a while. A month later my mother was in America. Unable to get a visa for me, she left anyway, but made sure I would be on a Children's Transport to England. When we said good-bye neither of us knew that it would be for seven years: By the time I rejoined her, I was an adolescent, and she a stranger.

My thoughts about the Holocaust did not gather momentum till after army service, in 1955. I had been drafted two years before and spent a funny and painful sixteen weeks of basic training at Fort Dix. During that period of methodical humiliation and physical exhaustion, I recovered "basic" feelings of a different kind—about the earth on which this strange training took place, about my dependence on sunrise and sunset. Solid, beautiful, encompassing, a sudden closeness to nature taught me more about companionship than the forced esprit de corps in the simulated hell the army provided. After the usual military mix-ups I ended in Heidelberg at Headquarters PID (Public Information). As an antidote to both army life and a country which had exiled or killed my relatives, I began to study Hebrew with another draftee—he was later to enter the Jewish Theological Seminary, a *hozer betshuvah* inspired by a vision of uniting, through Judaism, the wisdom of East and West.

We found a Holocaust survivor in Heidelberg with whom we read the Book of Job twice a week. As we knocked on the door of a dingy apartment, Herr Schreiber peered out, always with an anxious expression, as if expecting to be arrested again. His smile when he saw us was a relief. A Polish Jew, he had been through the camps and rarely talked about it. At that time (1954) the German government was not yet paying reparations or had not gotten around to him. Though in abject poverty, he was happy to be alive: a very small man with a ruddy, rotund face, who seemed supernaturally gentle and old. After my army service, during the first year of teaching at Yale, I wrote a play that included some of the stories he revealed. Basically, though, like many who had gone through far worse, I was building a life and not focusing on the past.

My grand scholarly project at Yale was a History of Interpretation which would do justice to the Jewish commentary-tradition in the context of patristics, allegoresis, and so on. I did not know at that time that David Hartman, my grandfather, a teacher of religion in Frankfurt, had published a doctoral thesis on Midrash and the Book of Ruth. None of this had a direct bearing on my duties at Yale: Courses on English poetry took most of my energy, although I smuggled in biblical texts. I suppose that, as in the army, I was working against the environment. T. S. Eliot was everywhere as the spiritual heir of Donne; I too was impressed by his ironic, liturgical rhythms, but disturbed by the uses to which his poetry was put. It reinforced a gentlemanly sort of Christianity that allied itself with the unmistakable Anglophile bearing of my senior colleagues in the seventeenth and eighteenth centuries. Those centuries were the prestige fields at Yale, attracting great donors as well as scholars, and overshadowing the adolescent and faintly disreputable Romantics. I tried applying to law school—in revolt, I suppose, and in hope that it would help my interpretation project: Law school would not accept me as a part-time student. I gave up my History of Interpretation, a task that needed total commitment, though twenty-five years later I was able to help in setting up Judaic studies at the university. Today Jewish and Hebrew texts can be learned either in the context of other literatures or in the context of Midrash: its exegetical inventiveness and colloquial force are still not fully appreciated in secular circles.

Throughout the fifties and sixties I remained future-oriented. Yet I often thought of the German-Jewish community that had been destroyed and wondered what kind of intellectual I would have become if I had grown up in the shadow of Franz Rosenweig, Martin Buber, Gershom Scholem, Ernst Simon, Abraham Heschel—not to speak of the Frankfurt School proper: Adorno, Benjamin, Fromm, and others. It was also, I suspect, a deep sense of separation that made Israel important for me. I have never been a conscious Zionist and went through none of the schools or youth movements fostering *ahavat Zion*. But already on my first visit, in 1952, Israel appeared to my feelings as an embodied dream. The sense of belonging to it, as if the land and not human parents had begotten me, especially an uncrowded, rural Jerusalem so close to the sky, intensified sensations that had bound me to the English countryside. This was starker, stonier, more primitive. I walked about with a barefoot mind, a spiritual vagabond having no sort of special Jewish identity, taking pleasure in every motion of sight and sound: goats and olive trees in Jerusalem, Mea Shearim with its market and numberless stubele; the mystery of the Old City, walled off, inaccessible; Safad, more Oriental still, its beggars, Hasids, and hole-in-the-wall shops; Tel Aviv, the city built from the ground up within the memory of many then living, where a young cousin of mine could date every new building and even tree in the neighborhood.

An organic relation to place is what I lacked and would never recover. I rarely experience strong feelings of attachment, whether to people or to soil. Israel was different. The soil I walked on felt both very old and very new: ancient beyond belief yet still to be planted, by the imagination too. Even the people moved me, from the Jekes (German Jews) to the black-suited Orthodox, and the aggressively secular, open-shirted kibbutz-niks. I was glad of the mingling and saw no need to take sides in an incredibly hardworking society where every group seemed to have its own rhythm. Enthusiastically I joined in, harvesting huge melons on my first day on a kibbutz, and was out with a sunstroke by noon.

We underestimate how important that feeling for place is as a physical memory. It is important for love, which often fuses person and place. But as *mystique* becomes *politique,* it can also grow into a fanatical passion: a self-sanctifying, place-bound nationalism that casts a murderous suspicion on the outsider. The Jew has been its major victim in the Diaspora. He is seen as an alien, however ancient and settled his claim. Those who cleave to Zion are not exempt from the dark side of that sacred passion. They must now confront it in themselves, in their own homeland and refuge.

It was toward the end of the 1970s that the survivors of the camps, now fully settled in America, with children grown up and grandchildren not far off, allowed the past a more conscious, public existence. Those who had entered the camps (or other extreme conditions) when their physical and mental resilience was at its prime (say, between fourteen and forty) had a better chance of survival. This age group was now close to sixty and some were over seventy. Most had rebuilt their families almost immediately without stopping to complete their formal education. The task of rebuilding had thrown them at once into making a living. Others became distinguished professionals, often returning to school at a later point. Now their children, the Second Generation, were beginning to seek a legacy.

To honor their parents meant also to honor the experience of their parents, however grim and burdensome it was. As children they had heard too much or too little. Both parents and children, moreover, were shocked by the growth of "revisionism," a phenomenon that became more aggressive in the 1970s. It denied that a systematic genocide had taken place. The deaths suffered in the Holocaust were attributed by revisionists to wartime conditions or exaggerated Jewish propaganda. Such malicious denial had to be met by an intensified act of witness. The movement encouraging ethnic affirmation also helped witnesses to speak out.

I too became directly involved at that time. What had haunted me all along, in addition to the genocide itself, was that it was not significantly opposed by local populations, who often even exploited it. I still felt German enough not to condemn the German character as such; other nationals had shown themselves indifferent or had actively promoted the crime. The exceptions —mostly compassionate individuals from all ranks of society, and even an entire village like Chambon or a nation like Denmark—only proved the rule. There was, then, the mystery of the bystanders as well as of the perpetrators; and among the bystanders were many well-educated persons (Max Weinreich called them "Hitler's professors") who condoned or even disseminated a racial theory that justified the exclusion of the Jews from public life.

The behavior of these intellectuals was especially incomprehensible. But then it all was; and I could not find an access-point for either study or activism. Yet had I really tried to find it? Or had I sheltered myself from too heavy a commitment by overestimating the mystery and pretending that thinking could not grasp the facts? It did not help that I saw around me many who depended on the *Shoah* to reinforce their religious or political identity.

My wife, Renee, now played a crucial role. Her story was one of the first to be recorded by the Holocaust Survivors Film Project, founded in 1979 at the request of New Haven survivors who wished to give public testimony. Born in Czechoslovakia, Renee and her deaf sister (a year younger) had been hidden on a farm near the Moravian border until their parents were deported to Auschwitz early in 1944. Payments for the children stopped and they were forced to return to Bratislava. The sisters (age nine and ten) arrived and found no one to shelter them—no Jews officially remained. After a few weeks they went to the police and asked to join their parents. They were sent to Bergen-Belsen.

One year in the camp was almost fatal. Liberated in April 1945, Renee was seriously ill with typhus: to this day she regrets not remembering the actual day of liberation. In 1948 she came to America from Sweden, where the sisters had been evacuated by the UNRRA and Red Cross.

Renee's participation in the Survivors Film Project roused my own interest. I discovered that the immediate cause for organizing it was the television series *Holocaust*. This film, so effective in West Germany, struck the survivors as a sanitized and distorted version of what they had suffered. The vow they had made not to forget—not to let the world forget—came back to them. The *Farband*, a Labor Zionist group comprising mainly East European immigrants, turned to a psychiatrist in New Haven (himself a survivor) and a television interviewer active in Jewish affairs. Dori Laub and Laurel Vlock, with the support of William Rosenberg, head of the *Farband*, and many in the New Haven community, began to assemble the means to videotape witnesses to the genocide.

What is a professor of English good for, if not to write a grant proposal? That is how I was drawn in; but the real reason for my increasing participation in this grass-roots effort was that I saw how important it could be for education. It gave me my point of access. I thought: Even the survivors are mortal. In ten or twenty years, how many will be left? For the time being we can ask them to tell their story in person, to talk to a classroom or to a community audience; but who will represent them when they are no longer among us? Historians establish the larger picture, while verifying every fact; they are rarely interested in transmitting stories, however impressive the latter may be as a revelation of personality and often in psychological and textured detail.

What I wanted was a restitution: the survivors not only re-calling what happened then, but their thoughts, *now* as well as *then*. The whole person, or as much as could be recorded in the space of two hours. Lanzmann's great film has set a standard for sophisticated and relentless inquiry, but the kind of open-ended, unprogrammatic interviewing practiced by the New Haven group is quite different. The interviewer, as Dori Laub has said, is a listener and a companion; he asks a minimum of questions in the hope that memories will emerge from a deeper, more spontaneous level.

It was also a way of compensating for the fact that most visual documentation of that period comes from Nazi sources. Our Holocaust museums are full of photos drawn from the pic-turebook of the murderers. The mind is exposed to images mag-nifying the Nazis and degrading their victims. The witness accounts are a view from the other side: They restore the sym-pathy and humanity systematically denied by Nazi footage. And even if, being recorded so many years after the event, they cannot be reliable in all respects, the passage of time also matures mem-ory. The video project does not impinge on the province of historians, who sift and compare sources, but seeks to open the hearts and minds of both high school students and adult audi-ences. They see the testimony of a thinking and feeling person, rather than of a victim.

It was during the Eichmann trial in 1960–61 that I first understood the power of personal witnessing. At that time I wrote "Ahasuerus," a poem that assimilated the witness account of a *Sonderkommando* member to the archetype of this legendary Wanderer, doomed to survive and conscious of everything. He would have preferred to die; but (in my version) his fear that he might be the last and only witness precluded death as a way out. While I glimpsed in many testimonies a mythic dimension learned from Jewish storytelling, or a poetry of realism that was a natural reaction to unbearable and meaningless suffering, I also saw that they were as authentic a representation as was possible in an audiovisual era—where exploitation is inevitable. An Archive of Conscience was needed both for educational purposes and for the sake of the media.

In 1982 Yale became the curator of the testimonies. The Revson Foundation enabled the university to establish a video archive in its central library. We had become a witness to the witness. What started as a grass-roots project could now develop into an oral history of national scope. (There are other important audiotape collections, "Voices from the Holocaust" that should also be indexed, coordinated, and so made accessible to education and research.) As I write this, close to the fiftieth anniversary of Kristallnacht, Yale's video-testimony project is being extended to Europe, and our archive has grown to over twelve hundred accounts.

Yet who can render the workings of memory? A Proust, perhaps, had he been born in a more tragic period and passed through the destruction. Everything we do seems, at times, inadequate and external. The interviews can be uneven; there are bad days; both witnesses and interviewers have resistances to overcome. In moments of doubt I take comfort from such writers as Primo Levi, Jean Amery, and Aharon Appelfeld. They tell us about weakness as well as courage, about the repression that occurred within the survivor, about a vital need to forget and the struggle against what has bitten into the soul. It is true but not all the truth that the survivors were neglected or that people could not bear to hear them. Silence shelters; even the most confessional writing communicates quietly, in its own space. There came a point when the survivors did not wish to talk. That time is past, although it is never entirely past. It required the "bribe" of life, that is, their children, and also the fear that the Holocaust would not be forgotten so much as denied or distorted, to bring the survivors back to the injunction: Thou shalt tell.

Ezekiel was forbidden to mourn the loss of the Temple in public. For many years after the Holocaust it seemed impossible to find an adequate form of public memory. Now it is possible, but still precarious. There are memorials to the memorials in Poland, funeral monuments made by piecing together vandalized tombstones. In Czechoslovakia the dome of a burned synagogue is set like a gravestone into a cemetery. At Worms, West Germany, you can admire the reconstructed medieval synagogue and the room where Rashi had his yeshiva. But these are cenotaphs. In the absence of a vital community the restored buildings and orphaned monuments recall painfully Hitler's Museum of a Vanished Race.

The most sensitive issue, both where there are Jews and where there are not, is how to communicate to the young what happened. The insemination of horror, or of horror and guilt, may produce terrible fantasies or else feelings of impotence. How does one teach a traumatic history without increasing inappropriate psychological defenses? The pedagogical question must be faced, especially when so many museums and educational programs are springing up.

Many times have I heard the nursery rhyme

> *Ring around the rosies,*
> *A pocket full of posies,*
> *Ashes, ashes,*
> *All fall down!*

without being aware of its sinister side, its possible origin in the Great Plague of the seventeenth century. The Opies, who mention that hypothesis in their *Oxford Dictionary of Nursery Rhymes,* have no proof. The catchy words absorb, so the hypothesis goes, that forgotten catastrophe: a red rash marking the disease, posies of flowers to ward off the smell of death and perhaps death itself, the burning of contaminated materials and corpses (though the version quoted by the Opies has "A-tishoo" not "Ashes"), and the sudden, macabre career of the plague. We don't trust such speculations, but they express our hope that deadly knowledge can be transformed from a traumatic into a bearable truth.

Our culture must look beyond the Holocaust, yet it can do so only by using ritual as well as realism. In the distant future we may stand before the most successful transformations as before certain traditional enactments: ceremonies, prayers, popular songs, even verses without an obvious reference to the tragedy. We need representations that do not founder under their weight of reality, that transmit more than images of victimage. In the search for authentic representations I believe testimonies can play a part. They are basic and archetypal, stories that are acts of facing in their very telling. A collective portrait is drawn and ordinary speech survives the burden of recollection.

In those testimonies there comes a moment when the loneliness is brought home: even into the home rebuilt with so much fervor and dedication. At family celebrations, such as a son's bar mitzvah, the survivor may realize that, among so many guests, the family from which he comes—all those aunts, uncles, cousins —is represented by no one except himself. That pang of loneliness remains; and it can swell to more than a pang, to a struggle with the Angel of Death, who threatens to vacate the entire achievement of a generation in which fathers and mothers started almost from scratch, like the patriarchs. It is as if they, the survivors, belonged to the dead after all.

At the end of the Israeli film *On Account of That War,* Halina revisits the death camp Treblinka, suffers a hallucinatory episode in which she acts out her struggle with the Angel, and returns home emptied rather than exalted, or exalted beyond the family. She realizes how much of her living strength has disappeared into a story she is able to retell or hysterically reenact, but not integrate into ordinary life. So we find that what is established on the flood is never established enough for the survivor.

I have not had to overcome so deadly a past. But sometimes in the midst of a bar mitzvah, when I realize once more how much communal experience is embodied in those prayers, I become enraged and argue with myself: How can you be so sad, so vengefully angry, just at this happy moment? I think of the sudden, pitiless removal of a family, or a community like the one in which I am praying, from their rooted and peaceful existence, to suffer a nakedness more terrible than Job's, and which resembles—if it can resemble anything—landscapes of hell in Christian painting. They are transported into that man-made hell, made naked, trampled on, massacred. It is not the image of death itself which gets hold of me, breaking past the safeguards, compelling imagination to look at that final transition. This Holocaust suddenness is worse than death, a denial of life so stark that it is hard to summon an affirmation to counter it, to decide that life, when such shame and desecration come to mind, remains worthwhile.

My bitter feelings, in the midst of a community's joy, focus on the killers who tried to extirpate an entire people, classifying them as unworthy to live. A people who are among the ancients of this world, not in age only but in continuity, not in continuity only but in wealth of learning, not in learning only but in a moral wisdom centered on the preservation of life, *pikuah nefesh*. Their morality, despite messianic-volcanic outbreaks, has tied them to life on this earth, a practical life, leavened by two thousand years of Bible reading and interpretation.

What happened cannot be explained by an intolerance of difference, or disgust for the pariah, or the need to blame and eliminate the victim. It really was violent evil rising up against a punctilious moral knowledge and an Ahasuerus-like conscience.

I am far from saying that Jews, who can be as stiff-necked, quarrelsome, and exclusive as any other group, have cornered the market on wisdom. They have their crazies, bigots, extremists, exploiters. And the Holocaust has hardened them: there are signs, especially in Israel, that the Bible can be a weapon turned against a world that is felt to be even more hostile now than *beyamim hahem,* "in those days."

Yet it is not a matter of the victims taking on features of the perpetrators, according to the pop psychology of unbenevolent observers. Israel is a state like any other and must defend itself. In the wake of the Holocaust, the 1967 and 1973 wars made its citizens intensely aware of the possibility of *hurban bayit shlishi,* the destruction of the Third Temple. Where else, within a context of such danger, do you find maintained a culture of argument and a system of values that prize study so much and do not see faith demanding a sacrifice of intellect?

I think of a Yiddish song like "Yankele," or of the service on the Sabbath, when the Torah scroll, handled like royalty, is opened and read to all, then carried into the congregation to show that it is a shared possession. It was the Jews' textual, not their territorial, ambition which cohered them, their refusal to kill the letter and to cancel the contract of their fathers and mothers with God. Yet this very people was taken out of its place and transferred—*raus, raus*—to that ultimate *Umschlag-platz,* the death camp, in a matter of days or hours. We were like a great tree that had weathered the centuries and in a day is uprooted, dismembered, and thrown to the flames. Each community in the Diaspora was a tree like that. There can be no replacement for those communities, though new centers have appeared in Israel, and with them a transplanting of new learning, new life, new problems. But the shadow of the destruction is not something that the joy of the newborn or the joy of what has survived can lessen.

A False Mustache,
a Frozen Swan:
The Holocaust
from a Distance

ROBERT PINSKY

1947, or maybe 1948. It is widely believed, as it will be for many years, that Adolf Hitler has escaped the ruins of Europe and is living a new life somewhere in the Western Hemisphere.

My parents are not quite thirty, an attractive small-town couple who have invited friends to the house for highballs. Flirtatiously she combs his forelock onto his handsome brow and with her other hand takes a pinch of her long brown hair and holds it under his nose.

"Everybody's looking for Hitler," she says, "and all the time he's right here on Rockwell Avenue."

He smiles shyly at their amused friends and flinches like a baby tickled on the neck. I can tell that the other couples admire

---

my parents for their physical grace, an admiration salted by the fact that everyone else in their set has tasted the postwar prosperity. Only Milford and Sylvia Pinsky still live in a rented apartment on the wrong end of town, just across the border from Little Africa. For all their prettiness and lightness, the name *Rockwell Avenue* is a thorn between them.

The high school basketball hero, a male version of the village beauty, Best-Looking Boy in the 1934 Long Branch Senior High School yearbook, was so far not as successful as Walt Weisman or Frank Holtz with their sunken living rooms and picture windows in West Long Branch. The impersonation, failure hiding in the mask of bodily grace, lurked somewhere in her audacious joke, the sexual teasing of that impromptu false mustache.

This memory of the name of Adolf Hitler comes far earlier and in a sense goes deeper than the newsreel images of emaciated bodies bulldozed into mass graves, ovens, the dark thousand-year-old eyes of survivors staring with an obscene, wary composure from bunks crowded and stacked like the rat cages in a pet shop. My mother's little gesture of arrogation may be part of a formative approach to the materials of history and culture. My first apprehension of Hitler is involved with a densely layered family joke. The irreverence, the recruitment of large matters to serve the involved needs of an individual life, the boldness, the eccentric cunning, appeal to me. Possibly, these qualities as a family heritage are related to the fact that, whatever it is I have found in the Holocaust, it is not the clear political or religious imperative some have derived from it.

They are qualities that remind me of the literature of Eastern Europe, with its grotesque comedy and violent fonts of emotion, a restless and mutual ambush between the outrages of history and the endurance of private life. Czeslaw Milosz and others have indicated that on the way to the massacre people sometimes carry along their old baggage, the lover, the boss, the brother-in-law, the toothache, the ambition, the bunion, the adultery, the revenge, the teapot. Crockery, indeed, is the theme of one of Milosz's most memorable postwar poems, "Song on Porcelain." In the central stanza, the poet walks past a torn, devastated landscape:

Before the first red tones
Begin to warm the sky
The earth wakes up, and moans.
It is the small sad cry
Of cups and saucers cracking,
The masters' precious dream
Of roses, of mowers raking
And shepherds on the lawn.
The black underground stream
Swallows the frozen swan.
This morning, as I walked past
The porcelain troubled me most.

In the economy of the poem, the tea service with its pastoral adornments perhaps represents Europe itself, but a Europe whose happy and elegant diversions are linked by powerful underground currents to the nightmare. The grotesque image of the frozen swan, like the image of my father as Hitler, suggests a complex binding together of hope and ugliness, love and despair, an approach to the nightmare that could be called ironic, rather than religious.

Both the poem and the early memory came back to me in 1980, on a tour of Eastern Europe sponsored by the U.S. State Department. I spoke and read poems to audiences put together from writers' unions, PEN clubs, embassy hangers-on, students, teachers, and (no doubt) spies, in such cities as Bucharest, Cracow, Szeged, Budapest, Iasi, Wroclaw: the murderous, frumpy terrain of the unimaginable. In that terrain, my mother's little gesture became the image of a response I couldn't quite formulate, to a series of enigmatic or subtly violating occasions.

For purposes of compression and disguise, imagine a composite and exaggerated country of deep Eastern sadness. The language is related to Finnish, to the Romance tongues by way of Rumanian, but also to Slavonic and Turkish—a Marx Brothers or Sid Caesar language, full of recognizable bits and slapdash imitations or mockeries, like the capital city itself, with its minor-key crumbling Grand Hotels and cynical echoes of Paris and Prague. Also Stalinist Moderne, yes, but because the country has for centuries succumbed readily to Romans, Turks, Russians,

Nazis, Russians again—so readily, and with such scant strategic importance, so few resources to plunder, that relatively little destructive force has been squandered on the capital city—it survives intact as an anthology of second-rate and derivative imperial architecture from every era.

Not a prosperous place. Even in the center, on the square surrounding the ironic little Arc de Triomphe, parking spaces abounded all day. Actual beggars appeared in front of the hotel, with not the familiar request for spare change, but the outstretched cupped hand and silent grimace of tradition.

Bribery, or rather, the use of one certain brand of American cigarettes as the true currency of persuasion, ruled everywhere. The cartons and packs, seemingly unopened through dozens of transactions with the actual tobacco nearly as theoretical as the metal in Fort Knox, appeared everywhere, symbols that the highest belief was reserved for intimate rather than official arrangements, a confidence in the rigidly prescribed image of the package, king-size only and never mentholated, tangible, a coinage so respected that only in such settings as the office of an extremely high official did I see a fresh pack ostentatiously opened: posed as in a magazine ad with four staggered virgin smokes extended seductively next to the coffee and cognac, exposed as if offhandedly for consumption.

At the other extreme, I asked for the bathroom at a roadhouse and on the other side of the door was the outdoors, a neat vegetable garden being hoed by the classic, suntanned Grimm's Tales crone dressed in black, nose touching her chin. She turned to me. I tried to pronounce the word I had seen over bathrooms: *"Toaletysny?"* She made her eyes wide and smiled, bringing two straight fingers to her mouth and puffing through them as she pronounced the American brand name. I gave her some smokes from the pack I had learned to carry for emergencies, and she directed me with gestures to the far side of an outbuilding.

The country's most successful exports have been artistic, including past glories of surrealism and the Yiddish theater. In the capital city's former Central Synagogue, the socialist state has established a Museum of Jewish History. Officially closed at the hour I was there, but Liz McGowan and Phil Dolan, the Cultural Affairs Officers, arranged for the curator to show us around. When Liz was at Vassar she dated a boy who had been the president of the class two years ahead of mine at Long Branch High School. A writer friend had warned me "the State Department people you like will all be CIA," but it was a comfort to have these two along as friendly spirits, as well as translators.

It also helped having two other tall people in the party, to keep me from feeling too gawky and overfed as I followed the curator, a dainty old man wearing an ancient suit and tie, a beret, and tiny house slippers. He showed us photographs and playbills in glass cases and in the upstairs gallery, where the women used to sit, costumes from famous productions of *King Lear* and *The Dybbuk*. Tristan Tzara, Guillaume Apollinaire, and Dionys Udzu in a restaurant, smirking at the camera. A linen tablecloth from that occasion, with holograph pornographic verses and doodles. Downstairs, we saw Torahs, shofars, siddur books, battered ritual ewers and baubles, and also souvenirs and archives of the oppresssion.

As the curator guided the diplomats and me, he was shadowed by an old lady who bickered with him in the classic manner of a Morris and Becky joke, a sideplay of nudges and impatient whispers as stylized as the commedia dell'arte: the international gesture of a hasty *yeah, yeah,* nodding the head in the double positive that makes a negative. Shushing the old lady, her husband or brother concentrated on me and seemed to slight Liz and Phil despite their superior, embassy-style clothes and grooming. Who did they tell him I am, in my college boy sweater? The old couple argued not in Yiddish but in the Urdu-Slavonic-Romance language of the country. Amused, Phil Dolan —a Slavic languages major at Notre Dame—explained that they were arguing about what might interest me.

Among memorabilia of the Nazi days, the curator pointed out preserved anti-Jewish posters and photographs of Jewish shops declared out of bounds. Behind us, the old lady sneaked up holding a framed document, what looked like a full-page ad in a tabloid. Banned authors, Phil translated. Patriotic citizens will demand that the contaminating works of the following Jewish authors be removed from the shelves of the homeland. Dozens of names, a few even I could recognize—and one, it became clear as the Morris and Becky routine got louder and faster, was the name of the very old man himself; he is or was an author.

Of children's books, Phil explained, following their chatter, very popular at the time. He and Liz watched as the old man beamed up at me, he and the old lady grinning expectantly and unanimously now, as if they had been nagging at one another only about the means to reach this moment. All four people were watching me—eh, what do I think? The old man named his concentration camp, still grinning. An air of expectation.

He was far from the first survivor of the Nazi onslaught I had met. In the world of my childhood synagogue on the Jersey Shore, there were several. I remember in particular a man called Yossel. Congregations like mine were populated on Sabbath mornings mainly by two groups: retired men rediscovering their piety and unwilling young boys yearning for freedom from the long, tedious services. My father, Walt Weisman, and Frank Holtz were at work. (Women, of course, were at home.)

Yossel with his toothless grin and his baggy clothes of a silent film comic had a unique place, somewhere between the boys and the graybeards. The old men treated him with a condescending affection. Sometimes they played small practical jokes on him—hiding the decrepit velvet bag where he kept his prayer equipment or offering him snuff doctored to make him sneeze. His meaningless perpetual smile gave the impression that he was feebleminded or shell-shocked. I could not tell, because he understood only Yiddish.

Though he couldn't speak with us, Yossel often lined up to pray with us boys, as if he felt more at ease there than with the old men who rocked from the waist and dipped their knees with exaggerated gestures while they prayed, affecting pompous cantorial sobs and grace notes. Once, encouraged by my grandfather, Yossel showed me the number tattooed on his forearm. I have no idea what country he came from or how he wound up on the Jersey Shore. He had no relatives. Some agency must have assigned him as a ward of our congregation.

The congregation accepted Yossel in what seemed an unreflecting way, a brusque, unsentimental, to some extent even an unfeeling embrace that assigned him his role—nor was that role a holy fool's: Yossel was not holy to us. Because the piety of the old men was centered upon the Torah, observance of the Law, Yossel was not sacred but an innocent who had suffered. For many in a later generation (though not for me) the suffering of those millions might be a holy charge, making Jewish survival sacred. The possibility of thus making a cult of the Holocaust perhaps did not present itself to those old men, immersed as they were in the rituals of their childhood. To make Jewish life sacred would be a redundancy. If they had thought about it, they might have argued that Armenians and others had been the objects of genocide, but only Jews had the Torah. And these men were themselves immigrants. Conceivably, the catastrophe Yossel had survived seemed to them merely an extreme extension of the cruelty and malevolence of Europe itself.

It was the idea of Europe that the curator called up—deep Europe, not the cultural edifice of T. S. Eliot's essays and not the Rome, Paris, London that I had visited from time to time since college, but the ancient grounds of conquest, rape, divisions, and enmities of peoples, the suppressed minorities, Slovenes and Estonians and Moldavians and Gypsies, the Rumanian minority in Hungary and the Hungarian minority in Rumania, the continent's name a reference to the violent carrying off of a virgin by a furious beast. The knowing, unreadable smile that the two survivors seem in my memory to share is like the hardy, bearlike expression that a denizen of the arctic turns toward a tourist from the temperate zones.

I murmured something about how astonishing his survival was. There was no point in faking an epiphany I did not feel. Could it be that though I had left Judaism behind me, without regret, as soon as I could, it had insulated me against that other religion of the Holocaust? I imagined that the gentile Americans from the embassy would have been gratified by some special show of emotion on my part.

I did not feel nothing. Unlike Yossel, the curator came with a filled-in European life before the atrocities—he was holding documentation of that life in his hands. To challenge my particular imagination the more (as he seemed to know) it was (unlike Yossel's) the life of a writer, one who conceivably sat in cafés with the likes of Tristan Tzara and Dionys Udzu. I was in the presence of people not unlike me, by birth and inclination, who had lived through the great and infamous storm. And finally, the curator and the old lady who hectored him were unlike Yossel in that they had not left: they still occupied the European terrain of hair-raising historical accounts and statistics, the actual terrain of the forever bone-chilling, barely touchable lore of the Holocaust. The contorted nationalisms and hatreds of Eastern Europe, preserved in the juices of the Soviet system, gave this lore a peculiar immediacy.

To show what I mean, I must abandon composites to cite some historical material about one country, as an example. Take Rumania. According to Raul Hilberg's exhaustive tome *The Destruction of the European Jews,* Rumanian military actions were characterized by "more than mere opportunism—an overpowering need to hurl oneself with all one's might at an enemy target." First, fighting as Germany's most important ally in the East, Rumanians died in large numbers in Odessa and Stalingrad. Later, when the Rumanians changed sides, they displayed the same desperate ferocity fighting against the Germans. It is as if the built-up emotions that drove Europe to tear and chew at itself in the war had reached a special concentration in this humiliated and corrupted corner of the Continent.

Hilberg states that in Jewish matters, too, the Rumanians showed a peculiar blend of individual opportunism and "something more."

> In Bukovina and Bessarabia . . . the Roumanians took the most drastic action. In these provinces the Roumanian authorities did not follow the usual pattern of concentrating the Jews and handing them over to the Germans; instead, the Bukovina and Bessarabia Jews were transported to what we might call the Roumanian "East"—the territory of "Transnistria.". . . In that territory the Roumanians maintained true killing centers. Besides Germany itself, Roumania was thus the only country which implemented all the steps of the destruction process, from definitions to killings.

There follows a description of mass murder and ingenious cruelties, sometimes carried out in so berserk a manner as to cause squabbling between the Rumanians and the Germans. The head of state, Marshal Antonescu, "was the only man in Europe besides Hitler who placed upon himself the burden of an order to commence a full-fledged killing operation."

The Transnistria centers represent, in Hilberg's term, "opportunism" on a national and official level. The measures taken in these centers, mainly starvation and mass shootings, successfully contributed to the destruction of Rumania's Jewish population, which in 1939 had been the third largest in Europe. Like the poetry of the passion of love, the literature of this suffering seems always capable of calling up from the depths of its reality new images and phrases:

> In the Vertujen camp the arriving Jews were told: "You have come in on two feet, and if you do not end your lives here, you will be allowed to leave on four feet only." In that camp the Jews were fed on a diet of cattle food that apparently resulted in paralysis. Levai writes that when the trial of war criminals opened in Bucharest after the war, a number of witnesses, including the Jewish ballerina Rebecca Marcus, "were indeed able to walk on all fours only." (Levai, *Martyrdom*, p. 68)

It is the enigmatic Eastern European extremes of passion and cynicism that I want to dwell on, however, to call them up without presuming to understand them. Lunatic behavior is expected in this context, but Hilberg describes something that seems possibly too bizarre for the category of "opportunism" to contain:

> Opportunism was practiced in Roumania not only on a national basis but also in personal relations. Roumania was a corrupt country. It was the only Axis state in which officials as high as minister and mayor of the capital city had to be dismissed for "dark" transactions with appropriated Jewish property. . . . The search for personal gain in Roumania was so intensive that it must have enabled many Jews to buy relief from persecution. The institution of bribery was, in fact, so well established that it was diverted for the benefit of the state: the Roumanian government permitted Jews to *purchase* exemptions from such anti-Jewish measures as forced labor and travel restrictions. However, what was true of personal opportunism in Roumania was true also of personal involvement in killings. Repeatedly the Roumanians threw themselves into *Aktionen*. [Formal extermination operations.] Witnesses and survivors . . . speak of scenes unduplicated in Axis Europe. Even in German reports there are criticisms of these operations, and in some cases . . . the Germans stepped in to halt killings that seemed offensive even to so hardened an establishment as the German army.

This account recalls the improvised currency of the single brand of American cigarette, trusted single-mindedly. I mean not simply the idea of corruption or bribery, but the formalized moral exchange rate that, beyond coexisting with the release of savage and long-stored-up passions, seems to be an extension of those passions into the fanatical account books of commerce. Both the assigning of a price to lives and a peculiar, distinctive passion in taking them were parts of a single cultural matrix that expressed itself in the camps of Transnistria. There an indigenous eastern or southern emphasis on individual fates and relations seemed to exceed in its passionate cruelty the purposes and regulations of the Nazis themselves.

Among the victims at Transnistria was the family of the Rumanian-born poet Paul Celan. His poems have been described as dismantling the German language from within, and as a response to the imaginable defeat of all language, culture, individual speech, poetry, by the facts of the great European mass murders of the 1940s which Celan, born in 1920, himself barely survived. Along with their numbers, a peculiar aspect of those horrors was their cultural intimacy: Europe killed and tortured Europe, the civilization brutalized itself. Culturally polyglot and therefore the more European (a Rumanian Jew who lived in France and wrote in German), Celan can also be described as the poet of the place where horror on the mass level comes up against horror on the intimate, personal level. His poem beginning "There was earth inside them, and they dug" (*Es war Erde in ihnen, und sie gruben*) concludes:

> *Es kam eine Stille, es kam auch ein Sturm,*
> *es kamen die Meere alle.*
> *Ich grabe, du gräbst, und es gräbt auch der Wurm,*
> *und da Singende dort sagt: Sie graben.*
>
> *O einer, o keiner, o niemand, o du:*
> *Wohin gings, da's nirgendhin ging?*
> *O du gräbst und ich grab, und ich grab mich dir zu,*
> *und am Finger erwacht uns der Ring.*

In English (as translated by Michael Hamburger):

> *There came a stillness and there came a storm,*
> *and all the oceans came.*

I dig, you dig, and the worm digs too,
and that singing out there says: They dig.

O one, o none, o no one, o you:
Where did the way lead when it led nowhere?
O you dig and I dig, and I dig towards you,
and on our finger the ring awakes.

The parody or evocation of a language lesson—*Ich grabe, du gräbst, es gräbt, sie graben*—is sardonic in an impersonal way, but nostalgic and childlike in a personal way, a polarity reflected also in the movement between the *einer* of love and the cold of *keiner*, between *niemand* and the familial intimacy of *du*. The digging of the doomed is futile, a digging toward mass obliteration, but the digging of the poem is toward an individual loss: "I dig"— or, since it is *ich grab mich*, "I dig myself"—"toward you." The poem digs through earth, annihilation, and language toward the intimate, personal pronoun of the familiar *you*.

In Celan's characteristic manner, difficult, allusive, withholding, irritably twisting and collapsing language around his one, obsessive subject, separate things are smoked over, while polarities are clear, especially the polarity between the universal and general, which is deathly, and the individual, which is all but completely obscured. Thus, "They dug and they dug," he writes. "And they did not praise God. . . . They dug and heard nothing more; they did not grow wise, invented no song, / thought up for themselves no language. / They dug."

This denial of transcendence at the beginning of the poem, evoking the meaningless labor of Transnistria, associates that labor with the grammar lesson in the language of death, I dig, you dig, they dig. On the other side, Celan posits an individual psychology within the mass, a sought-for, private *"du"* whose tokens are personal pronouns and a ring on a finger.

The poem digs to recover a particular life—we could call it the life of the poet's mother, killed in Transnistria, but that is merely speculative because the poem chooses, precisely, to make that life private as well as personal. This force of the private, the held back, in Celan's poems reminds me of the possibly embattled, often dark personal world behind the doors of Eastern Europe. Ironic even about the language it may happen to speak, as the poet is ironic about German, that life makes its public appearance briefly in the black market or "dark" market value of cigarettes, lives, hatreds. It is not the life of the official language, of the state or the schools or the newspapers.

A tangled pulling between public and private life is not exclusively Eastern European, of course, though I think it may be particularly distinct in that part of the world. It is a central, domesticated opposition of modern life. In its most benign—its neighborhood or regional or ethnic form—this opposition certainly is a staple of American life: on one side, the personal hospitalities and immigrant puritanisms and secret authorities of the Italian or Portuguese neighborhood, or the unspoken interdictions and charities of an isolated rural community. And facing all of that is the impersonal world of justice and administration, the official agencies and departments, the school assignments and building codes and credit requirements, the liberal edifice of the Law itself.

The idea of civilization, at each level of intensity, is the capacity to incorporate historical forces into personal gestures. Civilization is the amazing equipment that comes up with jokes and poems even about the death camps, which after all generated their own sardonic slang and comic lore. We tear ourselves to pieces, slowly, without mercy, and yet we dig, we conjugate the old verbs of intimacy again. This image of tearing the soil as the way we go on inventing ourselves after and even during the great catastrophe is perhaps more penetrating than the "building again" that Yeats opposes to the cataclysm of Europe in the mysterious ancient smiles of "Lapis Lazuli":

> *On all the tragic scene they stare.*
> *One asks for mournful melodies;*
> *Accomplished fingers begin to play.*
> *Their eyes mid many wrinkles, their eyes,*
> *Their ancient, glittering eyes, are gay.*

Yeats's imaginary Chinese sages and Celan's persistent hopeless diggers both represent endurance beyond the seeming end. So does the zany, obdurate figure who survives to hold up a framed clipping denouncing his work, for the edification of an American visitor: an allegorical representation of the civilizing gesture that starts over again endlessly, jostling and speaking in the very waiting rooms of Hell itself. On another and lower frequency, this unquenchable idiosyncrasy is replicated by my mother's joke, incorporating Adolf Hitler as folklore into the intricate and actual drama of her marriage. We cannot say what poem or even joke someone's imagination might someday come up with, no matter what the subject. (If nothing else saves us from silence, then our vulgarity will.)

A few days after the visit to the Jewish museum, Liz and Phil took me to visit a preserved concentration camp, the scene of the extermination of millions, two thirds of them Jews. There too the stubborn, ungeneralizable core of personality seemed forced to the surface.

The place had a cafeteria, a turnstile, an office where one paid admission, a bookshop. There were trailers where young people from a visiting German religious group, here for some sort of project, slept. The guide who showed us around was a young woman. Halfway through the tour she mentioned that the staff was rather down in the dumps because a coworker had died the night before. Mourning a single death in such a place seemed in itself an odd, meaningless irony. That first impression was overshadowed by the added information that the deceased woman, a commissary worker, was a former inmate. After the war, she had chosen not to leave and had lived for the last thirty-five years in an apartment converted for survivors from part of the original barracks.

Even the embassy people seemed startled. Liz McGowan said, "If I had been here, once I was out I would want to get as far away as possible. Why would anyone choose to stay here?"

The guide explained that the woman was French. Her family and friends had been wiped out. Here at the camp she had the free apartment as well as her government pension. Also, there were people she knew here, other inmates who had chosen to stay on, for similar reasons.

Precisely because on some deep level I did not understand this appalling information very well, I found something oddly restorative in it. Despite its horror it was also evidence of the concentration camp as a place, a place that went on existing as did other places, each with its balance between continuity and discontinuity. This woman's life was closed to me. Marx and Engels write that consciousness is from the start a product of society. Beginning with the division of labor, consciousness deceives itself that it is something other than consciousness of existing practice, the dialectic of production forces and social relations. Even supposing that one accepted this model of life, it is the staggering complexity of the dialectic that is underlined by individual lives: my young parents, wishing they lived in a single-family house; victims bribing or blundering their way to New Jersey or perishing under torture; others choosing after the ordeal to remain where they were.

As amazing as the extent and contortion of human cruelty are the twists of consciousness. Presentation of this fact in detail, precisely, in just proportion to the particular setting, is what gives Primo Levi's book *Survival in Auschwitz* its amazing force. In his compact, straightforward, and artful narrative, Levi enacts in the flesh the idea I have cited from Milosz, the idea of the great underground stream that flows between the works of Hell and the works of our hope and leisure, our images of desire. Here is all of the poem from which I quoted earlier. The setting is immediately after the war:

Song on Porcelain

Rose-colored cup and saucer,
Flowery demi-tasses:
They lie beside the river
Where an armored column passes.
Winds from across the meadow
Sprinkle the banks with down;
A torn apple tree's shadow
Falls on the muddy path;
The ground everywhere is strewn
With bits of brittle froth—
Of all things broken and lost
The porcelain troubles me most.

Before the first red tones
Begin to warm the sky
The earth wakes up, and moans.

It is the small sad cry
Of cups and saucers cracking,
The masters' precious dream
Of roses, of mowers raking
And shepherds on the lawn.
The black underground stream
Swallows the frozen swan.
This morning, as I walked past
The porcelain troubled me most.

The blackened plain spreads out
To where the horizon blurs
In a litter of handle and spout,
A lively pulp that stirs
And crunches under my feet.
Pretty, useless foam:
Your stained colors are sweet—
Some bloodstained, in dirty waves
Flecking the fresh black loam
In the mounds of these new graves.
In sorrow and pain and cost
The porcelain troubles me most.

There is something satisfying, decorous yet ironic, about the way Milosz treads steadily between elegant rhymes and revulsion, decorative art and violent death, the rubble of bourgeois domesticity and its bobbing back to the surface, as if endlessly renewable. The painted pastoral images, so false and sweet, seem endlessly capable of breaking and surviving. The frozen swan is an image both of death and of rigid, irrevocable fact. The elegance of swans, an almost kitsch perfection, adds a terrible comedy.

Once, at a poetry reading in California, I heard a woman hiss at this poem after it was read aloud: a single, heartfelt if bad-mannered escape of breath through teeth, in the middle of an otherwise approving crowd. I think she felt that the poet should have said it was the graves that troubled him most, not the porcelain. She might have preferred images of gold teeth broken from living jaws, the fingers of children chopped off for their rings—true images. But the poem notes that it is porcelain that cunningly attracts our attention and that in its permutations survives even the worst, however broken. In the understated laconic narrative of Levi, the agonizing chords and discords of Celan, in the shards of pretty crockery, we see the saving and various resourcefulness, almost the garrulity, of culture: nothing is precisely unspeakable, even though nothing can be plumbed or exhausted by speech. "Where did the way lead when it led nowhere?" says Celan. In this area, Milosz's poem suggests, it is sometimes our jokes and conjugations and false images—assuming that the image of harmony and ease is false—that tell the most about us.

After

DAVID SHAPIRO

It remains for me to be a shadow among shadows
to be one million times more shadow than the shadow
that will come and come again into your sunny life.
              —*Robert Desnos*

Scholem has said that commentary is a sacred activity of the Jewish people: a peculiar activity if one thinks that the revelation should be once and forever. He goes on to note that the Torah is also said in the esoteric tradition to show its "face" to each single Jew differently—let us thematize this as a profound pluralism at the heart of the mystic creativity of Kabbalah. The same must be said for the horror of the death camps. For every Jew, the meaning of this meaninglessness must be another face. It is also untrue that one can turn away from it, like the foolish son who is conjured each Passover as thinking himself separate from the Egyptian ordeal. No matter how much we might want to separate ourselves from this horror—and with most caution, out of respect for those who survived—we must actually speak for those, as Fackenheim is always reminding us, who were without speech: children thrown into the ovens. For those without speech there must be an attempt to speak. But I must add that I have not really seen the adequacy of any such speech. But here one might think of the favorite motto of Arthur A. Cohen: "It is not ours to finish the task, neither is it ours to abandon it." It is not ours to understand the horror of the "Tremendum," but it is upon us, it drowns us, even if we seem saved.

It occurs to me as my uncle, Gideon Chagy, praises the factual language of certain expositors, that I would indeed admire the writer who could simply show the Holocaust in its brute empirical reality. As John Felstiner has tried in certain translations of Celan to teach the reader German so that by poem's end the piece need not be translated, how much we could desire this work: On Not Translating the Holocaust. But we are condemned to translation and, in that sense, to mistranslation.

Scholem, speaking of Buber's luminous cotranslation of the Pentateuch into German, concludes with one of the darkest ironies I have met even in the dark precinct of this catastrophe: that Buber's triumph is only less positive in the historical era in which there is no longer a Jewish community wanting such a German version. This irony of the Hebrew scholar reminded me of the moments in my childhood in which my mother would speak laceratingly of the German language and its corruptions, of Ernst Toller and the poets who had renounced the syllables of their native language. I think of the moving modulations in Celan's last bitter poems, as if he wanted to burst from an imprisonment in German into Hebrew. These ideogrammatic movements that produce the perturbations of his amazing poems create, for me, a mystical condensation, a kind of linguistic Zionism. For Scholem and Celan, I am pleased to witness the movement in philology away from the Teutonic scholarship that too easily linked Greece and Germany. Reading Joseph Campbell's work on mythology, I am aware that even his strictures against racism do not seem menacing enough, and I am increasingly aware of my fear that the mythological approach in Jung may still be used dangerously. Part of the positivist in me knows that the Holocaust may perhaps best be glimpsed in its multiplicity and bareness, the factual multiplicity to which the prose of Levi points. Yet, in reading Helen Epstein's account of the multiplicity and unity of the survivors' children, I remind myself that there is a truth in naming, not foisting fanciful metaphor, but in naming those events that do, after all, become a monolith. The Holocaust is not metaphor or myth; it is the proper name for events that subvert language and myth. It is not that poetry becomes impossible after the Holocaust, but myth and its language and corruptions become dubious if not unbearable. Yet we know reality is unbearable without the consolations of metaphor and myth. This is what makes the strict interrogations of *Shoah* so bewildering and so bold.

Many times I have stared at the date of my birth and thought: I am a "peace baby," I am born after the catastrophe, after Hiroshima, after my father was stationed on a boat in Africa and learned the claustrophobia of war, after my mother escaped being bombed on a boat that crossed the dangerous Atlantic in 1940 from Johannesburg to New York, after the bombings and after the sustained and systematic murder of the Jews. Though I despise false periodicities and have learned to condemn such false ruptures as "postmodern" and all its satieties, it is hard not to picture oneself as an epilogue. No one should represent a generation, but if I may use the least royal we, we are the peaceful satieties, we are the lucky ones, born in the mildest of ghettos of Newark, raised amid American racism, growing up in Weequahic Park in the great postwar happiness. I was raised to enjoy chamber music and poetry. My older sisters had traveled in desk drawers through the country as part of a military doctor's itinerary. But my life was to be all too stabilized and haunted by the twin horrors of the Hitlerian past and the nuclear future. Too eschatological for some, the truth is that the forms of my happiness were always fitted between this elegiac residuum and the amazing illegible catastrophe that awaits. This is not to delete the thickness of bourgeois life in between, as when a New York poet once convincingly deposed a certain bohemian by insisting that "Everyone now wants to be bourgeois." But it is to insist that the shape of our particular middle-classness was deformed by the pressure and the principle of horror on all sides. It is not an accident that Jewish youth found it sensible to be a conscience during the Vietnam War. A war resister, professor now in Chicago, spoke at a class reunion twenty years later of his calm upon resisting even within Danbury prison and realizing, thrown into solitary, prison within prison, that he could endure the worst. But we all knew and know that we had not survived the worst. We were not survivors. The question remains: Were we malingerers in a false paradise of commodity-mad America that had sustained us with a shattering array of idols like empty food?

When Picasso's old best friend, the saintly Max Jacob, was hustled out of Paris toward the death camp wherein he finally died, Picasso had few words or heroic deeds for him. It is said that Picasso concealed any anguish behind the joke "Max is an angel and will leap over the prison walls." It is true that I have discovered in Picasso's putative whimsy an allusion to Jacob's prose poem, "Christmas Story," in which an angel reveals plans to a prisoner to afford an escape. Was the painter secretly alluding to Max's genius, to their former intimacy, and was the quotation more homage than whimsy? When I have raised this question to others, I have been convinced by a stern rejoinder that the remark does little credit to Picasso whether or not it alludes to Max's little poem. The terrible fact remains that we have wished our greatest aesthetic geniuses to have an ethical genius that has eluded them. Even the painter of *Guernica* might be condemned by his moral cowardice. . . . But as those who come "afterward," and "after" must be the title of our lives, who are we to cast this repellent stone at the French intellectuals? Some were heroic, some not. The Holocaust has become, over time, the source for all of us to learn the truth of altruism, how little there is, how much that little counts. For example, Beckett's quiet participation in the Resistance. Surely, *Guernica* itself is an act of altruism, after all. We do not know whether we can demand any more altruistic gestures from humanity than it has given us.

The music of this epoch, Adorno has warned us, must be an intransigent abrasiveness if it is to mean much to us beside adjustment. To some, this is an illogical posture and a mimesis of chaos. But surely, there is in harmony a kind of forgetting. Putting together too many things, let me say that I find a paradoxical reassurance in the very "noise" of our best poetry, art, and music.

Recently, Brian Swann and Ruth Feldman have translated a little volume of Primo Levi's poems. One might at first simply think that Levi was not a poet and that many of the pieces seem, at least in translation, insubstantial and more like psychological fragments than coherent wholes. I am impressed upon reading them, however, by their increasing aesthetic and ethical weight. The fragments point toward states of wholeness. Each piece is dated, and the dates remind one, perhaps as nothing else in Levi, of the act of writing poetry as a gesture of intransigeance in history, like the making of the most veristic documentary or document. The dates are indeed tattoos: February 1943; 28 December 1945. The poems have a melancholy almost unbearable, for Levi perhaps finally unbearable: " 'You multitudes with dead faces / On the monotonous horror of the mud /Another day of suffering is born.' / Tired companion, I see you in my heart." At the end of this collection, in the late postwar years, one senses as an intrusion the greater liveliness, a Cavafy-like wisdom of concreteness, an increasingly lighter set of possibilities. But always the central darkness is there, as in a poem to Eichmann, dated 29 July 1960—compare this dating mania with Picasso's Napoleonic sense of dating his paintings—"Oh son of death we do not wish you death." What Levi wishes on his "precious enemy" is the ideal insomnia haunted by the suffering of the innocents. There is a claustrophobic and penitential *terribilità* to this poem that is itself a terrible act of vengeance. The victim has survived in order to hurl this wretched one spiritually against the rocks of an impersonal Babylon. This poem is more searching and terrible than anything in Cavafy, say, and could not have existed in a naturalistic pose or prose. It is the menacing, crafted curse of the chemist-prophet. It smells of justice and is the counterweight to those horrors of the century, the Fascist poems of those who compared exploding children to roses. Levi's indelible denunciation is a defense of poetry and a requital of all falsely aestheticizing fascism.

I am living in Riverdale, part of the murdered city, part of the continental America. Around me observant Jews are going to shul. I see my own son for the first time in his yarmulke. On the phonograph, my grandfather is singing the *michtorm David* in an elegy for the Warsaw dead. My life is sheltered but vulnerable. I have learned the standards of Scholem and Meyer Schapiro, of the fidelity to truth-telling in their radiant works. On the desk is the Hebrew Bible my grandmother, founder of Pioneer Women Clubs, gave me on my bar mitzvah. When I go to pick up my clothes, I observe the blue numbers on the big arms of the proprietor. My little Hebrew remains from years at Bet Yeled. On my music stand Bloch's *Nigun,* dedicated to his mother's memory. Achron's *Hebrew Melody* and *Hebrew Lullaby,* with the Auer cadenza. I have never gone to Israel, since my relatives on a kibbutz rejected a summer's visit as arrogantly short. But I remember the sense during the explosive Six-Day War that I should go there to serve even if only in a pacific category, that I should never let Israel be imperiled. And I recall Arendt's syllogisms that Israel was most imperiled by her reliance on power politics when encircled by enemies. The American Jew is encircled by a strange variety of friend and the interior music of a tradition that is now devolving into a "mere" poetics. During a *yizkor* service, I am moved by the image of the bridge between the living and the dead, as the beloved dead seem to be visiting us with extended hands. I miss my theologian-friend Arthur Cohen, who died while writing his last text on the mystery of the resurrection, which he accepted because it was a scandal. I recall going to synagogue with my grandfather and watching with horror as someone—a child?—burned the Israeli flag. Fire! fire! fire! And later, fire on the American flag. Even a sheltered life sees the ungathered sparks and a few singed forms.

Like many sheltered American Jews, anti-Semitism has been to me at first a recited tradition more than a lived fact. I grew up in the "Jewish" ghetto of Newark (1947–63), where I knew a little the desiccating racism practiced against blacks; and I also knew and saw the brave attempts by many to mollify this condition. The racism of Newark, moreover, taught me what anti-Semitism must look like, and I must add that it was in the interracial choruses of Newark that I had my greatest experience of the universalism in which my parents believed. I did not see the sad rupture of black-Jewish politics until almost a decade later.

The anti-Semitism that chilled me most was lodged in the voice of Europeans, as when a worker told me at Cambridge that "Hitler should've finished 'em off sooner." The anti-Semitism I have discovered in European travels seems the most substantial, felt, vengeful, and bloody. And recently, the kind of disbelief in the Holocaust, even from so-called social scientists, has infuriated and challenged me. The revisionists who treat the Holocaust as a myth or text, aided by an infantile deconstructionism, or those who defend such promulgators on the basis of an absolute freedom of speech—all these have paradoxically strengthened my sense of still being an embattled Jew, Arendt's "pariah." I am not happy in being defined by the bigot. (My mother used to prepare with heartbreaking sincerity pluralist lectures, entitled "How to Respond to a Bigot.")

It has been said that it is good for a writer to have nightmares about this subject. I have found myself walking over the bridge in Riverdale while counting or trying to count to 6 million, like an obsessed conceptual artist intoning numbers. I have found myself suddenly seeing the black smoke from a nursing home as the black mist of children in Nelly Sachs' visions. It is startling to realize always that one is lucky, lucky, lucky to be alive, as the Italian artist Lucio Pozzi told me. When we recite our birth dates, it is significant that we are after. After. And shocking when confronted with dates so close to mine to realize how quickly and quietly one's life could have fitted into this horror. And the complacence to think this will not happen again. I agree with Marcel Ophuls, while praising Lanzmann's amazing images of horror, that the significance now of work on this subject is *defiance*.

Why is it that Eliach's collection of *Hasidic Tales* of the Holocaust seems to me the most eloquent and fiery of the many testimonies of the survivors? For me, the pure factuality of many witnesses, the almost impossible imperturbability that is striven for in the most noble passages of Levi, present too often a catastrophe *as if* without meaning. The Hasid who recounts the day in which the melody of a "nigun" keeps him dancing, until the snow under his feet is drenched in blood, is giving me something like the meaning of resistance. The theory of Viktor Frankl is that we survive through meaning: thus, logotherapy, building on the refusal to suicide. The Hasids in Eliach's amazing text survive the Holocaust with a sense that we are condemned to meaning. The stories are like the great Jewish prayer in which the martyr warns the deity that he is tempting him to lose faith. A woman rushes toward a hill after the war only to discover it is the mass grave at Bergen-Belsen under which her father was buried. She yields us a vision, a fact, and a paradoxical parable. Her story may be dismissed by some as visionary delusion, but to me in its distortions it reproduces the swirl of horror and redemption more closely than any neutralizing transcript. We write so often "against" metaphor and dream of a perfect language. It is almost too terrible to remember that, corrupted as our language is by the false figures of rhetoricians and sentimentalists, the body in pain demands a soul. There is no escape from metaphor. Even the word "literal" is a metaphor. I am convinced by the Hasidic tales that there is a vocabulary, archaic and fresh, for dealing with the extreme condition of meaning and its losses. For some, it will seem the figurative language of deluded faith. To others, it is the will to believe, stripped, pragmatic, amazed by horror as by glory. For me, it is a deposition of much of the unnaturally neutral positivism in the prose of our time.

With many, I think the very idea of a "personal response" to the Holocaust is both inevitable and enjoined and yet, in a certain sense, unbearable, seemingly wrongful. Who is the person who is strong enough to bear this catastrophe as a volunteer? I have, again like anyone, avoided the Holocaust as a subject, as a kind of personal taboo, since earliest childhood, and still am profoundly uncomfortable with the sense of it as a writer's "subject matter" unearned. The taboo is not unlike the naming of God or devil in certain sacred traditions. The issue was brought "home" to me very early and was discussed constantly in my home, both by Russian grandparents on both sides and by my own radical parents. I was so impressed by the reality of pogrom, ghetto, and death camp that I realized recently the abyss that distances me from those who can even tolerate others who disbelieve the *realia* of the Holocaust. To me, the evidence is as absolute as my skin, and the Holocaust has never been for me a parable, a metaphor, never anything less than an absolute. The Horror made so real, so unbearable, was not a subject for literature or poetry, not a subject for debate or moot court: a black hole from which no light issued. I have, thus, always been afraid that the smallest possible lightening of this black hole was a mollification, a sentimentalization. I am afraid that I have often detested the attempts, well-natured, to soften the blow by rhetoric concerning witness and memory. Rarely have I been happy with the presentation of the events. It is not just that there is no poetry after Auschwitz, as Adorno has said, but that this deletion must be a radical critique of all the arts: no artifice adequate, no music, no dance, no gesture. And the paradox of such self-consumption is such that I do not feel adequate even writing of the taboos, and I celebrate each victim's desire for witness. It does not mean that one is satisfied by any image of justice or witness. But as a believer in imperfections, I must be fair in acknowledging the unreasonableness of this taboo. And I find it increasingly reasonable to espouse an absolute promulgation of the bad news of the Holocaust. It is obvious to me now that the taboo regarding the Holocaust promotes in certain places such an ignorance that the reasonable will suspect a ploy. Was it not Hitler himself who was buoyed by the oblivion granted the Armenian disaster? Therefore, I have come to applaud those few witnesses, such as Levi, who come closest to the truthful resonance required in witnessing this black hole in history. Certain philosophers, such as Emil Fackenheim, seem to be able to bear to think it. An architect such as John Hejduk is strong enough to envision the penological architecture that must flourish after this hell and because of it. Almost every witness bends under the weight of the horror, and almost every rhetoric suspends true judgment. When I show my film classes *Night and Fog,* a few images seem sufficient, or one: the concrete ceilings of the death chambers clawed by the victims' hands. In my own life a few images have been sufficient for me to sense that I have come close to this nightmare.

When I was a teenager I had the privilege of sitting next to Elie Wiesel at a dinner at the home of my editor, Arthur A. Cohen. I was disturbed to watch the survivor as he slowly ate his meal in what seemed penitential patience. Arthur had spoken to me of the complex reaction of Elie to his father's death, and I was later to read in his books his terrible sense of the burden of surviving. I had been raised to question, and I questioned Elie that night about the Arendt thesis, then controversial, about the Jewish resistance and its adequacy. He gave me a wise and pained expression and spoke of the difficulty of acknowledging how every day one wanted and needed to protect a family and a way of life. I cannot present the precise metaphrasis of his response, but to me it annihilated forever the arrogance of her critique and substituted a disturbing human sense.

When I go to a shop in Riverdale, I ask a patron there what he thinks of the trial of Barbie. He raises an arm tattooed in the camps and makes the motion of swift execution. Again, for me, a gesture that annihilates rhetoric, the arrogance of my presumed pacifism, the poetry of justice. Not that I agree, but that momentarily I feel disbarred from speech. But who is disbarred from speech? Must not the sheltered American Jew speak?

The editor at first called this book *Sheltered Lives*. But I do not want to harp on the privileges of fin de siècle America as if one could possibly wish the catastrophe upon oneself except in dire ignorance. I am tired of the complaints of the conservative writers who, for example, suggest that Russian dissidents are superior writers because of their agon with the state. American writers have an agon, if they dispute the complacencies of empire, and the best have. The poet H.D. has a little "aesthetic" poem at the beginning of her career, "Sheltered Garden," where the virginal protagonist asks for a less cloistered life. It is important for all of us not to suggest a kind of Judaic equivalent of the fascist aestheticization of war. We do not ask for this suffering and accept it with all the involuntarism of Job or Jeremiah. The proper response is one of intransigeance, interventionism, and lamentation. The editor is correct to think of this as a story, however, and one that does indeed proceed discontinuously. I learned as a young man from a friend who was a survivor's child, and he taught me by letting the smallest of hints fall, as when he spoke of the terror of his mother during ordinary occasions, say, a thunderstorm. But my ignorance is such that I do not think that I understood until very recently how much this burden must have depressed this young thinker and how privileged I was, though my mother's story included her father's flight from Russia, fascism in Africa, and my father's participation in the war. The editor spoke of the dawning of this event upon one, and yet I must add that with each new document, with each new wave of anti-Semitism, the event continues to dawn upon me in my life. If the labyrinth of bureaucratic life was nearly ungraspable horror for Kafka, so is the ungraspable magnitude of this extraordinary, irreduceable evil.

My grandfather, to whose singing I am listening at this moment, fled the czar's army, put wax into his veins to simulate some painful condition, and escaped the Russia of pogroms and death. The sense in me from my childhood of the Jewish past is compounded of this image of distress and escape. When my mother once told me of fascists in South Africa who melted down my grandfather's recordings for bullets, I did not question the anecdote—believed in it too absolutely. But I believed in the justice and focus of the image like a Hasid. The metaphor would be that the fascists melted down the Jewish tradition for their bullets. But the immediate sanitizing positivist in me now demands something beyond images and metaphor.

Harold Rosenberg once spoke of the difficulty of film in making judgments. The problem, he sensed, in Ophuls' documentaries lies in the difficulty of making the aesthetic medium one of reason. There is no doubt that I have been most moved by the great veristic sculptors of film, Resnais, Ophuls, Lanzmann. But there is no doubt that there is both a need for the most reasonable judicial procedure, as with the surviving war criminals, and a need for the meditation upon the Holocaust that is a theological burden. Cohen's almost pantheistic sense in his meditation on "The Tremendum," his sense of meaning in meaninglessness, is a note toward an adequate philosophy of what he calls the "caesura." One may presume that Voltaire is smiling somewhere as we in our anguish discover a need for theodicy in this "caesura" of meaning, meaning in the suffering of children, but the need is there. *Only intransigeant memory protects the future of others.*

What remains for me is more than the Hasidic tales of the Holocaust, the songs of the survivors Celan and Sachs, but paradoxically the best of the poetry of our epoch. For me there is no poetry that survives that does not have as its dark margin the truth of this horror. For me, the Holocaust is the unspoken, tabooed meaning of all of our poetry, our painting, and our music. But the claim is irrationally large as Adorno's exclusions.

I dream of Germany and of being surrounded by the S.S. In my nightmare of heroism I scream in German: *Ich bin ein Jude.* When I wake in horror I consider Bruno Bettelheim's strictures concerning heroism. Bettelheim speaks even against the family of Anne Frank and how they were guilty of a passivity that led to their demise. Should they have gone into hiding when they could have resisted, gone into hiding more effectively separately, brought down an S.S. soldier or two at the end, etc.? Their false assumption, he insists, is that in a time of crisis and catastrophe they hoped beyond hope that all could continue normally. But what dismal arrogance of judgment does it take to remonstrate ex post facto with European and other Jewry? Is it not a grim geometric demonstration of Spinoza that all things wish to continue in their own form and that the Jewish family indeed attempted to keep to its peaceful norm? Yet one understands the militant rebuke.

It is this extraordinary evil that seems to displace all logic and in its own way, *more geometrico,* exists as the terrifying rebuttal to Spinoza's notion of the world as God. Spinoza's sense of shining immanence might have us completely in its thrall and, certainly, the one who placed spiders in a web and laughed to watch them fight might still have spoken of this colossal evil as an example of bondage to delusion and effects. But the pantheism here meets its colossal scandal, as does any monism that does not deal with "stubborn irreduceable evil." It cannot be wished away, it cannot be thought of as thought, and it can hardly be grasped except by a stubborn materialist intent on an effort Benjamin thought of, paradoxically, as the profane illumination of surrealism. Because this mighty horror is no dream, and truly annihilated, and annihilated difference, and it is in this spectacle of annihilation that we receive our persuasions away from Whitehead's "adventures" in ideas and civilization and zest, and toward such horrors and iniquities as the social prophets of the "Old" Testament made permanently fresh and straining. The vast evils of our time lead us to suspect that Freud was correct in his analysis of man as the aggressive animal par excellence and one who needed electric forms of sublimation lest he devour his children and his traditions. The Freud who put Civilization and its Discontents "like a lion in our path," and who escaped Hitler only to die miserably in profound exile while so many parts of his family were to die in the camps—Freud is the poet of this darkness, paradoxically, because he suggests the profound sexual deformation of this epoch and the too useless dreams of liberation from the body. Freud suggests the unblinking stare of the secular mind that refuses to be consoled.

Am I saying that wisdom, theological and political, lies within the victim? One might conceive of the opposite, rather, in Auden's Thucydidean formula that those to whom evil is done do evil in return. One of the arguments most rehearsed before me by anti-Israel rhetoricians is that the victims have been so hideously transformed as to render them incapable of moral clarity. Let us say that we are Hellenic enough to insist that wisdom is not the affair of those who have not suffered, that the suffering of Zion has indeed led to its varieties of wisdom, but that no State exists in an unchanging state of wisdom. Of course, the Holocaust is not now some sacred form of protection, nor certainly should it be used as a form of protection against political critique. But we insist again that those who have most darkly meditated upon the event have emerged with a form of tested sanity that is likely to be more than merely preservative. Our sense is that those who have not been impressed and deflected by radical evil—one thinks of our era's happy transcendentalists

—founder upon this lack. There can hardly be an aesthetics and ethics today that are not, in a sense, constructed out of the materials of this catastrophe. It deforms us as Darwin's bloody nature did his day. This is not to become, over time, a dogmatist of this Horror and to focus upon it as the only unshifting ground, but to know that much must be judged by its dark light. Like one who has suffered the death of a child and who, as Ben Jonson warns, will never love too much again, the Jew should forever have a quarrel with reality and, even as a restored Job, a skepticism in all restoration. Here, paradoxically, Arendt was correct in insisting that Israel not devote itself too confidently merely to realpolitik. The chapter after Job's restoration is the present chapter and here the folktale cannot furnish us a fideist continuance. The restored Job is still surrounded by enemies. Our analysis of the sheltered American Jew must conclude with the hope that he, too, has seen something, like the first photographs of genocide, and is changed forever by that intense truth.

Reading Delmore Schwartz's criticism, I came upon a sentence that for me could be the appropriate response to the Holocaust for an American poet. He speaks of his difficulty in understanding why Joyce should have identified so much with Jews and why the master stylist chose Jews both in *Finnegans Wake* and in *Ulysses* to be central protagonists. His answer, he says, came by way of art historian Meyer Schapiro, who suggested that the Jew for Joyce is both "alienated and indestructible." Schwartz paraphrases Schapiro's answer: " . . . he is an exile from his own country and an exile even from himself, yet he survives the annihilating fury of history." I discovered these sentences and wondered whether they could possibly have been written in the 1930s, like so many other precocious discursivities of Schwartz. But it is an essay from the 1950s and was written evidently in the darkness of the postwar years. Schwartz compares the poet and the Jew in indelible lines that for me lead to a renewed sense of the rapport between the liturgical lament and the secular style: "In the unpredictable and fearful future that awaits civilization, the poet must be prepared to be alienated and indestructible. He must dedicate himself to poetry, although no one else seems likely to read what he writes; and he must be indestructible as a poet until he is destroyed as a human being." Schwartz's unhappy consciousness is for us the most adequate response of one who tries to have faith and even love for his vocation, in the shadow of the worst. The adjective "indestructible" is particularly uncanny in the shadow of the seemingly all-consuming crematoria. And Schwartz's sanity prevails when he notes the mortality of the individual, the eternity of the vocation.

Remembering the Holocaust is our vocation. It is a paradoxical inversion of Spinoza's intellectual love of God as virtue. It is virtue itself in our time, our elegiac vocation to seek to understand what the theologian has called this Caesura, this Tremendum. It is an evil so huge that it produces a kind of reverse proof of the existence of God. It is an evil so terrifying that it becomes our most significant injunction to wrest a kind of atonal, disjunct meaning from it. It is for this the humiliated schoolteacher brings out a copy of the documentaries and attempts to stare at it again in the darkness. It is this that makes us want to understand the blue lettering of the tattoo on our neighbor's arm. It is for this reason that we applaud the rabbi in prisoner's clothing attempting to satirize the president when he makes a dismal gesture at Bitburg. It is for this reason that we are all involved in a kind of collaboration, a conspiratorial work so that the meaning of Israel will not be besmirched or beclouded by current events.

For me, poetry has always been aspiring to the condition of the liturgical elegies I heard my grandfather sing. A great cantor, Berele Chagy reached perhaps his greatest art in an improvised elegy for the dead of the Warsaw Ghetto. In this Bach-like fugal structure, I heard what for me in music was the true sense of anguish and dread and acceptance. Music for me is always aspiring to the condition of this passionate speech, and poetry is thus never truly cut off from music. Poetry for me of the New York School, for example, always was problematic when it was simply hedonistic or Lucretian, always close to being a secular abomination when it listed the ripest pleasures on the table, as if to ignore the horrors before the feasts. My poetry began with the image of the synagogue and chanting, even of the string quartet playing as if surrounded by bombs. I have in my own mind a sense that there was an infantile confusion in me between the possibilities of the nuclear apocalypse and the Holocaust. There is no doubt that I have judged every expression of art and artifice with this in mind: How does it measure to what has seemed the eschatological realities of the age? It is not Proust's musicality but the asthmatic prophet caricaturing an epoch that has been most coruscating for me in him. Kafka, the author who seems most realist for an age of this black labyrinth, I have also found to be the most obvious guide and friend. It is too sad, for all of us, that it is his diaries, his letters, as well as the most crushed of the parables, in which we find the photographic meditation on our system and the systems of persecution. If there has been any reason why Ginsberg's *Howl* or *Kaddish* particularly moved me as a boy, it was the sense that he was not merely an infant exaggerating the lament for friends, but actually performing a liturgical function in raising his voice for a part of Europe inside America. It is not a matter of the rational critique of such poetry's imprecision, the response to such poetry is at the least an indication of the emptiness of alternatives in an age that demanded mourning.

I was pleased to discover on my thirtieth birthday a Talmudic defense for the species of aphasia, agrammatism, sound disturbance, meaning disturbance, and the whole panoply of cubo-futurist devices that we identify with the elegiac in modern poetry. The mourner is relieved in ancient Jewish law of the following of many of the responsibilities of the mitzvot. The mourner in his despair is characterized by speechlessness. "How can the mourner," says Soloveitchik in luminous commentary, "pronounce the benediction or say amen if he is speechless?" (Legalism leads to a kind of comedy, where the weak mourner is urged, if he cannot summon the strength to tear his clothes, to have someone *tear it for him.*) But we may learn of the responsibilites and permissions of poetry from this. The poetry of aphasia and *kindersprache* is the cry of the mourner. The dead lie before us and we are spared; we are exempt also from the more symmetrical and the most balanced of our obligations. As a matter of fact, the formless *nigun* has become the obligation of our truer mourning. It is this Rimbaldien sense of a proper formlessness that is thus shown through Jewish law as compassion for per-plexed suffering man. The grand permissions of surrealism, as in the despairing love poem of Desnos, revised even in a death camp, are not often glimpsed as permissions to mourn. The agrammatism of this poetry is that of man who has nearly lost faith in himself. The palpabilities of poetry are elegiac possibili-ties. The task of poetry, as after the interment, is "to reestablish itself."

Paul Roubicek once suggested that the Heideggerian philos-ophy did not lead necessarily toward Nazism and the worst but did not contain enough substance to restrain from it. Our best poetry must be an instrumentality of self-restraint, a poetry of detail, detailed as our law and its permissions to mourn. In de-tail, in mourning and not melancholy, this poetry aspires to the condition of those private acts of heroism of which it is said only the Lord appreciates. Here we place a name such as Paul Celan and Primo Levi and Nelly Sachs.

I am in a little military garden in Europe, summer, 1973. With me, a French family, an engineer entranced by literature, his little children, my wife and his, as we delight in the miniature train running nearby like a carousel of pleasure. I stop to gaze at the walls of the cemetery and note, with my poor French, the poem I have most loved by Desnos: "I have dreamed of you so much, slept so much with your shadow, walked and talked with you so much, that now nothing remains of you but your shadow. It remains for me to be a shadow among the shadows, to be one million times more shadow than the shadow that will come and come again into your sunny life." My friend laughs, "The old surrealists now have good jobs and get the right poems on the walls." But I am staggered. The effect of these words, which I realize immediately emerge from the revision of a longer Desnos poem, is overwhelming. I see these poems in Desnos' hand in the death camp. I sense the heroism of this little love poem against all the ashes of the crematoria. The victory of this poem and its elegiac condensation seem complete. It is so much like Frank O'Hara's penetrating question: "But is the earth as full, as life was full, of them?" I am not speaking of consolation and its deceptions, but of the extraordinary eruptive possibilities of poetry "in a dark time." The obsessive shadow of Desnos in this little love poem, carved for the war dead, is an example of the victory of surrealism too often said to have failed. The oneiric in this poem is also its common sense: We are what haunts us, as Breton said. This, for me, was another dawning of the sense of the Holocaust and of the proper political response to it: the heroic intransigeant poem of love, if you will permit me a French flourish or classical figure and forgive the mistranslation from memory.

To conclude these fragmentary responses is to remember that they are, by nature, ongoing, partial hypotheses and hints. To many, there will be something almost obscene in the fact that so much of our focus is on the seemingly absurd aesthetic question of what kind of art must emerge after the Holocaust. Our pluralist answer will not seem too helpful, since we accept both the chiseled condensations of Celan and the veristic expositions of Levi's prose and the great film documents. There do not seem, thus, to be stylistic lessons to be learned from catastrophe. If anything, we are polarized toward two great masters; in Kafka and in Proust, we receive inner and outer prophets of the Holocaust. Both of them predict the systems of persecution, Proust from the scientific vantage point of the Dreyfus affair and its social sequels and Kafka with his uncanny and sublime analysis of the authoritarian momentum. The personal shelter for the writer in our time may be an architectural weave of Proust and Kafka. We know this may seem bare to some, but we affirm that from our tradition we accept both radiant belief and the investigation of belief itself, as in the pluralist work of Scholem and Schapiro. The unrelenting pressure of their radiant rationality drives us toward a great skepticism in systems and myths. As a relative irrealist, I ask no artist to go forth and unblinkingly confront the Holocaust. but I take it that the catastrophe of our epoch, called "the worst yet" by the ironical poet, stands as one of the fiery standards by which our lives and work must be judged. We do not address the issue of a second Holocaust, but we know that even triumphant assimilation cannot delete our sense of a haunting future which we ask in advance, like good Russian futurists, to resurrect us.

In 1954, my father tells me that my grandfather has died—I rush up the block to the synagogue. My grandmother, founder of Pioneer Women and Zionist, sobs to me that he would have so loved to see my bar mitzvah. Others tell me that he has died singing: the best death. My grandfather's art of liturgical singing had made him a hero both as a boy and as a chief cantor in Brooklyn and in South Africa. To me, the image of his davening at age five and his fleeing persecutions in Russia formed a tremendous and lifelong inspiration toward my poetry. So much of his art was arcane to me, but as I became a violinist his prayers became a canon. Drafted in 1968, I told a history professor at Columbia that my grandfather had fled Russia to escape the inevitable death of Jewish boys in the czar's army: that he had left his country during political tensions, had left South Africa when the fascists were taking control, and that I his grandson was preparing to leave America. After this slightly hysterical speech, the historian erupted with a bit of Dickensian glee, "Full circle, eh, Mr. Shapiro?" I didn't have to leave America, but I have sensed, during my study of the Holocaust, how the image of my grandfather and his brother fleeing Russia formed for me the earliest image of the survivor. The image of him mutilating his body, my grandmother's recitals of terrifying pogroms, her Zionism and love of literary Hebrew—all of these were principles and portents. My mother idolized him and spoke of him as a rare combination of genius and kindness. She even harped on his experimental side, as he and his friend Joseph Achron would listen to jazz in Harlem. The connection for me between music, poetry, and the indestructible Jew has been complete since childhood, when I screamed, it is reported, "That is my grandfather!" during a service. I see him walking slowly through the streets of Newark and hear his voice during our last family Passover: strong and untrameled and sweet, voice of the survivor, for me.

Helen

GRACE SCHULMAN

In my childhood, there was no actual peril. I wore starched pinafores, ate turkey with an attentive family, and lived only a walk from the Hayden Planetarium. On Saturdays, I was taken to Carnegie Hall. I went to good schools and expected to go to college. All the same, I sensed that some demon waited to destroy us all.

Even before "the war," as we called World War Two, I was acquainted with that fear. On the Knabe piano in the West Eighty-sixth Street apartment of my childhood, there were portraits of people who experienced danger and people who imagined it. Often I watched them move and invented stories about them, for my mother arranged and rearranged our family photographs in silver rectangles, in golden ovals with velvet mattes, and in brass squares with scroll-shaped edges. She collected those frames from junk shops on Third Avenue, and although she let them darken and develop shadowy crevices, she changed their locations the way a director places his actors, giving them life.

Some of the pictures were of my American relatives. Others were of living kin I had not met, such as my paternal grandparents. Having left Poland with two of their daughters in the 1930s, they raised vegetables and some livestock in Israel, and already possessed the grained, lizardlike skin of farmers with years of exposure to the sun and the wind.

Another photograph was of the family just before the move to Israel, when my grandparents and three daughters traveled from Warsaw to Danzig, then an autonomous city on the Baltic seacoast, to meet their son and his new wife. My father had asked that they assemble there rather than in Warsaw, which held memories of poverty and oppression. My parents had sailed for that encounter, and had returned from Berlin, on the S.S. *Bremen*'s last passenger voyage to America.

In that portrait, family members exaggerated their roles, as though they were the beams of a crumbling structure. My father stood stiffly with my mother, who blended adventurously with the foreigners despite the leggy stance, the knitted suit, and cloche hat of a New Yorker with generations of American Jews behind her. My father was emulating his father, who sat erect and stern, next to his smiling wife. Posing as authoritative, my grandfather was actually a reticent man given to a lifetime of study in the house. With them were the pretty aunts wearing man-tailored suits and neckties.

Still another photograph, an enlargement in an ivory frame, was of Helen, one of the aunts who, in the family picture, stood looking off to one side. "She was a lovely sprite," my mother said of her sister-in-law. "That time in Danzig, she had just earned her degree in medicine and wanted to cut loose. She sent postcards to all of her boyfriends (there were quite a few), and she scrawled, 'I love you very much' on every one."

To me, Helen's face was not simply carefree. Her gaze was soft and yet insistent; her smile was compassionate but icy. Her prim black dress was edged with maidenly lace and, unexpectedly, cut low. Like women I had seen in a movie of *Ivan the Terrible*, she had high cheekbones and wide-set eyes that were trusting and, at the same time, sharply inquisitive. Then as now, I have noticed that she looks older than her sisters and brother, and yet more vulnerable. Unlike them, she seems careless of her appearance, as though any risk is worth taking that will forgo surface vanities for deeper truths.

Often I glanced at her mouth, then turned away in terror. She seemed to be straining to speak to me, angrily, of hardship and pain, and of a fierce price she paid to be alive, even then, as a young woman in Poland.

I was drawn to Helen even before I learned, after the war, that Helen had died in the Warsaw ghetto uprising in 1943. Her picture remained where it was, and often my parents would pause to look at her. During that time, I must have stared at her frequently, for the piano was central to my family of musicians manqués. We all played, though woodenly, and while waiting for some heavenly sign that would improve my scales, I would wander to the bookshelves, where I heard my real music in volumes of poetry and, returning to the piano, fasten my eyes, somewhat desperately, on those photos. I remember Helen's name (actually Helena, but my parents Anglicized it), although I have forgotten many other names of the time. For me there were groups, such as children, classmates, relatives, workers, Democrats, Communists. Then there were individuals: Deborah, Persephone, Antigone, Helen.

Helen was the second oldest of three boys and three girls in my father's family of Łódź, a city south of Warsaw, in Poland. When their home was destroyed in an anti-Semitic demonstration, my grandparents fled with three of the children to Włocławek, while the oldest boy, Jan, Helen, and my father remained in Łódź to study. Jan died of a chest infection, having suffered poor health since he caught pneumonia while serving in the Polish army early in the century. He had fought in a skirmish when the Russians entered Poland in an effort to dominate that country. After Jan's death, Helen returned to her parents' home in Włocławek. Driven by fear, by the wish to be educated and the need to survive, my father left Poland for Germany and then England, where he studied law at the University of London before emigrating to America, then finished school at City College in New York. After brief careers as an actor and as a lawyer, he started a small advertising agency that he managed for the rest of his long life. A younger brother had joined my father here, and the sisters remained with their parents in Poland.

My grandmother, who opened a shop in Włocławek, sent Helen to medical school in Warsaw. Years later, when her brothers spoke of how she bandaged cuts and massaged her mother's shoulder, I resented their condescension. I assumed that she earned her education by earning higher grades than the others had. Her gentleness, I felt, was a myth: I envisioned her stealing apples from a shopkeeper who had ridiculed her for wearing drab clothes. I imagined she was annoyed with her brothers and her colleagues for valuing women doctors not because of their competence but for the doctor's role as nurturer. I do know that she was furious when professors called her "that one," asked her religion on examinations, and forced her to stand in back of an amphitheater during lectures even when there were empty seats.

My father told me that Helen had introduced him and his brother Jan to the poems of Adam Mickiewicz. He tried to teach me Polish when I was a child and, believing he had succeeded, recited that poet's ballad of love's triumph over reason, in words I did not understand. Years later, I gave him W. H. Auden's translation of the poem "The Romantic," and he read it aloud, but without the rough, emotive, declamatory strains that awakened me to poetry. The language sounded like a clarinet's low notes, like bells, and like arias in a production of *Boris Godunov* I had seen with my family. He, Jan, and Helen had shared German poems as well, notably Heine's and Goethe's, the acquisition of European languages being simpler for that border-inhabiting Jew than for his linguistically inept daughter. Although he was reluctant to speak of his past for fear of igniting anguish, he retained the poems all of his life and declaimed them in vehement tones. As for me, then as now my ear has been tuned to English poetry. Even in the years of those Polish recitals, I leaned toward my maternal grandfather's readings of Longfellow and Oliver Goldsmith. Nevertheless, those words I did not understand were, for me, the fire of language.

I imagined Helen speaking the poems my father had intoned, in that bellowing utterance close to song. I thought of her narrowing her eyes and trying to concentrate on the poems, trying to focus on her studies, trying to ignore the inequalities that were imposed on her. Later I realized she struggled through winters of chest colds and of hunger, her drafty room less of a trial than loneliness. Her worst pain, I know now, was in being deprived of a name and a voice by professors who taunted her and who made silence her price for attending school. At the time, though, before the war, I suppose I scanned Helen's photograph without comprehending why I sensed resentment. Next to her on the piano was a picture of me in a sailor's middy, writing alphabet letters in a notebook. We had the same eyes, the same cheekbones. I saw in her a darker version of myself.

Early in the 1930s, my parents learned that the family had emigrated to Israel. One of the sisters, Beta, joined a kibbutz, and the others settled nearby. Only Helen, who married Władek Gold, did not leave. She and her husband, both pediatricians, remained in Warsaw with their medical practices.

"Helen felt that she was needed in Warsaw," my mother said in around 1940, when I searched Helen's picture to fathom her decision. At the time Helen was lost to us, but her fate was still uncertain. "Helena Waldman-Gold," my mother mused. "That's what she called herself. She kept her maiden name by hyphenating it. I'm certain it was her wish to stay, and not anything Władek asked her to do. There were hundreds of children in that sector, and only a few doctors. She'd thought the Nazis dared not touch them in that position.

"It's complicated," my mother continued, as though trying to assure herself of some hidden wisdom in Helen's decision. "She was afraid, yes, but she felt she had as much right to her country as we do to ours. Her patients trusted her, and she wanted to help them with her skills. She thought it would be safe for her and Władek, and perhaps she was right. Perhaps they are still alive."

My father had a different view of Helen's choice. "Headstrong," he said. "If only she had listened. She never listened. So, go on. Be a hero." He glanced at me as he spoke, and I knew what he meant. All Jews must be cautious in order to survive, but Jewish women must bend to authority. It would have been better for Helen to believe her father's stern demeanor in the photograph, rather than in his actual meekness. She should have followed her husband, who, my father assumed, did not wish to remain in Warsaw.

I remember his remonstrance because it was the last time he discussed Helen's behavior. In the years that followed, he became depressed when he did things other than his work. There were times when he recited no poems and hardly spoke at all, for language only heightened his terror. Occasionally he would break the silence to utter undue concern about the warmth of my clothes or the safety of the local skating rink. Sometimes he would look at my hair, which I wore in long braids, as she had, and call me by her name.

My father's silences fell beyond the far reaches of my memory, and I can only reconstruct what I cannot recall of the Hitler period. For us in America, it was a time of distortion, when our ignorant suspicion gave rise to luminous horror fantasies. In that mysterious atmosphere, the evasion of hope was deemed more dangerous than denial, because more cowardly. Before the war, the news of persecution was gradual, and there was reason to think that some Jews might be spared. After 1941, we woke to the mass annihilation of millions of European Jews to find that our trust was gone and our fantasies were feeble imitations of the Nazi atrocities. By 1942, the newspapers were filled with rumors of death camps and mass graves and forced marches in the name of a proposed Final Solution for the Jewish populace.

In retrospect, the adults' illusions during the early and middle 1930s seem understandable in the light of scant facts, the perception that anti-Semitic acts were not born in the decade, and the climate of faith in America and in the world. In the family photograph taken in Danzig, my parents' faces shone with an optimism I have never understood but have always known to be genuine. Once my mother recalled, self-ironically, that when she and my father stopped in Berlin en route to New York, "They were beginning to play those German songs, and men in uniform wore armbands with swastikas. I asked your father what those swastikas were, and he said, 'I don't know. Perhaps they are meant to identify the blind.' "

Whether or not she recounted that incident in my childhood I do not know, but I'm certain it was central to my concept of the Nazis. Often I dreamed of blind uniformed men on blind horses leading a blind population, naked and on foot, to their death.

Reality was no less surreal, or so it seems to me now. In 1933, with Hitler's rise to power, my family knew the Nazis had burned books by Jews and non-Jews and had boycotted Jewish stores. In 1938, they were aware of Kristallnacht, "the night of broken glass," in Germany, when Jews were beaten and their store windows were smashed. They knew of the deportations of Jews in Germany and of the harassment of Jews in Poland even before the Nazi invasion of 1939. Helen's letters stopped coming at about that time, and my father enlisted Jewish organizations to find her. Recently I discovered a radiogram from Poland, dated December 15, 1939, addressed to my father and signed "Kuba Szejnberg," bearing the legend, "Delayed in USSR." The message read, "WALDMANOWNA LIVES ADDRESS UNKNOWN ANSWER QUICKEST." It was his last futile hope.

Memory began to assume sequential form for me during the war years, when refugees from France and Germany came to live in my neighborhood, struggling to put down roots in America. Many of the settlers were women, and I inferred that *refugee,* which rhymed with *flee,* meant *woman in flight,* or the woman who must run and hide before her rebellious demon stirred her to express disobedience to the man in her household who posed as the stern father image, such as the one in the Danzig photograph. They must leave, I thought, before the blue numbers appeared, those marks that were tattooed painfully on their arms in invisible ink to tell the compliant from the troublesome.

Once I asked my friend Joan Kenney, a gentile, if she and her mother had to hide until the war was over. I knew that her parents were divorced and that her father, who lived in London, might not see Joan until the war was over.

"Hide? No. We are safe here in America. That's what Mr. Wolf said today. Does your family have faith in America?" I could not ask my stricken father or my mother, who tried to shield him by diminishing the tragedy.

Despite the religious difference, I made little distinction between Joan's situation and mine, an impulse to which I may have been bred. My family detested discrimination and denied the importance of boundaries between people. By and large, they chose camps and schools that ignored those divisions as well. They believed that persecution of any minority group was a threat to any other, and maintained that conviction when events might have pressed for a partisan stance.

They persisted in that view even though they knew an anti-Semitism that I had not, as a child, encountered. My father remembered it from the Poland he left. After that, he experienced university prejudice in London. Then his best friend, a scientist, had been refused a teaching position at Yale. My father would throw down his newspaper when he read vitriolic speeches by Father Coughlin, and his face would darken when he heard radio reports of demonstrations by American Isolationists who blamed the Jews for America's having to enter the war. From polite gentiles, they heard so many insults to Jews, ranging from subtle to gross, that they prefaced all such conversations by identifying their religion. "I don't like the *galut* Jew," my father said, using a word that meant "exile." "The *galut* Jew tries to forget his heritage. That's a terrible mistake."

My mother's family were Zionists, her father a lawyer who, as president of a Brooklyn yeshiva, had run a series of poetry readings there by Hebrew writers, including Bialik, who visited in the twenties. On a wall over Grandfather's desk hung a framed letter from Supreme Court Justice Brandeis thanking him for his help in founding the village of Herzlia, which was then in Palestine. His wedding trip had been to Palestine, and when he died, my parents spared his aged mother by telling her he had gone to visit a kibbutz in Israel. For them, the cure for prejudice against blacks, women, Jews, and other minorities was to be found in the kibbutz, which promised justice for all.

It was only after the war, though, that Israel held that trust, both because of the formation of the state and the end of gloom. Our synagogue helped in that regard, and also assured me of women's privilege. It bore the unwieldy name of the Society for the Advancement of Judaism. At my bat mitzvah, Rabbi Ira Eisenstein asserted that freedom for one minority was freedom for all and that Israel would be the place for the new equality. He spoke of the Jewish heritage as a gift and of womanhood as a blessing. "Seize the day and follow your heritage," he told me from the pulpit. "Women are natural leaders, and wise women leaders are common in Jewish history. Besides, no boy could have sung your haftorah as well as you did."

That confidence, however, came years after we learned the terrible answers to what had occurred in Europe. During the war, only patriotic faith in our Allies would deliver us from evil. The war's despair taught my parents that restraint was the price paid for American sanctuary. Subdued as he was, my father admired Kafka and Rilke, especially in passages of anguish. Nevertheless, he found that silent resignation was his only armor for protecting his coherence as an individual in a world where protest had lost its meaning and where decency and even life depended on preserving one's own free square yard. Silence was essential in dealing with the Holocaust that haunted our home without ever entering it.

For some time after they knew of Helen's death, my parents collected books with photographs of Nazi desecration. They kept them on the shelves along with books they thought unsuitable for a young girl, hoping to avoid censorship while permitting me *not* to read about human devastation. The records of horror had *The Black Book* in their titles and were published between 1942 and 1946. One that I remember vividly was *The Black Book: The Nazi Crime Against the Jewish People.* * The bindings were black, as their names implied, and flimsy; the pages were brittle and yellow even when they were new.

Apparently my parents had no qualms about my reading Joyce's *Ulysses* and Lawrence's *Lady Chatterley's Lover,* or even books by Henry Miller and Frank Harris, for these were in a different room. On the Black Books' shelves were less literary erotic books, but they didn't stir when I reached for them. It was only when I looked at the Black Books that my mother seemed worried and told me once that I needn't feel I had to read them. It was then I associated the Holocaust with pornography.

The last of the books was filled with black-and-white photographs. I pored over the pictures: There were prisoners digging graves for other prisoners who were led to the pits, stripped, their hands covering their private parts. On mounds there were chains of naked, dead, emaciated bodies, bodies in hell, bodies distorted, tortured, misshapen. I thought of a painting I had

---

* Three of the books referred to here are, *The Black Book of Poland* (New York: Putnam, 1942); *The Black Book of Polish Jewry: An Account of the Martyrdom of Polish Jews Under the Nazi Occupation,* edited by Jacob Apenszlak, Jacob Kenner, and Isaac Lewin (New York: American Federation of Polish Jews, 1943); *The Black Book: The Nazi Crime Against the Jewish People* (New York: The Jewish Black Book Committee, 1946).

seen of *The Last Judgment* by Jan van Eyck, at the Metropolitan Museum of Art nearby. The painting had disturbed me, and when I studied the photographs, I knew why. As I stared at the camp victims, the corpses lost their distinctions and became one corpse, in one solid mass of horror. Only the faces were diversified, and Helen's face, in the picture I knew of her, was superimposed on each one. Gradually, as on film in developing solution, each face became Helen's. Then each face became mine.

When the Allied victory ended the nightmare image of the Holocaust, it also made that picture a concrete reality. A letter came from Beta, one of the aunts in Israel, who had news of Helen from a refugee organization. Still unable to speak of Helen, my father did not show the letter at home but did give it to Rabbi Eisenstein, who published it in the synagogue newsletter. Helen had moved to the Warsaw ghetto, where her husband had died in a typhoid epidemic. She believed she would be deported to a concentration camp, for there were rumors of the forthcoming ghetto liquidation. A survivor of Auschwitz, then in Israel, reported that he had known Helen in the ghetto. He said that he had seen her climb the tower of a municipal building, run to the ledge and pull down the Polish flag from its staff. With a strength that seemed to startle her, she ripped the flag into shreds. Then she stood for a while, holding the red cloth and smiling, before she was shot down by a Nazi guard. "It was an act of revenge on the Poles for having given her away," Beta wrote. "Her act gave that man courage to survive."

Even then, I had some murky knowledge of a truth that was to clarify in later years: Helen valued active death over a victim's life, and in her act she celebrated the dignity of life and affirmed the will to survive. As a Jew, she had to be governed by a doctrine that is central to our faith: "Therefore choose life, that thou and thy seed shall live."

> *We dance to songs*
> *in a world below ice, below time,*
> *sleepwalk to laws*
> *that manage our acts,*

I wrote years later in a poem, "Letter to Helen," assuming that she believed in the biblical injunction, whether or not she could summon it to memory. At the same time, the life she chose was built on a sequence of deeds, one following the other in a cause-and-effect relationship. She opted for the precarious life of a Jewish medical student in Warsaw; she elected to bear the hazards of Poland; and she risked her life to save her young patients. In choosing death, she held for the highest life she knew.

At the time, the news of Helen restored reason to us in New York. The facts did not lessen the impact of either the Holocaust or our personal loss, but they gave us a way to deal with both. My father's knowledge of Helen's death enabled him to read about other disasters. His silences abated as he examined the newspaper accounts, studied the Black Books, and began to absorb the extent of destruction. Although his scars were never to heal, he did resume a buoyant life. I remember him during those years of restoration. He would send roses and a book to a new friend or try to play a Chopin Nocturne and, recognizing failure, leap up and coax my mother and me to accompany him to Carnegie Hall. In time he grew well.

As for me, the distorted, dreamlike images of the Holocaust gave way to waking realities that were more painful, in some ways. At the war's end, when I first heard the word Holocaust, translated then from the French *"l'holocauste,"* I thought of a monster with a *"hollow caste,"* which, in one of the languages I could not learn, meant no face and no name, who came out of a bog and avenged himself by changing people into fragments of one body, faceless, voiceless, nameless. Defending us against it were comic-strip fighters with X-ray guns who would protect our Government and its Laws, Democracy and its Institutions, and Freedom. I saw life, then, as a struggle between social morality and supernatural evil, a battle that had been enacted in headlines and radio broadcasts.

As the details of horror accumulated force, I saw the monster with the "hollow caste" change into an evil system. The nameless mass altered to become victims, people slaughtered by actual people. Helen's deed had transformed our fantasies because she asserted her name. She fought back. She refused to be brought low. Her act offered a clear view of what we could not imagine. It gave us words for the unutterable.

As far as I dare speculate on matters of influence, I would say that Helen's death had much to do with my being a writer, but little to do with the kind of writer I became. Her fierce individuality enabled me to see myself and every other being as distinct from any other. My early fantasy of the victim as one solid mass of flesh changed, after her noble death, to a picture of separate bodies, torn, defiled, and desecrated, but human.

Nevertheless, her culture was not my culture. Her lofty example was no more aesthetic than my father's melodic recitations in Polish and German were literary experiences, sustaining though they were. A child of my time and place, I wrote out of gratitude to works that were composed in English and to the icons and the frescoes that had inspired them. I remember visiting a synagogue when I was a child and hearing in prayers a passionate sorrow I wanted to capture in language. My way of transforming that quality of sorrow was through English accents and rhythms, learned from Donne, Herbert, and, especially, Hopkins:

Mine, O thou Lord of life, send my roots rain.

It is a commonplace that one's deepest voice is that of another. I became myself when, hearing the music of Hopkins, I wrote in the voice of a Jew named Helen, praising life in her manner.

Helen's act taught me an integrity that was threatened during the postwar years. My enemy then was a steamroller like the radical "metaphysical" image in Marianne Moore's poem, "To a Steam Roller," who would "crush all the particles down/into close conformity, and then walk back and forth on them." It was a time when people were pressed into molds according to social utility: Women were thought to pursue writing only when they were free from household chores; men were poured into casts labeled "provider" and "authority."

My parents proclaimed their Jewish culture despite the backlash from fellow workers who made stereotypes of Jews and other minorities. I remember one of my father's visits to anti-Semitic clients, cotton-mill manufacturers in Durham, North Carolina. For months he had chafed at representing the mill owner, who accepted my father because he did not detect in him characteristics he disparaged. This gracious bigot invited my father to his home and announced that customarily he honored guests by asking them to say grace before evening meals. He called on my father, who reached for a silk, hand-rolled handkerchief, knotted it at the corners, placed it on his head, and said, "*Baruch atah adonai . . .*" then continued the prayer to the end. His host was startled, but curious. "It's the original," my father intoned. When my father told me the story, the handkerchief reminded me of Helen's Polish flag and all it taught us about the need to stand fast.

My father's assertion was no upheaval, but it did the job, and perhaps its modest scale was the only one suitable to his way of life. An actor turned businessman, he was at once alive to self-expression and bound by custom, torn between his sympathy for those in misery and his commitment to the necessities of his world. Although I understood his dilemma, I knew that I could never accept such a burden.

In the 1960s, when I was in graduate school, there was less pressure to conform. Patriotism, too, was less compelling. Even before Vietnam, the war in Korea, for example, had thrown to doubt the faith in a system that would set things right and the wisdom of trading lives for doctrine. The news of brutality from trusted sources lowered the status of what we called heroism. Abnormal prowess was suspect, for it was clear that World War Two was the last war for which a rationale could be found. And still, even as we aired our conviction that peace was the only acceptable standard, the Vietnam War grew out of control and beyond the range of our protests. For years we felt estranged.

During that period, my own poems were in crisis. To write of events that mattered, I had to maintain my trust in human rightness. I wanted to create grounds for hope and to invent reasons for confidence in worthy men and women. Around me artists, suffering for the oppressed, tried to rid their work of the imagery and archetypes that spoke for uniqueness. On the contrary, I had to believe in heroism. For me, song was praise.

For heroes I turned inward, to my imagination, and to literature. The standard, for me in those days, was Beowulf, the ruler of the Anglo-Saxon epic, who was, I believe, an exemplar of peace. Never appearing in battle scenes between human warriors, Beowulf fights not men but demons who visit evil on mankind. He destroys Grendel and, in an underwater cave, Grendel's mother, both fiends that are devouring the people; he slays a firedragon that has ravaged the country; he kills sea monsters that attack him while he swims to Finland. Beowulf ("bee-keeper") is a man who, above all, protects order against the monsters that threaten it, monsters that, in modern terms, can be seen as violent components of the self, irrational impulses that come up from some rank place and must be defeated. He was, I felt, a defender of tranquillity in a poem that cried peace even in times of slaughter.

Beowulf moves me to this day. In recent years, I saw in the British Museum glass cases filled with objects belonging to a seventh-century Anglo-Saxon king who may have been a prototype of Beowulf. The objects were found in the remains of a large boat in August 1939—curiously just before the blitzkrieg that preceded the war—at Sutton Hoo, on Suffolk's River Deben, near the North Sea.

My poem, "Sutton Hoo Ship Burial," ends:

> *As he loomed out of the sea to tell his story*
> *of mud-drenched creatures in the mind's black waters*
>
> *who thrashed ungoverned ghosts at the sea's edge,*
> *I find my house in a stone, my world in acorns,*
> *my solitude in galleys holding bowls,*
> *bronze stags, gold buckles, swords inlaid with garnets,*
> *stars locked in hollows, hidden and revealed,*
> *invisible, asleep, burning to live.*
> *In rocks I will know eels and sea-anemones*
> *before I surface into murderous air.*

Another of my fictional heroes was the protagonist of Bertolt Brecht's *Mother Courage,* the black marketeer in a corrupt system who sacrifices her own humanity to survive. Her daughter Kattrin, on the other hand, a mute who cannot overcome her virtuous impulses, climbs a ladder, sits on a roof, and plays a drum to warn the people of the enemy's approach. She is shot down. While Mother Courage finds ways of evading the evil system, innocent Kattrin confronts it. Her act is useless in a collective world, a world of victims.

At the time I considered the term "heroism" in the traditional sense, as an aesthetic designation, rather than to describe good deeds in the modern world. In classical tragedy, the hero is not simply a morally inspiring man or woman, but is one who holds fast to some permanent value beyond our practical needs. Their acts might alter our existence and affirm the cosmic order. The heroes of Sophocles, for example, protest against the limitations of being merely human. Each of them struggles with a "necessity" that, greater than any social problem, is the acknowledgment of life's smallness and is defeated by a "destiny" that is intrinsic to his character. The hero falls knowing, and restores universal harmony.

Since then, the notion of heroism has remained a luminous question. If the hero of classical tragedy is one who transforms the cosmic order, there is a notable lack of accord today as to what that order might be. People of different ideologies will disagree about stature. Recently, though, I have been attracted to deeds that affirm integrity in a world that would urge conformity. The hero's search for identity would be futile today in a society that encourages uniformity. Although no person can affect collective history, perhaps the outstanding individual can withstand those pressures and retain a singular vision.

When I consider that quest for identity, I think of Helen. What distinguishes her for me is that I remember her name, and I will. Her act was iconic, for it drew the imagination and engaged the memory. Her achievement was to be permanent, for it depended on her absolute conviction of right and wrong.

I picture her, always, standing on that roof, holding the torn Polish flag, knowing she would be shot, or would leap, to her death. Her gesture saved no one, nor did it alter the social order, let alone the cosmic one. Nor was her stance a protest in the name of an ideology. If she inspired other sufferers, I doubt that it was her goal. Helen was simply being what she was and doing what she had to do. She could not accept a passive death. She declined to walk, naked, to her death. The indignity of a concentration camp was a price she could not pay, not even for the hope of staying alive. Her very freedom, in fact, had forced her to climb those steps to her death, as though inertness had become repellent to her sense of life as a series of committed choices, and sinful to the conscience that sense had created.

Instructed by her example, my father did what he had to do, modestly but well. As for me, I learned from Helen's uniqueness the value of selfhood. Her courage established the importance of the freedom to act. As a link in a chain of faces, voiceless and nameless, I could not speak. Only with my face, my voice, and my name could I even begin to grope in the dark for words.

No Market
for Lamentations

DAVID ROSENBERG

1

I remember "The voice of the turtle." It was printed in large letters with curlicues, and perched on top: a pigeon. I was six years old and I knew turtles couldn't speak. Yet I never asked; everything about the atmosphere of the family Seder had double meanings, from the food and the plates to the songs and rituals. Parents were children—they made themselves drunk and put bed pillows on their chairs; and children were parents—they had the key prayer to recite and held the key to completing the service, the stolen matzah.

Each year I understood more, yet the mystery deepened: This was the year's most important family occasion and on it the grown-ups pretended to be children, more and more. By the time I was twelve I was articulate enough to ask my own questions: You don't really believe in miracles, you don't really believe that Elijah comes in to sip from his cup, so why do you pretend?

The first book I knew was the Haggadah. It was a real book, not a child's, because the adults all read from it in Zaydeh's serious language, Hebrew, then repeated it all in the King's English translationese. Before I could read, it was the first book I saw my parents read together, and my mother's parents. Later, I learned how this book was made, collaging centuries, making homes more poignant than temples, bringing down the balcony of the shul where the women and children were kept. It became my model for a book that I shamelessly dreamed of composing, more audacious and more humble than any other, against which all lesser books strained, awkward and overblown. The homely Haggadah, unlike Bibles, paraded no holiness, included jokes, songs in slang, and instructions for getting drunk.

If childhood is a time for collecting the problems we spend the rest of our lives solving, then mine all came together at the Passover Seder. There I could see whole, if not solve, the enigma of the parent and the child, discovering both contained within me. I couldn't understand whether the adults did or did not believe in the miracles, particularly of Elijah's entering the opened door. I received mixed messages, as if they wanted me to decide for myself. Part of us is pretending, but part of us is believing—so the parents seemed to be saying. Slowly I understood that both parts were within me, the child believing, and the adult I was growing into, pretending. Pretending belief—for the sake of protecting the child, his awe in the company of the grown-ups. Without the child's awe—his unmediated emotional response—the adult was limited; with it, a direct link remained to the Exodus miracles of liberation.

How severe is the adult limitation I learned only when struck by the Holocaust's evil a second time, at age twelve, a return of the repressed. It was then I recognized that smiling cousins and stern grandparents in pictures, family in the old country, were not those left behind or lost in a terrible calamity, but lives exterminated by their host civilization—much as if the adults at the Seder were to turn on the children. That would be the most frightening injustice, childhood—humanity, civilization—revealed as a cruel illusion. Yet that was what I understood the Holocaust was, and my response was a terrible anger, as now the adult in me—not the child—could only ask questions. How? Why? But how? But why?—the four questions.

I remember the exact Seder, my exact age, because it was the year after Bubbeh died, and I suddenly asked, where is my other Bubbeh? Childhood was no longer something I wore outside me, but within, protected by a little Jewish adult. Jewish, because that was what I connected with miracles: I had asked the questions, felt the Holocaust's dread approach me, and now would hide from the answers—I would choose, as an American, to put this behind me.

In my earlier, childish perception of the Haggadah, the threats of Egyptian recapture, of starvation in the desert, were overcome by God's hand. Later, at twelve, I still couldn't figure out how my family's fear of our American host civilization had been conquered (Mother spoke fondly of her childhood "democratic" Lithuania, Dad of his "democratic" Hungary). How were good Americans more reliable than good Europeans had been? More recently, I found all this too in the Haggadah. The parables of deliverance addressed each generation, along with further questioning, further levels and styles of interpretation. The little book was a mosaic of the world, from Persia to Prague, and of many ages.

Knowledge of the power of miracles, both then and now, came with Elijah: He stood for the family gone up in smoke, yet no one saw him die, no one could testify to his death, and so he was taken into heaven. We knew he wouldn't be coming back, like my cousins, but we pretended he would. That way, I was free to let the child within forget and play, since the memory of the cousins would always be coming back.

Still twelve, I remember dissolving in giggles, in league with my living cousin Walter as we laughed at the grown-ups, no doubt drunk ourselves. How could we laugh at them except that we already knew we were one of them? We laughed at *their* childishness. The Seders were fastidious, rare tablecloth and all, yet manners dissolved as the parents drank more and more wine. At a certain point, after the second or third cup, the decorum would miraculously disappear, and the matzah crumbs that were left on the plate from the previous ritual would be dumped onto the table in an extraordinary unconscious ritual: Each adult picked up his plate and knocked its side on the table, like a deck of cards, then shunted the crumbs aside with the back of his or her hand. Each year we waited to see this miracle, and each year it was so; only now, at twelve, my childhood awe was hidden in laughter.

Remembering the Holocaust, like the Passover Seder, was a reunion of family, living and gone, a healing of history back through every generation to—what origin? Liberation, freedom . . . There the Holocaust worked its way back, to revise that mood from awe to adult doubt. Yet the Seder remains filled with connections and set in a female place, the woman's domain: dining room, the kitchen, children under foot.

In that feminine realm, I came to understand the Haggadah as a woman's purse. Everything was in it, connecting us to origins, traces of the whole history carried around—dumped out on the table every year at Passover. The cups of wine and pillows were a satire against the Seder's weighty order, Greek and Roman customs turned on their head, mere fashion against the deeper history. The unofficial creative culture in Judaism—interpretation of interpretation, secular tales—had been considered a womanly realm, along with vernacular books of ethics and mysticism, the collections of personal prayers. Much of the Haggadah comes from this housebroken realm. On Passover Zaydeh acknowledged it, tossing off his own Yiddish paraphrasings.

The men and women drank equally, and the Seder's final act, to finish the tale with the almost crazy-drunk goal of "Next year in Jerusalem!" was often anticlimactic. Connection to others was the important agenda, and women knew it best. I always found that this was hard to accept by assimilated Jews, who had little patience for the *wandering* quality of the Seder, for touching all the bases. But my childhood awe found its adult equivalent firmly balanced in a woman's embrace of Passover rituals.

The purse that opened on Passover, spilling out on the table and in the Haggadah, will always signal my earliest connection to the Holocaust, the wonder of what's there mixed with the huge Elijah-like silence of what's missing, all who couldn't be grabbed up and brought here with us in one night.

2

"They didn't come back from the camp." Those were the first words of recognition, when I was at an age, six, for "camp" to be still an awesome place. I had gone to my first the previous summer, Camp Sunshine, where mothers with infants stayed also, came to tuck us older ones in, in the tents.

Being Jewish was already a problem for me, plotting escapes from the otherworldly yeshiva I attended in Detroit. At camp, I was estranged on Sundays; a public co-op, it still made chapel mandatory, confined to two choices, Catholic or Protestant. I was happy to learn that if you were Jewish you belonged to "Protestant." I already understood the word "protest."

It was around then I got the message in the family picture albums. "There's your Aunt Yanka, and there were her two daughters. And that man was her husband before Uncle Kalman." They never grew older, the daughters, forever young: "They didn't come back from the camp."

Only a few years ago, I discovered I was born on a Sunday, in that biblically austere Holocaust document, *Chronicle of the Lodz Ghetto*. I came across the entry that corresponded to my birth date in Detroit. "If they had to choose between Sunday and a regular workday, the workday would seem preferable to many a ghetto dweller. The hand does not waver in writing this down. The hand is guided by a brain that reliably preserves all impressions of the eye and ear. . . . Only for the dying is Sunday a day of rest. They can be seen through the curtainless windows —half of them ill, half of them starving—left alone on their fly-infested bedsteads."

Here was a new realm of illusion to mock civilization, learned only in my lifetime: the illusion of rest, to be added to the illusions of work and of order. All of it centered in that purposeful word, camp. To work: to be robbed of your body. Cleanliness: to enter the showers of gas. Work, rest, and cleanliness: Without this bedrock, can I write another word? I do, by embracing that kindred mind who watches his hand as he writes in Lodz in 1943. The mind and the hand divided—it is also the division between then and now. Then, civilization was a blanket under which few Jews escaped; now, I have the imagination to think "post-Holocaust" as my hand moves freely. Yet nothing divides my sense of then and now so well as the loss of hope in that word camp, with its dream of work for the Lodz ghetto. Losing the link to my childhood Camp Sunshine, I took a long time finding a lament. In between, the sixties offered a second childhood: Repressed despair was locked up like an enemy, pushed away with music, poetry, art. Now it's back but less scary to the adult, as despair's roots are visible history.

The film *Shoah* seemed the first attempt to represent that divide between then and now. It contrasts the visible present with memories of the past unseen but heard: the division I'd come to know between the hand that wrote and the mind that recorded, symbolized by my Lodz ghetto writer-father figure.

While I was living in Israel, a letter came from the American publisher of my book series, *A Poet's Bible*. I had proposed the Book of Lamentations as the next volume, and the reply explained that the house had consulted, was convinced no market existed for it. Telling this news, "No Market for Lamentations" became a catch phrase. We'd crack up, my Israeli friends and I: there was the innocence of America, perfectly encapsulated. But I was also American, so I did arrive at the market at last, proposing a book for *Yom HaShoah*—Holocaust Day.

In Israel, the lament on that day comes only from inhuman voices: air-raid sirens screaming through the country, as everything grinds to a halt for a minute. I felt free to search for some text to build on, found a treasured book of Jewish laments, *kinnot*. This Haggadah-like anthology collects laments based on the Book of Lamentations. Why not translate them as modern poems, in English? When I look at the published book now, I find its core in the image of the Lodz ghetto writer, writing on my day of birth—yet these lines were first written 2,500 years ago. "How good to find patience/to let rejected hope return//and how good to learn/to bear the burden young//to sit silent and alone/when the weight falls on your shoulders//to feel the weight of your maker/as all hope seems lost//to put your mouth to dust."

Facing myself as writer, I understood that when Freud counseled distrust of appearances he was offering the hope of useful work, a process of working-through. In psychoanalysis, memory and imagination can be employed to build bridges: to our child-hood islands of rejected hope.

3

The first thing I learned in elementary school was that nakedness or sensuality was primitive. I turned up my nose at pre-toilet-training smells, looked down upon classmates who peed at their desks. I can imagine what I thought but not what I felt then, because my feelings were repressed and I had not yet consciously known heartbreak. When I finally did know it, in a high school romance, as the feelings streamed back I lost instead some deli-cate spiritual instincts. In place of children still struggling for self-control, I now looked down on religion, banishing its bulg-ing trunks of culture to a mental basement. As if mistaking bad poetry for all poetry, I identified superstition and prejudice—basic elements of all culture—with religion itself, until modern poetry brought me back to the biblical poets.

But first I fell in love with a blond girl of Swedish Lutheran descent. It seemed to me she fell out of a child's picture-book. Now sixteen, I resembled a rootless orphan with no sense of time, no history behind me, all of it swept away—as if with that boundless postwar energy and its baby boom. A year later love vanished abruptly. That heartbreak brought primitive feelings flooding to consciousness. And this time, I set about thinking through those feelings, enough to become a writer of poetry.

Yet I belonged to a generation that turned its feelings out-ward, exposing the racism it found at the heart of American culture. On the defensive, this intolerance grew more subtle, unsolvable. Back in the sixties, a victory seemed possible, the "War on Poverty" echoing World War Two victory illusions; now we look further back in history, the Holocaust complicating perceptions of the war, just as racism reveals deeper historical roots. Then, though I campaigned in long hair against mental slavery, I saw little in history's mirror besides my poetic curls. Only now has the process of addressing the slave trade become urgently connected to a personal need: to address the recent European slave trade, the Holocaust's work-to-death slavery.

———

I made the rounds of Paris museums, a draft exile in the late sixties. I was perhaps more in exile than the subject of the doctoral thesis I pursued, Gertrude Stein: mine rendered me stateless, though it matched the fashion for dropping out. Europe had been through a great smashup in the war, and for a few years in the sixties, the creative culture at least acknowledged the amnesia. We didn't know why our memories were so short, only that the past was misrepresented by an outmoded culture. We knew we had walked away from a car wreck, though still didn't know we were suffering its trauma. So the alternative culture was obsessed with simply that, trauma, and devising ironic escapes into the present.

It would take some time for the fog to lift, to see my own parents' determination to repress the dread sights World War Two, when it was over, had left onstage. I grasped for the threads of a Jewish poetry, to avoid the illusion that the war was behind me. With the biblical poets, I found ways to lament the illusions with which narrative educates us: of an acceptable ending.

It felt like waking up when I found the turtledove again, as I published my own translation of the Song of Songs, portions from which are used in the Passover Haggadah:

> I was asleep
> but the soul within me
> stayed awake
>
> Like my heart—true to a timeless rhythm
> to which I still respond—
> listen, a gentle knocking
>
> like my heart's beating—
> *Open to me, my love*
> *my purest image, sister, dove*
>
> *all I can imagine—my head is drenched*
> *with dew, all my memories*
> *melt into you*

That awakening of passion, corresponding to Passover's heralding of spring, was a time for telling—for unlocking the mosaic of memories in the Haggadah, first of all handbooks for me.

4

Hundreds of rabbinic editions of the Passover Haggadah have been published, each with another set of interpretations. If I were at a loss to distinguish between interpretations and texts, I would be sheltered from history. A portion of liturgy that begins "Pour out Thy wrath" could then be mistaken for Jewish intolerance by anyone forgetting its poetry (it collages ancient verses from Psalms and from Lamentations). And once I heard a literary critic quote from Psalm 137 as an example of Jewish hatred. I looked up the Hebrew and the misquote shocked me into retranslating the psalm.

> O Lady Babylon
> Babylon the destroyer
> lucky man who holds you
>
> who crushes you
> who opens your mind
> to wither instantly in air
>
> who holds up your crying babies
> as if to stun them
> against solid rock.

I added an "as if" in the penultimate line, underlining the painfully ironic metaphors. If a scholar centuries from now quoted a song, "We Shall Overcome," as a call to violence—that would be the kind of nudge to study I had experienced.

Modern poetry makes you sensitive to the author behind every line, even as he or she dons a conflicting but transparent mask. So the further I read in biblical literature, the easier it became to see the scrappiness of its poets. Sainthood was far from their minds. The passion for knowing was combative, the fighting spirit reaching right up to God, wrestled with many places in the text. When I came across Andre Neher, the French writer, this sentence echoed back to childhood: "From the dust of the most abject misery to the most fascinating miracle by which human dignity is restored to all its grandeur, the night of the Seder forces man to face and fight himself." Wasn't this the fight between child and adult I'd always known?

To challenge myself, I offered to lead a Seder that year. It was an unusual one, more than fifty people seated around one hall-length table. They were primarily gay men and women who treasured a family experience, along with several Franciscan monks in habit—avid listeners. A few children were also there, and one boy of twelve began to mock me and the miracles I was interpreting—perfectly confirming my own feelings at his age. His mother was embarrassed, unable to control him. Others were trying to shush him also, yet I couldn't help egging him on. I stopped to explain to all: This boy is challenging me, and we all might stop and feel what that is like.

I was probably a stand-in for the boy's absent father. Freud credits Judaism with repressing death wishes (without ritualizing them) against the father. All children have felt these wishes in hot anger and repressed them. Yet bold traces of our fights with the father remain, vivid exchanges with God in the Bible, whether by Abraham or Moses, Sarai or Zipporah. And I was trying to turn this scene with a conflicted boy into further illustration. But his passion was real and mine was intellectual—I couldn't control him; he knocked over some plates and fled, his mother crying after him. So the Seder could not really be finished—the boy had stolen the matzah but not returned it, and we grown-ups were too polite to drink deeply.

With whom is a poem struggling, what muse, what ghost or lover?—I learned to ask myself that. When I asked it of Psalms, I found prayers grappling not with an ironic muse but a father. Job, Isaiah—they continue the contest with this father. And I kept translating until I reached Ecclesiastes, the symbolic wisdom of an old father, Solomon. I came full circle to my childhood in Hebrew school. Then, I absorbed and forgot the image of Herzl: a misty, romantic portrait at the head of the classroom. He looked like no rabbi or teacher I had known—windswept beard, shock wave of hair, eyes focused like a pilot's. Herzl came back to me as I worked on Ecclesiastes and thought of the poet behind it, his nonrabbinic, ironic cast of mind. At age eight, I had walked home from that Hebrew school through a largely black neighborhood—a culture I was also absorbing—in Detroit.

In those days I purchased leaves, to be pasted on paper trees with a hundred blanks, each green leaf a penny stamp. These trees were meant to help rebuild Israel, but they provided my first meditation on the Holocaust. They are symbols of renewal, we were told, new growth for the refugees. I thought how easy to replace a tree—that it wasn't like that with people. The conflict between a child's literal mind and adult irony blossomed in me here: I knew these trees were blues songs, as well. I only had to paste leaves on paper to plant a tree, I thought. No stamps and paper would do that for my European family.

I chose new fathers, versions of myself in opposition. Miles Davis, Thelonius Monk . . . Later there were poets; still later, Buber and Freud. And then the broken heart. Unknowing, I retreated into superficial relationships. Childhood passions resurfaced, even the synagogue. I found there, in place of the questing, a mothering tradition. The rabbis in the tradition of the Talmud and Midrash were often tender, otherworldly types, feminine in their devotion. I prayed the psalms in their way, creating a context for an all-hearing father.

But I couldn't accept this. The Holocaust had spoiled me, like a child handed merely pictures of all he desires. I had to struggle with mother and father. Nothing but irony seemed enriching, to complement the canonical Law. Yet the Torah records men's and women's struggles with God also with irony. I began to translate, starting with the most ironic portion of the text by the J poet. J is the name that for more than a century has characterized this author of the underlying narrative, running from Adam's creation to Moses's burial. I began in the book of Exodus because it was nearing Passover and I wanted to bring something to the Seder. I focused on God's own fear over how to meet—with Moses, with the priests, with the elders, with the people—in Sinai. Right away I knew I was touching the fear of the Holocaust in me. But it wasn't Moses's fear; it was something overwhelming, God's fear of causing death.

Why is God so anxious here, constantly changing the boundaries he invents? I sensed his alarm in coming too close to the physical substance of men and women. The only comparable fear I knew was to touch the Holocaust in its literal terror, a fear enlarged from looking at those smiling photographs of the murdered in childhood. I repressed it, until that first fear for my own life receded into images of life—into remembering those faces only as images on paper. Now I understood the terrible awe of encountering them in the flesh, of crossing broken boundaries. That was what my unprotected imagination first had to do, as a child.

> Mount Sinai was wrapped in smoke. God had come down in fire, the smoke climbing skyward like smoke from a kiln. The mountain, enveloped, greatly trembled.
>
> So God descended to Mount Sinai, to the summit. He called Moses to ascend to the top. Moses climbed up and God spoke to him, "Descend, hold the people's attention: they must not be drawn to God, to destroy boundaries. Bursting through to see, they will fall; many will die. Even the priests who approach God must be purified, detached—so they are not drawn to destruction."
>
> God spoke further, "Descend, arise with Aaron. The priests and the people should not come up, as boundaries destroyed will be their destruction.
>
> "They must be ready for the third day, the day God goes down, before the eyes of all, on Mount Sinai. The people will be a boundary, warn them to watch themselves, approach but not climb up, not touch the mountain. For those who overstep boundaries, death touches them, steps over their graves. . . ."
>
> God spoke to Moses, "Carve two stone tablets and at dawn prepare to ascend Mount Sinai. In the light of morning you will present yourself to me, there on the top of the mountain. No one goes with you, no one is seen anywhere on the mountain, no cattle or sheep are seen near it." In the morning Moses ascended to the summit as God desired, two stone tablets in his hands. . . .

The J poet's struggle with words indicates that God, like man, also fights for identity—can thus be a trusted partner with whom to cut a Covenant. I remembered the fight between child and adult within me at the Seders. God could bridge the divide, a parent knowing the roots of our greatest terror: broken boundaries between life and death. What did he do? God revealed his physical presence to our imaginations. I knew it in my hand on the page, struggling with translation, interpretation. He left to a human hand the authority of interpretation, even in the Lodz ghetto.

About the Authors

Max Apple was born in Grand Rapids, Michigan, in 1941. His books include *The Oranging of America and Other Stories* (1976), *Zip: A Novel of the Left and the Right* (1978), *Free Agents* (1984), a one-act play entitled *Trotsky's Bar Mitzvah* (1983), and his most recent novel, *The Propheteers* (1987). Mr. Apple has been awarded a National Endowment for the Humanities fellowship (1971), the Jesse Jones Award from the Texas Institute of Letters (1976 and 1985), and the *Hadassah* magazine Ribalow Award (1985). He has taught at Rice University since 1972 and has also taught at the University of Michigan, Reed College, and Stanford University. He lives in Houston.

E. M. Broner was born in Detroit, Michigan, in 1932. She has published two novels, *Her Mothers* and *A Weave of Women,* as well as three other books: *Summer Is a Foreign Land* (a play), *Journal/Nocturnal* (a novella and stories), and *The Lost Tradition: Mother and Daughters in Literature* (edited with Cathy N. Davidson). Her plays include *Body Parts of Margaret Fuller, Letters to My Television Past, The Olympics,* and *Half a Man.* Ms. Broner has won two National Endowment for the Arts awards, as well as two Michigan Council for the Arts grants and awards from the Michigan Foundation for the Arts, Wayne State University, and the Wonder Woman Foundation. She has taught at Wayne State University, as well as being a guest teacher at Haifa University, Sarah Lawrence College, New York University, and currently, Columbia University. She is at work on a novel entitled *The Repair Shop.* Ms. Broner lives in New York with her "painter-partner" Robert Broner. She has two sons and two daughters.

Jane DeLynn was born in New York City in 1946. She has published three novels: *Some Do* (1978), *In Thrall* (1982), and *Real Estate* (1988—chosen as a *New York Times* Notable Book of the Year). Her fiction has appeared in *The Paris Review, Christopher Street,* and *Washington Review of the Arts,* among others, and her articles have appeared in *The New York Times Magazine, Harper's Bazaar, 7 Days,* and *The Los Angeles Times Book Review.* Her theatrical works include *Hoosick Falls, Snob's Cabaret, The Cowgirl and the Blonde, The Monkey Opera (The Making of a Soliloquy),* and the recently completed farce *Dash & Lil, Julius & Ethel, & Tail Gunner Joe.* She has finished a new novel, *Don Juan in the Village.* Ms. DeLynn has won the Elizabeth Janeway Prize for Prose Writing (1967, 1968), the Book of the Month Club Writing Fellowship (1968), and the New York Foundation Fellowship for the Arts (1988). She currently lives in New York City.

Leslie Epstein was born in Los Angeles in 1933. He has published five books of fiction, including *King of the Jews,* and most recently *Goldkorn Tales.* A new novel, *Pinto,* will be published next year. He has also had essays and articles published in *Playboy, Esquire, The Atlantic, Harpers, Triquarterly, Salmagundi, Yale Review, Partisan Review, New American Review,* and others. Mr. Epstein has been both a Rhodes and a Fulbright Scholar, and has won a Guggenheim, a National Academy and Institute of Arts and Letters award for Distinction in Literature, and two grants from the National Endowment for the Arts. He is the director of the graduate creative writing program at Boston University. He lives with his wife and twin sons in Brookline, Massachusetts, and has a daughter at Yale.

Leslie A. Fiedler was born in Newark, New Jersey, in 1917. He is the author of *An End to Innocence* (1955), *The Art of the Essay* (1959, revised 1969), *The Image of the Jew in American Fiction* (1959), *Love and Death in the American Novel* (1960, revised 1966), *The Second Stone* (a novel, 1963), *The Last Jew in America* (1966), *Nude Croquet and Other Stories* (1969), *Collected Essays* (1971), *A Fiedler Reader* (1977), *What Was Literature* (1982), and a number of other books. He has received many awards, including a Rockefeller fellowship in the Humanities (1946–47), two Fulbright fellowships (1951–52, 1961–62), and a Guggenheim fellowship (1970–71). In 1988 he was elected to the American Academy of the Arts as a member of the Department of the Arts. Mr. Fiedler was on the faculty at the University of Montana at Missoula, 1941–64, and has been teaching English since 1965 at the State University of New York at Buffalo, including serving as departmental chairman from 1974 to 1977. Mr. Fiedler is married and has eight children, ranging in age from twenty-two to forty-seven. He lives in Buffalo, New York.

Herbert Gold was born in Cleveland, Ohio, in 1924. He has published many novels and collections of fiction, including *Fathers* (a novel, 1967), *Family* (a novel, 1981), *Lovers and Cohorts* (a collection of stories, 1986), and his most recent novel, *Dreaming* (1988). He has also written a number of essays, collected in *My Last Two Thousand Years* (1973) and *Travels in San Francisco* (1989), among other books. Mr. Gold has contributed to *The New York Times Magazine, The Atlantic, Harper's, Playboy,* the *Hudson Review,* and *Forthcoming.*

His awards include a Fulbright fellowship (1950–51), a Guggenheim fellowship (1957), a Ford Foundation grant (1960), the Commonwealth Club award for best novel (1982), and the Sherwood Anderson Award for Fiction from the State of Ohio (1989). He has taught at Stanford University, Cornell University, and the University of California (at Berkeley and at Davis). He is the father of five children, and lives in San Francisco.

Geoffrey Hartman was born in Germany and emigrated in 1939. He is the author of *The Unmediated Vision* (1954), *Criticism in the Wilderness* (1980), and other books. His most recent titles include the literary essays, *Easy Pieces, Bitburg in Moral and Political Perspective,* and, with S. Budick, *Midrash and Literature.* Among his many awards, he has received a Fulbright fellowship, a Guggenheim fellowship, a National Endowment for the Humanities fellowship, and the Christian Gauss Prize for *Wordsworth's Poetry* (1964). Mr. Hartman has taught at Yale University since 1955, and is the director of the Yale Video Archive for Holocaust Testimonies. He has also taught at the University of Iowa, Cornell University, the University of Chicago, Hebrew University in Jerusalem, the University of Zurich, and Princeton University. He has two children and lives in New Haven, Connecticut.

Alfred Kazin was born in Brooklyn, New York, in 1915. He attended the College of the City of New York and Columbia University. His many books include *On Native Grounds, A Walker in the City* (1951), *Starting Out in the Thirties* (1965), and *New York Jew* (1978). His most recent book, *Our New York* (with David Finn) is to be published in 1989. He has also served as editor for *The Portable William Blake* (1946), *F. Scott Fitzgerald: The Man and His Work* (1947), *Melville's Moby Dick* (1956), *Ralph Waldo Emerson: A Modern Anthology* (1958), *The Selected Stories of Nathaniel Hawthorne* and *Henry James's The Ambassadors* (1971). He was once the literary editor for *The New Republic.* Mr. Kazin's numerous honors include being the Phi Beta Kappa Orator at Harvard University in 1987, a fellow of the American Academy of Arts and Sciences, a member of the American Academy—Institute of Arts and Letters, and winner of the "Lion" award of the New York Public Library in 1988. He has taught at the New School for Social Research, Harvard University, New York University, and Hunter College, among others. He lives in New York City.

David Lehman was born in New York City in 1948. His published books include *An Alternative to Speech* (a collection of poems, 1986), *The Perfect Murder: A Study in Detection* (1989); a new book, *Operation Memory,* is forthcoming. Mr. Lehman has edited *Beyond Amazement: New Essays on John Ashbery* (1980), *James Merrill: Essays in Criticism* (co-edited with Charles Berger, 1983), *Ecstatic Occasions, Expedient Forms* (1987), and he serves as the series editor for the annual anthology *The Best American Poetry.* His poetry has appeared in *The Paris Review, The New York Review of Books, Partisan Review, The Yale Review, The New Republic,* and others. Mr. Lehman has published reviews, essays, and articles in *Newsweek, The New York Times Magazine, TLS, The Wall Street Journal, Partisan Review,* and a number of other periodicals. He has received grants from the Ingram Merrill Foundation and the National Endowment for the Arts, and various poems have won him the *Paris Review*'s Bernard F. Conners prize for 1987 and the Consuelo Ford Award from the Poetry Society of America in 1988. He was recently awarded a Guggenheim fellowship for 1989. He is a vice president of the National Book Critics Circle. Mr. Lehman lives with his wife and son in Ithaca, New York.

Alan Lelchuk was born in Brooklyn, New York, in 1938. His novels include *American Mischief* (1973), *Miriam at Thirty-four* (1974), *Shrinking* (1978), *Miriam in Her Forties* (1985), and *Brooklyn Boy,* due out in the fall of 1989, as well as a Young Adult novel, *On Home Ground* (1987). He co-edited the anthology *Eight Great Hebrew Short Novels* with Gershon Shaked in 1983. His short fiction has appeared in magazines such as *The Atlantic, Partisan Review, Forthcoming,* and *New American Review.* He has written articles for *New Republic, New York Review of Books, The New York Times Book Review, The Nation,* and others. He was the associate editor of Philip Rahv's *Modern Occasions,* a cultural quarterly, 1970–72. Mr. Lelchuk has been both a Guggenheim (1976–77) and Fulbright (1986–87, writer-in-residence at Haifa University) fellow. He has taught at Brandeis, Amherst College, and Haifa University, and is currently on the faculty of Dartmouth College. Mr. Lelchuk is married and has one son, and lives in Canaan, New Hampshire.

Julius Lester was born in 1939. Among fifteen published volumes are eight novels and story collections. His book *Lovesong: Becoming a Jew,* an autobiographical account of his conversion to Judaism, was nominated for the National Jewish Book Award. His books have been nominated for the National Book Award as well and received Notable Book of the Year citations from *The New York Times* and the American Library Association. He has won a Newberry Medal and the Lewis Carroll Shelf Award, and his books have been translated into seven languages. Essays have appeared in *The New York Times, Boston Globe, Village Voice, The New Republic,* and *The Nation,* among others. Mr. Lester has recorded two albums of original songs. A veteran of the Civil Rights Movement, his documentary photographs have been shown at the Smithsonian and are part of the permanent collection at Howard University. Mr. Lester has taught at the University of Massachusetts since 1971, and is presently a professor in the Department of Judaic and Near Eastern Studies. His most recent book is *How Many Spots Does a Leopard Have?,* a retelling of African and Jewish folktales.

Gordon Lish was born in Hewlett, New York, in 1934. He is the author of the novels *Dear Mr. Capote, Peru,* and *Extravaganza,* and of the short story collections *What I Know So Far* and *Mourner at the Door.* He is also the author of *English Grammar, The Gabbernot, Why Work,* and *A Man's Work.* He has served as editor for *Esquire, The Chrysalis Review,* and *Genesis West,* and is currently the editor of *The Quarterly,* as well as being an editor at the house of Alfred A. Knopf. He has brought out the anthologies *New Sounds in American Fiction, The Secret Life of Our Times,* and *All Our Secrets Are the Same.* Mr. Lish's honors include a Guggenheim fellowship in 1984. He was director of linguistic studies at Behavioral Research Laboratories, and has taught at Yale, Columbia, and New York universities. He is married and the father of four children, and lives in New York City.

Phillip Lopate was born in New York City in 1943. He has published seven books: the novels *Confessions of Summer* (1979) and *The Rug Merchant* (1987), the essay collections *Bachelorhood* (1980—winner of the Texas Institute of Letters' Award for best nonfiction book of the year) and *Against Joie De Vivre* (1989), the poetry collections *The Eyes Don't Always Want to Stay Open* (1972) and *The Daily Round* (1976), and a book about his teaching experiences, *Being with Children* (1975—winner of a Christopher award). His work has appeared in several anthologies, including *The Best American Short Stories of 1974, The Best American Essays of 1987,* several Pushcart Prize anthologies and *Congregation,* as well as in periodicals such as *The Paris Review, Vogue, The New York Times Magazine, Boulevard, Forthcoming, Mississippi Review,* and *American Film.* He has received a Guggenheim Fellowship, two National Endowment for the Arts literary grants, a New York State CAPS grant, and a Revson Fellowship in urban studies. He currently teaches in the graduate writing programs at the University of Houston and Columbia University, and divides his time between Houston and New York City.

Daphne Merkin grew up in Manhattan, and attended Barnard and Columbia University. Her novel *Enchantment* won the Edward Lewis Wallant Award for 1986. Her fiction has been published in *The New Yorker, Encounter,* and *Mademoiselle.* She has been the book and film critic for *The New Leader,* and her literary and film criticism has appeared in *Commentary, The New Republic, The New York Times Book Review,* and other periodicals. She is a contributing editor at *Partisan Review* and is an associate publisher at a New York City publishing house. Ms. Merkin lives with her husband on the Upper West Side of Manhattan.

Leonard Michaels was born in New York City in 1933. He is the author of two collections of stories, *Going Places* (1969) and *I Would Have Saved Them If I Could* (1975), as well as a novel, *The Men's Club* (1981). He is the co-editor, with Christopher Ricks, of *The State of the Language.* He has guest-edited various literary magazines and has contributed short stories, book reviews, memoirs, and critical essays to many publications. Mr. Michaels is currently completing an autobiographical work, and has recently co-edited *West of the West* and a second volume of *The State of the Language.* In 1967, he received an award from the National Foundation of the Arts; he was a Guggenheim fellow in 1970 and won a National Academy of Arts and Letters award in 1972. Also among his credits is the O. Henry Prize. He has been a professor of English at the University of California at Berkeley since 1969.

Mark Mirsky was born in Boston in 1939. He attended Harvard College and Stanford University. He has published the books *Thou Worm Jacob* (1967), *Proceedings of the Rabble* (1971), *Blue Hill Avenue* (1972), *The Secret Table* (1975), *My Search for the Messiah,* and *The Red Adam,* in addition to numerous magazine publications. Mr. Mirsky is completing a multivolume study of the city of Pinsk, forthcoming from Harvard University Press, as well as a memoir of his father. He has co-edited an anthology of Midrashic literature with David Stern, awaiting publication at the Jewish Publication Society. He is the editor of the magazine *Fiction.* Mr. Mirsky has taught English at the City College of New York since 1967, and lives in Manhattan with his wife, son, and daughter.

507

Marge Piercy was born in Detroit, Michigan, in 1936. Her fiction works include *Going Down Fast* (1969), *Small Changes* (1973), *Woman on the Edge of Time* (1977), *Vida* (1980), *Braided Lives* (1982), *Gone to Soldiers* (1988), and most recently, *Summer People* (1989). She has also published a number of collections of poetry, including *Breaking Camp* (1968), *Hard Loving* (1969), *Living in the Open* (1976), *The Moon Is Always Female* (1980), *Stone, Paper, Knife* (1983), *My Mother's Body* (1985), and recently, *Available Light* (1988). Also among her works are a play, *The Last White Class* (with Ira Wood, 1979), a collection of essays, *Parti-Colored Blocks for a Quilt* (1982), and an anthology, *Early Ripening: American Women's Poetry Now* (1987). Among her many awards and honors are the Avery Hopwood Award, the Orion Scott Award in the Humanities, the Borestone Mountain Poetry Award (twice), the Literature Award from the Governor's Commission on the Status of Women (Massachusetts), and a National Endowment for the Arts fellowship. She has taught, lectured, and conducted workshops at numerous universities and institutions in several countries. Ms. Piercy lives in Wellfleet, Massachusetts.

Robert Pinsky was born in Long Branch, New Jersey, in 1940. He is the author of three books of poetry, *Sadness and Happiness* (1975), *An Explanation of America* (1979), and *History of My Heart* (1984), as well as three of prose, *Landor's Poetry* (1967), *The Situation of Poetry* (1977), and *Poetry and the World* (1988). He is the co-translator, with the author, of *The Separate Notebooks, Poems by Czeslaw Milosz* (1984). His poems have appeared in publications including *The New Yorker, Paris Review, The New Republic, Occident,* and *Agni Review.* Also among his works is *Mindwheel,* a computer entertainment in prose and verse. Prizes and awards he has won include American Academy of Arts and Letters Award, a Guggenheim fellowship, a National Endowment for the Arts fellowship, and the William Carlos Williams Award. *The Want-Bone,* Mr. Pinsky's new book of poetry, will appear in spring 1990. He teaches at Boston University and lives in Newton, Massachusetts, with his wife and three children.

Francine Prose was born in New York in 1947. She is the author of seven novels, including *Judah the Pious* (1973—winner of the Jewish Book Council Award), *Hungry Hearts* (1983), and *Bigfoot Dreams.* Her fiction has appeared in *The New Yorker, The Atlantic, Mademoiselle, Antaeus, Commentary,* and *Tri-Quarterly;* she has also written a series of "Hers" columns for *The New York Times.* As well, she is the co-translator of a collection of Ida Fink's stories. Ms. Prose has won two National Endowment for the Arts awards and two New York State CAPS grants. She has taught at Harvard University, Sarah Lawrence College, the University of Arizona, and the University of Utah and in the Warren Wilson MFA Program for Writers. She lives in Krumville, New York, with her husband and two sons.

Barbara Rogan was born in New York in 1951. Her novels include *Changing States* (1981 in U.S. and England; Hebrew edition, Israel), *The West Bank Conspiracy* (1985, in Hebrew), and *Cafe Nevo* (1987 in U.S. and Holland; forthcoming in Israel). She is the co-author, with Barbara Newman, of *The Covenant: Love and Death in Beirut* (1989). The Barbara Rogan Literary

Agency was founded by her in 1975, in Tel Aviv, and subsequently added a New York office. Currently completing *Saving Grace,* a novel, Ms. Rogan lives in New York City with her husband and two sons.

Anne Roiphe was born in New York City in 1935. She has published five novels: *Digging Out* (1969), *Up the Sandbox* (1970), *Long Division* (1972), *Torch Song* (1977), and *Lovingkindness* (1987—winner of the Hadassah Fiction Award, 1988), and also has a novel in progress, *The Perplexed.* Her nonfiction works include *Generation Without Memory* (1981), *Your Child's Mind* (co-authored with her husband, Dr. Herman Roiphe, 1985), and *A Season for Healing* (1988). Ms. Roiphe's essays have been collected in several anthologies. She is the mother of three daughters and two stepdaughters, and lives in Manhattan.

Norma Rosen was born in New York City. She has published four books, *Joy to Levine!* (a novel), *Green* (a novella and short stories), *Touching Evil* (a novel), and *At the Center* (a novel). A fourth novel, *John and Anzia: An American Romance,* is to be published in November 1989, when a new edition of *Touching Evil* also appears. She has had short fiction published in *Commentary, The New Yorker, Forthcoming, Redbook, Ms.,* and *Orim,* among others, and her essays, including ten "Hers" pieces in *The New York Times,* have appeared in magazines including *The New York Times Magazine, Midstream,* and *Congress Monthly.* She is also the author of a play, *The Miracle of Dora Wakin.* Ms. Rosen's awards include the Eugene F. Saxton Award, a New York State CAPS grant, and a Harvard Fellowship of Bunting Institute. She has taught at Yale, Harvard, the University of Pennsylvania, and the New School for Social Research, and is currently teaching writing seminars at New York University and Barnard College. She lives in Westchester with her husband Robert; they are the parents of two children, Anna and Jonathan.

David Rosenberg was born in Detroit in 1943. Among his published books of poetry are *Disappearing Horses* (1969), *Paris and London* (1971), *The Necessity of Poetry* (1973), and several volumes in his ongoing *Poet's Bible* series. *A Blazing Fountain* (1978) and *Chosen Days* (1980) collect some of his verse translations, which include the Books of Psalms, Isaiah, Job, Lamentations, Ecclesiastes, and Judith. Mr. Rosenberg edited *Congregation: Contemporary Writers Read the Jewish Bible* (1987) and is the former editor in chief of the Jewish Publication Society of America. He has been a senior editor at publishing houses in Toronto, Tel Aviv, and New York, and for many years he taught at Toronto's York University. He edited the literary magazines *The Ant's Forefoot* (1967–73) and *Forthcoming: Jewish Imaginative Writing* (1982–84), both founded abroad. Mr. Rosenberg recently completed a literary translation of the Bible's original author, *The Book of J,* to be published next year in collaboration with the commentary of Harold Bloom. He is currently at work on *The Book of Kabbalah,* also with Mr. Bloom. Mr. Rosenberg lives in New York City.

Susanne Schlötelburg was born in Baden-Baden, West Germany, in 1959. Her essays and reviews appear often in *Die Zeit,* a national German weekly. Ms. Schlötelburg's doctoral dissertation, *Jewish Minds in the American Acad-*

emy: A Study in Intellectual Assimilation, is being readied for publication. She received her graduate degrees from Brandeis and the University of Heidelberg, and was a professor of English at the University of Mannheim. Among other courses, Ms. Schlötelburg has taught American Jewish history and culture, in Germany as well as the U.S. Currently, she teaches in the English Department at Harvard.

Grace Schulman is the author of *Burn Down the Icons* and *Hemisheres,* both collections of poetry that were widely published in magazines. New volumes of poetry and essays are nearing completion. She is also the author of the critical study *Marianne Moore: The Poetry of Engagement.* She was a co-translator of *Songs of Cifar and the Sweet Sea,* by Pablo Antonio Cuadra, and received the Present Tense Award for her translation of Israeli poetry. She is a former director of the Poetry Center of the 92nd Street YM-YWHA in New York City, and is the poetry editor of *The Nation* and a professor of English at Baruch College of the City University of New York. Her poems have appeared in *The New Yorker, Poetry,* the *Hudson Review, Forthcoming, The New Republic,* and other magazines. Ms. Schulman lives in New York with her husband, Jerry.

Lore Segal was born in Vienna, Austria, in 1928, and came to the United States in 1951. Her novels are *Other People's Houses* (1964), *Lucinella* (1976), and *Her First American* (1985), and she is at work on a new novel, *An Absence of Cousins.* She has also published five books for children: *Tell Me a Mitzi* (1970), *All the Way Home* (1973—nominated for the Caldecott Award), *Tell Me a Trudy* (1977), *The Story of Old Mrs. Brubeck and How She Looked for Trouble and Where She Found Him* (1978), and *The Story of Mrs. Lovewright and Purrless Her Cat* (1978). Her translations include *Gallows Songs,* by Christian Morgenstern (with W. D. Snodgrass, 1967), *The Juniper Tree and Other Tales From Grimm* (1973), and *The Book of Adam to Moses* (1987). Her works have appeared in *The New Yorker, Works in Progress, Story Quarterly, New American Review,* the *Quarterly Review of Literature, Commentary,* and more; several "Hers" columns for *The New York Times* appeared during 1987–88. Ms. Segal is a reviewer for *The New York Times, The Washington Post,* and *The New Republic,* among others. Her many honors include a Guggenheim fellowship (1965–66), a National Endowment for the Arts grant for fiction (1972– 73, and 1978–88), the Carl Sandberg Award for Fiction (1985), the Harold U. Ribalow Prize (1986), and the American Academy and Institute of Arts and Letters Award (1986). She has taught at Bennington College, Sarah Lawrence College, Columbia University, and Princeton University. Currently a professor of English at the University of Illinois at Chicago, she nonetheless lives in New York City. She is widowed and has two children.

David Shapiro has published many volumes of poetry, including *January, Poems from Deal, The Page Turner, Lateness,* and *To an Idea.* He has also published critical books on contemporary art and literature, including the prize-winning *Jasper Johns,* and was author of the first book-length critical study of John Ashbery. His most recent book of poetry, *House (Blown Apart)* (1988), will be followed by a book on Mondrian and translations of the Spanish poet, Rafael Alberti. In 1971 he was nominated for a National Book Award for

510

poetry and in 1977 received the National Academy and Institute of Arts and Letters' triannual prize for experimental poetry. Mr. Shapiro teaches art history and aesthetics at William Paterson College and Cooper Union, and has also taught at Columbia, Princeton, and Brooklyn College. He is married, has one son, and lives in Riverdale, New York.